8/1/07

For Prof. Ziadeh,
with best wishes.

Ron Shaham

LAW, CUSTOM, AND STATUTE IN THE MUSLIM WORLD

STUDIES IN ISLAMIC LAW AND SOCIETY

(*Founding Editor: Bernard Weiss*)

EDITED BY

RUUD PETERS AND KEVIN A. REINHART

VOLUME 28

Professor Aharon Layish

LAW, CUSTOM, AND STATUTE IN THE MUSLIM WORLD

Studies in Honor of Aharon Layish

EDITED BY

RON SHAHAM

BRILL

LEIDEN · BOSTON
2007

This book is printed on acid-free paper.

Library of Congress Cataloging-in-Publication Data

Law, custom, and statute in the Muslim world : studies in honor of Aharon Layish / edited by Ron Shaham.
p. cm. — (Studies in Islamic law and society ; v. 28)
ISBN-13: 978-90-04-15453-7
ISBN-10: 90-04-15453-1 (hardcover : alk. paper)
1. Islamic law—History 2. Justice, Administration of (Islamic law)—History. 3. Customary law (Islamic law)—History. I. Layish, Aharon, 1933- II. Shaham, Ron.

KBP50.L39 2006
340.5'9—dc22

2006050908

ISSN 1384–1130
ISBN-13: 978-90-04-15453-7
ISBN-10: 90-04-15453-1

PRINTED IN THE NETHERLANDS

CONTENTS

PREFACE

Ron Shaham

As a former student and then a colleague and a friend of Aharon Layish, it is a great pleasure to present this collective volume in his honor. The 'gestation period' of the volume was quite long, but, according to the Mālikī school of law, it did not exceed the maximum 'pregnancy' period, which is five lunar years. This school recognizes the phenomenon of 'the sleeping embryo' (*ḥaml nā'im*), that is, an embryo that, according to her mother's report, fell asleep in the womb and simply stopped developing. Such an embryo is expected to awaken some day, continue to grow, and ultimately be born. This volume differs from the sleeping embryo in that it did not sleep at all: it was awake and kicking all the time. Due to several hardships, however—academic, administrative, and financial—its expected delivery had to be postponed. Happily, here it is.

Aharon Layish is one of the leading authorities in the field of Islamic law. There is no need to elaborate here on his interests and achievements—they are very well portrayed in his academic autobiography. Rather, in what follows, I will highlight a few aspects of his work, offer some personal impressions, and, finally, express my gratitude to all those who contributed to this volume.

Layish is an adherent of the school of Joseph Schacht, who argued that the gates of *ijtihād* were closed during the tenth century. The scope of this debate goes beyond the legal field to encompass the more general debate on the decline of Islamic civilization after the first Islamic centuries ('the golden age'). Layish disagrees with the more recent school, led by Wael Hallaq, which holds that there has never been a consensus (*ijmāʿ*) among the jurists on the closure of the gates and that until the sixteenth century at least there were jurists (including some Shāfiʿīs and the Ḥanbalīs) who claimed the right of *ijtihād* and even called themselves *mujtahids* or innovators (*mujaddids*) (Hallaq 1984).

Layish's reservations focus on the claim that Hallaq based his thesis on legal theory (*uṣūl al-fiqh*) texts and on biographical dictionaries (*ṭabaqāt*) of the jurists, and not, or almost not, on positive law texts (*furūʿ al-fiqh*) (Layish 2004, 87 n. 7). It is one thing to talk about the right to engage in *ijtihād*, Layish argues, and a totally different thing to practice it. Layish's definition of *ijtihād* is strict. Following Schacht, he regards it as the creation of a new rule of law *by resorting to the sources of the law* (*uṣūl al-fiqh*) [emphasis added]. He argues that we do not yet have sufficient evidence to demonstrate that the *sharīʿa* body of positive law did in fact develop after the tenth century by way of direct reference to *uṣūl al-fiqh*: the Qurʾān and the Prophetic *Ḥadīth*, accompanied by analogical deduction (*qiyās*) from these textual sources and the acceptance of a new rule on the basis of the consensus of the scholars of a legal school (*madhhab*, pl. *madhāhib*). Recent studies have demonstrated, however, that the term *ijtihād* is multi-dimensional and that the *ʿulamāʾ* created a wide range of *ijtihād*s along a scale from *taqlīd*, strict adherence to *madhhab* doctrine, to *ijtihād muṭlaq*, the highest level of innovation performed by the founders of the *madhāhib* (see, for example, Hallaq 1984).

As demonstrated convincingly by Hoebink (1994), the disagreement between the two camps is largely mitigated by the fact that different scholars, Schacht and Hallaq included, use different definitions of the terms *ijtihād* and, more importantly, *ijmāʿ*. Layish is, however, correct in saying that more monographic studies based on *furūʿ* works are needed.

The studies of Aharon Layish on Islamic jurists' law (the *sharīʿa*) focus on the application of family law, inheritance, and pious endowment (*waqf*) in the everyday life of modern Muslim societies. He demonstrates particular interest in patterns of intergenerational transmission of property. He has written extensively on the family *waqf*, both Ḥanafī and Mālikī, as well as on the testamentary disposition (*waṣiyya*) and the gift (*hibā*). These three mechanisms have been traditionally used for circumventing the inheritance rules, based on the orthodox interpretation of some Qurʾānic verses. The social incentive for this circumvention has been to prevent the partition of the extended family's land plot, especially by female members of the family involved in exogamous marriages.

Layish analyzes the relationship between Arab customary law and the *sharīʿa*, which are two legal bodies that both compete against each other and complete each other from the early Islamic period onwards. Moreover, his work addresses the relationship between Arab customary law and the *sharīʿa*, on the one hand, and the legislation of the modern nation state, on the other. He found that Modern statutory legislation and its resort to codification contradicts the nature of the *sharīʿa* and creates new realities in the legal systems of Muslim states.

Being among the most distinguished scholars in his field, Layish contributed a number of important entries to the second edition of the Encyclopedia of Islam: 'marriage' (*nikaḥ*), 'divorce' (*ṭalāq*), inheritance (*mīrāth*), pious endowment (*waḳf*) and 'the *sharīʿa* court' (*maḥkama*). His contribution to these entries is in the sections related to the Middle East and North Africa in the modern era. His distinguished academic position is attested to by the fact that he has served on the editorial board of the most prominent journal in the field—*Islamic Law and Society*—since its foundation in 1994 and until today.

As a veteran student of the late Gabriel Baer, Layish pioneered the use of sharīʿa court records (*sijillāt*, sing. *sijill*) as a source for social and legal history. Indeed, most of Layish's studies are based primarily on this source: his first book on women and Islamic law in Israel (1975), his second book on the Druze family in Israel (1982), and his third book on divorce in the Libyan family (1991). Already in his first tome Layish developed a solid methodology for the integrated use of legal and judicial documents, governmental reports, official statistical reports, and newspaper materials to analyze the changes which Arab Israeli society underwent, focusing on familial patterns and gender relations.

Studies in which Layish evaluates the historical significance of the reforms conducted in the legal systems of modern Islamic states comprise the core of his scholarly work. In his important and frequently cited article, 'The Contribution of the Modernists to the Secularization of Islamic Law' (1978), Layish makes two highly critical claims: first, that the Modernist project of reformulating legal theory was an intellectual failure. Muḥammad ʿAbduh (d. 1905) and his followers did not succeed in articulating a new and coherent theory of *uṣūl al-fiqh* and they failed to define 'public welfare' (*maṣlaḥa*) as a source of law and the exact ways by which *maṣlaḥa* should function within legal theory. And, second, that the Modernists, unintentionally, enabled the *sharīʿa*'s secularization process by creating legal devices that made it possible for legislators to present statutory codified laws as emanating from the *sharīʿa*, when in fact those laws are purely secular. Among these devices is the eclectic mechanism, *takhayyur*, i.e., the combination of legal elements from various law schools, and 'patching,' *talfiq*, a more sophisticated form of *takhayyur*. The Modernists thus completely destroyed classical *sharīʿa* law without presenting an adequate substitute for it. It is noteworthy that at the time of its publication Layish's evaluation of legal Modernism was a revisionist one, since his teachers, J. N. D. Anderson and Noel Coulson, viewed some aspects of this project as an expression of 'neo-*ijtihād*' (Coulson 1964, Ch. 14; Anderson 1976, 52, 64–5; Layish 2004, 94). Later, Layish's opinion was adopted by other important scholars (see, for example, Hallaq 1997; idem 2004, 24–5, 46).

In a recent important article, 'The Transformation of the *Sharīʿa* from Jurists' Law to Statutory Law in the Contemporary Muslim World' (2004), Layish revisits the topic that he discussed in the 'Contribution of the Modernists.' His assessment of the Modernist project remained the same: it was a failure (ibid., 103). His main thesis is that the codification of the *sharīʿa* by state legislators, from the middle of the nineteenth century, brought about the transformation of the *sharīʿa* from a 'jurists' law,' i.e., one created by independent legal experts (the *ʿulamāʾ*), to a 'statutory law,' promulgated by a national-territorial legislature. This transformation has had profound implications, the most important of which is to deprive the *ʿulamāʾ* of their 'legislative' authority and to invest that authority in secular legislature.

Among the Middle Eastern nation states that were established in the post-WWI era, one can discern three types of legal models (excluding that of Turkey, which is a secular state): (1) a civil-law model was adopted by most states, including Egypt, Syria, Lebanon, Jordan, Iraq, and Iran. These states secularized all fields of law by importing Western-oriented codes (civil, criminal, commercial and international), to be applied by national courts. The only field left for the sharīʿa courts was family law, inheritance and *waqf.* Yet, family law too has been codified in an effort to improve women's rights within the family. (2) states such as Libya, Iran, Sudan and Pakistan, which had applied the first model following their national independence, decided, from the 1970s, to 'Islamize' their legal systems. It is important to note that these states do not intend to reinstate the *sharīʿa* by returning to the classical jurists' law regime. On the contrary: since they have had a relatively long and apparently successful experience with codification, they seek to preserve it as the main channel of 'Islamic' legislation. Codification offers efficient state control of the legal system as well as greater uniformity, consistency and predictability within the judicial system. Layish's study of this model (Layish & Warburg 2002) focuses on the Sudan which, under the rule of Numayri (ca. the mid-1980s), 'Islamized' various domains of the law, especially penal law. Finally, (3) the Saudi state, which has never reformed its legal system along Western lines, is still considered a continuation of the classical *sharīʿa* state. Layish has studied the Saudi Arabian legal regime in a number of articles (for example, 1987). This academic interest is expected, since Saudi Arabia offers the last and closest replica of the pre-modern *sharīʿa* state. Scrutinizing the modern Saudi Arabian legal regime, its judicial system, and the functioning of the *ʿulamāʾ* within it is therefore crucial for concluding whether classical legal theory and the classical mode of *ijtihād* are still operational.

Layish is also one of the leading scholars of the Israeli Arab-Islamic community. He published his first studies on Islamic law in Israel in the early 1960s and has continued ever since. Israel is a unique case in which the *sharīʿa* is applied in a non-Muslim state. The sharīʿa courts are part of the general judicial system. Until recently, these courts wielded the widest substantive jurisdiction compared to that of other religious courts, including the rabbinical courts (exclusive jurisdiction in almost all matters of personal status and *waqf*). In 2001 the Israeli parliament, the Knesset, legislated that the family courts (civil courts for family affairs, established in 1995) are authorized to adjudicate those family law affairs in which the sharīʿa courts enjoy exclusive jurisdiction, except for marriage and divorce.

The main law applied by the Israeli sharīʿa courts is the 1917 Ottoman Family Rights Law, which was based on the eclectic device. Also, Knesset laws which are explicitly directed to the religious courts oblige the sharīʿa court judges (qāḍīs), even if these laws contradict the *sharīʿa* substantively. Moreover, matters of personal status pertaining to Muslims are sometimes adjudicated in the civil courts, predominantly the High Court of Justice. It imposes on the *sharʿī* judiciary legal norms which occasionally may not be in harmony with the *sharīʿa* in matters of personal status pertaining to basic civil rights. It is possible that this policy will lead to the development of a dual legal system in matters of personal status according to the division of the judiciary: the sharīʿa courts will apply the codified *sharīʿa*, subject to the changes introduced by the Knesset legislation, and the civil courts will apply pure civil law.

The current generation of Israeli qāḍīs, which is the third generation since the foundation of the state, lacks formal *sharʿī* training. Headed by the president of the Sharīʿa Court of Appeal, Shaykh Aḥmad Nāṭūr, most are graduates of Israeli universities, either in law or in the humanities or social sciences. The attitude of the present generation of qāḍīs to the Knesset and the Supreme Court is ambivalent: on the one hand, they still have inhibitions towards these authorities, originating from the status of a Muslim-Arab minority in a state that defines itself as Jewish (in religious and national terms) and that is still in a perpetual conflict with the Palestinians. On the other hand, the qāḍīs, especially those who have had secular legal training and rich practical experience as attorneys, are aware of the fact that the *sharʿī* judiciary cannot operate independently from the general judiciary and that the *sharʿī* judiciary is bound by the Knesset's legislation and the judgments of the High Court of Justice. The qāḍīs of the present generation in the Sharīʿa Court of Appeal are anxious to preserve to the utmost the unique religious character of the *sharʿī* judiciary. Shaykh Nāṭūr holds that in the absence of a Muslim sovereign or legislative authority in Israel, the only way left to introduce reforms is by means of the legal circular and the judicial practice of the Sharīʿa Court of Appeal. Both these legal tools are inspired by the legislation and judicial practice in the Arab countries, especially Egypt (see Ido Shahar, Ch. 10 of this volume).

A forthcoming article, 'Adaptation of a Jurists' Law to Modern Times in an Alien Environment: The Case of the *Sharīʿa* in Israel,' based on a lecture delivered by Layish on March 16, 2004, at the Israeli National Academy of Sciences, includes his most recent take on the processes that Islamic law in Israel is undergoing. Layish argues that the qāḍīs in Israel have not created a new legal methodology capable of carrying on its shoulders the burden of the reform. Although they make extensive use of the principle of *maṣlaḥa*, it is doubtful whether they managed to raise it, on the theoretical level, to the rank of an independent source of law. The use of other methods, such as the literal interpretation of Qurʾānic verses and especially *takhayyur*, does not create a comprehensive, systematic and integrative methodology.

Layish estimates that neither the phenomenon of Anglo Muhammadan law nor that of *Droit musulman algérien* will repeat themselves in Israel. In British India there have been no sharīʿa courts since the late eighteenth century and the English courts applied Islamic law in light of the English common law. In French Algeria the sharīʿa courts were amenable to a French Supreme Court of Appeal, located in Algiers, and this court applied Islamic law in the light of the French principles of law. In Israel, by contrast, the Muslims have a complete judiciary that until recently enjoyed exclusive jurisdiction in almost all matters of personal status. Moreover, in contrast to Algeria, the Israeli High Court of Justice does not interfere in the judgments of the sharīʿa courts as an appellate court. So far, the *sharīʿa* in Israel has not developed along the pattern of the colonial tradition, though in academic discourse this notion is not totally alien.

His profound interest in Arab customary law as the main foundation on which the *sharīʿa* rests also led Layish to study the Israeli Bedouins at length. With the ongoing transformation from a nomadic society to a partly or fully settled society, the Bedouins have become closer to urban orthodox Islam. The *ʿulamāʾ* have been important agents in attracting Bedouins this way. The tensions between the three ingredients of Israeli law—Knesset legislation, the *sharīʿa*, and Arab customary law—have been studied by Layish in a number of articles, some of which were written jointly with the late geographer, Avshalom Shmueli. These studies are based on sharīʿa court documents, on legal opinions, and on documents of informal customary arbitration (*taḥkīm*), gathered by Layish in the Bethlehem area. A similar process to the Israeli one is analyzed by him with reference to Libyan nomadic populations in the process of sedentarization (1982).

To his students, Layish was a strict, meticulous, and demanding teacher. Many were intimidated by the first impression and retreated. Those who were patient enough to stay, and especially his research students, discovered a professor who was highly dedicated and caring for his students, and who was a good example of uncompromised reliability, fairness and honesty. Most impressive was the fact that every draft of an academic work submitted to him for review was returned to the author within a surprisingly short time, accompanied by a large number of detailed and thorough comments.

The present collective volume is based on a conference, titled 'Law in Islamic Societies: Historical Issues and Contemporary Developments,' conducted at the Hebrew University on June 10, 2002, in honor of Aharon Layish, upon his retirement from teaching. I would like to thank Prof. Amnon Cohen, the then-Director of the Harry S. Truman Research Institute for the Advancement of Peace, Idit Avidan, the Programs Director of that institute, Prof. Reuven Amitai, the then-Head of the Institute of Asian and African Studies at the Hebrew University, Prof. Steven Kaplan, then Vice Dean of the Faculty of Humanities of the Hebrew University, Nahum Regev, the Deputy

Dean of the Faculty, and, finally, Haggai Nahmias, a research assistant at the Truman Institute, for providing the funds and/or the administrative support that facilitated the conducting of that event. Some of the papers delivered in the framework of this conference by Israeli scholars, in addition to others invited from colleagues from abroad, constitute the academic crop included in this volume. I thank all the participants of that conference and the other contributors of chapters for their cooperation and support during the preparation of the volume. In order to enable the authors to improve their submissions, each draft chapter was read and commented on by an outside reader (or readers). I wish to thank all of them for their constructive comments.

The publication of this volume could not have taken place without the financial support granted by the Chaim Herzog Center for Middle East Studies & Diplomacy at the Ben-Gurion University and its Chairman Dr. Yoram Meital, the Institute of Asian and African Studies at the Hebrew University, headed by Prof. Meir Bar-Asher, the Nehemia Levtzion Center for Islamic Studies, also at the Hebrew University, directed by Prof. Reuven Amitai, and the Research Committee of the Faculty of Humanities, the Hebrew University, headed by Prof. Moshe Zimmerman. This support was mainly used for style editing. Many thanks are due also to Lisa Perlman for her excellent style editing of the volume.

Following his retirement from teaching, Aharon Layish has not slowed the pace of his academic work. On the contrary, he has accelerated it. He continues his extensive writing and travels the world, lecturing and collecting research material. His appetite for scholarship and his dynamism are a continuous source of inspiration for his younger colleagues. We wish him many years of good health and intellectual creativity.

ACADEMIC AUTOBIOGRAPHY

Aharon Layish

Looking back over my professional life, I realize that my choice of career was largely a product of chance. As a high school student in Haifa, at the Gymnasia Bialik, I planned to pursue a career in civil engineering at the Technion University, then one of the leading academic institutions in Palestine. What brought about a change of mind was the appearance at school of a new Arabic teacher, Mrs. Zahava Pir-Kister. Arabic was then a compulsory subject for graduation from secondary school and an option for the matriculation certificate. The impact of Mrs. Pir-Kister's personality and her dynamic style of teaching—in particular, her enthusiasm for Arabic language and culture—profoundly shaped the course of my life.

I was born in Suvalki, a small town in northeastern Poland (now on the Lithuanian border). When I was just a year old, in 1934, my parents, Grisha and Rosa Liskovski, under the pressure of political events, took my two brothers and me (I am the youngest) and emigrated to Palestine, leaving the rest of the family behind. They settled in Haifa. Seventy years later, in 2003, I visited the site of the demolished family residence in Suvalki on the occasion of a series of lectures on Islamic law delivered at meetings of the Committee of Oriental Studies, at the invitation of the Polish Academy of Sciences in Cracow.

Growing up in a mixed Jewish-Arab neighborhood gave me valuable insights into the Arab way of life, exposed me to colloquial Arabic, and aroused my intellectual curiosity, all of which influenced the direction of my subsequent studies at the university.

After two and a half years of compulsory military service, I started my undergraduate studies at the Hebrew University of Jerusalem (1953/54). Initially, my main interest was Arabic language and literature, and only the formal B.A. requirement of additional course work exposed me to Middle Eastern Studies. However, it soon became clear to me that I had no particular inclination for Arabic philology. At a lecture by the late Prof. D. H. Baneth, I vividly recall that, during the course of his elaborate commentary on the syntax of Abū 'l-Faraj al-Isfahānī's *Kitāb Riwāyāt al-Aghānī*, what caught my fancy in the text was the odd circumstance that a woman could repudiate her husband by changing the direction of the tent's entrance. For Baneth, this legal point was completely irrelevant.

After completing my B.A. degree, in Arabic language and literature and the contemporary Middle East, I came under the influence of Prof. Uriel Heyd, who encouraged my interest in Turkish culture with specific reference to the Ottoman reforms period (*Tanzimat*) and modern Turkey. To this end, I studied Ottoman and modern Turkish for four years. For my Master's degree, I specialized in the modern history of the Muslim countries and in Islamic civilization. I took my first steps in Islamic law under Prof. Shlomo D. Goitein, who introduced me to the history and legal methodology of this subject.

As a student, I joined the Israel Oriental Society and in 1955/56 was nominated secretary of the Society alongside Prof. Goitein, who served as President. In 1958, I joined the staff of the Bureau of the Prime Minister's Advisor on Arab Affairs. Eight years of intensive service in this government bureau (between 1963–66 as Deputy Advisor) dealing with Muslim and Druze affairs, e.g., communal organization, the judicial system and *waqf* administration, proved of immense utility to me when I later moved from the executive domain to an academic career. My friendly personal relations with Muslim and Druze religious functionaries, including *qāḍī*s, spiritual leaders, and *mutawallī*s, enabled me to acquire unique insight into their religious and social philosophy, and their daily legal practice. In particular, I acquired an intimate familiarity with Muslim and Druze legal documents and an appreciation for their social and legal significance as research sources. While I was still involved in government affairs, I wrote my M.A. thesis on Muslim communal organization in Israel, under the supervision of Prof. Gabriel Baer, and became acquainted with the *sijill* (records) of the *sharīʿa* courts.

My private life underwent a significant change in 1959 when I married Bilha Stein, a fellow graduate of the Department of Arabic Language and Literature, and settled down permanently in Jerusalem. Bilha, who had been a student of Prof. Meir Kister at *Hareali* high school in Haifa, would go on to head the Library of the Institute of Asian and African Studies of the Hebrew University on Givʿat Ram. Of our three children—Galia, Hadara and Dan—only Hadara chose to study Arabic at school. Her teacher, in Jerusalem, was Zahava Pir-Kister.

On resuming my studies as a research student at the Hebrew University in 1966/67, I read classical Islamic law with Prof. Eliahu Ashtor at the Faculty of Law. I decided to utilize the *sijill* as the principal source material in my research. Over the years, the use of legal documents for the study of social and legal history has been a challenging and stimulating intellectual enterprise. In the period 1971–72, with the assistance of a British Council fellowship, I pursued advanced studies in Islamic law at the School of Oriental and African Studies of the University of London, where I read Islamic inheritance law with Prof. Noel Coulson and Dr. Doreen Hinchcliffe and family law with Prof. Norman Anderson. My Ph.D. thesis, written under the supervision of Prof. Baer and approved by the Senate in 1973, dealt with the social status of the Muslim woman in Israel as reflected in the proceedings of the *sharīʿa* courts. The thesis focused on social history, the legal dimension here serving the interest of social analysis rather than being an end in itself.

Between 1966–68, I was Visiting Research Associate at the Shiloah Center for Middle Eastern and African Studies, Tel Aviv University and in 1967 I joined the Department of the History of the Muslim Countries and the Department of Islamic Civilization at the Institute of Oriental Studies (later renamed the Institute of Asian and African Studies) at the Hebrew University (Lecturer, 1973; Senior Lect., 1978; Assoc. Prof. 1981; Prof. 1989). During the period 1981–93, I was elected head of both departments several times and—after their unification—head of the Department of Islamic and Middle Eastern Studies. In addition, I taught Islamic law at the Faculties of Law of Tel Aviv University (1978–86, with short intervals) and the Hebrew University (1981–83, 1987–88); at the Department of Law at the School of Oriental and African Studies, University of London (1979–80); and at the Hagop Kevorkian Center for Near Eastern Studies, New York University (1989). In 1976–78, I was coordinator of the Middle East Unit at the Harry S Truman Research Institute at the Hebrew University.

From the very beginning of my research, I have been fascinated by the interaction between *sharīʿa* and custom (*ʿāda*, *ʿurf*), the former being a divinely revealed law, eternal, immutable and imposed on society from above, the latter being an unwritten law shaped on the ground by the collective practice of the community, outside the control of the central authority. The *sharīʿa* and custom have coexisted side by side for centuries in a state of perpetual tension, with occasional peaceful compromises with each other. Within this framework, the *qāḍī* plays a decisive role in bringing the Bedouin within the orbit of orthodox Islam. Having already been exposed to the interaction between *sharīʿa* and custom while writing my dissertation, I realized that the Muslim woman, especially in tribal society, is able to benefit from her *sharʿī* rights in matters of personal status and succession only to the extent that this is tolerated by custom (see List of Publications, sections 1.5; 3.1).

The same phenomenon emerges with greater clarity in legal documents collected from tribal arbitrators in the Judean Desert (1.6–8, 10, 13) and from the records of the Libyan *sharīʿa* courts (1.2–16). It is also manifested in the family *waqf*, the subject of several of my studies. In daily practice this institution is generally used first and foremost as an instrument for circumventing the *sharʿī* rules of inheritance in an effort to prevent the disintegration of the agnatic patrimony. Married females are deprived of their shares in the estate (or entitlement to the revenues of the *waqf*) out of fear that they might transfer their rights to their cognates (6.4, 7, 8).

Another topic that has been of special interest to me is the methodology for introducing reforms in contemporary Islam and the repercussions of the methodology and reforms on the nature of the *sharīʿa* and the family. In effect, the codification of the *sharīʿa* has resulted in its transformation from jurists' law to statutory law, and in the collapse of the traditional legal methodology (*uṣūl al-fiqh*) and the *fuqahā*'s historical role in the development of the *sharīʿa* (2.13). Paradoxically, the modernists of the school of Muḥammad ʿAbduh contributed significantly to the secularization of the *sharīʿa* by providing Middle Eastern parliaments in the twentieth century with traditional mechanisms, and hence *sharʿī* legitimacy for statutory legislation (2.3). It is intriguing to note that even the reinstatement of Islamic law in the Sudan under Numayrī was carried out through codification and legislation (2.2, 14). Reforms in matters of personal status and succession brought about the disintegration of the traditional Muslim patrilineal and patriarchal family (2.12). Of special interest here is the reaction of the *ʿulamāʾ*, especially the *qāḍīs*, to these reforms and the reasons for their cooperation with the state, as in the case of Saudi Arabia (2.4–6). A special case in point is the application of Islamic law in a non-Muslim state that entails interaction between the *sharīʿa* and custom, on the one hand, and statutory legislation, on the other (3.1–8; 6.2,7, 8).

My research on Druze family law has been a particularly stimulating intellectual venture. As is known, only those who are initiated into Druze scriptures have access to Druze religious law. Lebanon, under the French Mandate, was the first country to codify Druze family law (1948). The Druze spiritual leadership in Israel adopted Lebanese law with two important modifications: Ḥanafī doctrine was replaced by Druze custom and Lebanese statutes were replaced by Israeli statutes. The codification of family law was indispensable to its application in the religious courts of the newly recognized community. Needless to say, I was fortunate in being able to conduct research on Druze family law, succession, wills and *taqiyya* on the basis of the records of these courts. In particular, I was amazed by the daily practice of adapting religiously-inspired rules, such as the prohibition of polygamy, the prohibition of reinstating one's divorced wife and freedom of testamentary disposition, to the agnatic patterns of Druze society, on the one hand, and by the *qāḍīs*' efforts to mitigate religious prohibitions in light of modern reality, on the other (5.1, 12, 15).

Over the last ten years, I have been working on the Sudanese Mahdī's legal methodology, its sources of inspiration and its application, as reflected in proclamations, rulings, and legal opinions issued by the Mahdī from the time of his manifestation in 1881until his death in 1885. These documents entail far-reaching deviations from traditional legal theory and Islamic substantive and procedural law. Thus, the Mahdī denied systematic analogy (*qiyās*) and the consensus (*ijmāʿ*) of the *fuqahāʾ*, replacing them with inspiration (*ilhām*) from the Prophet Muḥammad. Similarly, he abolished the consolidated law of all schools. This was a striking attempt to create a theocracy based on the Prophet's model. To this end, the invention of a new legal methodology was instrumental (2.9, 11, 15).

I am currently working on an Arabic scroll—20 meters long—containing the registration of some thirty transactions of different kinds, e.g., *waqf*, sale, lease and succession, in the region of Aleppo over a period exceeding 100 years, from the late fourteenth century to the beginning of the sixteenth, produced by three generations of descendants of a Mamluk *amīr* (hence *awlād al-nās*). This family saga sheds additional light on the *waqf* as an instrument for the preservation of the agnatic patrimony, on women's capacity to own and dispose of property, on relations between the founder and his Mamlūks, and on the role of the *waqf* in social welfare in a society in transition from a Mamlūk military elite to a civil elite (6.10). *Waqf* documents shed important light not only on social history but also political history, as has been demonstrated in the case of Sulṭān Selīm I's *waqf* in favor of a Ṣūfī shaykh settled in Dayr al-Asad, a small settlement on a strategic road between Acre and Safed. This legal document illustrates the Ottoman policy of colonization of recently conquered areas by means of Ṣūfī monasteries (6.5).

My sabbaticals abroad were very useful for the implementation of my research projects.

As a Visiting Fellow at Clare Hall and Member of the Law Faculty, University of Cambridge (England), in 1979–80, I studied Bedouin legal documents collected from tribal arbitrators in the Judean Desert. A stay, seven years later, at Eliot College, University of Kent in Canterbury (1986–87), with the support of a Marks fellowship, was devoted to research on Libyan documents collected by the anthropologist Prof. John Davis from the Sharīʿa Courts of Ajdābiya and Kufra (Libya). I was able to continue my research on this project as Associate at the Institute of Social Anthropology, University of Oxford, with the support of an Israeli Visiting Fellowship provided by St. Antony's College. A stay at New York University, in 1989, as a Visiting Fulbright Professor allowed me time to concentrate on legal documents pertaining to Muslim family *waqf* in Jerusalem.

As a research fellow at the Centre of Middle Eastern and Islamic Studies of the University of Leiden in 1995, with the support of Nederlandse Organisatie voor Wetenschappelijk Onderzoek (NWO) Fellowship (1995), and at the Centre of Middle Eastern and Islamic Studies, University of Bergen within the Cultural Agreement (the Specialists Program) between Norway and Israel (1996, 1997), I was able to pursue research on the Sudanese Mahdī's legal methodology on the basis of his documents. In July 2002, I retired from the Hebrew University.

Retirement provides ample opportunity for self-examination. Occasionally, I wonder whether I should have concentrated on one major subject rather than spreading myself over a variety of subjects and regions. Be that as it may, in terms of scholarship, this is a purely academic question, for I simply could not resist the temptation of undertaking new intellectual ventures. I was fortunate to have access to an abundance of rare documents and archives. In most cases this was not the result of a special effort on my part, but rather a matter of sheer luck. To fully exhaust the research potential of this material, a long life and good health are indispensable. I have enjoyed every moment of my research; there is nevertheless one regret: I should have obtained a degree in general (Israeli) law. A thorough command of a legal discipline is essential for research on the social and legal history of Islamic law as well as for comparative study. I have been fully aware of this lacuna in my training for many years, but I was too busy with instructional commitments at the university and too anxious to promote my own research to be able to realize this ambition.

I am deeply grateful to the Hebrew University of Jerusalem for providing me with the opportunity to explore the entrancing world of research and I am particularly indebted to my teachers, colleagues and students at the Hebrew University and abroad. I should like to single out my teacher and colleague, Prof. Pessah Shinar, for his intellectual inspiration and warm friendship.

At the request of Muslim and Druze litigants, the Ministry of Justice or the civil court, I occasionally issue legal opinions on matters pertaining to personal status, succession, *waqf*, homicide and bodily assault (the latter, on the basis of tribal law). These opinions are based on legal literature and research experience. I regard them as intellectual exercises, the object of which is to find appropriate solutions to daily problems, that is, to adapt legal norm to the practical requirements of modern society. On these occasions I can easily identify with the *muftī*'s challenge. In one case, my opinion regarding paternity out of wedlock under the *sharīʿa* was instrumental in shaping a new constitutional norm (civil paternity) by the Supreme Court.

My affiliation with the Israel Oriental Society was interrupted for a short period during my stay at the Prime Minister's Office. All in all, I have served the Society as the editor of its Hebrew journal, *Hamizrah Hehadash*, *The New East* (1976–92), as deputy chairman of the Executive Committee (1981–98), as its chairman (1998–2004) and as its president (2004–06). In 1993, I joined the editorial board of the newly-founded journal, *Islamic Law and Society* (Brill, Leiden).

In 1979, I coordinated the S. Neʿeman Workshop (at the Technion) on the Implications of Peace for the State of Israel, with special reference to the Israeli Arabs; the report was submitted to the Prime Minister. Between 1991–2004, I was a member of the executive committee of *Sikkuy*, the association for the advancement of equal opportunity for Arabs in Israel.

I express my thanks to my colleagues who participated in the conference to mark my retirement: "Law in Islamic Societies: Historical

Issues and Contemporary Developments" sponsored by the Harry S Truman Research Institute for the Advancement of Peace and the Institute of Asian and African Studies, at the Hebrew University on June 6, 2002, and to those who contributed most interesting essays for this wonderful volume.

My student and colleague, Dr. Ron Shaham, who initiated both the conference and this volume, has been my best investment in the academy. I retired with the certain knowledge that there is someone to replace me in instruction and research on the meeting point between Islamic law and society. Roni will do it his own way, paving new roads and leaving his personal imprint on research and instruction.

Finally, I am profoundly grateful to my wife, Bilha, for much patient understanding, moral support and encouragement all along the way.

LIST OF PUBLICATIONS
Classified by subjects in chronological order

Aharon Layish

1. Sharīʿa *and Custom*

Books and edited issues of journals

1.1 (Ed.) *Bedouin Law: The Impact of Sharīʿa on a Tribal Society*. Special issue of *Hamizrah Hehadash* 33 (1991) (in Hebrew).
1.2 *Divorce in the Libyan Family. A Study Based on the* Sijill *of the* Sharīʿa *Courts of Ajdābiya and Kufra*. Jerusalem: Magnes Press & New York: New York University Press, 1991.
1.3 *Legal Documents on Libyan Tribal Society in Process of Sedentarization. A Selection of Decisions from the* Sijills *of the* Sharīʿa *Courts of Ajdābiya and Kufra*. Part 1: *The Documents in Arabic*. Wiesbaden: Harrassowitz, 1998.
1.4 Sharīʿa *and Custom in Libyan Tribal Society. An Annotated Translation of Decisions from the* Sharīʿa *Courts of Ajdābiya and Kufra*. With an essay on "Orality, Language, and Culture in Arabic Juridical Discourse," by Alexander Borg. Leiden: Brill, 2005.

Articles and chapters

1.5 "*Sharīʿa* and Custom in the Muslim Family in Israel," *Hamizrah Hehadash* 23. 4 (1974), pp. 377–409 (in Hebrew).
1.6 (with A. Shmueli) "Custom and *Sharīʿa* in the Bedouin Family according to Legal Documents from the Judaean Desert," *Bulletin of the School of Oriental and African Studies* 42.1 (1979), pp. 29–45.
1.7 "Challenges to Customary Law and Arbitration: the Impact of Islamic Law upon Settled Bedouin in the Judaean Desert," *Tel Aviv University Studies in Law* 5 (1980–82), pp. 206–21. Also in *Cathedra* 20 (1981), pp. 81–96 (in Hebrew).
1.8 "The Islamization of the Bedouin Family in the Judaean Desert as Reflected in the *Sijill*s of the *Sharīʿa* Court," in *The Changing*

Bedouin, ed. E. Marx and A. Shmueli. Brunswick, N.J.: Transaction Books, 1984, pp. 39–58.

1.9 "Customary *Khulʿ* as Reflected in the *Sijill* of the Libyan *Sharīʿa* Courts," *Bulletin of the School of Oriental and African Studies* 51.2 (1988), pp. 428–39.

1.10 "The *Fatwā* as an Instrument of Islamization of Tribal Society in Process of Sedentarization," *Bulletin of the School of Oriental and African Studies* 54.3 (1991), pp. 449–59. Also in *Hamizrah Hehadash* 33 (1991), pp. 120–31 (in Hebrew).

1.11 "*Dār ʿAdl*—Symbiosis of Custom and *Sharīʿa* in a Tribal Society in the Process of Sedentarization," *Jerusalem Studies in Arabic and Islam* 18 (1995), pp. 198–213.

1.12 "*Sharīʿa* and Tribal Custom in Libya: Was Tajdīda Married to Two Husbands?" *Archív Orientální* 63 (1995), pp. 488–503.

1.13 "The Fatwa as an Instrument of Accommodation," in *Islamic Legal Interpretation. Muftis and Their Fatwas*, ed. M. Kh. Masud, B. Messick and D. S. Powers. Harvard University Press, Cambridge, Mass., 1996, pp. 270–77 (revised version of 1.10).

1.14 "The *Qāḍī's* Role in the Islamization of Sedentary Tribal Society," in *The Public Sphere in Muslim Societies*, ed. M. Hoexter, S. N. Eisenstadt, and N. Levtzion. New York: SUNY, 2002, pp. 83–107.

1.15 "*Shahādat naql* in the Judicial Practice in Modern Libya," in *Dispensing Justice in Muslim Courts: Qadis, Procedures and Judgments*, ed. M. Kh. Masud, R. Peters and D. S. Powers. Leiden: Brill, 2006, pp. 493–514.

1.16 "Interplay between Tribal and *Sharʿī* Law: A Case of Tibbāwī Blood Money in the Sharīʿa Court of Kufra," *Islamic Law and Society* 13.1 (2006), pp. 63–75.

1.17 "Islamization of Custom as Reflected in Awards of Tribal Arbitrators in the Judean Desert." Paper submitted to Princeton Conference on Customary Law, New Jersey 13–14 May, 2006.

2. *Legal Reformism and* ʿUlamāʾ

Books and edited issues of journals

2.1 (Ed.) *Renewal* (Tajdīd) *and Reform* (Iṣlāḥ) *in Islam.* Special issue of *Hamizrah Hehadash* 31 (1986) (in Hebrew).

2.2 (with Gabriel R. Warburg) *The Reinstatement of Islamic Law in Sudan under Numayrī. An Evaluation of a Legal Experiment in the Light of Its Historical Context, Methodology, and Repercussions*. Brill: Leiden, 2002.

Articles and chapters

2.3 "The Contribution of the Modernists to the Secularization of Islamic Law," *Middle Eastern Studies* 14.3 (1978), pp. 263–77. Also in *Hamizrah Hehadash* 26 (1976), pp. 1–14 (in Hebrew).
2.4 (with Aviva Schussman) "Dialogue between Saudi *ʿUlamāʾ* and European Jurists and Scientists," *Hamizrah Hehadash* 28.1–2 (1979), pp. 74–80 (in Hebrew).
2.5 "*ʿUlamāʾ* and Politics in Saudi Arabia," in *Islam and Politics in the Modern Middle East*, ed. M. Heper and R. Israeli. London: Croom Helm, 1984, pp. 29–63.
2.6 "Legal Reform in Saudi Arabia as a Mechanism to Moderate Wahhābī Doctrine," *Journal of the American Oriental Society* 107.2 (1987), pp. 279–92. Also in *Hamizrah Hehadash* 31 (1986), pp. 104–37 (in Hebrew).
2.7 "Islamic Law in the Contemporary Middle East," *Occasional Papers* 3, Centre of Near and Middle Eastern Studies, University of London, April 1989.
2.8 "Maḥkama, 4. The Arab Lands and Israel in the Modern Period," *The Encyclopaedia of Islam*, 2nd ed. VI (1991), pp. 22–9, 31–42.
2.9 "The Legal Methodology of the Mahdi in the Sudan, 1881–85: Issues in Marriage and Divorce," *Sudanic Africa* 8 (1997), pp. 37–66. Also in *Hamizrah Hehadash* 40 (1999), pp. 38–51 (in Hebrew).
2.10 (with Ron Shaham) "Tashrīʿ," *The Encyclopaedia of Islam*, 2nd ed. X (2000), pp. 353–54.
2.11 "The Legal Methodology of the Mahdi in the Sudan as a Mechanism for Adapting the *Sharīʿa* to Political and Social Purposes," in *Mahdisme et millénanrisme en Islam*, éd. Mercedes Garcia-Arenal. *Revue des Mondes Musulmans et de la Méditerranée*. Série Histoire 91–92–93–94 (2000), pp. 221–38.
2.12 "Reformist Matrimonial Legislation and the Collapse of the Muslim Patrilineal Family," *Awrāq* 21 (2000), pp. 57–80.
2.13 "The Transformation of the *Sharīʿa* from Jurists' Law to Statutory Law in the Contemporary Muslim World." *Die Welt des Islams* 44.1 (2004), 85–112. Also in *Intertwined Worlds of Islam. Essays in Memory*

of Hava Lazarus-Yafeh, ed. N. Ilan. Jerusalem: Ben-Zvi Institute of Yad Izhak Ben-Zvi and the Hebrew University of Jerusalem, 2002, pp. 393–412 (in Hebrew).

2.14 "Ḥasan al-Turābī's Contribution to the Modernization of Islamic Legal Methodology," in *Islamic Legal Thought: Jurists and Their Works*, ed. Susan Spectorsky, David S. Powers and Oussama Arabi (forthcoming).

2.15 "The Sudanese Mahdī's Legal Methodology and Its Ṣūfī Inspiration." *Jerusalem Studies in Arabic and Islam*. Special issue in Honor of Yohanan Friedmann (forthcoming).

3. *Islamic Law in Israel*

Book

3.1 *Women and Islamic Law in a Non-Muslim State. A Study Based on the Decisions of the* Sharīʿa *Courts in Israel.* New York: John Wiley & Jerusalem: Israeli Universities Press, 1975.

Articles

3.2 "Muslim Religious Jurisdiction in Israel," *Asian and African Studies*, vol. 1 (1965), pp. 47–79. Also in *Hamizrah Hehadash* 13.1–2 (1963), pp. 19–38 (in Hebrew).

3.3 "*Qāḍīs* and *Sharīʿa* in Israel," *Asian and African Studies* 7 (1971), pp. 237–72. Also in *The ʿUlamāʾ and Problems of Religion in the Muslim World*, ed. G. Baer. Jerusalem: Magnes Press, 1971, pp. 293–315 (in Hebrew).

3.4 "Communal Organization of the Muslims," in *The Arabs in Israel: Continuity and Change*, ed. A. Layish. Jerusalem: Magnes Press, 1981, pp. 102–22 (in Hebrew).

3.5 "Maḥkama, 4. The Arab Lands and Israel in the Modern Period," *The Encyclopaedia of Islam*, 2nd ed. VI (1991), pp. 29–31.

3.6 "The Status of the *Sharīʿa* in a Non-Muslim State: the Case of Israel," *Asian and African Studies* 27 (1993), pp. 171–87.

3.7 "Bequests as an Instrument for Accommodating Inheritance Rules: Israel as a Case Study," *Islamic Law and Society* 2.3 (1995), pp. 282–319.

3.8 "Adaptation of a Jurists' Law to Modern Times in an Alien Environment: The *Sharīʿa* in Israel." *Die Welt des Islams*, 46.2 (2006), pp. 168–225. Also in *Proceedings of the Israel Academy of Sciences and Humanities*, 9.2 (2005), pp. 13–51 (in Hebrew).

4. *Muslim Family Law*

Books and edited issues of journals

4.1 See 3.1.
4.2 See 1.2.
4.3 (Ed.) *Marriage, Divorce and Succession in the Muslim Family*. Theme issue of *Islamic Law and Society* 2.3 (1995).
4.4 See 1.3.
4.5 See 1.4.

Articles

4.4 "Women and Succession in the Muslim Family in Israel," *Asian and African Studies* 9.1 (1973), pp. 23–62.
4.5 "Mīrāth, 2. In Modern Islamic Countries," *The Encyclopaedia of Islam,* 2nd ed. VII (1993), pp. 111–13.
4.6 (with Ron Shaham) "Nikāḥ, II. In the Modern Islamic World. 1. The Arab, Persian and Turkish Lands of the Middle East," *The Encyclopaedia of Islam*, 2nd ed., VIII (1995), pp. 29–32.
4.7 See 3.7.
4.8 "Ṭalāḳ, II. Reforms in the Modern Middle East and North Africa," *The Encyclopaedia of Islam*, 2nd ed., IX (1998), pp. 155–57.

5. *Druze Family Law and Community*

Book

5.1 *Marriage, Divorce and Succession in the Druze Family. A Study Based on Decisions of Druze Arbitrators and Religious Courts in Israel and the Golan Heights*. Leiden: Brill, 1982.

Articles and Chapters

5.2 "Druze Communal Jurisdiction in Israel," *Hamizrah Hehadash* 11.4 (1961), pp. 258–62 (in Hebrew).
5.3 "Women and Succession in the Druze Family in Israel," *Asian and African Studies* 11.1 (1976), pp. 101–19.
5.4 "Compensation to the Divorced Woman in the Israeli Druze Family," *Israel Law Review* 12.3 (1977), pp. 330–43.
5.5 "The Prohibition of Reinstating a Divorced Wife in the Druze Family," *Bulletin of the School of Oriental and African Studies* 41.2 (1978), pp. 258–71.
5.6 "Islam as a Source of Law in the Druze Religious Courts, *Israel Law Review* 14.1 (1979), pp. 13–30. Also in *Hamizrah Hehadash* 26 (1976), pp. 149–61 (in Hebrew).
5.7 "Polygamy and the Druze Family in Israel," *Journal of the American Oriental Society* 99.1 (1979), pp. 58–63. Also in *'Iyuney Mishpaṭ* (*Law Review*) 5.3 (1977), pp. 573–80 (in Hebrew).
5.8 "Dower in the Israeli Druze Family," in *The Druse. A Religious Community in Transition*, ed. N. Dana. Jerusalem: Turledov Publishing, 1980, pp. 77–111.
5.9 (with Nissim Dana) "The Law of Personal Status of the Druze Community in Israel," in *The Druse. A Religious Community in Transition*, ed. N. Dana. Jerusalem: Turledovc Publishing, 1980, pp. 147–75. Also in *The Druzes*, ed. N. Dana. Ramat Gan: Bar-Ilan University Press, 1998, pp. 225–77 (revised version in Hebrew).
5.10 "Communal Organization of the Druzes," in *The Arabs in Israel: Continuity and Change*, ed. A. Layish. Jerusalem: Magnes Press, 1981, pp. 123–39 (in Hebrew).
5.11 "Religion, Custom and Secular Legislation in the Druze Family," *The Druzes in Israel, Occasional Papers on the Middle East*. New Series 6. Haifa: The Jewish-Arab Center, University of Haifa, 1984, pp. 55–69 (in Hebrew).
5.12 "*Taqiyya* among the Druzes," *Asian and African Studies*, vol. 19.3 (1985), pp. 245–81.
5.13 "Continuity and Change in the Druze Family," in *Families in Israel*, ed. Lea Shamgar-Handelman and Rivka Bar-Yosef. Jerusalem: Academon, 1991, pp. 125–33 (in Hebrew). Also in *The Druzes*, ed. N. Dana. Ramat Gan: Bar-Ilan University Press, 1998, pp. 131–40 (in Hebrew).
5.14 "The Status of Islamic Law in the Druze Family in a Non-Muslim State as Reflected in Judicial Practice," in *Syncretistic Religious*

Communities in the Near East, ed. K. Kehl-Bodrogi, B. Kellner-Heinkele and A. Otter-Beaujean. Leiden: Brill, 1997, pp. 139–53.

5.15 "The Druze Religious Will as a Political Instrument," in *Alevi Identity—Cultural, Religious and Social Perspective*, ed. T. Olsson, C. Raudvere and E. Özdalga. Istanbul: Numune Matbaası, 1998, pp. 137–50.

6. *Waqf*

Edited issue of journal

6.1 (Ed.) *Social and Economic Aspects of the Muslim Waqf.* Theme issue, *Islamic Law and Society* 4.3 (1997).

Articles

6.2 "The Muslim *Waqf* in Israel," *Asian and African Studies* 2 (1966), pp. 41–76. Also in *Hamizrah Hehadash* 15.1–2 (1965), pp. 38–56 (in Hebrew).

6.3 "A *Sharʿī Waqfiyya* in Favour of the Ashkenazi Community in Jerusalem," in *Jeruslem in the Modern Period*, ed. E. Shaltiel. Yaacov Herzog Memorial Volume, Jerusalem: Yad Ben-Zvi, 1981, pp. 249–54 (in Hebrew).

6.4 "The Mālikī Family Waqf according to Wills and *Waqfiyyāt*," *Bulletin of the School of Oriental and African Studies* 46.1 (1983), pp. 1–32.

6.5 "*Waqf*s and Ṣūfī Monasteries in the Ottoman Policy of Colonization: Sulṭān Selīm I's *Waqf* in Favour of Dayr al-Asad," *Bulletin of the School of Oriental and African Studies* 50.1 (1987), pp. 61–89. Also in *Cathedra* 35 (1985), pp. 17–52 (in Hebrew).

6.6 "The Druze Testamentary *Waqf*," *Studia Islamica* 71 (1990), pp. 127–54.

6.7 "The Muslim *Waqf* in Jerusalem after 1967: Beneficiaries and Management," in *Le waqf dans le monde musulman contemporain* (*xix*^{e}–*xx*^{e} *siècles*), ed. F. Bilici. Institut Français d'Études Anatoliennes, *Varia Turcica*, xxvi (Istanbul, 1994), pp. 145–66. Also in *Hamizrah Hehadash* 34 (1992), pp. 95–114 (in Hebrew).

6.8 "The Family *Waqf* and the *Sharʿī* Law of Succession in Modern Times," *Islamic Law and Society* 4.3 (1997), pp. 352–88.

6.9 "Waḳf, 5: In the Modern Middle East and North Africa," *The Encyclopaedia of Islam*, 2nd ed. XI (2000), pp. 78–81.

6.10 "*Waqf* of *awlād al-nās* in Aleppo at the End of the Mamlūk Period as Reflected in a Family Archive." Paper submitted to the Conference on *Waqf* Law, Harvard Law School, Cambridge, Mass., May 26–28, 2006.

7. *The Arabs in Israel and Palestine*

Books and edited issues of journals

7.1 (Ed.) *Muslims and Christians in Jerusalem*. A special issue, *Hamizrah Hehadash* 28.1–2 (1979) (in Hebrew).
7.2 (Ed.) *The Arabs in Israel: Continuity and Change*. Jerusalem: Magnes Press, 1981 (in Hebrew).
7.3 (Ed.) *The Arabs in Israel: Between Religious Revival and National Awakening*. Special issue, *Hamizrah Hehadash* 32 (1989) (in Hebrew).
7.4 (Ed.) *The Arabs in Jerusalem. From the Late Ottoman Period to the Beginning of 1990s—Religious, Social and Cultural Distinctiveness*. Special issue, *Hamizrah Hehadash* 34 (1992) (in Hebrew).

Articles

7.5 A. Liskovski [Layish], "Resident 'Absentees' in Israel," *Hamizrah Hehadash* 10 (1960), pp. 186–92 (in Hebrew).
7.6 "Social and Political Changes in the Arab Society in Israel," in *The Palestinians: People, History, Politics*, ed. M. Curtis, J. Neyer, Ch. L. Waxman and A. Pollack. New Jersey: Transaction Books, 1975, pp. 81–7. Also in *The Arabs in Israel: Continuity and Change*, ed. A. Layish. Jerusalem: Magnes Press, 1981, pp. 241–47 (revised version; in Hebrew).
7.7 "The *Sijill* of Jaffa and Nazareth *Sharīʿa* Courts as a Source for Political and Social History of Ottoman Palestine," in *Studies on Palestine during the Ottoman Period*, ed. M. Maʿoz. Jerusalem: Magnes Press, 1972, pp. 514–21. Also in *Cathedra* 1 (1976), pp. 141–47 (in Hebrew).
7.8 "Muslim Religious Institutions in the West Bank under Jordanian Rule," *Medina, Mimshal Wi-[y]Ḥasim Benleumiyim* 11 (1977), pp. 97–108 (in Hebrew).

8. *Miscellanea*

Books and edited issues of journals

8.1 (Ed. with Y. Gershoni and B. Neuberger) *Africa: Islam, Christianity and Judaism.* Studies in Honor of Nehemia Levtzion. Special issue, *Hamizrah Hehadash*, 40 (1999) (in Hebrew).

Articles

8.2 "Uriel Heyd's Contribution to the Study of Legal, Religious, Cultural and Political History of the Ottoman Empire and Modern Turkey," *Bulletin of the British Society for Middle Eastern Studies* 9.1 (1982), pp. 35–54.

8.3 "Notes on Joseph Schacht's Contribution to the Study of Islamic Law," *Bulletin of the British Society for Middle Eastern Studies* 9.2 (1982), pp. 132–40.

CHAPTER ONE

THE *MUKHTAṢAR* OF AL-KHIRAQĪ AND ITS PLACE IN THE FORMATION OF ḤANBALĪ LEGAL DOCTRINE

Nimrod Hurvitz

The aim of this chapter is to analyze al-Khiraqī's *Mukhtaṣar* and on the basis of this analysis to argue that, in contrast to a view prevalent among modern historians, Ibn Ḥanbal's legal opinions constitute a crucial element in the legal doctrine of the Ḥanbalī *madhhab*.

For decades, modern historians of the Ḥanbalī *madhhab*, such as Henri Laoust, Joseph Schacht, Muḥammad Abū Zahra and Susan Spectorsky, assumed that Aḥmad b. Ḥanbal (d. 241/855) laid the foundations of the Ḥanbalī legal doctrine (*EI*[2], s.v. Ḥanābila, 3: 158; Schacht 1964, 63; Abū Zahra 1949, 168–87; Spectorsky 1993, ix–xi). Laoust, for example, states that Ibn Ḥanbal's followers drew their doctrine from their master's recorded opinions: "Ḥanābila . . . denotes the followers of the school of theology, law and morality which grew up from the teaching of Aḥmad b. Ḥanbal (d. 241/855 [q.v.]) . . . had begun to be codified even during the lifetime of their author."[1] Recently, however, scholars such as Christopher Melchert, Wael Hallaq, and Patricia Crone cast doubts on Ibn Ḥanbal's contribution to the legal doctrine of the *madhhab* named after him (Melchert 1997, xxv; Crone 2000, 10; Hallaq 2001, 39–42). This position was stated most emphatically by Melchert: "No more should textbook-writers tell us the eponyms founded their schools . . ." (Melchert 1997, xxv). In a more specific remark about the Ḥanbalīs he argues that "Al-Khallāl might justly be called the founder of the Ḥanbalī school (Melchert 1997, 137)."[2] In what follows I would like to challenge this new narrative which claims that Ibn Ḥanbal played a minor role in the formation of Ḥanbalī doctrine. Much in line with Laoust,

---

[1] *EI*[2], ibid. A similar assessment is also found in Laoust 1959, 74.

[2] For a similar opinion on Abū Bakr al-Khallāl, see Crone 2000, 10, and Hallaq 2001, 41.

Schacht, Abū Zahra and Spectorsky, I consider Ibn Ḥanbal's contribution to the evolving Ḥanbalī doctrine to be of crucial importance. However, I would like to go beyond the mere naming of eponyms. To understand the process by which the Ḥanbalī doctrine evolved, we need not look for a single individual that founded it, but rather for a group of scholars who put the rough contours of doctrine in place and refined it over the generations. The heart of the matter is therefore: how did generations of Ḥanbalī jurists collect, edit, compile, and interpret Ibn Ḥanbal's legal opinions? This collective, intergenerational project will be examined here through the crucial link of Ibn Ḥanbal's *masāʾil* and al-Khiraqī's *Mukhtaṣar*.[3]

One of the central arguments that the revisionists of the history of the Ḥanbalī *madhhab* present is that Abū Bakr al-Khallāl ought to be ascribed the role of founder. There are two problems with this proposition. The first is that his contribution to the Ḥanbalī legal tradition was of little consequence. Al-Khallāl was no more than a strongly driven and thorough collector of Ibn Ḥanbal's *masāʾil*; he never met his master and thus was totally dependent on the mediation of Ibn Ḥanbal's direct disciples who recorded their teacher's legal opinion. Judging by the *Ṭabaqāt al-Ḥanābila* (a fifth/eleventh century Ḥanbalī biographic dictionary), decades before al-Khallāl began traveling and collecting Ibn Ḥanbal's *masāʾil*, hundreds of the master's disciples had written down his legal opinions. Approximately a dozen of these *masāʾil* collections became compendia, several of which are extant and accessible.[4] It is precisely because so many of Ibn Ḥanbal's contemporaries made the effort to preserve his opinions that al-Khallāl was able to compile a huge multi-volume compendium of his opinions on law and theology, and probably a variety of other topics. Yet, although he compiled the biggest single collection of Ibn Ḥanbal's *masāʾil*, a compendium that was consulted many centuries after his death, it seems that he never took the additional, creative step to put together a document that shows any independence of mind. In the words of Michael Cook, "Khallāl made it his life's work to collect the responsa of Ibn Ḥanbal (d. 241/855); he scarcely

[3] For an important discussion about jurists' authority and *mukhtaṣars*, see Brockopp 2002.

[4] On such compendia, see Laoust 1959, 75–7; also *EI*², s.v. Aḥmad b. Ḥanbal, 1: 274. Another survey of transmitters is found in Abū Zahra 1949, 176–81.

figures as an authority in his own right" (Cook 2000, 88). Although al-Khallāl's *masā'il* collection was preserved for several centuries, it did not generate commentaries (or, considering its size, abridgements), and it seems that this compendium was not a basic component of the Ḥanbalī curriculum.

By contrast, the pivotal document in the Ḥanbalī legal tradition, one that served as the basis for the training of Ḥanbalī jurists as well as eliciting numerous commentaries, is the *Mukhtaṣar* of Abū al-Qāsim al-Khiraqī (d. 334/946). According to Laoust, the *Mukhtaṣar* "was to enjoy a considerable success and to contribute to the education and formation of numerous generations of legal scholars (*EI*², s.v. al-Khirakī. See also Abū Zahra 1949, 185–87)." A few decades after it was authored (conjectured to have been between 317/930 and 334/945) it aroused debates among the leading Ḥanbalī jurists. In Ibn Abī Ya'lā's (d. 560/1131) *Ṭabaqāt* it is stated that the renowned jurist Ghulām al-Khallāl (d. 363/976) remarked that he did not see eye to eye with al-Khiraqī on sixty issues, while Ibn Abī Ya'lā claims that they differed on ninety-eight legal questions (Ibn Abi Ya'lā 1952, 2: 76). Be the number as it may, it is clear that a generation after al-Khiraqī's death scholars studied his writings and deemed it important enough to record points of disagreement. Furthermore, less than a century after the *Mukhtaṣar* was composed, leading Ḥanbalī scholars began to write commentaries about it, the best known being *al-Mughnī*, by Ibn Qudāma (d. 620/1223) (Ibn Qudāma 1970).

But there is a more significant issue at stake than the misplaced honor of the *madhhab* founder. The search for the ultimate *madhhab* founder misses a crucial historic dynamic: intergenerational relations, and their impact on the elaboration and transmission of Ḥanbalī legal doctrine. The issue is not which single individual founded the *madhhab*, but how the collective efforts of two or three generations shaped the *madhhab*'s doctrine. It is widely accepted among historians of Islamic law that the eponyms were seen as authorities by their disciples, yet, at the same time, they were not viewed as absolute authorities with whom one could not disagree. In the words of Schacht: "... by the middle of the second century of the *hijra* many individuals, instead of working out independent doctrines of their own, began to follow the teaching of a recognized authority in its broad outlines, while reserving to themselves the right to differ from their master on any given point" (Schacht 1964, 57). This combination, of following a teacher and at the same time reserving "the right to differ" from him, points to a complex situation in which both teachers and disciples contributed and shaped *madhāhib* doctrine.

Like other eponymous founders, Ibn Ḥanbal's authority was recognized by his disciples, but it did not always lead to blind imitation. Among his disciples we come across two types of reactions: the first emphasizes their esteem for his decisions and the second approached his legal decisions with respect, but also with a modicum of reservation. Among the first type were his early disciples who recorded as many of his answers to legal questions as possible, despite his objections to such documentation. A similar attitude can be detected in the work of al-Khallāl, who compiled questions and answers indiscriminately. The second type included jurists like al-Khiraqī, who in the course of transforming Ibn Ḥanbal's *masāʾil* into a *Mukhtaṣar* made some difficult choices regarding which of Ibn Ḥanbal's decisions he would ignore and occasionally even contradicted the eponymous founder. Although both of these reactions are part of the general process in which the Ḥanbalī legal doctrine was elaborated, I am of the opinion that the most crucial step in this process is the interaction between the works of al-Khiraqī and Ibn Ḥanbal, if only because it led to the *Mukhtaṣar*, the foundational text of Ḥanbalī jurisprudence, and generated dozens of commentaries, as well as being used by numerous students of the Ḥanbalī legal tradition. The remainder of this chapter will be devoted to examining Ibn Ḥanbal's *masāʾil* and the manner in which al-Khiraqī worked with them.

Ḥanbalī *Masāʾil*

Ibn Ḥanbal's opinions and conversations were thoroughly documented by his supporters. The *Ṭabaqāt al-Ḥanābila* mentions 577 individuals from the first generation of Ḥanbalīs, most of whom are described as having memorized or written something that Ibn Ḥanbal said or taught. In fact, it seems that the main criterion for being included in the *Ṭabaqāt al-Ḥanābila* was possessing one of Ibn Ḥanbal's *masāʾil* or *ḥadīth*. Ibn Abī Yaʿlā, the author of the *Ṭabaqāt al-Ḥanābila*, repeatedly refers to knowledge that each disciple gained from his contact with Ibn Ḥanbal. As a consequence we read over and over again that so and so 'transmitted from our imam several matters—*naqala ʿan imāminā ashyāʾ*,' 'heard from Abū ʿAbdallāh [i.e., Ibn Ḥanbal] *masāʾil—samīʿ min Abī ʿAbdallāh masāʾil*,' or 'transmitted from our *imām* faultless *masāʾil—naqala ʿan imāminā masāʾil jiyādan*.'[5] Based on of such remarks one gets the impression that it was very common for individuals who sat in Ibn Ḥanbal's circle to memorize and transmit his answers.

Of the numerous admirers who quoted Ibn Ḥanbal, at least a dozen compiled his *masāʾil*. ʿAbd al-Malik al-Maymūnī (d. 274/888) had a compendium of Ibn Ḥanbal's *masāʾil* that is described thus: "He had *masāʾil* on the authority of Abī ʿAbdallāh, [compiled] in sixteen volumes, two of which were huge volumes, one hundred pages or around this, in splendid penmanship (*bi-khaṭṭ jalīl*)" (Ibn Abi Yaʿlā 1952, 1: 213). On ʿAbdallāh b. Aḥmad b. Ḥanbal's (d. 290/903) collection we read that "he had an abundance of faultless *masāʾil* on the authority of his father" (ibid., 1: 183). We also learn that Muhannā b. Yaḥyā al-Shāmī (d. 248), one of Ibn Ḥanbal's earliest adherents, was very proud of the rare *masāʾil* of Ibn Ḥanbal that were at his disposal. It was on his authority that "ʿAbdallāh b. Aḥmad wrote over ten volumes of faultless *masāʾil* that go back to his father. [Such *masāʾil*] were not transmitted to ʿAbdallāh from his father and were not in the possession of anyone else" (ibid., 1: 345). References to large, multi-volume compendia of *masāʾil* appear more than once in the *Ṭabaqāt al-Ḥanābila* and suggest the efforts and pride that were associated with *masāʾil* collections among Ibn Ḥanbal's adherents.

The clearest testimony to the efforts that Ibn Ḥanbal's disciples invested in documenting his legal opinions are five extant *masāʾil* collections: one, compiled by Isḥāq b. Ibrāhīm b. Hāniʾ (d. 275/889), whose two-volume *masāʾil* collection is described in the *Ṭabaqāt al-Ḥanābila* as six volumes of Aḥmad's *masāʾil* (ibid., 1: 108). A second, by Abū Dāwūd al-Sijistānī (d. 275/889), the renowned *ḥadīth* collector, is depicted as one 'who quoted our imam on several matters' (ibid., 1: 160). A third was compiled by Isḥāq b. Manṣūr al-Kawsaj (d. 251/865), who put together the *masāʾil* of Ibn Ḥanbal and Ibn Rāhwayh.[6] The fourth and fifth *masāʾil* collections were compiled by his sons ʿAbdallāh and Sāliḥ, both avid collectors of their father's comments and opinions.[7] The focus of all five collections was legal

[5] These depictions appear dozens of times in Ibn Abī Yaʿla's *Ṭabaqāt*. See, for a random set of examples, idem 1952, 1: 42–5.

[6] I have not seen this collection. A partial translation and information on the manuscript are found in Spectorsky 1993, 2, 143–254.

[7] On ʿAbdallāh, see Laoust 1959, 77; also Abū Zahra 1949, 177. For his extant *masāʾil* collection, see ʿAbdallāh b. Aḥmad b. Ḥanbal 1981. On Ṣāliḥ, see Laoust

topics, although some of them dealt with theological issues, history and opinions about the quality of transmitters. Four of the five are organized by topics (the exception is Ṣāliḥ's collection). The thematic order of these compilations should not surprise us since we read that other disciples organized Ibn Ḥanbal's *masāʾil* according to themes. For example, it is written of al-Athram that he "quoted from our *imām* numerous *masāʾil* and he classified them and organized them into chapters" (ibid., 1: 66; Spectorsky 1993, 7–8).

Ibn Ḥanbal's disciples did not merely collect and record his *masāʾil* and *ḥadīth*, they also circulated them among themselves. In the abovementioned anecdote Muhannā passed on ten volumes to ʿAbdallāh b. Aḥmad b. Ḥanbal. In other cases the knowledge was passed on to much larger audiences. The most infamous case of wide-scale promulgation of Ibn Ḥanbal's legal opinions is that of Isḥāq b. Manṣūr al-Kawsaj: in the *Ṭabaqāt al-Ḥanābila* we read that when al-Kawsaj heard that Ibn Ḥanbal rescinded the *masāʾil* that were in his possession, he "collected these *masāʾil* in a bag, carried it on his back and walked by foot to Baghdād" (Ibn Abī Yaʿlā 1952, 1: 114). This event, which is obscure in the Ḥanbalī text, is clarified by al-Khaṭīb al-Baghdādī, who claims that all this happened because al-Kawsaj angered Ibn Ḥanbal when it was reputed that he had sold the *masāʾil* (Spectorsky 1993, 6; particularly n. 6). It is not clear if this allegation is true, but it does indeed seem very likely that he was discussing and teaching the *masāʾil*. Another less scandalous case is that of Ḥanbal b. Isḥāq, Ibn Ḥanbal's cousin. It is written in his entry that "he left for ʿUkbara and read to them (the inhabitants) his *masāʾil*. And he also went to Wāsiṭ and I (Abū Bakr al-Khallāl) met him in Wāsiṭ and heard from him a few (*yasīra*) *masāʾil*. Later, I heard his *masāʾil* in ʿUkbara from our ʿUkbarī *aṣḥāb* (who conveyed them on his authority)" (Ibn Abī Yaʿlā 1952, 1: 143). These two stories about al-Kawsaj and Ḥanbal suggest that already in Ibn Ḥanbal's lifetime his legal thought was documented and taught in different areas of the Islamic world.

Perhaps the most fascinating feature of this collective documentation enterprise was that Ibn Ḥanbal himself opposed it. Ibn Ḥanbal's criticism of disciples who wrote his opinions appears in the *Ṭabaqāt al-Ḥanābila* several times. In the entry of Aḥmad b. al-Ḥusayn of

1959, 76; also Abū Zahra 1949, 176-77. For his extant *masāʾil* collection, see Ṣāliḥ b. Aḥmad b. Ḥanbal 1999.

Samarrā' the following exchange is reported: "A man said to Abī ʿAbdallāh: I want to write these *masā'il* for I fear I shall forget them. Aḥmad replied: Do not write a thing. I oppose the writing of my opinions. Once, he noticed a man writing and the man had several boards in his sleeve. [Ibn Ḥanbal] said: Do not write my opinion, because in a certain moment I answer a question in one manner and the next day I change my answer" (ibid., 1: 39). According to this argument, Ibn Ḥanbal's disciples wrote their master's *masā'il* for practical reasons—as an aid to memorizing them. At the same time, Ibn Ḥanbal forbade documenting his legal opinions because he was aware of the fluidity of his own opinions and did not want them to be treated as rigid legal solutions. These opinions are echoed in another conversation that was held between Ibn Ḥanbal and one of his most respected disciples, ʿAbd al-Malik b. ʿAbd al-Ḥamīd al-Maymūnī. In the course of that discussion Ibn Ḥanbal states: "But this is merely opinion (*ra'y*), because it is stated in the morning and it is changed later. Then he said to me: Look at Sufyān and Mālik, when their books and *masā'il* were written and published: how many mistakes were in them? It is merely opinion, today he thinks one thing and the next day he changes his mind. And an opinion can be mistaken . . . This conversation took place between him and me several times" (ibid., 1: 39, 57, 214, 263, 329). Although Ibn Ḥanbal upheld his position and scolded the disciples who wrote his opinions, it seems that he was well aware that they continued to disregard his instructions.

Clearly, the *Ṭabaqāt al-Ḥanābila*'s references to hundreds of devotees who recorded Ibn Ḥanbal's opinions and the extant *masā'il* collections indicate that they blatantly opposed his instructions on this matter. By disobeying his explicit instructions they undermined his authority; yet, paradoxically, this act of disobedience was performed for the sake of enhancing his authority. As can be expected, later generations also played up Ibn Ḥanbal's jurisprudential authority and built upon it the Ḥanbalī doctrine. From the perspective of this article it is less vital to examine how the disciples' disobedience enabled future generations to construct his standing as the founder of the Ḥanbalī legal doctrine than to observe the intensity with which they argued against Ibn Ḥanbal, their willingness to disregard his explicit instructions, and the seriousness with which they took the project of preserving his opinions.

The biographies of the first generation of Ḥanbalīs reveal that already in Ibn Ḥanbal's lifetime hundreds of individuals wrote or memorized his *masāʾil* and *ḥadīth*, dozens brought together whole volumes of his legal opinions, and several transmitted these *masāʾil* to scholars in different parts of the Islamic world, while others were scandalized by the behavior of their colleagues and Ibn Ḥanbal himself criticized such endeavors. Yet, Ibn Ḥanbal's steadfast opposition highlights just how serious and wide ranging was the scope of documentation. Clearly then, when al-Khallāl and al-Khiraqī (as well as dozens of other second- and third-generation scholars) joined the circle of Ḥanbalī jurists, they had a solid basis to work on. Al-Khallāl's contribution was in collating the largest collection of Ibn Ḥanbal's opinions. However, it was al-Khiraqī, using the existing *masāʾil* collections that were in circulation among the Ḥanbalīs, who transformed this huge mass of opinions into an abridged, manageable text that would become the mainstay of Ḥanbalī legal doctrine.

The Masāʾil–Mukhtaṣar *Link*

In the opening lines of the *Mukhtaṣar*, al-Khiraqī writes, "I have summarized this book on the basis of the *madhhab* of *imām* Abī ʿAbdallāh . . ." (al-Khiraqī 1964, 3). This terse remark indicates that by the first decades of the fourth/tenth century, a jurist like al-Khiraqī thought there was a Ḥanbalī *madhhab*, that this *madhhab* had a doctrine that was distinctly its own, and that its contents were in a state that needed further work and organization. For the historian of Ḥanbalī doctrine, this remark triggers several questions: What was the body of Ḥanbalī doctrine that al-Khiraqī summarized? What did he include and what did he omit in the course of this process? And what is the nature of Ibn Ḥanbal's influence on this doctrine? In the next section I assume that the Ḥanbalī doctrine to which al-Khiraqī refers is the huge, disorderly corpus of Ibn Ḥanbal's *masāʾil*. Therefore, I will examine how al-Khiraqī worked with Ibn Ḥanbal's *masāʾil* and constructed the abridged text. It is clear that the analysis put forth in this study has its limitations, for several reasons. First, we do not have at our disposal all the sources that were available to al-Khiraqī, so the reconstruction of the process by which he wrote the *Mukhtaṣar* will not be complete. Second, this study focuses on one chapter of the *Mukhtaṣar* and therefore we need to be cautious about what it represents.

The nexus between the *masāʾil* and the *Mukhtaṣar* will be examined here through an analysis of one chapter from al-Khiraqī's

Mukhtaṣar, the *Bāb zakāt* (or *ṣadaqat*) *al-fiṭr*, which deals with the injunction to give provisions to the poor at the end of the fast of Ramaḍān.[8] The legal basis for this obligation is found in the *ḥadīth*, and therefore all Muslims consider it compulsory (though its exact legal standing is debated). This chapter was chosen because it reveals several important features of al-Khiraqī's work and his attitude towards Ibn Ḥanbal's *masāʾil.*

Translation

Bāb zakāt (interchangeable with *ṣadaqat*) *al-fiṭr* (al-Khiraqī 1964, 56–7)

1. He said: *zakāt al-fiṭr* is [an obligation placed on] every freeman and slave, male or female from among the Muslims. [The amount of *zakāt al-fiṭr* that is given is] one *ṣāʿ* [a cubic measure of varying magnitude] identical to the *ṣāʿ* of the Prophet (PBUH), which is five *arṭāl* and a third, of any nourishing grain or fruit.[9]
2. If the Bedouins [*ahl al-bādiya*] give [one *ṣāʿ*] of cheese, it is approved if this is their food. And Abī ʿAbdallāh [Ibn Ḥanbal]—*raḥimahu Allāh*—preferred to issue dates.[10]
3. It is not permitted for someone who is capable [of giving] dates or barley or wheat or raisins or cheese to issue something else.[11]
4. It is forbidden to give the value [of the *zakāt al-fiṭr* in cash].[12]
5. The time to issue [*zakāt al-fiṭr*] is when one goes to the place of prayer. If one presents it a day or two earlier, it is allowed.[13]
6. It is obligatory to issue [*zakāt al-fiṭr*] on one's behalf, and for his family if he has more food than a day and a night.[14]

---

[8] For a brief description of *zakāt al-fiṭr*, see s.v. Zakāt, *Short EI*, 654–56, mainly 656.

[9] Regarding the amount to be issued, most jurists agree that it is one *ṣāʿ*. However, according to Ibn Qudāma 1970, 2: 648 and Ibn Rushd 1995, 2: 135, Abū Ḥanīfa and some of the early jurists thought that in the case of wheat (*burr*), the amount to be given is only half a *ṣāʿ*.

[10] On the principle, see Ibn Ḥanbal 1981, 169. On Ibn Ḥanbal's preference, see ibid., and Sijistānī 1353/1934, 85. On the preferences of Ibn Ḥanbal, Mālik and Shāfiʿī, see Ibn Qudāma 1970, 2: 655.

[11] There is disagreement over the right to give other types of foodstuffs. Among the Mālikīs and Shāfiʿīs are jurists who argue that one can give from the foodstuffs that are in wide use in one's land. See Ibn Qudāma 1970, 2: 657 and Ibn Rushd 1995, 2: 134.

[12] For Ibn Ḥanbal's opinions, see Ibn Ḥanbal 1981, 171; Sijistānī 1353/1934, 85.

[13] For Ibn Ḥanbal's opinions, see ibid.

[14] For Ibn Ḥanbal's opinions, see Sijistānī 1353/1934, 86.

7. The owner of a *mukātab* [a slave who buys his freedom] is not obliged [to issue] *zakāt* [on the *mukātab*'s behalf].[15]
8. The *mukātab* is obliged to give *zakāt al-fiṭr* for himself.
9. If a group owns a slave, each of the owners is obliged [to issue] one *ṣāʿ*. There is a transmission on the authority of Abū ʿAbdallāh [Ibn Ḥanbal] [according to which] the group as a whole is obliged to give one *ṣāʿ*.[16]
10. *Ṣadaqat al-fiṭr* will be distributed to those who are allowed to receive *ṣadaqat al-amwāl*.[17]
11. It is permitted to give a group what is obligatory for a single person, and to give to a single person what is obligatory for the group.
12. It is agreeable to issue [*zakāt al-fiṭr*] for an embryo, ʿUthmān b. ʿAffān (R.A.ʿA.) issued [*zakāt al-fiṭr*] for an embryo.[18]
13. If someone possesses the amount that is needed to issue the *ṣadaqat al-fiṭr* and he has a debt (of a similar amount) he is obliged to issue [the *zakāt al-fiṭr*], the exception being when he is required to settle the debt, then he is exempt from the *zakāt*. *Wa-Allāhu aʿlam.*

The following analysis of the *Bāb zakāt al-fiṭr* will touch on three main issues: The choices made by al-Khiraqī; references to Ibn Ḥanbal; and legal reasoning. Over half of the rulings in this *Bāb* were debated by Islamic jurists. As a result, the jurists articulated several acceptable legal solutions. This study reveals that when al-Khiraqī was faced with these options, he almost always chose Ibn Ḥanbal's position. Along with the similarity of al-Khiraqī's doctrine to that of Ibn Ḥanbal, he also mentions Ibn Ḥanbal by name several times. Moreover, both al-Khiraqī and Ibn Ḥanbal rely on the same jurisprudential principles, which set the Ḥanbalīs apart from many other jurists, i.e., with their heavy reliance on the Prophet's companions (*Ṣaḥāba*). These three characteristics suggest that al-Khiraqī

[15] For Ibn Ḥanbal's opinions, see Ibn Ḥanbal 1981, 168. There is disagreement about this. Shāfiʿī, Abū Ḥanīfa and Ibn Ḥanbal argue that an owner is not obliged to pay for his *mukātab*, while Mālik assumes that he should.

[16] Ibn Ḥanbal's second opinion appears in Ibn Ḥanbal 1981, 168.

[17] They disagreed over who may receive the *zakāt al-fiṭr*. Mālik, Shāfiʿī and Ibn Ḥanbal limit it to Muslim paupers, while Abū Ḥanīfa includes the poor of the *ahl al-dhimma*.

[18] For references to ʿUthmān's conduct, see Ibn Ḥanbal 1981, 170; Sijistānī 1353/1934, 86.

operated within an existing Ḥanbalī tradition and at the same time influenced it.

When al-Khiraqī composed the *Mukhtaṣar*, the Islamic legal system was already a highly elaborate and complex intellectual system. Numerous legal problems were raised by generations of jurists and a plethora of answers were given. Although the echoes of these debates are not mentioned in the *Mukhtaṣar*, when we browse through Ibn al-Qudāma's *al-Mughnī* we learn that there is a long history of disagreements and discussions between Islamic jurists, and hence numerous opinions and legal solutions from which al-Khiraqī could have chosen.

According to Ibn Qudāma and Ibn Rushd's *Bidāyat al-Mujtahid*, the discussions regarding *zakāt al-fiṭr* raised six open-ended questions. 1. Is the *zakāt al-fiṭr* a religious duty (*farḍ*, as is the opinion of most jurists), or a mode of behavior (*sunna*, as the opinion of Mālik's later students) (Ibn Qudāma 1970, 2: 645; Ibn Rushd 1995, 2: 129)? 2. Are the *ahl al-bādiya* (a position held by a handful of early authorities) exempt from payment (Ibn Qudāma 1970, 2: 653)? 3. What types of foodstuffs were considered legitimate *zakāt al-fiṭr* (the Mālikīs and Shāfiʿīs permitted all sorts of foodstuffs if they were abundant in someone's land, while Ibn Ḥanbal allowed only those mentioned in the *ḥadīth*) (ibid., 2: 657; Ibn Rushd 1995, 2: 134)? 4. Who should give the *zakāt al-fiṭr* for a man's wife—the wife or her husband (Mālik, Shāfiʿī and Ibn Ḥanbal opted for the husband; Abū Ḥanīfa thought the wife should pay for herself) (Ibn Qudāma 1970, 2: 670–71; Ibn Rushd 1995, 2: 130)? 5. Who should pay for the *mukātab* (Shāfiʿīs, Ḥanafīs and Ḥanbalīs thought the owner is not obliged, Mālik thought that the owner is the one who should pay) (Ibn Qudāma 1970, 2: 675; Ibn Rushd 1995, 2: 133)? And, finally, 6. Who should receive the *zakāt al-fiṭr* (Mālik, Shāfiʿī and Ibn Ḥanbal considered only Muslims as legitimate recipients while Abū Ḥanīfa thought it could be given to *ahl al-dhimma*) (Ibn Qudāma 1970, 2: 690; Ibn Rushd 1995, 2: 137)? These are the questions that prompted disagreements among a host of early Islamic jurists. In all of these matters, al-Khiraqī chose Ibn Ḥanbal's solution as his own and inserted these positions into the *Mukhtaṣar* as clear-cut instructions regarding proper conduct.

The similarity between Ibn Ḥanbal's *masāʾil* and the statements in the *Mukhtaṣar* are also evident in cases that were not debated. For example, both Ibn Ḥanbal and al-Khiraqī deal in a comparable manner with the question of substituting conventional foodstuffs with something else that is of identical value. In the *Mukhtaṣar* it appears as follows: "If one gives a substitute that is equal in value (*al-qīma*), it is not permitted." In the *masā'il* of ʿAbdallāh it is presented thus: "I heard my father reject [the possibility] to give a substitute of equal value in the case of *zakāt al-fiṭr*, he said: I fear that giving a substitute is not permitted" (Ibn Ḥanbal 1981, 171). Abū Dāwūd al-Sijistānī reports a similar reaction: "Ibn Ḥanbal was asked, and I heard, giving [as *zakāt al-fitr*] *darāhim* [coins]? He said: I am afraid it is not permitted, it contradicts the *sunna* of the Prophet (PBUH)" (al-Sijistānī 1353/1934, 85).

Both texts echo a corresponding legal position: it is forbidden to substitute the foodstuffs with anything else, including money or objects of identical value. However, the *masā'il* and *Mukhtaṣar* differ in literary form. The *masā'il* is a record of oral exchanges that describe conversations between Ibn Ḥanbal and anonymous interlocutors and the answers that are ascribed to him are presented as his own personal opinions. By contrast, the statements in the *Mukhtaṣar* are impersonal instructions that are not ascribed to anyone and, as such, they create an aura of authority.

Another difference between these two texts is that in the *masā'il* Ibn Ḥanbal explains the legal basis behind his opinion, whereas in the *Mukhtaṣar* legal reasoning is omitted. When Abū Dāwūd al-Sijistānī cited Ibn Ḥanbal as saying that giving money instead of *zakāt al-fiṭr* contradicted 'the *sunna* of the Prophet', he was presenting to his listener the reasons behind the legal solution he chose. At the same time, he was opening this position to criticism: the mere fact that Ibn Ḥanbal brings into the discussion the legal reasons behind his position enables his listener to think about alternatives. By contrast, in the *Mukhtaṣar* we rarely come across explanations. There could be several reasons for this, the most likely being that brevity is one of the genre's conventions.

Although Ibn Ḥanbal's influence on al-Khiraqī's *Mukhtaṣar* is evident, al-Khiraqī did not simply summarize and integrate Ibn Ḥanbal's positions mindlessly. In one case, that of the *zakāt* of a slave, al-Khiraqī actually contradicts Ibn Ḥanbal's opinion. The issue at hand is the amount of *zakāt al-fiṭr* that is due for a slave who is owned by several owners. There are two options: that each of the owners gives one *ṣāʿ* or that all the owners together give one *ṣāʿ*, which means that each of them gives a certain fraction of a *ṣāʿ*. According to the *masā'il*, Ibn Ḥanbal held to the second option. ʿAbdallah reports: "I asked my father about a slave who is owned by two men, how will they issue his *zakāt*? He said: Each one will contribute a half, half a *ṣāʿ* half a *ṣāʿ*" (Ibn Ḥanbal 1981, 168). Furthermore, later accounts of Ḥanbalī doctrine, such as Ibn Qudāma's *al-Mughnī*, refer to this position as the 'apparent' (*ẓāhir*) opinion of Ibn Ḥanbal. However, despite Ibn Ḥanbal's explicit position, al-Khiraqī writes: "If a group owns a slave, each of the owners is obliged [to issue] one *ṣāʿ*. There is a transmission on the authority of Abū ʿAbdallāh [Ibn Ḥanbal] [according to which] the group as a whole is obliged to give one *ṣāʿ*." Thus, although Ibn Ḥanbal's opinion was documented and was well known to his disciples, al-Khiraqī contradicts this position and opens with his own opinion, stating that each of the owners is obliged to give a full *ṣāʿ*. He could have ignored Ibn Ḥanbal's opinion, but chose to present it to the reader, and in so doing he exposed his difference of opinion with his master. If we compare al-Khiraqī's exposition regarding the *zakāt* of collectively owned slaves with the rest of the legal prescriptions in this chapter, it is noticeable that when al-Khiraqī agrees with Ibn Ḥanbal's position, he does not mention his master's name. However, when he disagrees with Ibn Ḥanbal, he mentions him by name and presents the contrasting opinion. In and of itself, such a presentation demonstrates that Ibn Ḥanbal was, on the one hand, a truly important factor in the development of doctrine, because in most cases al-Khiraqī adopts his position; and when he does not, he says so and exposes this difference of opinions before his readers. On the other hand, it also indicates that Ibn Ḥanbal was not an absolute authority whose word was final, and whose disciples would not differ from him. Such an attitude is an example of Schacht's observation on the relationship between masters and disciples—who, on the one hand, have an aura of authority but, on the other, are not blindly obeyed by their disciples.

A second instance in which Ibn Ḥanbal's name appears in *Bāb zakāt al-fiṭr* is when al-Khiraqī wants to clarify one of the idiosyncrasies of his legal outlook. The question at hand is what type of foodstuff is acceptable as *zakāt al-fiṭr*. The common, widely known and widely accepted answer, based on a *ḥadīth*, is dates, barley, wheat, raisins, and cheese. This position is mentioned in a variety of sources. However, after stating the commonly known legal position, al-Khiraqī adds a piece of information that does not, in fact, contribute to our knowledge and understanding of what is permitted or forbidden. Apparently Ibn Ḥanbal preferred to give dates as *zakāt al-fiṭr*. This two-leveled presentation of both the formal legal position and the informal preference of the master already appears in the *masāʾil* (Ibn Ḥanbal 1981, 169; Sijistānī 1353/1934, 85). It is not very clear why there is any need to mention Ibn Ḥanbal's preference at all, though when we read Ibn Qudāma's *al-Mughnī*, we learn that several of the great jurists had their own preferences. For example, Mālik preferred to give pressed dates (*ʿajwa*) and Shāfiʿī and Abū ʿUbayd favored wheat. It is in this context that al-Khiraqī decided to specify Ibn Ḥanbal's preferences. However, the more telling element in this discussion is not the inclination of each of these jurists, but the way they justify their preferences. Shāfiʿī's followers claim that he chose wheat because it was the most expensive in 'his time and place', and that it was desirable (*mustaḥabb*) to give the most expensive foodstuff (Ibn Qudāma 1970, 2: 655). Ibn Ḥanbal chose dates because this is what the Prophet and the *Ṣaḥāba* gave out most often, and he wanted to follow in their footsteps.

The justifications given to each of these preferences introduces another widely known aspect of the Ḥanbalī legal doctrine—its reliance on the *Ṣaḥāba* as a central means for reaching legal decisions. Reliance on reports from the Ṣaḥāba, which is ascribed above by Ibn Qudāma to Ibn Ḥanbal, appears also in al-Khiraqī's *Mukhtaṣar*, when he discusses giving *zakāt al-fiṭr* in the name of an embryo: "It is agreeable to issue [*zakāt al-fiṭr*] for an embryo, ʿUthmān b. ʿAffān (R.A.ʿA.) issued [*zakāt al-fiṭr*] for an embryo" (see note 18) ʿUthmān b. ʿAffān, the third of the four Rāshidūn and a respected *ṣaḥabī*, is referred to by al-Khiraqī as a means to justify a certain mode of behavior. Note that in this case, again, the discussion is not about an obligation but rather about a commendable form of conduct. Apparently, the law does not oblige to give *zakāt al-fiṭr* for an embryo. And if there is no injunction to do so, there is also no reason to insert this piece of information into the *Mukhtaṣar*. However, the position that is mentioned here appears in the *masāʾil* of Ibn Ḥanbal, both in that of ʿAbdallāh and that of al-Sijistānī, and it seems that due to the attention that it received there, al-Khiraqī chose to mention it in the *Mukhtaṣar*. It also seems that precisely because it is not a clear-cut legal prescription, but a recommendation, al-Khiraqī chose to mention the basis of its justification—one of the esteemed *Ṣaḥāba*.

There are other instances in which Ibn Ḥanbal mentions the *Ṣaḥāba* in the *masāʾil*. For example, when he is asked about the precise moment that one should give the *zakāt al-fiṭr*, Ibn Ḥanbal comments that the renowned Ibn ʿUmar (son of ʿUmar b. al-Khaṭṭāb, the second of the Rāshidūn caliphs) gave the *zakāt al-fiṭr* two or three days before the *fiṭr* (the breaking of the fast) (Ibn Ḥanbal 1981, 171). However, in this case, al-Khiraqī omits the names and descriptions of the *Ṣaḥāba* from the *Mukhtaṣar*. It is not clear why he mentions some *Ṣaḥāba* by name in one case and not in the other.

Conclusion

The legal doctrine of the *madhāhib* is the outcome of changes and adaptations over many years. Each generation adds a layer by compiling existing *fatāwā*, issuing new ones, and commenting on the existing authoritative texts of the *madhhab*. This process has been studied and described extensively, and is widely accepted by historians of Islamic law (Hallaq 1994; Masud, Messick & Powers 1996, 3–32). What is debated is the relative contribution of the different generations, particularly that of the eponymous founders and the first generations of their disciples.

This study focused on the contributions of Ibn Ḥanbal and his disciples to the formation of Ḥanbalī legal doctrine. In contrast to the prevailing new interpretations of *madhhab* history, which belittle and even discard Ibn Ḥanbal's contribution, this inquiry concludes that Ibn Ḥanbal's legal opinions served as the main source for the later developments of Ḥanbalī doctrine. The numerous conversations between Ibn Ḥanbal and his disciples, which were recorded in *masāʾil* collections, were abridged and transformed into a manageable working manual by al-Khiraqī. Hence, I argue that the most creative development in the formation of Ḥanbalī doctrine (other than Ibn Ḥanbal's legal opinions) is the creation of a *Mukhtaṣar* based on al-Khiraqī's editorial policies and opinions. His decisions regarding what to include or omit from the huge reservoir of Ibn Ḥanbal's opinions, and the occasional insertion of his own opinions, determined the contents of the foundational text of Ḥanbalī legal doctrine, the *Mukhtaṣar*.

Al-Khiraqī's achievement fits two historical developments that have been described by Wael Hallaq and Norman Calder. In his discussion of *madhhab* authority, Hallaq observes that the "ubiquitous plurality became increasingly circumscribed by the beginning of the fourth/tenth century . . ." (Hallaq 2001, 61). The fourth/tenth century, in which al-Khiraqī wrote, was an intermediate stage between the relatively pluralistic and intellectually fluid third/ninth century, in which new *madhāhib* were established, and the fifth/eleventh century, which "marks the end of the period in which the activity of *takhrīj* was extensively practiced" (ibid., 75). In other words, the fourth/tenth century was the phase in which the contours of the Islamic legal system were put in place. In the Ḥanbalī case it was al-Khiraqī who articulated the document that would become the foundational text of the *madhhab*.

The circumscription of opinions by which Hallaq characterizes the fourth/tenth century is reflected in the types of literary products that make their appearance in that period. According to Calder, some time before the fourth/tenth century, "a movement from a jurisprudence which is a predominantly oral and socially diffuse informal process towards a jurisprudence which is a complex literary discipline . . ." occurs (Calder 1993, 164). The literary expression of this process is the shift from a 'scholar's notebook' to 'institutional redaction' (ibid., 163). The editorial work that al-Khiraqī did with the *masāʾil* of Ibn Ḥanbal, which probably served their compilers as private notebooks, and the production of a *Mukhtaṣar* that became the pivotal text of Ḥanbalī legal doctrine is an example of this transition, from a scholar's notebook to an 'institutional redaction.'

The circumscription of legal opinions and the shift from personal notebooks to widely studied redactions are complementary processes. Both describe important aspects of the formation of a fixed body of *madhhab* doctrine, and both enable us to analyze how second and third generations of Ḥanbalī jurists transformed Ibn Ḥanbal's opinions into the foundation of Ḥanbalī doctrine.

CHAPTER TWO

LAW AND CUSTOM IN THE MAGHRIB, 1475–1500: ON THE DISINHERITANCE OF WOMEN*

David S. Powers

At the time of Muhammad's birth, ca. 570 C.E., the Arabian peninsula was predominantly polytheistic, tribal, nomadic and stateless. By the time of the Prophet's death in 632, polytheism had given way to monotheism, tribal ties had been attenuated by attachment to the new religio-political community known as the *umma*, and the peninsula was united into a single state structure for the first time in its history. True, the nomads remained nomads, although their energies would soon be directed outwards and channeled into the activity of *jihād*. Over the course of the next 100 years, the conquering tribesmen were exposed to a process of sedentarization, and, by the year 750, large numbers of the descendants of the original Arab conquerors were monotheists living in the villages, towns, and cities of the Islamic state.

Islamic tradition characterizes the historical transformations that occurred during the first centuries of Islam in terms of a dichotomy between Islam or submission to God, on the one hand, and *jāhiliyya*, on the other. The term *jāhiliyya*, a neologism derived from *jahl* (ignorance or barbarism), connotes the perceived state of affairs in Arabia prior to the career of the Prophet; and it evokes the beliefs, way of life, and social practices of the inhabitants of the Arabian peninsula prior to the emergence of Islam. The transition from *jāhiliyya* to Islam is marked chronologically by the hegira from Mecca to Medina in the year 1/622; everything before that date is *jāhilī*, everything after it, *islāmī*. By extension, the word *jāhiliyya* came to signify the state of affairs that preceded Islam in all of the lands whose peoples

* I wish to thank Tilman Hannemann, Annelies Moors, Aharon Layish, and Ron Shaham for their comments on earlier drafts of this essay. All remaining errors are mine.

eventually accepted Islam. As the conquests spread from Syria, Iraq, and Egypt to the Maghrib, Iran and Central Asia, many if not most of the inhabitants of these areas came to regard their past in terms of *jāhiliyya*. In fact, the process of Islamization was slow and uneven, and, in many areas of the Muslim world, it was never fully completed: at different times and in different places practices regarded as *jāhilī* have risen to the surface and threatened the order of what the guardians of orthopraxis regard as a truly Islamic society.

The first Muslims brought with them not only a new religious ideology based on the notion of the oneness of God (*tawḥīd*) but also a distinctive way of life characterized by a religious cult (prayer, alms-giving, fasting, and pilgrimage), dietary prescriptions, sartorial customs and detailed instructions for practices relating to marriage, divorce, and inheritance. Across time and space, Muslims have followed this religious ideology and its attendant social practices to a greater or lesser extent. In many Muslim societies, one finds a tension between tradition and innovation, official Islam and popular Islam, urban life and rural life, practices labeled Islamic and those labeled *jāhilī*.

In a Muslim society, every believer, male and female, should be able to perform the five pillars of Islam—the testimony of the faith, prayer, fasting, alms-giving, and pilgrimage—and every Muslim is expected to adhere to the rules and regulations of Islamic law. Throughout Islamic history, it has been the responsibility of the leader of the Muslim community—prophet, caliph, *imām*, or sulṭān—to make it possible for his Muslim subjects to live their lives in submission to God by adhering to the prescriptions of Islamic law or *sharīʿa*. For the most part, Muslim rulers have shared this responsibility with the *ʿulamāʾ*, scholars trained in the law who have the authority to assess a particular action or behavior as Islamic or un-Islamic. For the past 1400 years, the *ʿulamāʾ* have served as the guardians of urban, orthodox, official Islam, and it is they who are charged with the task of identifying and rooting out those practices which, in their opinion, are either reprehensible innovations (*bidaʿ*, sg., *bidaʿ*) or vestiges of *jāhiliyya*.

I propose here to examine the tension between Islam and *jāhiliyya* in the central Maghrib at an undisclosed date in the last quarter of the ninth/fifteenth century. This tension centers on a dispute over inheritance practices, as documented in a *fatwā* preserved in the *Miʿyār* of Aḥmad al-Wansharīsī (1981–83, 11: 293–98), who died in

914/1508. Although we do not know the name of the *mustaftī*—the person who asked the question—or his place of residence, we do know that the question was addressed, in the first instance, to Abū Sālim Ibrāhīm al-ʿUqbānī, one of al-Wansharīsī's teachers in Tlemcen before the latter's departure for Fez in 874/1469, and that two other Tlimsānī *muftī*s also issued responses to it. Al-ʿUqbānī no doubt issued his response prior to 874/1469; in any event, his *fatwā* must have been written before 880/1475–6, the year of his death.

Before proceeding, it will be helpful to examine the basic outlines of the Islamic inheritance system, known in Arabic as the *ʿilm al-farāʾiḍ*' or 'science of the shares'.

The ʿIlm al-Farāʾiḍ *or Science of the Shares*

The Qurʾān treats the topic of inheritance at great length and in considerable detail. Q. 4:8 establishes that both men and women have the right to inherit: "Men have a share in what parents and relatives leave behind at death and women have a share in what parents and relatives leave behind. Be it large or small, a legal share is fixed."[1] 4:11–12 and 176, known as 'the inheritance verses', award specific fractional shares of the estate to a range of male and female heirs, i.e., one or more daughters, a mother, a father, one or more siblings, a husband, and one or more wives.

During the first century AH, these verses served as the textual foundation upon which Muslim jurists constructed the system for the devolution of property known as the '*ilm al-farāʾiḍ*' or 'science of the shares'. Renowned for its mathematical complexity, the science of the shares imposes compulsory rules for the division of a minimum of two thirds of any estate; bequests are limited to one third and may not be made in favor of one or more heirs without the consent of the others. Thus, a person contemplating death may not, in theory, designate one or more of his (or her) relatives as a testamentary heir nor may he transmit real assets in integral units to one or more heirs. Instead, the estate of the deceased is divided into fractional shares and distributed to those persons who qualify as heirs according to the science of the shares. Consider, for example, the

[1] All translations of the Qurʾān in this essay are based on Ali 1993.

case of a man who dies leaving a wife, daughter and son and whose estate is comprised of a house, plot of land and a mill. According to the science of the shares, the wife will inherit 1/8 of the house, plot of land, and mill, the daughter 7/24, and the son 7/12. Left unattended, the properties in question will become increasingly fragmented over time as the fractional shares become smaller and smaller (see further *EI*[2], s.v., Mīrāth; *EQ*, s.v., Inheritance; Powers 1986).

The treatment of females as heirs is one of the distinctive features of the Qurʾānic inheritance verses. Islamic tradition teaches that during the *jāhiliyya* women did not have the right to inherit and that one purpose of the Qurʾānic legislation was to improve the status of women. Accordingly, the Qurʾān awards shares of the estate to daughters, mothers, sisters and wives (Powers 1986, 10–18, 190–202). The right of a woman to inherit from her father, brother or husband has important economic consequences. In the above-mentioned example, if the widow remarries and her second husband is from a family, clan, or tribe different from that of the first, she will effectively alienate 1/8 of her first husband's estate; similarly, if the daughter was unmarried at the time of her father's death and she subsequently marries and takes up residence with her husband and his family, she will effectively alienate 7/24 of her father's estate.

The Qurʾānic inheritance verses were revealed in Medina and the science of the shares developed in the area that is today the Middle East. The particular shape taken by this system surely was influenced by historical factors such as the Arab conquests, economic expansion and the accumulation of large fortunes by influential members of the early Muslim community (ibid., 113–43, 212–16). As the conquests abated, however, the science of the shares remained fixed in the form that it had taken during the first century AH. Based upon Qurʾānic verses regarded by Muslims as a direct manifestation of the Divine Will, the science of the shares is simultaneously universal, on the one hand, and timeless and immutable, on the other. Thus, as the Muslim state expanded and spread in a westerly direction across the Maghrib and into al-Andalus and in an easterly direction into Central, South and Southeast Asia, the science of the shares should have replaced any local inheritance practices previously in force.

It is not difficult to imagine the tension that developed between the science of the shares and local inheritance customs, especially in those regions in which property was controlled by the male patriline.

Pious Muslims faced two challenges: how to prevent the progressive fragmentation of property; and how to prevent the alienation of property by out-marrying females. Generally speaking, they responded to these challenges in three ways: (1) by developing social strategies that neutralize the negative consequences of inheritance law (e.g., cousin marriage); (2) by developing legal strategies that make it possible to circumvent the letter of the law without violating its spirit (e.g., gifts *inter vivos*, nominal sales, family endowments) (Powers 2002, chaps. 4 and 6); or (3) by ignoring the science of the shares and distributing property in accordance with local norms and customs. Many Muslims no doubt came to regard these strategies as part of their vision of what constitutes *sharīʿa*.

From al-Andalus to Indonesia, Muslims throughout history have adopted one or another of these approaches, sometimes with the assistance of the *fuqahāʾ*, many of whom, it should be noted, were themselves property owners. Muslim jurists helped proprietors to circumvent the science of the shares by teaching that the inheritance rules take effect only on property owned by the deceased at the moment he (or she) enters his final deathbed illness; a proprietor is thus free to dispose of his property in any way that he wishes prior to that moment. The law places no restrictions on the amount of property that a person may alienate during his lifetime, and a Muslim therefore may shift assets to his desired heir or heirs by means of a sale, gift, acknowledgement of a debt or by establishing a familial endowment—on the condition that these transactions are in conformity with the requisite legal formalities. In the above-mentioned example, the father, before entering his final death sickness, might have arranged for his daughter to marry his brother's son; or he might have transferred the house, plot of land and mill to his son as a gift *inter vivos*, effectively disinheriting his wife and daughter; alternatively, he might have gifted the house to his wife and daughter and the plot of land and mill to his son; or he might have chosen any other strategy that suited his needs and wishes (see Powers 2001).

The third response to the challenges of inheritance law is to ignore the science of the shares altogether and to transmit property according to local customary law. We know from anthropological studies that in many Muslim communities females generally do not inherit real property (although they do inherit gold, silver and other movables). In some Muslim communities, it is customary for females to cede their inheritance rights to their brothers in return for compensation, either monetary or non-monetary, e.g., protection in the event of divorce or death of a husband (Moors 1995, 53 ff.; cf. idem 2004; Maher 1974; Layish 1975).

At the same time that the disinheritance of women may solve certain key economic issues, it raises grave ethical and moral questions. From a theological perspective, all wealth—whatever form it may take—ultimately belongs to God. The inheritance rules enshrined in the Qur'ān are regarded by Muslims as a reflection of the divine will. Q. 4:11–12 open with the weighty pronouncement, "God commands you concerning your children . . ."; these two verses justify the specific fractional shares mentioned therein on the grounds that humans are incapable of determining the relative entitlement of their heirs ("Your fathers and your sons, you know not which of them are closer to you in usefulness"), and they conclude by characterizing the inheritance shares as a decree of God (*farīḍatan min Allāh*). The next two verses of the Qur'ān, 4: 13–14, promise eternal reward to whoever follows these rules and eternal damnation to whoever violates them.

> These are the limits set by God, and those who follow the commandments of God and the Prophet, will indeed be admitted to gardens with streams of water running by, where they will forever abide; and this will be success supreme.
>
> Those who disobey God and the Prophet and exceed the bounds of law will be taken to Hell and abide there forever and shall suffer despicable punishment.

Clearly, the instruction to distribute an estate in accordance with the rules specified in the Qur'ān is not only a legal requirement but also a religious duty. It is the individual obligation (*farḍ ʿayn*) of every Muslim to observe these rules, and, strictly speaking, any Muslim who fails to do so violates the precepts of his (or her) religion; indeed, he disobeys God and His Prophet.

Now if it were the case that one or perhaps a handful of Muslims in a particular community occasionally violated the Qur'ānic inheritance rules, there might be no cause for alarm. But what happens when an entire community of Muslims ignores these rules over a period of several hundred years? This is precisely the question raised in the request for a *fatwā* sent to the Tilimsānī jurist Abū Sālim Ibrāhīm al-ʿUqbānī at an unspecified date in the last quarter of the ninth/fifteenth century.

The Provenance of the Question: Bilād al-Qibla

The *istiftā'* or request for a *fatwā* is formulated in general and abstract terms, referring only to "the case of a country" (*mas'alat balad*) without further specification. Fortuitously, as al-Wansharīsī was copying this *fatwā* into what would become the *Mi'yār*, he made a brief editorial intervention, specifying that the question emanated from "*bilād al-qibla*" or "the lands of the *qibla*" (ibid., 11: 293, ll. 18–20).

The location of '*bilād al-qibla*' is not immediately apparent. The word '*qibla*', of course, signifies the direction in which Muslims turn while praying, i.e., towards the Ka'ba in Mecca. The phrase 'the lands of the *qibla*' might therefore refer to Mecca and its environs, which, during the last quarter of the ninth/fifteenth century, were part of the Mamlūk empire. It is unlikely, however, that a person living in the Hijaz or elsewhere in the Mashriq would have sent a question about the disinheritance of women to a *muftī* living in Tlemcen.

In his *Ta'rīkh*, Ibn Khaldūn used the phrase '*bilād al-qibla*' to signifiy the region that stretches across the northern fringes of the Sahara desert, from the Zab mountains below Constantine to the Awres and Hudna mountains, the High Plains and the Saharan Atlas, until reaching Sijilmasa, the gateway to the south.[2] Since pre-Islamic times, this broad expanse of territory has been inhabited by people who call themselves Imazighen (sg. Amazigh, literally, 'free or noble man'), a rural people, many of whom lead a nomadic existence, speak their own Hamito-Semitic language, and, for the most part, operate outside the authority of the nominal rulers of the territory in which they live. Nominally Muslims, the Imazighen reportedly pay little attention to the subtleties of religious doctrine, although they do manifest a distinct inclination to Khārijism. It is thus no wonder that the Sunni '*ulamā'* of the Maghrib dubbed them '*barbar*', hence, our term, 'Berbers' (*EI*[2], s.v. Berbers).

The Imazighen are tribesmen and their social structure is based, at least in theory, upon the principle of tribal segmentation. Among nomads, semi-nomads and peasants, familial relationships stretch outward in concentric circles from the extended family to include:

[2] For access to these references, go to http://www.alwaraq.com; then to Ibn Khaldūn 1967.

(1) a lineage, (2) a clan, (3) a tribe, and (4) a confederation of tribes (on these terms and their meanings, which may vary from one society to the next, see Eickelman 1981, 85 ff.). The inner circle of the extended family is patriarchal, patrilineal, and patrilocal. The principles of tribal segmentation have important consequences for the holding and use of land. In theory, the fields cultivated by peasants are held as private property (*mulk*). In practice, however, the land is generally held in common: if a family unit wishes to sell its share of common land, the clan or village may exercise its right of preemption (*shufʿa*). Similarly, the nomads and semi-nomads who control the lowland valleys and hills of the semi-arid high plains—which, in theory, belong to the state—enjoy extensive rights over these properties, including the right to occupy and cultivate the land, the right of usufruct and, of critical importance to the present investigation, the right to transmit the land exclusively to male heirs. The inheritance practices of the Imazighen are regulated by Berber customary law, which operates to keep familial or tribal property collective and undivided by limiting the right to inherit to male agnates and *by systematically excluding females*. The exclusion of females is justified by the argument that if a woman were to marry out of the family and yet inherit from a blood relative, her husband—a 'stranger'—would gain access to the property of a patrilineal descent group other than his own. These arguments are equally relevant in an urban context (Ruedy 1992, 24; cf. Bargaoui 1998; Boulifa 1925, 264–66, 334–36; Aït-Zaï 1995, 305–12—to be used with caution).

Having established that the term '*bilād al-qibla*' refers to the mountainous region above the northern edge of the Sahara desert, inhabited by Berbers and stretching from the Zab mountains in the northeast to Sijilmasa in the southwest, let us attempt to identify with greater precision the location in which the question may have originated. One fact is uncontestable: All three responses were issued in Tlemcen, in its heyday the hub of the Saharan transit trade and arguably the most important intellectual and cultural center in the central Maghrib. In the ninth/fifteenth century (as today), there were large concentrations of Berbers in the central Maghrib, especially in Grand Kabylia and the western part of Lesser Kabylia, approximately 500 km. east of Tlemcen, on the border between the ʿAbd al-Wādid and Ḥafsid states. As noted, the tribesmen of these regions systematically exclude females from inheriting (Patorni 1895, 315–20). The word 'Kabylia' is derived from the Arabic '*qabāʾil*' (sg. *qabīla*), which means 'tribes'. Thus, when al-Wansharīsī indicated that the question emanated from *bilād al-qibla,* he may also have had in mind the *bilād al-qabā'il,* i.e., 'the lands of the tribes', referring to Kabylia and its Berber inhabitants. Alternatively, he may have had in mind another area of the central Maghrib inhabited by significant numbers of Berbers, e.g., Oran or the coastal region between Algiers and Annaba. Be that as it may, until such time as evidence to the contrary is produced, we adopt as a working hypothesis that the inhabitants of the *bilād al-qibla* mentioned by al-Wansharīsī were Berber tribesmen of the Central Maghrib.

The Istiftā'

Although our source does not identify the *mustaftī,* it is clear from the formulation of the question that he was a jurist and that the issue at hand was a matter of concern not only to private individuals but also to the state and its ruler.

The *mustaftī* begins by stating that the current inhabitants of an unidentified country (*balad*) have been colluding (*tawāṭa'a*) to prevent women from receiving their inheritance shares for a period of approximately 400 years, going back to the fifth/eleventh century. Although the practice was contested and many *fatwā*s reportedly were issued about it, the problem had persisted over time without resolution. Indeed, the practice of disinheriting women had now become a political issue at the highest levels of the state. The governor or ruler (*al-wālī*) of the area, characterized by the *mustaftī* as a pious Muslim determined to enforce the *sharī'a* and to correct an injustice (*istarshada ilā al-ḥaqq*), was demanding that all landed property and residences in the possession of their de facto owners be restored to their lawful owners. His proposal to expropriate Berber lands appears to have encountered stiff resistance, as reflected in the *istiftā'* (Wansharīsī 1981–3, 11: 293, ll. 19–22).[3]

[3] The unnamed ruler mentioned in the question would have been an agent of either the Ḥafsid or 'Abd al-Wādid sultan. The Ḥafsid ruler of the eastern Maghrib during last quarter of the ninth/fifteenth century would have been either Abū 'Amr 'Uthmān (r. 1435–88) or Abū Yaḥyā Zakariyā' II (r. 1489–94); the 'Abd al-Wādid ruler of the central Maghrib during this same period was Abū 'Abd Allāh Muḥammad IV (r. 1468–1504). If we assume that the unnamed ruler was carrying out the will of his sovereign, then one or the other of these sultans was prepared to intervene

The *mustaftī* articulates the interest of the men whose lands were threatened with expropriation and of the people who were opposed to the ruler's proposed course of action. How is it possible, he asks, retroactively to restore the properties in question to their lawful owners (ibid., 11: 293, ll. 22–3)? His position with regard to the action proposed by the ruler emerges clearly from his enumeration of five obstacles to its successful implementation:

(1) It is difficult if not impossible to identify the true heirs because their rights have been denied to them continuously over the course of many generations.
(2) The original shares have been appropriated by men and recycled, presumably among men, from one generation to the next.
(3) It would be difficult to identify the exact number and identity of the women who have been deprived of their inheritance shares over a period of 400 years and who therefore have a claim to those shares.
(4) Over the course of a lifetime, a woman may inherit at successive points in time from different members of her family. In order to calculate the size of her inheritance from each one of these individuals, one would have to know the exact constellation of heirs at the moment on which a particular member of the family died and also the exact order in which they died. Practically speaking, such knowledge is unattainable.
(5) Many of the men who allegedly appropriated the inheritance shares of their sisters or female relatives recycled the properties through purchase and sale, with the result that those properties can no longer be identified (ibid., 11: 293, l. 23–294, l. 1).

The problem is insoluble, the *mustaftī* asserts, because the facts of the case are uncertain, for it is impossible to determine the identities of the individuals who are entitled to the inheritance shares and/or the exact properties, or shares thereof, to which they are entitled. Undeterred, the ruler of the country was determined to

in tribal affairs and to risk the antagonism of the tribesmen. He proposed to rectify the problem by seizing the properties in the hands of its current holders, redistributing them to their rightful owners, and re-setting the inheritance clock, so to speak, so that, in the future, property might be transmitted from one generation to the next in a lawful, *shar'ī* manner. If so, he failed to anticipate the objections of the *'ulamā'*, who intervened in the dispute on the side of the de facto property holders, upholding their rights against the power of the state.

expropriate the property in the possession of the current holders. Is it permissible for him to do so, the *mustaftī* asks, and what is the legal status of the property that is currently in the possession of the inhabitants of this country: lawful, unlawful or somewhere in between (ibid., 11: 294, ll. 1–2.)?

The *mustaftī* engages in some legal reasoning of his own, reducing a large and complex problem to a smaller one of more manageable size. He proposes that the problem be considered from the perspective of just one (male) individual. Some of the property in the possession of this individual may have been lawfully inherited, whereas other property may have been acquired unlawfully, either currently or in the past, through the expropriation of inheritance shares from female members of his family. How does one distinguish the lawful property from the unlawful and what action, if any, may the ruler take with regard to property that was acquired unlawfully? The *mustaftī* distinguishes two hypothetical situations or circumstances:

1. If *all* of the property in the possession of a particular individual has been acquired unlawfully, then the ruler is under an obligation to seize this property and either to distribute it as charity or use it in some manner that will be of general benefit to the Muslim community.
2. If, however, only a *preponderance* of the property in the possession of a particular individual has been acquired unlawfully, then the ruler is enjoined from seizing it and redistributing it. As support for this conclusion, the *mustaftī* cites a statement attributed to Ibn Rushd (d. 520/1126) in his *Muqaddimāt* (ibid., 11: 294, ll. 2–6).[4]

Clearly, a vicious cycle had been created: According to the *mustaftī*, most if not all of the property held by the inhabitants of the region in question ca. 880/1475–76 had been acquired unlawfully or its status was a matter of dispute; but the identity of the true owners of the property was indeterminable. If, as the *mustaftī* concedes, it is impossible to do justice with respect to the past, might it not be possible to do justice with respect to the present and the future? Is the imām empowered to put an end to the vicious cycle, on the grounds of public interest, by issuing a judgment (*yaḥkum*) on behalf of each

[4] On the general problem of lawful and unlawful property and what to do about it, see ʿAbd al-Jabbār, ca. 1965, 14: 451 ff. I am grateful to my colleague Maurice Pomerantz for drawing my attention to this text.

and every (male) property owner, declaring that the property currently in his possession does in fact belong to him and henceforth may be inherited from him in the future in a lawful manner by his male (and, presumably, female) heirs (ibid., 11: 294, ll. 7–9)?

Three Responses

Three responses to the question are preserved in the *Miʿyār*, that of Abū Sālim Ibrāhīm al-ʿUqbānī, and, in addition, those of two of his younger colleagues in Tlemcen: Abū ʿAbdallāh Muḥammad al-Sanūsī, and Abū ʿAbdallāh Muḥammad b. ʿAbdallāh al-Tunsī al-Tilimsānī.

1. *The Response of Abū Sālim Ibrāhīm al-ʿUqbānī*

Al-ʿUqbānī, the chief qāḍī of Tlemcen and scion of a family of distinguished jurists (Makhlūf 1975, 1: 265, no. 977), begins his response by drawing attention to the *mustaftī*'s formulation of the question, which, he asserts, is flawed, for two reasons: (1) The *mustaftī* confused the underlying principles and the specific rules that apply to the question and failed to stipulate the "soundest" course of action, despite the fact that he possessed the requisite legal knowledge to do so (hence my inference that the *mustaftī* was himself a jurist); and (2) he also cast aspersions on the inhabitants of a specific Muslim country, attributing to them behavior which, if confirmed, would require their expulsion (*ikhrāj*)—presumably either from their lands or from the Muslim community (ibid., 11: 294, ll. 10–13).

Turning to the charge of disinheritance, al-ʿUqbānī expresses greater interest in the religio-ethical implications of the question than he does in its practical aspects. He is willing to concede that at a given point in time and in a given place there may be a certain number of impious individuals who seek to deny women their right to inherit. Surely, however, the great majority of the Muslim inhabitants of the country in question are pious men, and it is inconceivable that pious Muslims would conspire to prevent anyone from inheriting one of the 'shares of God'. Even if one were to concede, for the sake of argument, that they did conspire to do so, surely there had always been a religious leader (*qawwām bi-umūr al-dīn*) in that country who upheld the interests of Islam, clung fast to the religion and was qualified to provide the women in question with whatever help and assistance they needed. Thus, al-ʿUqbānī took a position on the facts of the case, rejecting as implausible—indeed, as *unthinkable*—the charge that the people of this country were disinheriting women at present and had been doing so for hundreds of years in the past (ibid., 11: 294, ll. 13–15).

Echoing one of the points raised by the *mustaftī*, al-ʿUqbānī notes that even if the inhabitants of this country were in fact disinheriting females, any claim with respect to the distant past would be difficult to substantiate. It is hard enough for an individual to reconstruct his genealogy with regard to the recent past. How much the more so with regard to the distant past, i.e., 400 years ago (ibid., 11: 294, ll. 15–17)!

Be that as it may, the consequences of the alleged violation of Qurʾānic law were grave, indeed, potentially fatal. Al-ʿUqbānī explains that if the inhabitants of a country did in fact conspire to violate a religious obligation that applies to the community as a whole (*farḍ kifāya*), then it would be lawful to fight them (*qitāl ahl al-balad*). In the present instance, however, the obligation is not communal but individual. That is to say, each and every one of the Muslim inhabitants of this country in question has an individual obligation (*farḍ ʿayn*) to convey the 'shares of God' to their lawful recipients, males and females. If one or more Muslims nevertheless conspires to disinherit women and refuses to give them the shares to which they are entitled, the obligation to fight these Muslims is even greater than the obligation to fight those Muslims who have failed to perform a communal obligation. However, it would be absurd to fight fellow Muslims—even if the *muftī* does not say so—leaving it to his interlocutor to draw this conclusion on his own and convey it to the ruler (ibid., 11: 294, 11. 17–19).

Having clarified the flaws in the *mustaftī*'s formulation of the question, al-ʿUqbānī now announces that with the assistance of God he will attempt to penetrate the mind of the *mustaftī*, clarify his real intentions, and arrange the relevant legal issues in their proper order, so that each point might be treated in the appropriate manner. This is the true beginning of his response to the question. It is noteworthy that al-ʿUqbānī now shifts his attention exclusively to the unidentified ruler who wished to seize the properties in question and restore them to their rightful (female) owners; from this point on in his response, the men who allegedly had disinherited women, and, even more so, the women who allegedly had been disinherited, recede into the background (ibid., 11: 294, ll. 19–25).

The *muftī* begins by citing a statement attributed to the Prophet Muḥammad, as recorded in the *Ṣaḥīḥ*s of al-Bukhārī and Muslim:

> Verily, that which is lawful is clear and that which is unlawful is clear, and between them are the things that are ambiguous, [things] about which many of the people have no knowledge. Thus, if someone is wary of the ambiguous things (*shubuhāt*), his religion and honor are sound; but if someone engages the ambiguous things, he does what is unlawful, like the shepherd around the sacred precinct (*ḥimā*) [in which it is forbidden to graze] who is on the verge of falling into it. Verily, every king has a sacred precinct. Verily, the sacred precinct of God is his forbidden things (*maḥārim*). Verily, the body contains an organ (*muḍgha*): if [the organ] is sound, the entire body is sound, but if it is corrupt, the entire body is corrupt; verily, it is the heart (ibid., 11: 295, 11. 1–6; cf. Bukhārī 1862–98, Īmān, bāb 40; Muslim 1930, al-Musāqāt, bāb 20, no. 4178).[5]

The enigmatic prophetic statement establishes a tripartite typology of actions: lawful, unlawful and ambiguous. Actions that are lawful or unlawful are clearly marked in the Qurʾān, e.g., "Prescribed for you are . . ." or "Forbidden for you are . . . ." Occupying an intermediate zone between the lawful and the unlawful are actions that are neither one nor the other, i.e., they are ambiguous. What attitude should be adopted by a pious Muslim—such as the unnamed Muslim ruler—towards activities that fall into this intermediate category? The *ḥadīth* establishes that a Muslim who engages in actions assessed as ambiguous does something that is unlawful. The Prophet explained why this is so by invoking two metaphors: the first posits that a person who engages in actions assessed as ambiguous resembles a shepherd who is on the verge of entering a sacred precinct in which it is forbidden to graze (on this metaphor, see Abū Yūsuf

[5] The term *shubuhāt* used in this *ḥadīth* is surely related to the term *mutashābih* which occurs in Q. 3:7, even if our *muftī* does not make this connection. Q. 3:7 opens as follows: "He has sent down this Book which contains some verses that are *muḥkamāt*, which are the mother of the Book, and others *mutashābihāt*. As for those in whose hearts is deviation, they follow what is *mutashābih*, seeking *fitna* and seeking its interpretation; but none knows its meaning except God . . ." The message is clear: The believer is advised to avoid engagement with ambiguous verses.

1969, 43). In a similar manner, the ownership of every object is protected by a sacred enclosure that marks off God's forbidden things (*maḥārim Allāh*), and any Muslim who penetrates this sacred enclosure in an effort to appropriate an object that belongs to God engages in an action that is forbidden. The second metaphor is based on the heart: if a person's heart is sound, then all his actions will be sound; but if his heart is corrupt, then all his actions will be corrupt. Here the *muftī* is sending a direct message to the ruler, suggesting that the relationship between the heart and the body is analogous to that between the ruler and the body politic or state. Thus, if the ruler is corrupt, the entire state is corrupt.

This *ḥadīth* is the centerpiece of al-ʿUqbānī's response. The legal status of the disputed property falls into the middle category of "ambiguous things about which many of His creation have no knowledge." Ambiguity is a sign of confusion. A Muslim who attempts to observe and execute the precepts of his (or her) religion may become confused when it is necessary to declare an action either lawful or unlawful. Certain actions clearly must be declared lawful and others clearly must be declared unlawful. In some instances, however, the lawfulness and unlawfulness of the action in question may offset one another, so that there is no preponderance of one over the other. In that case, the action is equivocal (Wansharīsī 1981–3, 11: 295, ll. 7–11; cf. ʿAbd al-Jabbār ca. 1965, 14: 453).

The legal status of equivocal actions, the *muftī* observes, is a matter of scholarly disagreement. According to some, an equivocal act is unlawful and should be avoided; according to others, it is lawful and its practice is permissible; according to still others, the assessment of its status should be suspended, presumably until such time as its equivocalness has been resolved. Support for the first two of these three positions can be found in the aforementioned *ḥadīth*. Those who hold that an equivocal act is unlawful rely on the phrase, "If someone engages the ambiguous things (*shubuhāt*), he does what is unlawful". Those who hold that an equivocal act is lawful rely on the phrase, "like the shepherd around the sacred precinct", i.e., although the sacred precinct itself is unlawful, whatever is outside of, or surrounds, the sacred precinct is lawful. Adherents of this latter position nevertheless concede that it is desirable—albeit not obligatory—to avoid even the things that surround the sacred precinct. As for those who hold that the assessment of the act should be suspended, they argue that engagement with *shubha* is reprehensible (*makrūha*); this is equivalent, the *muftī* comments, to saying that the action is lawful, because an action that is reprehensible resembles an action that is permitted, even if its omission entails a reward (ibid., 11: 295, ll. 11–17).

Next, al-ʿUqbānī cites an unnamed *imām* (*baʿḍ al-aʾimma*) who formulated the issue at hand in terms of epistemology and intention. According to this *imām*, the uncertainty that a person may experience regarding the legal status of an act is one of three types:

1. Someone is initially certain that an action should be treated as unlawful but subsequently becomes uncertain about whether or not it continues to be unlawful. According to the *imām*, any action that falls into this category should be treated as unlawful, because it is unlawful to engage in an activity except on the basis of certainty, and it is not possible to pass from the certainty of unlawfulness to the uncertainty of lawfulness.
2. Someone knows that an action is lawful but later comes to suspect that it has been declared unlawful. According to the *imām*, any action that falls into this category should be treated as lawful until such time as its unlawfulness becomes a matter of certain knowledge.
3. Someone does not know if a particular action is lawful or unlawful. There are two possibilities: (a) it is either lawful or unlawful; or (b) there is no indicator that points to its lawfulness or unlawfulness. In either case, the best course of action is to remain above suspicion (*al-tanazzuh*) by avoiding the action in question (ibid., 11: 295, 11. 18–25).

If I understand al-ʿUqbānī correctly, he is suggesting that it would be wrong for the unnamed ruler to implement the proposed policy of expropriating properties in the possession of the current owners and returning them to their lawful owners—women, past and present—because he cannot know, with certainty, that the current holders of the properties are *not* the lawful owners. It is noteworthy, in my view, that al-ʿUqbānī approaches the question entirely from the perspective of the unidentified ruler and the men who currently are in possession of the disputed property. As for the women whose rights allegedly had been denied for a period of over 400 years, the *muftī* says not a word about them.

2. *The response of al-Sanūsī*

A second response to the question was issued by Abū ʿAbdallāh Muḥammad al-Sanūsī, who was born some time after 830/1426–7 and died in 895/1489–90, fifteen years after al-ʿUqbānī died. Al-Sanūsī, who served as qāḍī of Tlemcen, was a distinguished jurist and theologian who wrote a large number of treatises on issues relating to faith and religious beliefs (*ʿaqāʾid*). He is remembered as "the shaykh of the scholars, ascetics, and the pious (*al-asātidha al-ʿibād*)". He was a Sufi who received the cloak of investiture from his master, al-Walī Ibrāhīm al-Tāzī, and who combined theoretical knowledge (*ʿilm*) and good deeds (*ʿamal*). It is noteworthy in the present context that he was an expert in the field of logic (Makhlūf 1975, 1: 266, no. 984; on law and logic, see El-Rouayheb 2004).

Like al-ʿUqbānī, al-Sanūsī focuses his attention on the unnamed ruler's proposal to expropriate the disputed properties. He begins his response by making three general points: (1) One may not strip a person of his ownership rights on the basis of a mere 'possibility' that is unaccompanied by a sign or indicator that points to unlawfulness; (2) there is no ambiguity with regard to the ownership of land or structures, and the ownership of both types of property is therefore 'lawful'; and (3) in the present case, certain knowledge and probable knowledge combine to refute the claim of unlawfulness (Wansharīsī 1981–3, 11: 296, ll. 2–5).

The *muftī* suggests that claims about current practices must be distinguished from those about the past. Whereas it may be possible, he concedes, to establish that the current inhabitants of the country in question are disinheriting females, it is impossible to establish that this practice has been continuous over a period of 400 years. To substantiate this assertion, he engages in a logical demonstration: he proposes that his readers assume, for the sake of argument, that females at the present time do *not* inherit real property. What inference, if any, can be drawn from this 'fact'? On the one hand, one may infer that the females in question have been unlawfully disinherited and one may further posit that this is a local practice or custom with roots in the distant past. At the same time, however, it is also possible to infer that women do in fact inherit real property, but that, for whatever reason, they fail to summon witnesses to verify the inheritance. The epistemological and evidentiary value of both inferences are weak, the *muftī* concludes, because they are based on the assumption of continuity with regard to the past (*istiṣḥāb al-ḥāl*; ibid., 11: 296, ll. 6–10). In other words, we cannot safely reason our way back from knowledge of the present to knowledge of the past.

Unlike al-ʿUqbānī, al-Sanūsī does refer to socio-economic aspects of inheritance practices. He observes that there is no mention in the question of certain widespread and acceptable practices, as, for example, a woman's renouncing her inheritance shares in return for compensation; a woman's ceding her inheritance rights to male relatives, especially, he says, in periods of economic prosperity; and a man's providing maintenance for his sister with wealth generated by an inheritance share that she previously had ceded to him (ibid., 11: 296, ll.12–14).

Like al-ʿUqbānī, al-Sanūsī is incredulous with regard to the allegation. He states that the general presumption (*al-aṣl*) is that men do not force women to renounce their inheritances. In support of this presumption, he engages in another logical demonstration: Suppose that men have in fact been forcing women to renounce their inheritances for as long as 400 years. If so, why is it that these women have begun to speak up only now, hundreds of years after the practice allegedly began; and why is it that they remained silent throughout the intervening period? Surely a woman who, 400 years ago, was unjustly deprived of her inheritance had a better chance of recovering her shares at the time of their unlawful expropriation than do her descendants at the present time. The fact that women apparently did not lodge a complaint immediately after the violation allegedly occurred serves as an indicator that the Muslims in question have in fact been distributing inheritances in a lawful manner. To this argument, al-Sanūsī continues, one may object: perhaps the women in question were coerced to renounce their inheritances against their will and—although he does not say so—were threatened with repercussions if they chose to speak up in public. Al-Sanūsī concedes that although this might happen in isolated cases, it is *unthinkable* that all of the women in this country could be compelled to relinquish their inheritances, especially since the country in question is, he says, *balad al-ḥukkām*, i.e., a country in which the rule of law is observed—a point that sheds some light on al-Sanūsī's understanding of gender relations (ibid., 11: 296, ll. 14–22).

In sum: men have acquired the property that is currently in their possession without anyone contesting their right to do so. This confirms their entitlement to these properties, and they therefore may engage in lawful commerce with them. In support of his position, al-Sanūsī observes that God does not require Muslims to penetrate to the hidden and interior aspect (*nafs*) of a matter or to determine the original legal status of a property that he acquires at the time of its acquisition (ibid., 11: 297, ll. 1–3).

Al-Sanūsī concludes his response by referring to the suggestion that the unnamed ruler might seize the properties in question on the basis of a mere 'possibility' (*iḥtimāl*). This is absurd, he argues, because if one were to act upon the basis of a tenuous insinuation (*wiswās min al-iḥtimāl*), then no person's wealth would be secure. In the end, the determination of the lawfulness or unlawfulness of the property in one's possession is a matter between every individual and his Maker, and every person must make an individual decision upon the basis of either certain knowledge or preponderant knowledge: If it becomes clear that a particular property does in fact belong to a third party, then the current holder of the property should convey it to its true and rightful owner; if the current holder is unable to do so (e.g., because the rightful owner is no longer alive), then he should distribute the property as charity. As for property whose ownership is uncertain, the current holder should make every possible effort to remain above suspicion (*tanazzuh*), that is to say, he should act on the basis of what is most secure in all of his affairs (ibid., 11: 297, ll. 3–9). In either case, it should be noted, an individual's right to property is protected against interference by the state.

3. *The response of al-Tunsī*

The third response was issued by another distinguished jurist, Abū ʿAbdallāh Muḥammad b. ʿAbdallāh al-Tunsī al-Tilimsānī, who died in 899/1493–4, five years after al-Sanūsī and three years prior to al-Wansharīsī's completion of the *Miʿyār*.[6]

Al-Tunsī begins his response by reiterating the distinction drawn by al-Sanūsī between claims relating to the present and those relating to the past. He states: If, at the present time, it is possible to identify the true owner of a property and also to identify the specific

[6] Al-Tunsī studied in Tlemcen with Abū al-Faḍl al-ʿUqbānī and Ibn Marzūq al-Ḥafīḍ. His students included Ibn Marzūq al-Sibṭ, al-Zawāwī, and Abū al-ʿAbbās b. Dāʾūd al-Andalusī—the latter praised him as the most knowledgeable of the scholars with whom he had studied in Tlemcen (Makhlūf 1975, 1: 267, no. 986).

property that belongs to her, then ownership of the property may be transferred to its true owner, in accordance with judicial practice (*ʿamal*) and legal doctrine (*fiqh*)—presumably by tracing the devolution of the property in question from one person to another in accordance with the inheritance rules. Suppose, however, that the alleged violation took place in the distant past and that it is impossible at present to identify the true owner of a particular property; and suppose further that it is established that the current holder of the property is not the true owner and that the property passed from one generation to the next by means of inheritance, so that the current holder is merely the *de facto* owner of the property. In this case, one follows the opinion of Ibn Rushd, according to whom, if someone acquires property, and no one contests his ownership of it, then his ownership of the property in question is confirmed, either absolutely or on the basis of uncertainty (*shubha*).[7] As a Western lawyer might put it: possession is 9/10 of ownership.

Al-Sanūsī concludes his response with another citation from Ibn Rushd on the subject of inherited property the majority of which is either lawful or unlawful (ibid., 11: 297, ll. 17 ff., where the term *mustaghraq* occurs; on this term, see Osswald 1993, chaps. 7 and 8).

Return to Jāhiliyya

It is reasonable to assume that at the end of the ninth/fifteenth century, the Berber tribesmen of the central Maghrib, especially those living in the rural countryside, the highlands and the mountains, were only thinly islamicized. Their native language was Berber and most had little or no knowledge of Arabic. Although they may have observed one or more of the five pillars of Islam, they had little or no knowledge of the subtleties of law or theology.

Of particular relevance to the present investigation, the Berbers held fast to their customary law and, specifically, to the longstanding practice of excluding women from inheriting. If this practice could be substantiated, then the Muslim ruler of this territory would

[7] "He said: *Shubha* refers to their inheritance of that which is in the liability of the person who is inherited from (*fī maḍmūni mawrūthihim*)" (Wansharīsī 1981–3, 11: 297, 11. 10–17).

be duty bound to take military action against the violators of Qur'ānic law and/or to expel them from their lands. Clearly, the issue was politically sensitive and potentially explosive, and it required careful and, no doubt, circumspect treatment. This may explain why the *mustaftī* refers to the problem in general and abstract terms (*mas'alat balad*), why al-Wansharīsī identified the location of the dispute as the expansive *bilād al-qibla* (rather than the more narrowly circumscribed *bilād al-qabā'il* or Kabylia); and why the question was the subject of not one but three responses issued by distinguished jurists over a period of nearly a quarter of a century.

How did al-ʿUqbānī, al-Sanūsī, and al-Tunsī accomplish their objective? Upon what sources did they rely to legitimize their views? Did they succeed in producing an authoritative statement of the law? It is noteworthy, to my mind, that the three *muftī*s make only passing reference to the established sources of legal authority, Qur'ān, *ḥadīth*, and the doctrine of earlier jurists. As for the Qur'ān, not one of the three *muftī*s mentions any of the verses that treat the subject of inheritance. They ignore Q. 4:8, which establishes that both men and women have the right to inherit; they do not cite the three 'inheritance verses', Q. 4:11, 12, and 176, which award specific fractional shares of the estate to male and female heirs; and they are silent about Q. 4:13–14, which define these fractional shares as the 'limits' (*ḥudūd*) of God, promising reward in the Hereafter to whoever observes these limits and punishment in Hell to whoever disobeys them. As for the *ḥadīth*, al-ʿUqbānī does cite one, but it has nothing to do with the inheritance rights of women or men. Otherwise, the three *muftī*s ignore the large body of prophetic dicta about inheritance, e.g., the well-known statement attributed to Muḥammad, "It is better to leave your heirs rich than to leave them destitute, begging from others. Any expense that you incur, seeking thereby the face of God, will be rewarded—even the morsel of food that you put in your wife's mouth" (Muslim 1930, 11: 76). As for juristic authority, al-ʿUqbānī refers to disagreements among certain unnamed scholars, again, having nothing to do with inheritance; and al-Tunsī does cite Ibn Rushd, although not about inheritance.

If these three jurists disregarded the standard sources of legal authority, upon what did they base their respective opinions? Here, the true basis of their responses is logic, legal presumptions and assumptions about human behavior. The reader will recall that al-Uqbānī began his response by reformulating the question that had been sent to him. Unlike the *mustaftī*, who framed the question in terms of the tension between law and custom—men were depriving women of their inheritance rights—al-ʿUqbānī, and following him, al-Sanūsī and al-Tunsī, successfully shifted the focus of the question to the lawfulness, or lack thereof, of the unnamed ruler's proposal to seize the properties from their current holders and restore them to their 'true' owners. Al-ʿUqbānī claimed that he had the ability to penetrate the minds of the people in question and that he knew what pious Muslims would or would not do (the *aṣl* or legal presumption is that men do not disinherit women); in the unlikely event that his assumption were mistaken, religious leaders no doubt would have handled the problem. The assumption that men have in fact been disinheriting women would lead to the absurd conclusion that it is necessary to take military action against fellow Muslims. Upon examination, it emerges that the behavior of the alleged perpetrators cannot be qualified as lawful or unlawful, but rather is ambiguous or equivocal. The allegation cannot be supported with hard evidence. Thus, the preferred course of action is to avoid taking any action whatsoever and thus to remain above suspicion. Let the status quo be maintained.

Al-Sanūsī reasons his way to a conclusion in a similar manner. To his mind, the epistemological certainty produced by the fact that people at present are in possession of landed property outweighs the mere 'possibility' that these properties had been acquired unlawfully in the distant past. He favors logical demonstration, e.g., we cannot reason our way back from knowledge of the present to knowledge of the past. It may appear as if men disinherit women, but the surface picture hides a more complex reality (women may concede their inheritance rights to their brothers or other male relatives). The starting point of any investigation should therefore be the legal presumption (*al-aṣl*) that men do not force women to renounce their inheritance rights. This presumption is supported by another logical demonstration (if women were in fact denied their inheritance rights in the past, they would have spoken up). In a Muslim society it is *unthinkable* that men would do the things that they are accused of doing. If the ruler were to pursue the proposed course of action, the result would be chaos, and no one's property would be safe from confiscation by the state. The question of whether or not the property in one's possession has been acquired lawfully or unlawfully is a private matter between each individual and his Maker, not a public matter between the individual and his ruler.

Finally, al-Tunsī argued that if it cannot be established with certainty that the *de facto* owner of property is its *de jure* owner, one follows Ibn Rushd's observation that long-term and uncontested possession of property is equivalent to ownership.

According to all three jurists, the uncertainty and confusion associated with the practices in question are too great to justify action by the ruler against the alleged violators of Qur'ānic law. The *status quo* should be maintained. Although their responses were not based upon Qur'ān and *ḥadīth*, the *muftī*s did provide *sharʿī* justification for the customary practices, with the result that, if and when a similar question arose in the future, men could point to the three *fatwā*s analyzed here as justification for their actions.

This surely was not the first time that a Maghribī *muftī* had been asked for his legal assessment of the relationship between Islamic inheritance law and local customary law. Nor would it be the last. Some 250 years later, in the middle of the eighteenth century, the disinheritance of women lay at the heart of politico-religious conflicts in the central Maghrib, in the course of which one Berber tribe, the Ait Betrūn, issued an official proclamation in which it was affirmed, *inter alia*, that daughters, sisters, and orphans may not inherit (Patorni 1895, 315–20; Hacoun-Campredon 1921). And the disinheritance of women continues to the present time (Moors 1995). Thus, the three *fatwā*s analyzed here represent points on a continuum of an ongoing discussion of the incongruities and gaps between Islamic law and customary law with respect to female inheritance rights, and, more generally, the gap between Islam and *jāhiliyya*.[8] In the future, scholars of Islamic law will want to engage in a systematic analysis of this discourse across time and space.

[8] In the eighth/fourteenth century, a *mustaftī* asked a jurist living in Bijāya about an unidentified person "in the midst of the Muslims" who pronounces the credo of the faith, prays, and fasts, yet is ignorant of the meaning of the basic elements of Islamic theology (Wansharīsī 1981–3, 2: 382–4; this *fatwā* is discussed briefly in Hannemann 2002, 223).

CHAPTER THREE

WOMEN AS EXPERT WITNESSES IN PRE-MODERN ISLAMIC COURTS*

Ron Shaham

> O believers, when you contract a debt one upon another for a stated term, write it down . . . And call in to witness two witnesses, men; or, if they be not men, then one man and two women, such witnesses as you approve of, lest one of the two [women] err, then the other will remind her (Qur'ān 2: 282)
>
> Women are defective in terms of logical capability and religiosity (Prophetic tradition)
>
> The testimony of women is permitted with regard to what men are incapable to watch (Prophetic tradition)

Historical and Comparative Background

This chapter focuses on the role of ordinary women, in general, and midwives, in particular, as providers of expert testimony concerning the intimate parts of the female body. In Muslim societies, in which females had to be segregated from unrelated males, it was preferred that a female treat an ailing female, especially if the malady or wound were located in the intimate parts of the body. Legal texts instruct male physicians to teach women how to take care of other women. Only if a female practitioner is not available, and the life of the female patient is in danger, is a male physician allowed to treat her (Sarakhsī 1993, 10: 156–57; Bos 1993, 305–6).[1]

* Author's note: early drafts of this chapter were presented in various academic forums. I thank all the participants of these forums for their comments. I also thank my graduate students at the Hebrew University for helping me to struggle with some of the Arabic texts analyzed in this chapter. Nimrod Hurvitz, Avner Giladi, Liat Kozma, Aharon Layish, and especially David Powers, read earlier versions of the chapter and provided helpful substantive and editorial comments. My gratitude to all of them.

[1] According to Sonbol (2003, 79–80), the hospitals (called Maristans) were divided into separate departments for females and males. Only female physicians and

Our current knowledge of the functions of midwives in Muslim societies is insufficient, and Islamicists can only envy the rich source material and scholarly literature on this topic in early modern Europe. In early modern Europe, most midwives were mature women, married or widowed, who started to practice after their children had grown up. Most were trained in some form of apprenticeship, formal or informal; most were of middle-class status, married to artisans, craftsmen, tradesmen or farmers, for whom the practice of midwifery, although not essential for the household income, was a useful addition (Marland 1993, 4; Bar-On 2000, 66–7; Baumgarten 2000, 50, 55). We are not yet able to construct a broad profile of the average pre-modern[2] Muslim midwife, although they doubtless provided essential services and gained their expertise through informal apprenticeship (Toledano 1998, 76; Lane 1954, 509–11).

In pre-modern Muslim societies, midwifery was considered essential for ensuring the survival of a newborn baby (Sarakhsī 1993, 10: 156; Ibn Khaldūn 1958, 2: 368–70).[3] Some of the legal sources mention that a husband may not prevent his wife from working as a midwife (Zaydān 1994, 7: 291–92). The work of midwives in hospitals (called Maristans) was considered a low-status job, although those who served as midwives in the harems of elite households apparently enjoyed a higher status (Ahmed 1992, 84, 115; Shatzmiller 1994, 353). It is not clear if these practitioners were organized in formal guilds, as male artisans were, or if midwifery was recognized as a female occupation.[4]

---

midwives worked in the female department. When a male physician's opinion was needed with regard to a female patient, a female physician or a midwife reported her condition to the male physician, who then diagnosed the patient without physically inspecting her. Sonbol does not provide any references for this statement.

[2] Throughout the article, I use the term 'pre-modern' for the period before the nineteenth century.

[3] The Egyptian Mālikī jurist Ibn al-Ḥājj al-ʿAbdarī (d. 1336) criticizes midwives for ignoring the basic rules of hygiene while treating the newborn, and for their systematic refusal to cooperate with each other, thereby risking the health of mothers and infants (ʿAbdarī n.d., 3: 282–91). In the same manner, the Shāfiʿī Ibn Ḥajar al-Haytamī (d. 1567) links infant mortality to the irresponsible treatment of midwives in the course of deliveries (Giladi 1992, 77).

[4] Three studies, all based on the sharīʿa court records of Ottoman Jerusalem in the sixteenth century, present contradictory evidence. Al-Yaʿqūb ('Nāḥiyat al-Quds al-Sharīf fī al-Qarn al-ʿĀshir al-Hijrī/al-Sādis ʿAshr al-Mīlādī,' Masters thesis, the Jordanian University, 1986, quoted in Abū Salīm 2000, 66–7) argues that there was a guild for midwives; Sonbol (2003, 74) does not mention a specific midwives guild and argues (p. 79) that in 1555 there were five midwives in Jerusalem; Cohen

In spite of the patriarchal reluctance to rely on the testimony of women, regarded as suspect, midwives in early modern Europe served as expert witnesses, in addition to their main role in assisting women to deliver babies. For example, Quaker midwives served as both arbitrators and witnesses in domestic disputes and in cases of sexual misdemeanor, rape, incest, infanticide or physical abuse. Moral integrity and religious conformity were demanded from midwives for ensuring their suitability to testify in court, to question the mothers of bastard children *in extremis*, and to decide on cases of ante-nuptial fornication or infanticide (Marland 1993, 7).[5]

The function of midwives in early modern Europe as the right hand of municipalities and judges in preserving the societal morality code was probably similar to their function in Muslim societies. For example, in the beginning of the fifth century AH, there lived in the city of Tuṭiyla (east of Cordoba) a woman who had a full beard, similar to that of men. She traveled freely and acted like a male. Nobody paid attention to the matter until the local qāḍī ordered a few midwives to inspect her. They refrained from doing so due to her appearance, but the qāḍī reiterated his order. They determined that she was a female, whereupon the qāḍī ordered that her beard be shaven, that she wear female attire, and that she not travel unless accompanied by a male relative (Yāqūt 1866, 1: 853).

In this study, I use legal and historical sources to analyze the involvement of ordinary women and midwives in expert witnessing in pre-modern Muslim societies. I see two points of interest here. The first is legal, that is, the attitude of Muslim jurists to expert testimony, in general, and to female expert testimony, in particular—a topic that is not adequately covered in research. The second, the social aspect, is the relationship between the legal status of women as expert witnesses and their social status in patriarchal societies. I start with a preliminary consideration, i.e., the attitude of Islamic law towards the testimony of women in general.

(2001, 186) did not find a midwives' guild and mentions that the historian 'Abd al-Karīm Rāfiq did not find names of women in lists of guilds from Ottoman Damascus and Aleppo. As for nineteenth-century Egypt, Baer (1964, 33, 171) found the midwives (*dāyāt*) in the guilds' list, but he observes that he is not sure if the intention is to an organized guild or to a mere mention of a female occupation.

[5] For additional information, see the articles of Harley, Wiesner and Ortiz in the volume edited by Marland.

The Attitude of Islamic Law towards the Testimony of Women

The position of women in Muslim societies, and particularly in Islamic law, is reflected in the rules of evidence. Generally speaking, Muslim jurists are reluctant to rely on the testimony of women. Most jurists agree that the testimony of women is unacceptable entirely not only from all criminal (*ḥudūd*) and penal (*ʿuqūbāt*) cases, but also from claims of marriage and divorce, because those fields encompass issues dealing primarily with the human body and its status. As for financial matters, according to a literal interpretation of Qurʾān 2: 282, the ideal is the testimony of two males; if, however, there is only one male witness, it is permitted to substitute a second one with two females. The traditional rationalization for the 2: 1 equation is that females are forgetful and imprecise in relating details. The two female witnesses remind each other about the details of the contract, thereby complementing one another and together producing a full testimony, equal to that of one man.[6]

A few recent studies have tried to break this monolithic patriarchal narrative by proposing a modernist reading of the verse. Fadel, for example, argues that post-Ayyubid Sunnī jurists were concerned about the existence of two discourses concerning female testimony. The first, which he calls 'normative', recognized the equality of women to men as transmitters of tradition (*ḥadīth*) and as *mujtahids*.[7] The second, called 'legal-political,' discriminated against women as witnesses and judges. Since it was impossible to justify this gap on the grounds of the natural intellectual inferiority of women, some jurists, such as al-Qarāfī (Mālikī; Egyptian; d. 1285) and Ṭarābulusī (Ḥanafī; Syrian; d. 1440), developed social-oriented justifications for the gap (Fadel 1997, 186–93, 199–201; ʿAlwānī 1996, 173–79). This

[6] For primary legal sources which discuss the inter- and intra-school controversies on this topic, see Ibn Qudāma 1990, 14: 126–30; Ibn Rushd 1996, 2: 559; Asyūṭī n.d., 2: 438; Ibn Qayyim n.d., 90; Zaydān 1994, 5: 340–41, 441. For secondary sources, see ʿAlwānī 1996, 190–92; Fadel (1997, 194) places the legal issues in which the testimony of women is accepted along a 'private-public' continuum. Women's testimony is acceptable in private disputes (financial) but not in disputes that require public recognition (criminal, penal, marriage and divorce). Fadel (ibid., 197–99) also refers to the Ḥanbalīs, Ibn Taymiyya (d. 1327) and his student Ibn Qayyim al-Jawziyya (d. 1350), who argued that a judge should be allowed to rely on the testimony of men or women, as long as the evidence is credible, thereby rejecting the standard two-women-equal-one-man rule.

[7] For historical evidence on women's involvement in the transmission of traditions and in legal studies, see Berkey 1992, 168–69, 173–75, 180–81.

interpretive line, which was probably not dominant, was revived by the modernist Muḥammad ʿAbduh and his followers, who argued that the testimony of females is discounted because women have traditionally exercised domestic occupations that prevent them from developing memory skills, precision in details and proficiency in public matters, such as contracts (Riḍā 1999, 3: 103–5).[8]

Muslim jurists are reluctant to rely on the legal testimony of females and hold that such testimony may not be considered as 'basic evidence' (*ḥujja aṣliyya*). There is, however, one field in which the testimony of women is essential and enjoys a privileged status, i.e., that relating to the hidden parts of the female body (in legal jargon: 'under the dress', *taḥta al-thiyāb*). This is the only field in which Islamic law, on the grounds of necessity (*ḍarūra*), permits women to testify alone and not alongside a male (Sarakhsī 1993, 6: 48, 106; 17: 82). The necessity is created by the fact that males are prohibited from viewing the intimate parts of the female body.

The jurists disagree about the events involving females which men are forbidden from watching. For example, Abū Ḥanīfa, the eponym of the Ḥanafī school (d. 767), held that males who are foreign to a woman might watch her breast-feeding, and therefore they could testify about it. Similarly, he held that males may not witness a birth, but they may give testimony about the first cry of the newborn (*istihlāl*). It seems, however, that Abū Ḥanīfa's is a minority opinion and that most jurists prohibited men from witnessing breast-feeding and the *istihlāl* (Ibn Qudāma 1990, 14: 135).

It is reasonable to divide female testimony regarding the female body into two types: in the first, the female supplies standard eye-witnessing to events in which she participates and which are closed to foreign men, such as birth and breast-feeding. Every adult and reliable Muslim female is qualified to supply this direct evidence. In the second type, a female expert witness who has medical knowledge or is a midwife can supply testimony of opinion concerning events that she has not observed directly (e.g., sexual intercourse), on the basis of signs found on the inspected woman's body. These two types of evidence are different, the first being direct and the second indirect;

[8] Sayyid Qutb (1999, 1: 374–75) retreats from the 'social' explanation for the lack of equality between a male's and a female's testimony and returns to the traditional explanation, linking this lack of equality to the impulsive and emotional nature of women.

the juristic discourse on female testimony, however, does not make a systematic distinction between them and both are discussed in the same chapters. In addition, with respect to almost any kind of testimony or inspection related to the female body, the juristic literature labels expert women by a variety of terms: 'a woman' (*imraʾa*) or 'women' (*nisāʾ*); 'a just woman' (*imraʾat ʿadl*); 'women trusted by the qāḍī' (. . . *mimman yathiqu [al-qāḍī] bihinna*); and, frequently, 'a midwife' (*qābila*, pl. *qawābil*). We may infer from this that the provision of testimony concerning the female body was not preserved exclusively to midwives.

Female testimony concerning signs found on another woman's body locates the testifying female in the category of an expert witness (*khabīr*, or *mukhbir*, as against a regular witness, *shāhid*) who provides a report (*khabar*, or *taqrīr*) to the court, based on her opinion. The Ḥanafī jurist al-Sarakhsī (d. 1097), discussing the case of a convicted female adulterer who pleads that she is pregnant, instructs the qāḍī to delay the application of the *ḥadd* punishment, here stoning, and to have women inspect her. He reasons that the qāḍī should consult with experts whenever he faces difficulty (*wa-mā yashkulu ʿalā al-qāḍī fa-innamā yarjiʿu fīhi ilā man lahu baṣar fī hādhā al-bāb*) and he compares the inspecting woman to a male expert, *qayyim al-mutlafāt*, i.e., a person who is an expert in estimating the decrease in the value of damaged property (Sarakhsī 1993, 9: 73–4).

A few prominent traditions serve as the framework for the juristic discussion of female testimony regarding the hidden parts of the female body (Ibn Qudāma 1990, 14: 134–37; Sarakhsī 1993, 6: 49–50; Ibn Qayyim n.d., 90–6). According to a tradition transmitted by the Prophet's companion Ḥudhayfa b. al-Yamān (d. 656), the Prophet allowed the testimony (*shahāda*) of a midwife concerning birth. According to another tradition, ʿUqba b. al-Ḥārith married Umm Yaḥyā b. Abī Ihāb, and following the marriage a black female slave claimed that she had breast-fed both ʿUqba and his wife, which meant their marriage was prohibited. ʿUqba sought relief from the Prophet, arguing that the slave was lying. The Prophet, however, dismissed his claim and held that he had to separate from his wife on the basis of the slave's testimony. In another tradition the Prophet said that the testimony of females (*shahādat al-nisāʾ*) is permitted with regard to events that males are forbidden to observe.

These traditions gave rise to two juristic attitudes. The first, attributed to the Mālikī and Shāfiʿī schools, requires anywhere between two and four female witnesses, on the grounds that such testimony falls within the scope of the term '*shahāda*'. Those who hold this view argue that the fact that the traditions use the term '*shahāda*' (and not '*khabar*'), and also the term 'female' in the plural rather than the singular, proves that all the standard rules of evidence apply here, excluding the requirement that the witness be a male. The number of female witnesses should therefore be at least two, though Shāfiʿī (d. 820) requires four, according to the standard equation of 'one male equals two females' (Ibn Abī al-Damm 1987, 316–18). In support of their view, these jurists state that the fact that the female expert is required to be a free Muslim proves that the testimony she provides is a standard *shahāda*. In an attempt to refute their opponents from the Ḥanafī school (see below), the Shāfiʿī jurists argue that even the latter prefer two experts to one, for the sake of caution and certainty, thereby implying that they consider the testimony of a female expert as a *shahāda*.

The second attitude, associated with the Ḥanafī and Ḥanbalī schools, permits reliance on the testimony of one female, on the grounds that such testimony is not a standard *shahāda* but a *khabar*, namely a report, similar to the transmission of a tradition. This approach is based on the following grounds: (a) some traditions speak about the testimony of one female in this context, as, for example, that of ʿUqba b. Ḥārith concerning the black slave wet-nurse. The Ḥanafī Sarakhsī, a supporter of this approach, responds to the difficulty emanating from the fact that certain traditions use the term 'females' rather than 'a female' by arguing that 'females' may be treated as a generic noun (*ism al-jins*), which may be interpreted as both singular and plural (Sarakhsī 1993, 6: 49; Ibrāhīm 1985, 173); (b) in refutation of al-Shāfiʿi's stand, the Ḥanafī scholars argue that the rule that 'one male equals two females' is applicable only to financial claims in which females testify alongside males, and is inapplicable to claims pertaining to the female body, in which females testify alone (Ibn Qudāma 1990, 14: 136); and (c) Sarakhsī argues that from a socio-moral perspective, there is a necessity (*ḍarūra*) to minimize the shame and disrespect caused to a female by allowing only one female (rather than two) to inspect her. Responding to the polemical argument of the Shāfiʿi jurists, the Ḥanafī jurists say that they do not require reports from two female experts, yet if it happens that a woman is inspected or observed by more than one female expert, without her objection, then neither will they object, since the double inspection lends greater certainty to the report. The need to minimize the inspected female's shame, the Ḥanafī scholars add, justifies the waiving of two requirements of the witness: gender (female instead of male) and number (one witness instead of two), but it does not justify waiving the requirement of freedom, since an inspection by a free female does not cause greater shame to the inspected female than that by a slave. The female expert must therefore be free (Sarakhsī 1993, 6: 49–50).

The second approach, by permitting reliance on one female expert, creates an analogy between expert female testimony and the transmission of traditions (*riwāya; riwāyat al-akhbār*) (ibid., 6: 49; Ibn Qudāma 1990, 14: 136; Ibn Qayyim n.d., 94). The analogy is as follows: in a situation of necessity, only one female expert is required to inspect the intimate bodily parts of another female and report about it, as in *ḥadīth* transmission, where only one person (female, for our purposes) heard the saying of the Prophet and reported it to others. A tradition or report going back to a single authority, called *al-aḥād*, stands in contrast to the ideal, a *mutawātir* report, i.e., a *ḥadīth* that has been transmitted through multiple channels of transmission and in which each level of transmission (*ṭabaqa* or *daraja*) includes several transmitters, not one. Epistemologically, a *mutawātir* report produces certain knowledge, while *al-aḥād* produces only probable knowledge. Nevertheless, Muslim jurists permit reliance on *al-aḥād* report as a source for *ijtihād* (Hallaq 1997, 60–5; *EI*[2], s.v. Khabar al-wāḥid).

Thus, the second approach creates an analogy between two situations, that is, a single female's report concerning the intimate bodily parts of another female, on the one hand, and the transmission of a tradition by a single female, on the other. In both situations, necessity justifies the relaxation of two evidentiary requirements, i.e., the masculinity of the witness and the number of witnesses. In both cases the 'necessity' is apparently created by scarcity, either of experts or of *ḥadīth* transmitters. It follows that the testimony of a female concerning another female's body is defined as *khabar*, the appropriate term for a *ḥadīth* report, and not as *shahāda*, the appropriate term for judicial testimony. Sarakhsī tries to answer the question whether a female expert's testimony on another female's body is a *shahāda* or a *khabar* by arguing that it has characteristics of both (*khabar min wajh wa-shahāda min wajh*) and that there is an ambiguity (*shubha*) in this respect. On the one hand, it is a *shahāda*, because the female witness must be a Muslim and free, she must use the formulary 'I testify' (*ashhadu*) in the framework of a judicial procedure, and her testimony has a binding effect (*ilzām*) because the qāḍī bases his decision on it. On the other hand, it is a *khabar* because the requirements of gender (female instead of male) and number (one witness instead of two) are dropped (Sarakhsī 1993, 6: 49; 16: 143–44; Ibrāhīm 1985, 173).

It should be emphasized, however, that even those jurists who allow a single female's report do so not because it is desirable but only out of necessity, i.e., the scarcity of experts. Ibn Ḥanbal (d. 855) is a case in point. Contradictory sayings were attributed to him. In some he rejected reliance on the report of a single midwife, while in others he permitted it on the grounds of necessity. However, the clear impression conveyed by all the reports attributed to him is that he strongly supported reliance on as many midwives as possible, preferably three or four, and that he was reluctant to rely on the report of a single female witness (Ibn Qayyim n.d., 91–2).[9]

I turn now to the types of event or physical inspection in which female experts may be involved.

Virginity

In patriarchal societies, virginity is the main criterion for the fidelity of unmarried women, the symbol of a woman's honor (*ʿirḍ*) and, consequently, of the honor (*sharaf*) of her male agnates and of society at large. Presenting evidence of a bride's virginity, such as a blood-stained bed sheet, is a central part of the wedding ceremony. Until recently it was customary in rural Egypt to summon midwives to break the hymens of brides with their fingers, thereby establishing the purity of the bride for the sake of the groom, the families involved and the local community (Longinotto & Hunt 1990).[10]

---

[9] I argue that the jurists are satisfied with one expert witness mainly because of the scarcity of experts. My understanding is different than that of Johansen (2002, 175, 188–89), who claims that one expert is sufficient because he does not testify or make an oath, but expresses his opinion on the basis of knowledge. I intend to discuss this topic more extensively in my book on expert witnesses in Islamic law (in process).

[10] In what seems to be a legendary story, the Maghribi historian al-Ḥimyarī (d. 1494) relates that in Aswan there lived Nubian women who were so tall and strong that no man could deflower them and, therefore, the assistance of midwives was needed to enable the consummation of marriage (Ḥimyarī 1984, 58).

The inspection of an unmarried woman's virginity has often been initiated by her patrilineal kin in cases in which they suspected that she has lost it. In his study of Aleppo in the eighteenth century, Marcus relates that one resident was so disturbed by public reports that his unmarried daughter was no longer a virgin that he had four midwives establish the girl's innocence and their expert testimony was duly recorded in an official court document (Marcus 1989, 323–24). In nineteenth-century Cairo, girls who ran away from home and lived in the streets, but who were later found, were inspected by midwives, either at the request of their male agnates or after they claimed that they had been raped while on the streets (Fahmy 1998a, 35; idem 1998b, 59–61).[11]

Following the consummation of marriage, the groom might claim that he found his bride a non-virgin, contrary to what he had been promised. Rare historical evidence of the involvement of midwives in such a case is provided by *al-Miʿyār* of al-Wansharīsī (1981, 3: 32–5).[12] In the second half of the fourteenth century, a husband who lived near Granada complained to the qāḍī that upon consummating his marriage, he found his wife to be a non-virgin. The wife denied the allegation, claiming that the marriage had not been consummated and that she was still a virgin. The qāḍī ordered two midwives to inspect the wife. One of them found her deflowered. The other did not inspect the wife independently, but merely corroborated the testimony of her colleague, explaining that the husband himself might have caused the loss of virginity. On the basis of this testimony, the qāḍī dissolved the marriage on the grounds of physical defect (*ʿayb*) in the wife, and ordered her mother to return to the husband the dowry that had been transferred to her. The mother appealed the verdict to another qāḍī, to whom she presented the written testimony of another knowledgeable midwife from the city of Andarash who had inspected her daughter and found her a virgin. Referring to the performance of the first two midwives, the second qāḍī said

[11] For additional evidence concerning Ottoman Cairo, see Sonbol (2003, 80), who bases herself on a court document from Bāb al-ʿĀlī court in Cairo in 1736. See also Baghdadi (1998, 90–1) on the testimony of midwives regarding virginity, abortion and infant mortality; and (ibid., 116, n. 35) on a qāḍī who, following a complaint by a mother concerning the deflowering of her minor daughter, sent two women who inspected the girl and found her still a virgin.

[12] I thank my colleague and friend David Powers for referring me to this text, allowing me to read his analysis of the case and discussing it with me.

that the fact that they had not inspected the wife on the morning following the consummation of marriage, but only a few days later, made it impossible to determine whether the loss of virginity was recent or not, since it is well known that the wound caused by the loss of virginity heals quickly. He stated that the testimonies of the two midwives were therefore useless. The qāḍī added that late Mālikī jurists opposed virginity inspections because it is difficult to establish the truth on the basis of these tests, especially of late, when the profession of midwifery, which requires a high degree of certainty and a strong religiosity, had lost much of its credibility.[13]

In another case that centers on the consummation of marriage, this time from Ottoman Cairo, the father of a minor wife sued his son-in-law, arguing that the latter had violated their marriage agreement not to consummate the marriage for three years (probably until the girl reached puberty), thereby causing her physical harm. After the husband denied the allegation, the qāḍī sent a female expert (*khabīra*) to examine her. When she verified the claim, the qāḍī instructed the husband to divorce his wife (Farḥāt 1988, 83–4).

The verification of a wife's virginity is also required when she files a suit against her husband, demanding to dissolve their marriage on the grounds of his impotence. If the husband denies the claim, the qāḍī grants him respite of one lunar year to prove his sexual potency. If the wife repeats her claim after that time, but the husband argues that he has succeeded in having sexual intercourse with her, the qāḍī sends the wife to a reliable woman (or, if possible, two) for inspection. If they find her to be a non-virgin (*thayyib*), the husband's claim is accepted together with his oath. If they find her to be a virgin, she has the choice between dissolving her marriage or staying with her husband (Sarakhsī 1993, 10: 156–57; Ramlī 1893/94, 1: 60; Qadrī 1928/29, art. 301; Abū Zahra 1957, 357). Elsewhere I have discussed the application of these procedures in the judicial practice of twentieth-century Egypt (Shaham 2003, 136–38, 140–41).

Another situation in which the verification of a woman's virginity is required is adultery (*zinā*). If four males testify that a woman fornicated, but she denies the allegation and claims that she is still a virgin, most jurists (including the Ḥanafīs, Shāfiʿīs and Ḥanbalīs)

[13] In early modern Europe, surgeons argued that midwives failed to distinguish between virgin and non-virgin women and also between pregnant and non-pregnant ones (Bar-On 2000, 130, 155, 212).

hold that female experts (one is sufficient for the Ḥanafīs and Ḥanbalīs) should inspect her. If her claim is verified, she and her partner are relieved from the *ḥadd* punishment for adultery and the witnesses are exempted from the *ḥadd* punishment for false accusation of adultery (*qadhf*), on the grounds of ambiguity (*shubha*), since it is possible that the woman was penetrated but that her virginity remained intact or that the hymen has grown anew, or that the expert who inspected her falsely stated that she was still a virgin. The Mālikīs and the Ẓāhirīs oppose this view, holding that such testimony by women cannot prevent the application of the *ḥadd* punishment.

The Ḥanafī Sarakhsī refers to a situation in which females inspect the corpse of an 'adulteress' after she has been executed by stoning and find her a virgin or an adulteress whose sexual organ has been blocked since birth (*ratqāʾ*). Sarakhsī explains that such evidence is not sufficient to require the witnesses who testified against the 'adulteress' to pay blood money to her relatives, since female testimony does not constitute 'complete evidence for creating an obligation to pay compensation money' (*shahādat al-nisāʾ lā takunu ḥujjatan tāmmatan fī ilzām ḍamān al-māl*) (Sarakhsī 1993, 9: 50; Zaydān 1994, 5: 106–8; Powers 2002, 77).

An additional situation in which the verification of a woman's virginity is required is when the sale contract of a female slave stipulates that she is a virgin, but the buyer claims that she is not. If the buyer sues the seller, demanding to return the slave and get his money back, and if the slave is found to be a non-virgin, his claim should be granted (Sarakhsī 1993, 13: 99–100).

Competence for Sexual Intercourse

Ascertaining the physical ability of a wife to engage in sexual intercourse with her husband is needed, for example, when the father of a minor wife, acting as her guardian, refuses to hand her over to her husband, arguing that she is not physically capable of sexual intercourse. Responding to a question relating to such a situation, the seventeenth-century Palestinian *muftī* Khayr al-Dīn al-Ramlī says that if the girl is accustomed to appearing in public (literally: to exit her house, *mimman takhruju*), she should be summoned to court. If the qāḍī finds, on the basis of her look, that she is able to engage in sexual intercourse, her father must hand her over to her husband.

If the girl does not appear in public, the qāḍī sends reliable women to inspect her in her house. Another case concerns a wife who complains that her husband forces her to have intercourse with him too often and that she is not physically able to sustain it. In both cases two female experts inspect the wife and their report informs the qāḍī's decision (Ramlī 1893/94, 1: 32; Jazīrī 1980, 4: 215, respectively).

Pregnancy

A pregnant divorcee or widow is required to observe a waiting period (*ʿidda*) until she gives birth, and is entitled to receive maintenance during that period from her ex-husband or from his heirs, respectively, and the child later enjoys inheritance rights. According to al-Shāfiʿī and Ibn Ḥazm (d. 1064), if the ex-husband or the heirs of the deceased husband deny that the woman is pregnant, the qāḍī should send four trustworthy midwives to inspect her. If they find her pregnant, her ex-husband or his heirs must pay her maintenance. If not, her claim for maintenance is rejected. If the midwives testify that she is pregnant, but it later becomes clear that they lied or were mistaken, she must return the maintenance and any clothes that she has received from her ex-husband (Shāfiʿī 1903, 5: 220; Ibn Ḥazm 1984, 10: 62). Midwives and physicians were involved in pregnancy tests in numerous court cases dealing with disputes of this nature in twentieth-century Egypt (Shaham 2003, 140–44).

The Mālikīs regard pregnancy as circumstantial evidence of adultery, for which the *ḥadd* punishment may be applied, under the following circumstances: (a) if the pregnant woman is not married; (b) if she is married but her husband is a minor or has been castrated; (c) if she gives birth less than six months after the date of her marriage (that is, less than the minimal gestation period); (d) if she is a slave and her owner denies that he has slept with her. Such a woman might be saved from the *ḥadd* punishment if she brings evidence that she has been raped. The Ḥanafīs, Shāfiʿīs and Mālikīs, however, reject the application of the *ḥadd* punishment under these circumstances if the accused woman denies the fornication or if there is ambiguity (*shubha*) concerning the alleged act (Zaydān 1994, 5: 113–14). According to Sarakhsī, if a woman convicted of fornication argues that she is pregnant and her claim is verified by the testimony of a female expert (preferably two) who inspected her, the application of the *ḥadd* punishment is postponed for two years, the maximum duration of pregnancy according to the Ḥanafī school, during which time the woman is imprisoned. If she fails to give birth during that period, the *ḥadd* punishment is applied (Sarakhsī 1993, 9: 73–4. Cf. Bar-On 2000, 62).[14]

A pregnancy test is also required in the case of a pagan female slave owned by a pagan owner who becomes pregnant by her pagan husband, who then converts to Islam. The question is whether her owner should sell her, since her future child will follow the religion of his father and will therefore be a Muslim. The Ḥanafī Ḥaṣkafī (d. 1677) holds that the owner is not required to free the slave until she gives birth, because the birth may not take place after all, due, for example, to miscarriage. Ibn ʿĀbidīn (d. 1836) presents a different view, holding that if experts (*arbāb al-khibra*; he probably means here midwives) find irrefutable signs (*al-ʿalāmāt al-qāṭiʿa*) of pregnancy, the owner is required to free her before she gives birth, unless it is feared that the fetus will die in her womb (Ibn ʿĀbidīn 1966, 3: 657).

Termination of Pregnancy by Abortion

Musallam, in his study on birth control in pre-modern Muslim societies, argues that abortions were used for various practical reasons, among them birth control (Musallam 1983, 68–71). He does not mention the involvement of midwives in abortions, but we have some evidence from other sources that they did. One report from mid-nineteenth-century Egypt, contained in investigation protocols of the police, relates to the case of the white slave Şemsigül, who was purchased by a slave-dealer in Istanbul, impregnated by him and brought to Cairo. The slave-dealer's wife, who wished to prevent Şemsigül from having the baby, summoned a midwife, first to verify her suspicion that Şemsigül was pregnant and then to perform an abortion, probably by the use of drugs. However, the midwife reported

[14] Ibn Taghrībirdī (1963, 4: 185) relates that the Fatimid caliph al-Ḥākim bi-Amri Allāh, after being informed that the behavior of his unmarried sister, the Princess Sitt al-Mulk, was immoral, sent midwives to verify that she was not pregnant (*li-istibrāʾihā*). On the historical background of that episode, see Lev 1987, 324.

that the pregnancy was too advanced for an abortion (Toledano 1998, 60–1).[15]

In judicial contexts, the determination of the stage of development of the aborted child is essential for deciding on its legal and financial rights, or those of its relatives. According to the jurists, the embryo goes through three stages of development, each forty days in duration: (1) the semen (*nuṭfa*) stage; (2) the blood clot (*ʿalaqa*) stage; and (3) the lump of flesh (*muḍgha*) stage. After the conclusion of the third stage, i.e., after 120 days have passed, the fetus is ensouled and is therefore considered a human being. It should be noted that the *muḍgha* is first 'unformed' (*ghayr mukhallaqa*), i.e., it is a lump of flesh that does not carry clear signs of human organs, and later it becomes 'formed' (*mukhallaqa*) (Qurʾān 22: 5).

Midwives were sometimes summoned to give their opinion as to whether the aborted fetus was 'formed' or 'unformed'.[16] In the context of penal law, if a woman aborts due to physical injury caused to her by an offender, and if the aborted child is 'formed', it is considered a fetus (*janīn*) and its relatives are therefore entitled to blood money (*diya* or *ghurra*). If it is 'unformed', there is no entitlement for *diya* but a lesser compensation (*ḥukūmat ʿadl*) is possible.[17]

For the Ḥanbalīs and the Shāfiʿīs then, a *muḍgha* which resembles a human being or in which the form of some organs has become clear is considered a fetus (*janīn*). However, the jurists of these two schools also consider as an embryo a lump of flesh that has the hidden form (*ṣūra khafiyya*) of a human being that midwives can identify. The Shāfiʿī jurist Nawawī (d. 1277), for example, explains that if the aborted material is only blood or blood clot, the waiting period of the divorced mother is not ended. But if the material carries signs of a human being, such as a hand, a finger or a nail, then the waiting period is ended. If there is no sign of a human being, but expert women (*ahl al-khibra min al-nisāʾ*) testify that it is clear to them that

[15] See Marcus (1989, 201) on few cases of initiated abortions conducted in eighteenth-century Aleppo. On the involvement of midwives in abortions in early modern Europe, see Bar-On (2000, 64, 100).

[16] See Sonbol (2003, 80) on midwives in eighteenth-century Cairo who were sent by the courts to investigate cases of forced abortions.

[17] For the definitions of *diya* and *ḥukūmat ʿadl*, see Zaydān (1994, 5: 427–40). In addition to penal liabilities, a 'formed' aborted fetus is entitled to religious burial. If a female slave who conceived from her master aborts a 'formed' fetus, she is entitled to her freedom at the time of her master's death (Musallam 1983, 57).

the material carries the hidden form of a human being, then the waiting period should be regarded as complete, even if laymen are not able to discern this form. If the midwives are in doubt, the qāḍī should not rule on the termination of the waiting period (Nawawī 1992, 6: 352–53). The Ḥanafīs, on the other hand, do not recognize the lump of flesh as an embryo if the form of a human body is not clear, even if trustworthy midwives testify that it is a human being (Zaydān 1994, 5: 382–85).[18]

Birth

I referred earlier to the controversy among the schools of law concerning reliance on the testimony of one woman. Shāfiʿī, the main opponent of such reliance, and other jurists who joined him, denied the soundness of the *ḥadīth* according to which ʿAlī b. Abī Ṭālib permitted reliance on the testimony of one midwife (Ibn Qayyim n.d., 92–3). More interesting is the fact that the Ḥanafīs, who are the main supporters of such testimony, disagree among themselves. Let us begin from the point of agreement among them. Consider the case of a married woman whose pregnancy is not visible (*ẓāhir*) and is not confirmed by her husband prior to delivery. If the husband denies that she has given birth, both Abū Ḥanīfa and his two disciples, the Ṣāḥibān, Abū Yūsuf (d. 798) and Muḥammad al-Shaybānī (d. 804), agree that the testimony of one reliable free Muslim woman concerning the delivery is sufficient for establishing the husband's paternity of the newborn (Qadri 1928/29, art. 348). If the husband affirms that she has given a birth to a child, but claims that the child presented by his wife is not the one born to her (in legal terms, he denies the identity, *taʿyīn*, of the child), a reliable midwife's testimony regarding the child's identity is sufficient to establish the father's paternity (ibid., art. 348; Abū Zahra 1957, 394–95).

In the above-mentioned case, the woman whose delivery is denied is married. Consider an alternative case, in which the woman is a

[18] The Mālikīs apply the status of *janīn* to the *ʿalaqa*, if it is on the verge of becoming a *mudgha*. They test the *ʿalaqa* by pouring boiled water on it. If it does not melt, the criterion is satisfied (Sarakhsī 1993, 6: 27). On the differences among the law schools on this topic, see also Ibn Rushd (1996, 2: 502–3).

divorcee or a widow who observes her waiting period and her ex-husband or his heirs, respectively, deny that she has given birth. Abū Ḥanīfa requires the regular number of witnesses (two males, or one male and two females) concerning the delivery, while the Ṣāḥibān (joined by Ibn Abī Laylā) are satisfied with the testimony of one midwife.[19] Abū Ḥanīfa argues that here—contrary to the above-mentioned case of a married woman—the woman terminated her waiting period by giving birth and thereby became a stranger to her husband. Since the testimony of one woman is not sufficient to establish the paternity of a stranger, two witnesses are required. To the contrary, the Ṣāḥibān argue that by delivering the child the mother has not yet become estranged from her husband and therefore the testimony of one female witness is sufficient for establishing the delivery.

Sarakhsī understands the controversy between Abū Ḥanīfa and the Ṣāḥibān differently. According to him, all three agree that the testimony of one midwife is sufficient if the divorce is revocable, because such a divorce does not terminate the marriage bond until the expiration of the waiting period. They differ concerning the irrevocably divorced mother. It seems that Ibn ʿĀbidīn adopts al-Sarakhsī's interpretation (Sarakhsī 1993, 6: 48, 16: 144, 30: 128; Ibn ʿĀbidīn 1966, 3: 545, 546, 548; Abū Zahra 1957, 394). It is interesting to note that in the same scenario, if the husband's (or his heirs') denial of the delivery has been preceded by their confirmation of the pregnancy, or if the pregnancy was visible, Abū Ḥanīfa holds that the testimony of the midwife is redundant and that the testimony of the mother, in addition to her oath, is sufficient. However, the Ṣāḥibān follow their above-mentioned view, i.e., that the testimony of a midwife is required (ibid., 395). If the husband or his heirs confirm the delivery but deny the child's *taʿyīn* (see above), both Abū Ḥanīfa and the Ṣāḥibān are satisfied with the testimony of the midwife concerning the child's identity (Ibn ʿĀbidīn 1966, 3: 545; Qadrī 1928/29, art. 349).

Another topic treated in Ḥanafī texts concerns a master who states that he will free the first child born to his female slave; the slave gives birth and a woman testifies about the delivery, but the master

[19] Qadrī Pasha (1928/29, art. 349) adopts Abū Ḥanīfa's view. On the Opinion of the Ṣāḥibān, see Kāsānī 1910, 3: 216–17.

argues that the child was born to another slave and therefore becomes his (the master's) slave. Abū Ḥanīfa requires the regular number of witnesses concerning the child's identity as a condition for his release from slavery. The Ṣāḥibān are satisfied with the testimony of the midwife who attended the delivery. Abū Ḥanīfa reasons that since the evidence provided by a midwife is accepted only on the grounds of necessity (*ḥujja ḍarūriyya*), it should be limited to the delivery itself and to the specific rules relating to birth, namely, the establishment of motherhood and paternity. The emancipation of slaves, Abū Ḥanīfa argues, is a separate topic not related to the birth itself, and therefore the regular number of witnesses is required. But the Ṣāḥibān argue that a midwife's testimony is acceptable with regard to the paternity of the infant, and that, by analogy, it should be accepted with respect to other rights related to the birth (Sarakhsī 1993, 7: 135–36).[20]

The First Cry of the Newborn (Istihlāl)

The first cry of the newborn child is a clear indication of his or her being alive. From a legal perspective, if the baby dies immediately after birth, it is important to know whether s/he made the first cry before dying. If so, its relatives are required to make an internment prayer over the baby and s/he enjoys inheritance rights. Abū Ḥanīfa and the Ṣāḥibān agree that the testimony of the midwife (and, according to the Ṣāḥibān, also the testimony of the mother) is sufficient for establishing the obligation of prayer, because the issue of prayer is a religious matter (*amr al-dīn*), and the testimony of one woman (*khabar al-marʾa al-wāḥida*) is complete evidence (*ḥujja tamma*) in such matters, like the testimony of two women concerning the new moon (*hilāl*) of Ramadan (Ibn ʿĀbidīn 1966, 7: 74; Sarakhsī 1993, 16: 144).

As for an infant's inheritance rights and also the entitlement of his relatives to the payment of blood money, if the mother gave birth prematurely as a result of being beaten,[21] all three agree that

[20] The same controversy between Abū Ḥanīfa and the Ṣāḥibān occurs in the case of a husband who stipulates that his wife's divorce is conditional upon her giving birth; after she gives birth and a midwife testifies about it, he denies that she has given birth. The question is whether the divorce takes place on the basis of the midwife's testimony (Sarakhsī 1993, 6: 105–6).

[21] In the context of the entitlement of the relatives of the aborted fetus to blood money, the Mālikīs consider the first cry as the exclusive sign of life of the aborted

the mother's testimony concerning the first cry is unacceptable, due to the fact that she has a direct interest in the baby's inheritance rights or the payment of blood money. But they differ concerning the number of witnesses required: Abū Ḥanīfa requires a regular number of witnesses concerning the first cry (two males, or one male and two females) because inheritance involves personal rights (*ḥuqūq al-ʿibād*), and therefore may not be established by the testimony of women, if men are available. The Ṣāḥibān are satisfied with the testimony of two women, or, according to some versions, even one, on the grounds of necessity, i.e., the fact that males are not permitted to attend the event (Ibn ʿĀbidīn 1966, 2: 227; Sarakhsī 1993, 16: 144; Ibn Qayyim n.d., 94–5).[22]

The testimony of midwives concerning the first cry of a newborn child involves financial interests and was therefore a practical procedure, as attested to in legal formularies (*shurūṭ*) (*EI*[2], s.v., Sharṭ). In *al-Muqniʿ fī ʿIlm al-Shurūṭ* by the Andalusian jurist al-Ṭulayṭulī (d. 1067), we find a formulary entitled "a document concerning the first cry of a baby who screamed and then died". It includes a declaration by the witnesses according to which they know the pregnant widow. Anticipating her delivery, the woman summoned to her house an unspecified number of trustworthy midwives. They testified on the details of the birth (date, duration) and that the newborn child screamed (*istahalla ṣārikhan*) until the end of night or a specific hour, and then died (Ṭulayṭulī 1994, 340–41).

Suckling

Affinity through breast-feeding from the same woman creates an impediment to marriage. If there is a dispute as to whether the candidates for marriage suckled from the same breast, those jurists who consider breast-feeding to be an event solely attended by women, for example the Ḥanbalīs, are satisfied with the testimony of one woman, on the grounds of the *ḥadīth* concerning the black wet nurse in the case of ʿUqba b. al-Ḥārith.

child. Shāfiʿī and Abū Ḥanīfa accept in addition to the first cry any indication of life, such as movement, sneezing or breathing (Ibn Rushd 1996, 2: 502–3).

[22] On the number of required women according to other schools, see al-Asyūṭī (n.d., 2: 439).

The Ḥanafīs, who consider the event of suckling as accessible to both men and women, require a regular number of witnesses, that is, the testimonies of two males or one male and two females. The Ḥanafī position is supported by traditions ascribed to ʿAlī b. Abī Ṭālib, Ibn ʿAbbās and ʿUmar b. al-Khattāb, who claimed that reliance on the testimony of the wet nurse in this context would create a dangerous precedent, enabling any woman who wishes to take revenge against a specific couple to argue that she has breast-fed both. The Ḥanafīs also argue that the annulment of a contract involving ownership, such as marriage, requires the testimony of men.

The Mālikīs and other jurists hold a middle position. They argue that men should abstain from attending breast-feeding, since female breasts are among 'the attractions of females' (*maḥāsin al-nisāʾ*), which, according to Allāh's order, should be concealed from male strangers. But if they watch it, the damage caused is less severe than that created by watching a female's genitals. They therefore require the testimonies of two women, who are equivalent to two men in these circumstances. Al-Shāfiʿī requires the testimonies of four women (Ibn Qayyim n.d., 90, 93–6; Ibn Rushd 1996, 2: 560; Sarakhsī 1993, 5: 137–38; Asyūṭī n.d., 2: 439).

Physical Defects in Female Slaves

Physical defects or diseases in slaves that are concealed by the seller and not reported to the buyer at the session in which the sale contract is concluded constitute legal grounds for the annulment of the sale or a reduction in the price of the slave. With regard to male slaves, the procedure should involve physicians, who, following the buyer's complaint, inspect the slave and report to the qāḍī on their findings; and slave dealers, who advise the court on whether the medical findings justify the annulment of the sale, or, alternatively, on the reduction in the market value of the slave. As for female slaves, female experts take the role of physicians if the defects or the maladies are located in the intimate parts of the slave's body (Ibn Farḥūn 1986, 2: 81–2).[23]

[23] Ibn Farḥūn requires that the female be an expert in medicine (*māhira bil-ṭibb*). For the juristic discussion of specific physical defects in female slaves, see Ṭulayṭulī (1994, 169–71); Sarakhsī (1993, 13: 107 ff.); Asyūṭī (n.d., 1: 70–1).

Pregnancy is considered a defect in a female slave, if the seller fails to inform the buyer about it at the time of the sale. In one case from Ottoman Egypt, a black slave was defined as "clean from any sharʿī defect" in the sale contract. The buyer later found that she was pregnant and sued the seller. The qāḍī summoned two midwives who examined the slave in court and reported that she was already three months pregnant. The qāḍī annulled the sale and the slave was returned to the seller (ʿĪsā 1998, 318). As with pregnancy, the fact that the slave gave birth prior to the sale, if concealed from the buyer, might constitute a defect (Sarakhsī 1993, 13: 99–100).

Consider a case discussed by Ḥanafī jurists in which the buyer discovers that the seller concealed from him the fact that the slave has a hidden physical defect (the same case refers also to pregnancy and birth). Women inspect the slave and determine that the defect is old and must have existed before the sale. Abū Ḥanīfa holds that the regular number of witnesses is required to establish that the defect was created when the slave was still in the possession of her original owner, but different opinions are attributed to Abū Yūsuf and al-Shaybānī. Ibn ʿĀbidīn, summarizing this controversy, argues that if the dispute between the seller and the buyer occurs prior to the transfer of the slave to the buyer, some Ḥanafī authorities hold that the testimony of one female expert concerning the defect or the pregnancy is sufficient to annul the sale and return the slave to her original owner, while others hold that the refusal of the seller to support his version by swearing an oath is also a pre-condition for annulment; if the dispute occurs subsequent to the transfer of the slave, all authorities agree that testimony of a female expert and the refusal of the seller to make an oath are both required for the annulment of the sale. The underlying reasoning is that a sale in which the merchandise has already been conveyed to the hands of the buyer is a 'strong' contract (*ʿaqd qawiyy*), which may not be annulled solely on the basis of 'weak' evidence (*ḥujja ḍaʿīfa*) provided by women. Defining the preponderant opinion of the school, Ibn ʿĀbidīn says that both the testimony of a female expert (preferably two) and the refusal of the buyer to support his version by swearing an oath are necessary for annulling the sale, whether the dispute takes place prior to the transference of the slave or subsequent to it (Ibn Nujaym n.d., 6: 46–8; Sarakhsī 1993, 13: 110–11; Ibn ʿĀbidīn 1966, 5: 31–2).

The use of female experts in this context was part and parcel of Mālikī judicial practice. The Mālikī jurist and qāḍī Ibn Farḥūn

(d. al-Madina, 1397) reproduces a judicial ruling by Ibn Ziyād, a Mālikī qāḍī from Cordoba in the ninth century,[24] who ordered a female slave to be returned to the slave dealer who had sold her, on the basis of testimony provided by a reliable woman. The witness stated that the physical defect found on the slave existed prior to the date of the sale and therefore justified her return to the buyer. A latter Mālikī jurist and qāḍī in Cordoba, Ibn Sahl (d. 1093), criticized this judicial practice on the grounds that it considered the female expert as a witness, a physician and a jurisconsult (*muftiyya*) simultaneously. According to Ibn Sahl, the female expert should be restricted to reporting on her findings, without any further judicial recommendation. Then, the qāḍī should consult slave-dealers on whether the findings constitute a defect. Then *muftīs* should hand down an opinion about the annulment of the sale and the judge should rule accordingly. It seems that Ibn Sahl's criticism of the practice does not necessarily reflect the jurists' displeasure with the fact that female experts played an important role in the adjudication processes involving female slaves. Rather, he levels the same criticism against male physicians who, after inspecting defects in male slaves, do not limit their reports to the qāḍīs to their medical findings, as should be, but refer also to the legal implications of the findings, which is the task of slave dealers and *muftīs* (Ibn Farḥūn 1986, 2: 81–2).

Physical Damage and Forensic Evidence

In the context of penal law, female experts (*ahl al-maʿrifa min al-nisāʾ*) inspect women who suffered physical damage to the intimate parts of their bodies and they report about the size of the wounds and their severity, as a prerequisite for fixing the amount of blood money (ibid., 2: 85). In 1647, a man came to the sharīʿa court in Jerusalem and informed the qāḍī that his wife had been killed by the collapse of the roof of their house. Four women, summoned to the house by the husband, examined the body and testified in court that they found her head and face swollen from the falling debris and saw no signs of violence caused by the husband. On the basis of this testimony,

[24] This is probably Aṃad b. Ziyād who refused to bow to the authority of the masters without allowing his own reasoning to adjudicate first (Hallaq 2001, 59).

the court found that the husband bore no responsibility in his wife's death (Sonbol 2003, 30). The fact that the husband summoned four female witnesses is of interest. He was perhaps a Shāfiʿī, or he was interested in a large number of witnesses to make the case of his innocence as strong as possible.

Conclusion

Muslim jurists are unanimous that only women should testify about the intimate parts of the female body which men are forbidden from observing. The controversy among the jurists focuses on the number of female witnesses required for this task. At one end of the spectrum are the Ḥanbalīs, who base their position on traditions according to which the Prophet permitted the reliance on the testimony of one midwife. It is clear, however, from several traditions attributed to Ibn Ḥanbal, that he preferred reliance on the testimony of two female experts, and, if possible, even three or four, for the sake of certainty. He was willing to accept a single female's expert testimony only if it was impossible to find an additional expert. Put differently, the Ḥanbalī position is based on a two-fold necessity: first, the prohibition on males to testify about the intimate parts of the female body; second, due to a scarcity of female experts. At the other end of the spectrum are the Shāfiʿīs, who require four female witnesses, thereby applying the basic evidentiary rule which holds in financial matters, namely, that 'one male equals two females'. The Shāfiʿī position demonstrates basic mistrust of female testimony and an attempt to minimize the potential damage which might result from the reliance on such testimony.

The differences between Abū Ḥanīfa and his two students, the Ṣāḥibān, are instructive. Abū Ḥanīfa consistently holds a restrictive interpretation with respect to female expert testimony. First, he seeks to narrow down the list of events that are closed to male viewers. Second, he holds that the testimony of a single female expert is sufficient only with regard to the actual event in which she participates (such as birth) or with regard to any legal status created directly by the event (for example, maternity and paternity). Such testimony is insufficient with regard to legal rights that emanate only indirectly from the event. For example, if a husband stipulates that his wife's divorce is conditional upon her giving birth, and he later denies the fact that she subsequently gave birth, Abū Ḥanīfa holds that the divorce does not become effective on the basis of the midwife's testimony because the testimony of a single female is insufficient in divorce cases.

The juristic discussion on female expert testimony is part and parcel of daily practice. This is evidenced, *inter alia*, by the fact that the discussion is located not only in treaties devoted to positive law (*furūʿ*) but also in more 'practical' genres of the legal literature, such as collections of legal opinions and works of legal formularies. Although further research, especially in historical sources, is needed, I think that it is possible to make some generalizations. First, Muslim laymen have willingly made use of the services of midwives for a variety of needs: for example, to get help when a baby was about to be born or when an abortion was needed; to conduct a virginity test when there was a need to clarify family honor; and to conduct an investigation of criminal events in which females were the victims (such as rape), as a preliminary step to the filing of a penal lawsuit. Second, state functionaries such as the qāḍī (and perhaps also the *muḥtasib*) have used female experts or midwives as a central tool for monitoring and safeguarding public morality. They sent them to conduct investigations and bodily inspections in cases in which women were involved, and their reports formed the basis for court decisions and subsequent punishment.

Giladi, who studied the role of wet nurses in medieval Muslim societies, argues that a patriarchal legal system is willing to acknowledge the modest amount of social power that women possess as a result of their life-giving functions as wet nurses (Giladi 1999, 88). This is true for midwives as well. In the sharīʿa court, which is a patriarchal arena dominated by males, women have functioned both as litigants and as witnesses, albeit from a position inferior to that of men. Their expert testimonies were tolerated, but only because they were indispensable for safeguarding the morality code set by men. As a result of their exclusive role as expert witnesses on the female body, they have succeeded in securing a certain degree of social power and control for themselves, but this power and control should be weighed in the context of a patriarchal power-relationship.

In the course of the nineteenth century, the profession of midwifery underwent dramatic change. In Egypt, for example, with the establishment of modern medical systems directed by the centralist state, the theoretical and practical training of female medical practitioners (*ḥākimas*) shifted into schools established by the state and the *ḥākimas* were incorporated into state apparatus. Male physicians penetrated the field of midwifery and birth was removed to hospitals (Kuhnke 1990, 122–33; Sonbol 1991, 80–1, 88–9, 101–2, 129–30; Fahmy 1998a, 23; Fahmy 1998b, 41–6, 50–2, 55–7, 59–62; Sonbol 2003, 12, 223–24). All these developments, however, are beyond the scope of the present study but they open new doors to further research in this little-explored field.

CHAPTER FOUR

QĀḌĪ, *MUFTĪ* AND RULER: THEIR ROLES IN THE DEVELOPMENT OF ISLAMIC LAW

Miriam Hoexter

The notion, reiterated in traditional literature, that Islamic law remained stagnant from its crystallization, around the tenth century, and until the reforms of the twentieth century has occupied scholars in recent decades. In their studies, many called into question this undifferentiated notion. They showed that, challenged by new problems, Islamic law did in fact develop in the course of centuries, providing innovative and original solutions. The solutions, and therefore the development of Islamic law, were usually attributed to *muftī*s—jurisconsults who composed *fatāwā: responsa*, learned opinions on points of law (e.g., Hallaq 1994; idem 1996; Calder 1996; Johansen 1993; Powers 1993, esp. 105–6).[1] Scholars debate whether *muftī*s and their *fatāwā* collections or author-jurists who composed the collections of substantive law—*furū*ʿ, *shurūḥ*—should be credited with the preeminent role in the process of development, or which of the two influenced the other (Hallaq 1994; idem 1996, 128–30; Calder 1996, esp. 143, 163–64. See also Johansen 1993, 31–6).[2] What they do all seem to agree on, however, either explicitly or by default, is that qāḍīs (judges), and certainly rulers, played no role whatsoever, or at best a very minor and insignificant one, in the development of Islamic law.[3]

[1] On the history of *iftā*ʾ, see Masud, Messick & Powers 1996, 3–15. The first collection of *fatwā*s appeared in the second half of the tenth century—ibid., 9. On the typology of *muftī*s and their levels of competence, see ibid., 15–20; Calder 1996.

[2] Both Hallaq (1996, 129) and Calder (1996, 142) are aware of the fact that the *muftī* and the author of the *furū*ʿ collection might in practice be the same person.

[3] For the important role of *muftī*s compared to qāḍīs in the doctrinal development of law from the early ʿAbbāsid period onwards, see Schacht 1964, 74–5. Hallaq (1994, 55) explicitly states that, "After the second/eighth century, the contribution of judges appears to have been halted, and the elaboration of law seems to have become almost exclusively the province of the *muftī*." Johansen (1993, 33–5) assigns to the *fatwā*-literature a much more important contribution to the formation of new legal doctrines than to the qāḍī's judgments, basing his argument on the uncertainty as to the actual application of their judgments. In other discussions

Indeed, by the time the classical doctrine was formulated, qāḍīs and rulers were deprived of much of their initial authority in doctrinal matters. Qāḍīs played an important role in the development of Islamic law in the Umayyad period (661–750). In this early period, qāḍīs were responsible for the elaboration of the incipient law. For this purpose they relied on a combination of independent reasoning (*ra'y*), ethical norms based on the Qur'ān, customary practices and various elements adopted from legal systems of their geographical environment. However, the qāḍīs lost this role in the course of the eighth century, and certainly with the crystallization of the Islamic legal doctrine and the four Sunnī schools of law, at the beginning of the tenth century.[4] Interpretation of the law was henceforth to follow the hermeneutic methodology laid down in the literature of *uṣūl al-fiqh* (roots, sources of law). Since the doctrine did not recognize legal precedents as a source of law, judicial decisions delivered by qāḍīs had no authority beyond the particular case they adjudicated.[5] Thus, after the crystallization of the four schools of law, the *fuqahā'*—scholars of the legal doctrine and the science of law—that is, the *muftī*s[6] rather than the judges, became the interpreters of the doctrine and its exponents.

The role of rulers in legal issues, like that of the qāḍīs, underwent changes in the course of the first centuries of Islam. During the ʿAbbāsid period and certainly after the *miḥna* (inquisition, 218/833 to 234/848), a kind of *modus vivendi* was reached between the *fuqahā'* and the ruler: the former were recognized as the bearers of the norms and basic values of the *sharīʿa* and its authoritative interpreters; the rulers, for their part, were made responsible for implementing the *sharīʿa* in the territories under their control.[7]

---

of the subject, the possibility that qāḍīs or rulers played a role in the development of the law is not even considered.

[4] Schacht 1955b, 35–40; idem 1964, 15–27, esp. 25–6; Juynboll 1983, 77–95; Coulson 1964, 28–35; Hallaq 1994, 55. Crone (1987) attributes all legal authority, legislative and adjudicative, to the early caliphs. Motzki (2002) places the beginnings of Islamic law based on the *uṣūl* in the last few decades of the first/seventh century.

[5] On the Mālikī *ʿamal*, see p. 71 below and n. 13. See also n. 43.

[6] See Hallaq 1994, 55 and n. 122, based on Ghazālī as quoted by Ḥājjī Khalīfa: "*ʿilm al-fatwā* was often equated, and at times was used synonymously with *fiqh*."

[7] Crone and Hinds 1986, esp. 80–97, 109–10; Hurvitz 2002; Hoexter 2002. See also Coulson's formulation: "ʿAbbāsid policy had endorsed the idea that the Caliph was the servant of the law, not its master; legal authority was vested in the scholar-jurists and not in the political leader" (Coulson 1964, 52). On the period before the *miḥna*, see also Zaman (1997), who argues that the *miḥna* did not change

Given that the point of departure of the scholars referred to was the classical doctrine and that they based their studies on material that implemented this doctrine, attributing an almost exclusive role in the development of Islamic law to those who composed this material was almost a foregone conclusion.

My aim in this article is to open a debate on whether this conclusion holds true in the face of practice or whether it represents the whole picture. In what follows I shall try to define at what stage and in what manner qāḍīs and rulers participated in the evolutionary process of Islamic law.

Two comments are in place before I enter the discussion. The major problem in discussing these issues is that of the sources. Contrary to the wealth of *fatāwā* and *furūʿ* literature, there exists no parallel literature comprising either qāḍīs' judgments or rulers' decisions. Qāḍīs' judgments were registered in local sharīʿa courts for purposes of follow-up on specific cases. However, since Islamic law is not a case law, there was no real need to catalogue them systematically or publish them in the form of collections.[8] The same was true for rulers' decrees. Based on his *siyāsa sharʿīyya* competence, decrees issued by a ruler were binding in the territory under his control, and, at least theoretically, only as long as he lived. As suggested by their name, they were supposed to be compatible with the *sharīʿa* and some jurists even considered them to be part of it. However, these decrees did not in fact assume normative *sharʿī* authority (Heyd 1973a, 198–207; Johansen 1979, 54–61, idem 1981, 302; Coulson 1964, 129–30, 172; idem 1957, 51; Hoexter 1995. For the Mālikī school of law, see Yanagihashi 1996). However, decisions taken by both rulers and qāḍīs occasionally left traces in *fatāwā* and *furūʿ* literature, and it is on this material, or rather on these traces, on which my study is based. I shall concentrate on the Ḥanafī school of law

permanently the caliphs' authority in matters of law and that they continued to be a part of the religious circle in which the law was interpreted. On the nature of this *modus vivendi*, see more on pp. 78–9 below. Exceptions to the above *modus vivendi* were rulers who declared themselves *mahdīs* (divinely guided rulers who would restore Islam to its original perfection). I shall not deal with them in this article.

[8] One of the reasons advanced by Hallaq to explain why qāḍīs' registers from pre-Ottoman periods failed to survive was the absence of "practical, theoretical or literary use" for their originals—see Hallaq 1998, esp. 434–35, and compare Milliot 1953, 169–71 on the existence of collections of *ʿamal* in the Mālikī school, where judicial precedence enjoys a special status (see n. 13, below).

and on the pre-modern era. My examples will be taken from the Islamic endowment institution—the *waqf*—particularly from two issues: cash-*waqfs* and *istibdāl*—exchange transactions in *waqf* property.

The second comment refers to the definition of the subject. The framework of my study is the development of Islamic law, the changes and new interpretations which gained *sharʿī* approval in the writings of those authorized to interpret the law. I shall therefore not include in this study developments which did not find their way into the corpus of Islamic law, such as decisions by courts of law established by rulers (*maẓālim*).

The involvement of qāḍīs and rulers in the development of Islamic law was connected to two central issues: the way custom—*ʿurf, ʿāda, taʿāmul, taʿāruf*—was absorbed in the law, and the problem of *ikhtilāf*—differences of opinion among *fuqahāʾ*.

The principal incentive for the development of the law in the course of centuries was the need to face problems arising from social and economic change. Many of the solutions provided to these problems included an innovative element.[9] Clearly, all solutions had to be brought into the framework of the *sharīʿa*, that is, they had to be worked out in accordance with *sharʿī* legal methodology. Although it was never universally recognized as a fifth source of law on a par with the four traditional ones, custom appears in collections of *fatāwā* and *furūʿ* as a principal argument or justification for introducing changes in the law. The prominent role of custom as a vehicle of change has been emphasized by a number of scholars,[10] and it is

[9] Interestingly, examining the types of *fatwās* included in *furūʿ* works, Hallaq found that a central consideration was relevance to contemporary needs. That much of Ḥanafī legal doctrine was formulated by later jurists who modified early doctrines in order to bring them in line with changing conditions of society is attested by both Ibn ʿĀbidīn and Khayr al-Dīn al-Ramlī—Hallaq 1994, 48–50.

[10] E.g., Ibn ʿĀbidīn 1301/1884; Libson 1997 (see 132 n. 3 for an extensive bibliography on the subject); *EI*[2], s.v. ʿUrf 1. (G. Libson); Johansen 1993; Coulson 1996; Milliot 1953, 156–67; Gerber 1999, 105–15; Hallaq 2002. For the gradual integration of custom in the law, see Libson 1997. Libson concludes that custom was recognized as a source of law in the sixteenth century, with Ibn Nujaym—see ibid., esp. 142, 154–55. On this question, see also Ibn ʿĀbidīn 1301/1884, 3. For Coulson (1996, 261) custom is "a legal principle of subsidiary and supplementary value." However, he concludes (p. 265) "that on none but the highest theoretical plane can it be denied that custom is an important source of law in the world of Islam." For Hallaq (2002, 40), custom was never recognized as an independent and formal legal source and never managed to occupy a place equal to the so-called supplementary sources in the hierarchy of legal sources. For local and general custom, see Ibn ʿĀbidīn 1301/1884; Johansen 1993. For interpretations of Ibn ʿĀbidīn 1301/1884, see Gerber 1999, esp. 105–10; Hallaq 2002.

conspicuous to anybody familiar with *fatāwā* and *furūʿ* literature. The following are but some examples from this literature justifying the reliance on custom: al-Sarakhsī (d. 483/1090) stated that "what people have been accustomed to and is not invalidated by an [explicit] text is permitted . . . based on the *ḥadīth*: 'Whatever is considered good by the Muslims is good in the eyes of God'"—*mā taʿārafahu al-nās wa-laysa fī ʿaynihi naṣṣ yubṭiluhu wa-huwa jāʾiz . . . li-qawlihi ʿalayhi al-ṣalāt waʾl-salām mā raʾāhu al-muslimūna ḥasanan fa-huwa ʿinda Allāhi ḥasanun* (al-Sarakhsī n.d., 12: 45). According to Ibn Nujaym (d. 970/1561), "what is known through custom is like [i.e., as binding as] what is stipulated by law"—*al-maʿrūf ʿurfan kaʾl-mashrūṭ sharʿan.*[11] al-Ḥaṣkafī (d. 1088/1677) argues that "custom overrides analogy, based on the *ḥadīth*: 'Whatever is considered good by the Muslims is good in the eyes of God'"—*al-taʿāmul yutraku bihi al-qiyās liʾl-ḥadīth mā raʾāhu al-muslimūna ḥasanan fa-huwa ʿinda Allāhi ḥasanun* (al-Ḥaṣkafī 1386/1966, 4: 364).[12]

I believe that qāḍīs played an important role in the process of incorporating customs into the body of the law and thus in the development of Islamic law. Louis Milliot, studying the Moroccan *ʿamal* (judicial practice) (Milliot 1918, 23–31, Annexe II, 109–17; idem 1953, 167–78), pointed to the close connection between court decisions and the incorporation of custom, inconsistent with the dominant doctrine, into the body of law in the Mālikī school. In the Ḥanafī school, qāḍīs' decisions did not attain the formal doctrinal recognition of the Mālikī *ʿamal.*[13] However, by the very nature of their office, judges of the Ḥanafī school as well were faced with situations that called for innovative decisions that involved reconciling changing circumstances or local practices with the letter of the *sharīʿa*

[11] Johansen 1993, 30, n. 5, quoting Ibn Nujaym 1322/1904–05, 99. Slightly different versions of the same appear frequently in the literature, e.g., *al-maʿlūm biʾl-ʿurf kaʾl- maʿlūm biʾl-sharṭ; al-maʿlūm biʾl-ʿurf kaʾl-mashrūṭ biʾl-sharṭ*—al-Sarakhsī [1324]–1331/[1906–1907]–1912–1913, 15: 90, 130. See also references quoted by the authors mentioned in n. 10, above.

[12] See also, e.g., Kāsānī (d. 587/1191) 1328/1910, 6: 220; al-Marghīnānī (d. 593/1197) 1316/1898–99, 5: 51; Bābartī (d. 786/1384) 1316/1898–99, 5: 51; Ibn al-Humām 1316/1898–99, 5: 51. See also references quoted by the authors mentioned in n. 10, above.

[13] On the status of *ʿamal*, see Milliot 1918, 20–31 and Annexe II, 109–17; idem 1953, 167–78; *EI*², s.v. ʿAmal (Berque); Coulson 1996. See also *EI*², s.v. Nāzila. Milliot and Coulson argue for *ʿamal* as case-law or positive law. Berque, based on Moroccan exegesis, concludes that it has regulative force and "is virtually a pragmatic law. But it remains subject to doctrinal criticism which can at any moment revoke it." See also n. 16, below.

law.[14] Although a qāḍī's ruling was valid only for the specific case under his review, the accumulation of judgments in the same vein resulted in the innovation acquiring an informal status of what I would call 'an established custom.'[15] *Muftīs* and/or composers of *furūʿ* collections seem to have usually stepped in at a later stage only, after the innovation became an established custom. They gave the new solution its proper *sharʿī* framework and argumentation which made it part of the substantive law.[16] Mandaville's study of the cash-*waqf*s in the Ottoman Empire (Mandaville 1979) is a pertinent example of the process just described. Endowments of cash were problematic on two accounts: first, in principle, *waqf* laws allowed the endowment of immovables only, except for a number of movables—not including cash—allowed on the basis of precedents attributed to the time of the Prophet. Second, benefits from cash endowments were

[14] Qāḍīs were free to interpret texts by themselves. They could but did not have to consult a *muftī*. How frequently they actually did is a moot question. Even when they did, qāḍīs did not have to follow the *muftī*'s opinion (see, e.g., Schacht 1964, 74; Heyd 1969, 56; idem 1973a, 187; Gerber 1999, 79) and certainly had to form their own opinion when presented with two opposing *fatwās* by litigants. Not infrequently, this resulted in different decisions by different judges concerning the same case (see, e.g., Coulson 1996, 266). The distinction between qāḍīs and *muftīs*, in as far as their legal education and intellectual ability are concerned, is somewhat artificial. In fact many of the famous *muftīs*, certainly but not exclusively in the Ottoman Empire, functioned as qāḍīs at some stage of their life, e.g., Abū Yūsuf (d. 798) (*EI*^{2}, s.v. Abū Yūsuf (J. Schacht)); Takī al-Dīn al-Subkī (d. 1355) (Haram 1996, 72–3), al-Ṭarsūsī (see his title '*qāḍī al-quḍāt*' in his 1344/1926, 1). al-Ṭarsūsī's detailed description of the steps to be taken by a judge before authorizing an exchange transaction (pp. 114–15) attests to a personal experience as a judge. For Ottoman examples, see Mandaville 1979, 296. From the early seventeenth century, the career path of all Shaykhs al-Islam included serving in various qāḍī positions (e.g., Gerber 1999, 30).

[15] See Coulson 1996, 269, who called it 'established practice', and see also n. 16, below.

[16] Milliot described how the qāḍī, who was continually confronted with a custom which was in conflict with *sharīʿa* law, at some point, grudgingly, sanctioned it, on grounds of public interest (Milliot 1953, 175–76; Coulson 1996, 268–69). There are a number of similarities between the above description and Milliot's description of the way custom penetrated into the law: (a) repetition of judgments sanctioning the custom until the custom gradually became 'established practice' (this is Coulson's way of rendering what Milliot called 'jurisprudence fixée' or 'stabilisée'—Coulson 1996, 268–269; Milliot 1953, 175–76; idem 1918, 26–7, 116); (b) the need for doctrinal sanction (Milliot 1918, 25; idem 1953, 175); (c) the fact that the process was gradual and relatively long (ibid., 176). The main difference between the Mālikī and Ḥanafī schools was in the way the 'established custom' was incorporated into the law. In the Mālikī school, a customary rule was incorporated in the law by the jurisprudential process (ibid., 175). Upon its recognition as an established practice, the new rule, originally based on custom, was henceforth founded on judicial precedent—"Lorsque la pratique des tribunaux sera bien fixée en ce

inevitably connected with the problematic issue of interest and usury. Mandaville found that cash-*waqf*s originated in the legal practice of Ottoman courts that, from the early fifteenth century, authorized such endowments. Cash-*waqf*s became very popular in Anatolia and Rumeli in the second half of the fifteenth century and in the course of the sixteenth century.[17] However, only in the forties of the sixteenth century did they give rise to a vehement controversy among the *ʿulamāʾ*. This was, to quote Mandaville, "long after there was any chance for a reversal of the practice" (Mandaville 1979, 298). A *fatwā* was then issued by Shaykh al-Islām Abū al-Suʿūd, the chief *muftī* of the Empire (in office: 1545–1574), authorizing cash-*waqf*s.[18] He also composed a long essay, mainly intended for scholars, justifying his ruling on the grounds of its being a popular custom (*taʿāmul, taʿāruf*) and *istiḥsān* (juristic preference) and, as Mandaville put it, "with a tone of 'Let's be practical', an appeal to common sense" (Mandaville 1979, 297–98).[19] As we shall see a little later, this by

sens, il y aura jurisprudence . . . La règle de droit, originairement fondée sur la coutume, s'appuie désormais sur le précédent judiciare" (ibid., 176; Coulson 1996, 269). The process in the Ḥanafī, just as in the Mālikī school, was actually based on judicial precedents. However, since judicial precedence was not recognized as a source of law by the Ḥanafīs, custom was incorporated into the doctrine by different methodological tools (e.g., *istiḥsān, ḍarūra*, 'changing times', *taʿāmul*, etc.; see references in n. 10, above, and n. 19, below). Judicial precedence was not mentioned by any of the Ḥanafī sources I have seen as a tool justifying the inclusion of custom in the law.

[17] Mandaville 1979, 290 n. 3. See also ibid., 296 and particularly 297, where he quotes Abū al-Suʿūd's *fatwā* on the popularity of cash-*waqf*s and on the fact that "judges past and present . . . ruled in favor of its permissibility . . . and no one has spoken out against this." Abū al-Suʿūd himself validated many cash-*waqf*s when he served as judge of Istanbul, between 1533 and 1537—see Imber 1997, 144. On the popularity of cash-*waqf*s in the sixteenth century, see also Barkan and Ayverdi 1970.

[18] The controversy started when in 1546 or 1547, at the instigation of Chivizade Mehmed, the Military Judge of Rumelia, the sultan issued a decree declaring cash endowments unlawful. Abū al-Suʿūd then issued the above mentioned *fatwā* and persuaded the sultan to issue a decree validating cash endowments—see Repp 1986, 254–55; Imber 1996, 144–45. On this decree and on Shaykh al-Islam, see below.

[19] Mandaville 1979, 298 translates *istiḥsān* as 'welfare of the people'. It is true that *istiḥsān* was often used when practical considerations, particularly the welfare of society required an innovative ruling. However, the term essentially refers to legal methodology, which is usually translated as 'juristic preference', i.e., the personal preference of a jurist, which is an accepted, though minor or supplementary source of law, and overrides analogy (*qiyās*). Customs were often integrated into the legal system by using *istiḥsān* (see Libson 1997). On the various definitions and interpretations of *istiḥsān*, see Makdisi 1996; *EI*[2], s.v. Istiḥsān and Istiṣlāḥ (R. Paret); Hallaq 1997, 107–11; Gerber 1999, 92–104, esp. 93 n. 5 where he translates al-Sarakhsī's definition of the term.

itself did not solve the differences of opinion on the subject of cash endowments (see pp. 78–81 and notes 35, 37, below). In the present context, this example illustrates the important role of qāḍīs' repeated decisions in creating an 'established custom' and thus in initiating developments in the law. Only at a later stage did it become a subject of doctrinal controversy, led, only naturally, primarily by *muftī*s.[20] That the endowment of cash was an established custom was Abū al-Suʿūd's main argument for its incorporation into the doctrine.

The problem of *ikhtilāf*—differences of opinion among *fuqahā'*—prompted the involvement of rulers in the development of Islamic law. Different rulings on many issues existed even among the founders of the Ḥanafī school. The phenomenon persisted in later times, when new solutions were required, either because certain problems had not been addressed by the founders of the school or when a solution offered by the latter no longer suited changing circumstances. Not infrequently, *muftī*s of the same school issued different, even opposing *fatwā*s on the same issue. In their endeavors to fight indeterminacy, the best scholars could hope for was for one of the proposed new solutions to attain the status of 'the preferred view' (*al-rājiḥ*) or 'the correct, the sounder, preferred view' (*al-ṣaḥīḥ, al-aṣaḥḥ al-mukhtār*) of a particular school of law. This process could take a long time, even centuries. However, even then it did not invalidate different or opposing rulings, particularly when the latter originated with one of the founders of the school (*ẓāhir al-riwāya*). One example of a ruling that attained such a status concerns the authorization for a founder of an endowment to add a stipulation (*sharṭ*) in the *waqfiyya* (deed of endowment) allowing him to exchange the asset he endowed for another property. Abū Ḥanīfa's (d. 150/767) two famous disciples differed on the issue. Muḥammad al-Shaybānī (d. 189/805) ruled

[20] For the gradual doctrinal admission of court practice in another matter—the recognition of written documents as valid evidence—see Tyan 1945; Schacht 1955a, 79; Coulson 1996, 267. An interesting case of an extraordinary contribution of qāḍīs' judgments to the introduction of custom in the *sharīʿa* in Israel is discussed by Layish. While in the case discussed above a *muftī* completed the process initiated by qāḍīs, in Israel, since 1948, there has been a shortage of experts in Islamic law who could do the same. Because of the unique circumstances of the Muslim legal system in Israel, "the balance between the two elements [the judicial decisions of qāḍīs and the legal opinions of *muftī*s] has been upset, and the importance of the qāḍī as a shaper of material law is increasing"—see Layish 1971, esp. 271. See also idem 1974, idem 1993. I am grateful to the anonymous reader for drawing my attention to the Israeli case.

that the endowment was valid, but the stipulation was void. Abū Yūsuf (d. 182/798) allowed the stipulation on the basis of *istiḥsān* (al-Khaṣṣāf—d. 261/875–1322/1904, 22; al-Sarakhsī n.d., 12: 41–2, 44). At least from the twelfth century (with Qāḍīkhān, d. 592/1196), Abū Yūsuf's ruling attained the status of *al-ṣaḥīḥ*—the correct ruling—and some scholars added that the ruling was accepted by consensus (*ijmāʿ*) (Ṭarsūsī—d. 758/1356–57–1344/1926, 109–12; Ibn al-Humām—d. 861/1457–1316/1898–99, 5: 58–9; Ibn Nujaym 1311/1893–94, 5: 239; Ibn ʿĀbidīn—d. 1252/1836–1386/1966, 4: 384; idem 1311/1893–94, 5: 239).[21]

On other occasions scholars had difficulties reaching agreement. One example is that of the exchange of *waqf* property other than by the founder's specific stipulation. Abū Yūsuf's was the most permissive position on the subject. He allowed exchange transactions of endowed assets, whether dilapidated or in perfect condition, on the sole condition that the exchange be in the interest (*maṣlaḥa*) of the endowment, that is, that it be economically advantageous to the *waqf*. Although other scholars did not agree with his permissiveness, Abū Yūsuf's ruling was apparently widely followed in the first few centuries of Islamic history (Ṭarsūsī 1344/1926, 112–14). At least from the fourteenth century onwards, the literature is replete with complaints against the proliferation of exchange transactions. Endowments, the jurists claimed, either lost assets altogether or suffered economic damage as a result of exchanges of good, productive properties for worthless assets. The blame was invariably put on ignorant and corrupt qāḍīs or greedy *waqf* administrators or rulers, who secured the cooperation of corrupt witnesses and qāḍīs in order to carry out their evil designs (al-Ṭarsūsī 1344/1926, 109, 114; Ibn Nujaym 1311/1893–94, 5: 223, 241; Ibn ʿĀbidīn 1386/1966, 4: 388.).[22] The scholars' main concern was to limit exchange transactions to the bare minimum. Some of the more radical suggestions obviously never

---

[21] The fact that Qadrī 1902, article 129 simply states that this was the rule, points to its wide acceptance by Ḥanafī scholars. According to Ibn ʿĀbidīn 1386/1966, 4: 384, the right situation was that the above stipulation was permissible *ʿalā al-ṣaḥīḥ wa-qīla ittifāqan*—"as the preferred ruling and some say by agreement." See also idem 1311/1893, 94, 239, where he brings some examples of scholars who opposed this ruling.

[22] The one concrete example of abuse repeatedly cited is that of the Mamluk ruler al-Mālik al-Nāṣir Faraj (r. 801–15/1399–1412) and the *amīr* Jamāl al-Dīn Yūsuf, assisted by the *qāḍī al-quḍāt* Kamāl al-Dīn ʿAmrū b. al-ʿAdīm cited in al-Maqrīzī (d. 845/1442), 1270/1853–54, 2: 296. See also Abū Zahra 1971, 14–16.

met with widespread agreement and were dropped. Such was, for instance, the fate of al-Ṭarsūsī's call to all Ḥanafī qāḍīs to completely "close the gates of *istibdāl*" (al-Ṭarsūsī 1344/1926, 115) and Ibn Nujaym's suggestion to forbid exchanges for money (*istibdāl bi'l-darāhim*) altogether (Ibn Nujaym 1311/1893–94, 5: 241).[23] Other means to the same end met with general approval by authors of *fatwā*s and *furū'* literature. Such was the suggestion to withhold from *waqf* administrators the right to make exchange transactions and require that each proposed transaction be authorized by a qāḍī (al-Ṭarsūsī 1344/1926, 112–15; Ibn al-Humām 1316/1898–99, 5: 59; Ibn Nujaym 1311/1893–94, 5: 240; Ibn 'Ābidīn 1386/1966, 4: 386). Another suggestion, recommended by many scholars, consisted in making the approval of an exchange transaction by a qāḍī conditional on the existence of an element of duress (*ḍarūra*) in addition to verifying its economical benefit to the *waqf* (*maṣlaḥa*). The general tendency of scholars, and particularly the inclusion of the duress element, obviously went counter to Abū Yūsuf's permissive attitude. Ibn al-Humām was decisive on this point, when he declared that an exchange transaction—whether according to the founder's stipulation or not—is allowed in cases of duress only (Ibn al-Humām 1316/1898–99, 5: 58–9). Other scholars obviously had a problem opposing Abū Yūsuf outright.[24] One way of dealing with the problem, which was apparently adopted by many scholars, was to separate the discussion of the conditions under which the judge was allowed to authorize an exchange from the discussion of exchange transactions of good properties (*al-'āmir*). We thus find, on the one hand, a set of rules governing the conditions under which the qāḍī

---

[23] Another suggestion was to restrict the right to authorize exchange deals to *qāḍī al-janna* 'interpreted as one who has knowledge and experience' (*dhū al-'ilm wa'l-'amal*)—see Ibn Nujaym 1311/1893–94, 5: 241, who attributes this suggestion to Ṭarābulsī (d. 922/1516–17). On the history of exchange deals in general, see also Abū Zahra 1971, 167–85.

[24] al-Ṭarsūsī (1344/1926) did not include duress in his definition of the question put to him, which was simply: Is it allowed to exchange an endowed asset for a better one or not (pp. 109, 112)? When he got to explaining how the qāḍī should act, he opened by assuming that the case put before the judge was one of duress. In his detailed explanation, however, he referred only to steps to be taken by the judge to ensure that the interests of the *waqf* (*maṣlaḥa*) be secured and said nothing about proving duress (pp. 114–15. Compare with the procedure in Algiers, which included verification of the duress element as well—Shuval 1996. For the same in the case of perpetual leases, see Hoexter 1984). He finished the discussion, as we have seen, with a suggestion to discontinue exchange transactions altogether.

may authorize an exchange. Basically, they focus on the need to prove the existence of the two principles of *ḍarūra*—duress—and *maṣlaḥa*—the safeguard of the *waqf*'s interests. For example, a qāḍī may authorize an exchange deal only when the endowed asset is completely dilapidated and produces no income; the transaction must be just and advantageous to the *waqf*, that is: the value of the incoming asset must be at least similar to that of the outgoing asset. On the other hand, and quite apart from the above set of rules, we find another set of four cases in which the exchange of good, undilapidated assets (*al-ʿāmir*) is permitted. Of these cases, only the fourth concerns us here. It reads: when a person wishes to exchange an endowed asset for an asset which produces more income or is of better quality (*aḥsan waṣfan*) (another version reads: better located—*aḥsan ṣuqʿan*), it is permitted according to Abū Yūsuf and *fatwā*s should follow his ruling (*wa-ʿalayhi al-fatwā*), as in Qāriʾ al-Hidāya's *fatwā*s.[25] This conflicted with the first set of rules, allowing the exchange of completely dilapidated assets only, and left the door wide open for exchange deals involving good properties. In the course of several centuries, no general agreement was thus reached to declare that Abū Yūsuf's permissive stipulation concerning *istibdāl* of good, undilapidated assets was no longer the Ḥanafī school's preferred view (*al-rājiḥ*). The absence of a legal authority, recognized by all adherents of a school of law, which is at the heart of the problem of *ikhtilāf al-fuqahā'*, thus resulted in legal indeterminacy.

Attempts to tackle the problem of *ikhtilāf al-fuqahā'* by means of *mukhtaṣars*—abridged, code-like manuals including only the most authoritative rules of a legal school (*EI*², s.v. Mukhtaṣar (A. Arazi & H. Ben Shammai); Fadel 1996)[26]—or by the appointment, under the Mamluks, of four chief qāḍīs, each of whom ruled according to his own school of law (Rapoport 2003), obviously did not solve the problem. Two ways which seem to have worked consisted the one in the

[25] For the separate discussions, see Ibn Nujaym 1311/1893–94, 5: 240–41 and Ibn Nujaym 1322/1904–05, 76 quoting Sarrāj al-Dīn Abū Khafṣ (d. 829/1426), the author of *Qāriʾ al-Hidāya*. See also al-Ḥaṣkafī 1386/1966, 4: 386 and 388; Ibn ʿĀbidīn 1386/1966, 4: 386 and 388. The same separation is found in Qadrī, 1902, arts. 133 and 135. As to the change in the reference to Abū Yūsuf's ruling in al-Ḥaṣkafī, 1386/1966, 4: 388, Ibn ʿĀbidīn 1386/1966, 4: 388 and Qadrī, 1902, art. 135 see pp. 81–2 below. For the details of both sets of rules, see Ibn ʿĀbidīn 1386/1966, 4: 386–88 and Qadrī, 1902, arts. 133–43.

[26] For reasons why the *mukhtaṣars* could not achieve this goal, see also Hallaq 1996, 133–35.

involvement of the ruler, the other in the establishment of a permanent consulting body next to the qāḍī.

I have referred above to the *modus vivendi* reached between rulers and *fuqahā᾽* in the course of the ʿAbbāsid period. Rather than severing relations between the two parties, or dissociating their interests, this *modus vivendi* called for respect, cooperation and mutual dependence of rulers and scholars. Respect and acknowledgement of their role as exponents of the *sharīʿa* made rulers seek the advice of *fuqahā᾽*, usually in the form of a *fatwā*, on important decisions of war and peace and other political issues. The cooperation of *fuqahā᾽* with the ruler, in his capacity as protector of the community of believers (the *umma*) and responsible for the implementation of the *sharīʿa*, took many forms. Although the ruler did not usually interfere with the daily administration of justice, his cooperation was needed for instance in the fight against all kinds of people accused by the *fuqahā᾽* of preaching doctrines at odds with the mainstream Sunnī doctrine, and certainly for the enforcement of capital punishment on them.[27] Involving the ruler, usually in cooperation with some of the prominent scholars of the day, in difficult legal decisions was not an Ottoman invention.[28] It seems, however, that with the Ottomans this solution was elevated to the level of a system. By means of a combination of a *fatwā*, issued by the chief *muftī* of the realm, and a sultanic decree, they sought to solve problems of legal indeterminacy. Shaykh al-Islam—the chief *muftī* of the Ottoman Empire—was the head of the Ottoman legal establishment. Naturally, his *fatwā*s carried much weight. However, they were not binding on the qāḍīs of the Empire, and thus could not, by themselves, put an end to differences of opinions among the *ʿulamā᾽*.[29] The sultan, for his part,

---

[27] For examples, see Talmon-Heller 2002.

[28] See, e.g., Zaman 1997 for the early ʿAbbāsid period and Talmon-Heller (2002, 50) for Syria in the thirteenth century.

[29] On Shaykh al-Islām, see Heyd 1973a, 183–87; Repp 1986; Imber 1996; idem 1997; Gerber 1999, 60–4. All sources agree that his *fatwā*s were not binding on the judges. On the popularity, respect and practical use made of *fatwā* collections of Shaykhs al-Islam, see Imber 1996, esp. 142. According to Heyd (1969, 56), several Shaykhs al-Islam ruled that disregard of *fatwā*s, especially those issued by them, made a Muslim liable to punishment (*taʿzīr*) and even reduced him to the status of infidel (*kāfir*) and a judge who failed to act in accordance with them deserved to be dismissed from office. It seems very doubtful that these rulings were ever carried out. Rather, they attest to the fact that Shaykhs al-Islam encountered difficulties in imposing their legal opinions on both the public and qāḍīs, unless, of course, they were accompanied by a sultanic decree.

was responsible for the implementation of the *sharīʿa* in the territories under his control. As such, his order was binding on the qāḍīs of the Empire.[30] Heyd's study of the collection of *fatwā*s by Abū al-Suʿūd enlightens us on the kind of cooperation between the chief *muftī* of the Empire and the sultan and its relevance to the problem of *ikhtilāf al-fuqahāʾ*. The procedure followed by Abū al-Suʿūd was to suggest to the sultan that "for the sake of the order of religion and State" the opinion of a certain scholar of the past should be followed. It was up to the sultan to approve his suggestions.[31] Heyd found that a major group of these suggestions consisted of matters on which jurists of the past had disagreed. Abū al-Suʿūd's aim was "to ensure that the individual cadi is . . . not permitted freely to choose whose opinion he will follow, but obliged to adjudicate in accordance with the sultan's directives" (Heyd 1973a, 185). It was the sultan's prerogative to choose and impose on the qāḍīs of the realm "whatever opinion he considers preferable for the good of the State or of society or for any other reason" (ibid.).[32] Obviously, the initiative, the content of the suggestions, as well as the legal argumentation in favor of the proposed ruling should be attributed to the chief *muftī*. However, the sultan's decree, addressed to all the qāḍīs of the Empire, was needed in order to obtain the expected result—putting an end to legal indeterminacy in the Empire.

The cooperation of the chief *muftī* with the sultan clinched the *ikhtilāf* on cash-*waqf*s and *istibdāl* at least on the practical level. In 955/1548, a sultanic decree ordered the qāḍīs of the Empire to authorize cash-endowments. The decree was accompanied by Abū al-Suʿūd's *fatwā*, which, as we have seen, was based on custom (*taʿāmul*,

---

[30] See Heyd 1973a, 187. That this is how the general public saw it—see Mandaville 1979, 295, 308, particularly the letter sent by the Ṣūfī leader Bali Baba to the sultan, begging him to issue a sultanic order which will solve the *fuqahā*'s dispute.

[31] This explains the title of the collection: *Maʿrūḍāt Abī al-Suʿūd Efendi*—"The Matters Submitted by Ebu al-Suʿūd Efendi to Sultan Süleymān the Lawgiver"—see Heyd 1973a, 183.

[32] On the cooperation of Abū al-Suʿūd with the sultan, see also Imber 1997, esp. 106–10. In exceptional cases the chief *muftī*s referred in their *fatwā*s to opinions expressed by jurists belonging to schools of law other than the Ḥanafī—the official Ottoman school of law. In some cases the sultan was even asked permission to apply the principle of *istiḥsān*—see Heyd 1973a, 186. Theoretically at least, sultanic decrees were valid during the lifetime of the sultan who had enacted them and had to be approved by a new ruler. In practice they were usually confirmed—ibid., 172, 184. On the durability of the decisions on the two cases at hand, see below.

taʿāruf) and *istiḥsān*.[33] The same combination sought to clinch the issue of *istibdāl*. A sultanic decree, dated 951/1544–45, declared that, as against Abū Yūsuf's view, no exchange was henceforth permitted, unless it received a special authorization by the sultan.[34] Abū al-Suʿūd's *fatwā* was in this case based on *tarjīḥ*—opting for one opinion as the preferred ruling, without, however, invalidating other opinions (Horster 1935, 42–3; Imber 1997, 158; al-Ḥaṣkafī 1386/1966, 4: 388; Ibn ʿĀbidīn 1386/1966, 4: 388).

Both decrees and *fatwā*s found their way to the *furūʿ* literature. Only naturally, they were not recognized as overriding opinions, putting an end to theoretical *ikhtilāf*. However, their content was basically accepted and thus provided a practical solution to the problem of indeterminacy.[35] Discussing the exchange of undilapidated properties (*al-ʿāmir*), both al-Ḥaṣkafī and Ibn ʿĀbidīn mentioned the content of the sultanic decree and the *fatwā*, based on *tarjīḥ*, as the rule that should be followed.[36] Ibn ʿĀbidīn's commentary concerning cash-*waqf*s is particularly interesting. As we have seen, the authorization of cash-*waqf*s was based on custom. Relating to the *fatwā* and the sultanic decree, al-Ḥaṣkafī endorsed the ruling, adding some examples from earlier jurisconsults. Ibn ʿĀbidīn, commenting on al-Ḥaṣkafī's work, added a reservation to this general authorization, which he based on the same argument which served Abū al-Suʿūd. As Ibn ʿĀbidīn put it, the endowment of cash (like that of other

[33] See p. 73 above. That a sultanic decree was issued is mentioned, e.g., in Mandaville 1979, 308; in Abū al-Suʿūd's *Maʿrūḍāt*—see Horster 1935, 41–2; in al-Ḥaṣkafī 1386/1966, 4: 364. The sultanic decree is quoted in al-Kafawī's (d. 990/1582) manuscript, partially translated in Repp 1986, 255. Repp, as well as Imber (1997, 144), also give the exact date of the decree. According to the decree, quoted in Repp, the sultan relied on *fatwā*s of several distinguished scholars and office-holders, including Abū al-Suʿūd.

[34] Besides preventing embezzlement and loss of properties to the *waqf*, Imber (1997, 158) points to what he considers a more important aim of the decree: the prevention of trusts acquiring, without the sultan's consent, lands belonging to the royal demesne.

[35] The legalization of the cash-*waqf* continued to be disputed by some scholars. However, based on the above *fatwā* and sultanic decree and supported by official *ʿulamā*ʾ, cash endowments were made in large numbers in Anatolia and Rumeli in the following centuries—see, e.g., Mandaville 1979, 305–7; Gerber 1994, 105–6; Çizakça 1995.

[36] Both al-Ḥaṣkafī (1386/1966, 4: 388) and Ibn ʿĀbidīn (1386/1966, 4: 388) stated that Abū al-Suʿūd's *fatwā* was based on *tarjīḥ* and that it and the sultanic decree concerned good and undilapidated assets (*al-ʿāmir*). Ibn ʿĀbidīn further explained that they referred to the exchange of a good asset (*al-ʿāmir*) when the income dropped but the asset did not become completely unprofitable.

specific movables) was valid only in places where it had been an established custom. As far as cash-*waqf*s were concerned, their endowment had been the custom in the center of the Empire (*Bilād al-Rūm, al-Diyār al-Rūmiyya*), but not in "our country" (*fī bilādinā*), meaning Syria (al-Ḥaṣkafī 1386/1966, 4: 364; Ibn ʿĀbidīn 1386/1966, 4: 364).[37]

The sixteenth-century decisions on both issues were mentioned in the two semi-official codifications of *waqf* law, published towards the end of the nineteenth century, which have been widely used by qāḍīs: Qadrī's codification in Egypt and the Arab countries and Hilmi's in the centre of the Ottoman Empire. On cash-*waqf*s, Qadrī followed Ibn ʿĀbidīn's lead when he stated that the permission to endow cash depended on the custom (*ʿurf*) of each region. It was allowed in countries where this had been the custom and was not permitted in countries in which no such custom existed (Qadrī 1902, art. 60). In Hilmi's codification, which was mainly designed for use in the heartlands of the Ottoman Empire, where the endowment of cash had been very popular, cash-*waqf* simply appeared as one of the endowable movables (Hilmi 1922, art. 350). As for *istibdāl*, Qadrī summarized the four exceptional situations in which the exchange of undilapidated properties were allowed. The difference between his rendering of the fourth case and that of Abū Khafṣ is telling. It unmistakably demonstrates the effect of the sultanic decree accompanied by Abū al-Suʿūd's *fatwā*. Concerning the fourth case, Qadrī

---

[37] Ibn ʿĀbidīn lived in Damascus. He actually argued that cash endowments, like endowments of other specific movables, should be considered *ʿurf khāṣṣ* (custom of a specific region). From the context of the controversy concerning cash-*waqf*s it is quite clear that the purpose of the sultanic decree was to legitimize past and future cash endowments where they were popular, rather than to introduce cash-*waqf*s or propagate this particular kind of endowments elsewhere. For a study analyzing reactions by Syrian *ʿulamāʾ* to what they considered Ottoman "excesses" incompatible with the *sharīʿa*, see Rafeq 1994. See Johansen 1993 on how a particular *ʿurf khāṣṣ* spread and was finally generally accepted. Whether, or to what extent, endowing cash spread to Arab lands, seems to be a moot question. At least, it seems not to have been as widely spread as in Anatolia and Rumeli. For instance, studies on endowments in Aleppo, all based on court records and Kāmil b. Ḥusayn al-Ghazzī's *Nahr al-Dhahab*, do not mention cash endowments—e.g. Marcus 1989, Meriwether 1999 (her only mention of cash endowments is on p. 254, n. 7, referring to Mandaville's study); Roded 1979; Rafeq 1994, 9 ("the voluminous sharīʿa court records in Ottoman Syria make no reference to the application of *waqf al-nuqūd* in that country"). Mandaville 1979, 308, esp. n. 61 found four cash endowments, one from each of the sixteenth, seventeenth, eighteenth and nineteenth centuries in al-Ghazzī's work. Masters (1988, 162) claims, however, that the court records of Aleppo contain many references to cash endowments. Çizakça (1995, 313, based on Masters) concludes that cash endowments were widespread in Aleppo.

mentioned Abū Yūsuf's opinion, allowing the exchange of an endowed property on the sole grounds of economic advantage to the *waqf*, adding, however, that "the preferred view is that this is not permitted"—*wa'l-rājiḥ ʿadam al-jawāz*—thus referring to Abū al-Suʿūd's *tarjīḥ* (Qadrī 1902, art. 135 and compare p. 77 above and n. 25). Hilmi, for his part, stated that exchange transactions (unless by the founder himself) were conditional on the authorization of the sultan. As reference to this article he cited the sultanic order of 951/1544–45 (Hilmi 1922, art. 416 and see, particularly, note to article 416 on p. 123).

An alternative way to overcome the problem of *ikhtilāf* was devised in the Maghrib and, as far as I know, was practiced exclusively in Algeria and Tunisia under Ottoman rule. In both territories an institution named *majlis ʿilmī* (in Algiers) and *majlis sharʿī* (in Tunis) was established with the purpose of discussing problems whose solution was disputed among the local *ʿulamāʾ*, or issues for which the literature did not provide an answer.[38] Requests to authorize exchange transactions and perpetual leases of endowed assets were of the first mentioned nature and were thus usually brought before this institution. The *majlis ʿilmī* of Algiers was convened once a week, on Thursdays, in the Great Mosque of the town. From the end of the seventeenth century it was composed of four members: the Ḥanafī and the Mālikī *muftīs* of Algiers and the qāḍīs of the two schools of law. The Ḥanafī members represented the official Ottoman school of law, while the Mālikīs represented the school of law to which the majority of the Algerian population adhered. A representative of the ruling authority in Algiers was present in the deliberations of the *majlis*. His main duty was to bring the decisions taken by the *majlis* to the ruler's attention. His presence seems to have been instrumental in ensuring that discussions in the *majlis* did not get out of hand, that is, to discourage vociferous, even violent, disputes among its members.[39] Examining the way the Algerian *majlis* functioned

[38] For the Algerian *majlis*, see Hoexter 1984, 256–58. See also Shuval 1996. On the Tunisian institution, see Brunschvig 1965. The following passage is based on these essays. On other *majālis* resembling the *maẓālim* courts in both towns, see ibid. (for Tunis) and Hoexter 1982, esp. 126. The difference between the various *majālis* in Tunis is not absolutely clear.

[39] The ruler of Tunisia exercised control of the *majlis* and at times even headed its meetings—see Brunschvig 1965. It is not clear which of the various *majālis* was headed by the ruler. See also ibid. for the vehement conflicts within the *majlis* of Tunis.

when cases of perpetual leases (*ʿanāʾ*) and exchange transactions (*muʿāwaḍa* in the Maghrib) were brought before this institution, it was found that the details of each case were discussed by its members and some of the procedural steps took place in their presence. Once all the procedural points relevant to a case were performed to the satisfaction of the *majlis* and a judgment was required, the case was referred to the relevant qāḍī, who alone had the authority to pronounce judgment (Hoexter 1984; Shuval 1996). The principle, whereby the function of adjudicating was exercised by a single judge,[40] was thus maintained. The *majlis* had an advisory or consultative role only. However, while a *fatwā* was not binding on the qāḍī, he could hardly ignore the advice of the *majlis*. The *majlis* thus secured uniformity of adjudication in Algiers. Over and above its advisory competence in specific cases, it seems that the *majlis*, in cooperation with the ruler, was responsible for decisions of a more general character, amounting to a change of policy. I have shown elsewhere (Hoexter, 1997; idem 1998, 104–43) that for a long time exceptional transactions in *waqf* properties in Algiers, that is, perpetual leases and exchange deals, were kept to a minimum. However, due to a combination of social and economic circumstances, a new policy was adopted sometime in the second half of the eighteenth century. Its aim was to facilitate the proliferation of these exceptional transactions. In the case of exchange deals, the new policy consisted in allowing for the exchange of productive assets or properties which were not completely dilapidated, and insisting that the transaction be of clear economic advantage to the *waqf*. For all intents and purposes this policy meant the re-adoption of Abū Yūsuf's permissive rulings.[41] This policy persisted in Algiers for the remaining decades of Ottoman rule.

The *majlis* system, which to the best of my knowledge had no equivalents in the Mashriq, probably originated in al-Andalus where consultation (*shūrā*) of the qāḍī with *muftī*s was institutionalized. There, as well as in Morocco, special advisors (*mushāwarūn*) were appended to each court. They formed 'the qāḍī's council' (*shūrā*), were consulted on difficult cases, issued *fatwā*s at the qāḍī's request and were

[40] *EI*², s.v., "Ḳāḍī (E. Tyan). A collegiate system was applied only in the *maẓālim* courts.

[41] Shuval (1996, 61) mentions a *fatwā* appended to one of the exchange documents in which the content of Abū Yūsuf's ruling is quoted verbatim. However, it is not mentioned in the article (and perhaps not even in the *fatwā*) that the author's ruling was based on Abū Yūsuf's view.

thus an essential component of the Mālikī judicial system. As in the case of the Algerian *majlis*, in Morocco too, the role of 'the qāḍī's council' remained purely consultative (Masud, Messick & Powers 1996, esp. 10–11; Tyan 1960, 230–36; *EI*^{2}, s.v., Ḳāḍī (E. Tyan); Marin 1985; Powers 1994). The combination of qāḍīs and *muftīs* of two different schools of law was, however, unique to *majālis* in Algiers and Tunisia under Ottoman rule.

Conclusion

al-Qarāfī, a thirteenth-century Mālikī *muftī* (d. 684/1285), in his study of the differences between *muftīs* and qāḍīs, described the qāḍī's function, i.e., adjudicating, as creative or original (*inshāʾī*). He compared the *muftī*'s mission to that of a *ḥadīth* transmitter or an interpreter, and characterized it as informative (*khabarī*) (al-Qarāfī 1967, esp. 29, 84; Jackson 1992; idem 1996, 170–77; Masud, Messick & Powers 1996, 19).[42] My argument is that although the validity of the qāḍī's judgments was basically restricted to specific cases (*khāṣṣ*), his creative work, and mainly the accumulation of judgments in the same vein, created a status of established customs. In many cases the qāḍī's endeavors were designed to address problems resulting from changing socio-economic circumstances and the solutions were not always compatible with traditional *sharʿī* rulings. These solutions, arrived at by the creative endeavors of qāḍīs, were often adopted by authors of *fatāwā* and *furūʿ* collections. Having recourse to the appropriate legal methodology, they translated them into normative *sharʿī* language. In so doing they often relied on the notions of 'custom' or 'changing times' as tools facilitating the introduction of changes in

[42] al-Qarāfī's characterization of the *muftī* and the qāḍī should be understood in connection with the binding nature (*ilzām*) of the qāḍī's judgment compared with a *fatwā*, which is a legal opinion, that may either be accepted or rejected—see also Ibn al-Qayyim al-Jawziyya—d. 751/1350—1969, 1:37, 39; Heyd 1969, 56; Masud, Messick, Powers 1996, 19 and n. 22. Jackson (1996, 174) explains that what al-Qarāfī meant when he referred to the judge's decision (*ḥukm*) as *inshāʾ* (which Jackson translates as origination) was that it created a status, or according to al-Qarāfī "This (binding and unassailable) status is a thing that comes into existence after the judge's ruling, not before." This does not mean that *muftīs* and author-jurists were not creative in the broader sense of the word. For the nature of creative thinking concerning the development of the law after the post-formative period, see, e.g., Schacht 1964, 73; Hallaq 1996, 128; Calder 1996, esp.156–57.

Islamic law. In other words, while qāḍīs initiated many of the developments in Islamic law, the authors of *fatāwā* and *furūʿ* collections provided the change with authoritative formulation. They thus sanctioned the change beyond the specific case and endowed it with general (*ʿāmm*)—though not binding—authority, which made the new ruling applicable, within the specific school of law, to all equivalent cases.[43]

The role of qāḍīs in the development of Islamic law was thus in the initiation of change, that is, at the starting line of the process of change; the role of rulers was at the closing end of the same process, that is, in their contribution toward providing and enforcing solutions to *ikhtilāf al-fuqahāʾ* on issues relevant to the development of the law. In the Ottoman center the ruler exercised this function in cooperation with, and most probably in response to the initiative of the chief *muftī* of the Empire, whereas in the Ottoman Maghrib the same function was exercised by the *majlis*, comprising *muftī*s and qāḍīs and controlled by the ruler. Adding an examination of some practical aspects to those of doctrine, my conclusion is, thus, that the development of Islamic law was a result of a joint effort by qāḍīs, *muftī*s and rulers.

[43] On the general authority of the *fatwā* compared with the specific nature of the qāḍī's judgment, see, e.g., Ibn al-Qayyim al-Jawziyya 1969, 1: 39. Interestingly, Imber (1996, 149) argues that by means of a *fatwā* of Shaykh al-Islam in reply to a qāḍī's question "court cases could, in a sense, come to form legal precedents."

CHAPTER FIVE

OTTOMAN QĀḌĪS IN DAMASCUS IN THE 16TH–18TH CENTURIES

Michael Winter

This chapter examines the chief Ottoman qāḍīs of Damascus. It is based mainly on the chronicles and biographical dictionaries of contemporary Damascene *ʿulamāʾ*, all of whom were thoroughly familiar with the Ottoman judicial system. Indeed, they, or members of their families, often served as deputy judges in the law courts, enhancing their knowledge of the details of the system. Their loyalty was given first and foremost to their community and by extension to the Ottoman Empire, the only Muslim government they knew (with the exception of Shams al-Dīn Muḥammad b. Ṭūlūn, the great scholar and historian who chronicled the last decades of the Mamluks and the first decades of the Ottomans in Damascus. He lived from 880/1475 to 953/1546). These writers were bilingual (again with the exception of Ibn Ṭūlūn, who spoke only Arabic) and occasionally traveled to the Ottoman capital. Culturally and socially they were Arab and Damascene, but this did not conflict with their loyalty to the Empire.

The Main Sources

Among the primary sources for our subject are the centennial dictionaries, all written by members of well known *ʿulamāʾ* families: Najm al-Dīn al-Ghazzī's *al-Kawākib al-Sāʾira fī Aʿyān al-Miʾa al-ʿĀshira* in the tenth/sixteenth century and his *Luṭf al-Samar wa-Qaṭf al-Thamar min Tarājim Aʿyān al-Ṭabaqa al-Ūlā min al-Qarn al-Ḥādī ʿAshar* for the first generation of the notables of the eleventh/seventeenth century. From approximately the same time we have Ḥasan al-Būrīnī's *Tarājim al-Aʿyān min Abnāʾ al-Zamān*. The centennial dictionary for the eleventh/seventeenth century is Muḥammad Amīn al-Muḥibbī's *Khulāṣat al-Athar fī Aʿyān al-Qarn al-Ḥādī ʿAshar*, and for the twelfth/eighteenth century

Muḥammad Khalīl al-Murādī's *Silk al-Durar fī Aʿyān al-Qarn al-Thānī ʿAshar.*

The Judicial System under the Mamluks

In the Mamluk Empire there were in Cairo, the capital, and in the major provincial towns, including Damascus, four chief judges, each representing one of the Sunnī *madhhab*s, the schools of Islamic law. Formally, from the beginning of the Mamluk Sultanate, the four were of equal status and each qāḍī was referred to as *Shaykh al-Islām.* In reality, however, the Shāfiʿī chief qāḍī was far more influential and powerful than his colleagues, owing to the fact that his *madhhab* had considerably more followers than the other three.

The top qāḍīships in Damascus were a virtual monopoly of a few old and prominent local families. Yet no Shāfiʿī house of *ʿulamāʾ* was as successful as the Banū al-Furfūr, which gave the city two outstanding chief judges and several other high-ranking officials as well. For a quarter of a century Shihāb al-Dīn Aḥmad b. Furfūr was, with but a few interruptions, the chief qāḍī, until his death in 911/1505. He won the distinction of being the only judge who was appointed by the Mamluk sultan as the Shāfiʿī *qāḍī al-quḍāt* both in Cairo and Damascus simultaneously.

Walī al-Dīn b. al-Furfūr, Shihāb al-Dīn's son and successor cuts an even more imposing figure. Upon the death in Cairo of the chief Shāfiʿī qāḍī, his young son was immediately named to inherit his position in Damascus, and all the positions, honors and benefits that went with it. Totally undeterred by his youth (he was about sixteen at the time), he quickly increased the number of his deputies.[1]

The Ottoman Occupation of Damascus and the First Chief Qāḍīs

After the Ottoman conquest of Syria in Shaʿbān 922/August 1516, Walī al-Dīn adjusted quickly to the new regime. He gave an eloquent *khuṭba* in the presence of *Yavuz* Sultan Selīm, the Ottoman ruler. In his sermon, he called Selīm "Sultan of the Two Noble

[1] For the situation of the judicial system in late Mamluk Damascus, see Winter 2004.

Sanctuaries" (*sulṭān al-ḥaramayn al-sharīfayn*), thus being the first to honor the Ottoman sultan with that title, even before the Hijaz accepted Ottoman suzerainty (this happened only after the Ottoman conquest of Egypt early the following year). In the next *ʿīd al-Fiṭr* prayer, Shams al-Dīn Muḥammad b. Ṭūlūn, the most important chronicler of the period who witnessed the conquest and the first decades of Ottoman rule in Damascus (Conermann 2004), observed that Ibn al-Furfūr performed the service according to the Ḥanafī rite to suit the new masters' custom. It was soon rumored that Ibn al-Furfūr had converted to the Ḥanafī *madhhab*, though he remained a Shāfiʿī (Ibn Ṭūlūn 1964, 2: 71).

The first encounters of the people of Damascus with the Ottoman administration and the judicial system were negative. To the people of Syria, and later Egypt, the Ottomans seemed strange and unjust. There were inevitable cultural differences between Turks (*Arwām*, *Rūmī*s, in the terminology of the time) and Arabs (*awlād ʿArab* or *abnāʾ ʿArab*), despite the fact that the new masters were Sunnī Muslims like the previous regime and the overwhelming majority of the local population. Ibn Ṭūlūn recounts that he wanted to communicate with his Ottoman colleagues, but the language barrier prevented it (ibid., 31). In time, this problem largely diminished, since many Turkish *ʿulamāʾ* learned to speak Arabic and Arabs acquired proficiency in Turkish.

The first Ottoman qāḍī whom Sultan Selīm appointed was Zayn al-ʿĀbidīn Muḥammad al-Fenerī. He named his local deputies in the courts to represent the four *madhhab*s. He introduced new arrangements that were considered as infringing on the rights of the local judicial personnel. For example, he ordered the *shuhūd*, the professional witnesses or notaries, to do their work only at his residence.[2] The Ottomans charged special fees on all contracts to be paid to the qāḍī and his assistants. What infuriated people most were the special marriage taxes—100 *dirham*s in the case of a virgin and 25 for a woman who had been previously married. The various fees were known as *yasaq*, the Ottoman law, which was implicitly in conflict with the *sharīʿa* according to the views of the Arab jurists of the time.[3] It seems that the issue disappeared after a while. It is

[2] Ibid., 41. In Cairo, Ibn Iyās (1961, 5: 417–18) reports both similar procedures and complaints.

[3] Ibn Ṭūlūn 1964, 2: 30. For the anger which the marriage taxes caused in

reported briefly under the year 931/1524 or 1525 that the tax marriage (*yasaq al-nikāḥ*) was abolished, since the people could not afford to marry or divorce (Ibn Ṭūlūn 2002, 180).

In line with their customary procedures in newly conquered territories, the Ottomans conducted a survey of all taxable properties. As a Muslim government, the Ottomans recognized the validity of the rights of people holding titles to private properties (*amlāk*) or as beneficiaries of pious foundations (*awqāf*), either as direct recipients of *waqf*-generated revenues or as directors and trustees of such funds. Each person was ordered to present his or her legal documents to prove the claim. The documents were then translated into Turkish. At the next stage, a fee of 25 *dirhams* was levied, and the case was referred to the chief imperial *ḳāżīʿasker* who was present in Damascus at the time. Upon receiving his approval, the applicant had to pay an additional 500 *dirhams* if the holder was a trustee of a *waqf*. In other cases, the fee was 100 *dirhams*.[4] As we see in the registers of these surveys, the holders of the documents were also required to bring witnesses to support their claims as descendants of the founders of the *waqf* or as the property owners.[5] It was pronounced in the name of the Ottoman qāḍī that all those who held a position of trusteeship of *waqf* should come to settle the accounts of the two last years. People were very angry, particularly at the Ottoman qāḍī. ʿAbd al-Qādir al-Nuʿaymī, the author of *al-Dāris fī Taʾrīkh al-Madāris*, a famous historical work about the educational institutions in Damascus, and an expert on the *awqāf* of Damascus, refused to show his registers to the Ottomans (Ibn Ṭūlūn 1964, 2: 73).

In Muḥarram 924/January 1518, Sultan Selīm entered Damascus on his way to Istanbul after conquering Egypt and establishing Ottoman rule there. He prayed in the city's al-Ṣāliḥiyya suburb, in the mosque that he had built near the tomb of Muḥyī'l-Dīn Ibn al-ʿArabī (d. 638/1240), the great controversial Andalusian mystic whom the Turks venerated. Again, Ibn al-Furfūr delivered the sermon. In Ṣafar 924/February 1518, Selīm appointed him as the chief qāḍī of

Cairo, see Ibn Iyās 1961, 5: 224, 418, 427 (where a Maghribi student of religion called the marriage tax '*yasaq al-kufr*', 'the infidels' tax'), 460.

[4] Ibn Ṭūlūn 1964, 2: 33, 34, 36. It is noteworthy that at that time the annual salary of a clerk in a religious institution was approximately 120 *dirhams*.

[5] *Defter* provides many examples to suggest that this was the usual procedure of having the claims to the *waqf* and *milk* rights recognized by the government.

Damascus. He was in charge of the deputy qāḍīs in the town, and was also given authority over all the judges from Gaza to Ḥomṣ, that is, over all of central Syria and Palestine.[6] That was the same policy by which Selīm appointed Jānbardī al-Ghazzālī, a former emir in the Mamluk high command who had betrayed his sultan. The Ottomans soon regretted that appointment, since as soon as Selīm died in 1520 and was succeeded by the young Süleymān, al-Ghazzālī rebelled. Ibn al-Furfūr escaped to Aleppo and was later named the chief qāḍī of that city. It was said about him that "he was the last Arab qāḍī (*min awlād al-ʿArab*) of Aleppo" (ibid., 310). The same would be true about his terms as the qāḍī of Damascus. In the long run, the Ottomans learned their lesson, and did not give such wide powers to their governors or qāḍīs in the province. It is unusual that Selīm appointed Ibn al-Furfūr, a Shāfiʿī and an Arab. This too was not repeated.

During his short term as a sultan, al-Ghazzālī named as chief qāḍī Sharaf al-Dīn b. al-Mufliḥ al-Ḥanbalī, a member of another old Damascus family of scholars and judges. He participated in the ceremony of al-Ghazzālī's ascent to the sultanate. When the Ottomans arrived in Damascus after crushing the revolt, Ibn Mufliḥ was promptly incarcerated in the Citadel. Ibn al-Furfūr, who was reinstalled as the qāḍī of Damascus, interceded for him, and he was set free (Ibn Ṭūlūn 2002, 107, 128).

Ibn al-Furfūr was an avid, imaginative and original builder and developer. In 932/1526, he started to build a market and a bathhouse in front of Bāb Jayrūn; both were named after him. He applied original methods, without using clay, to make the structures fireproof. He also built an elevated (*muʿallaqa*) *madrasa* in the middle of his market above a water pool. In addition, he began building a bridge over the Yazīd River. He removed the copula on the Shaysh Arslān sepulcher that was in danger of collapse and replaced it with a stronger one. Nearby he erected his own sepulcher (*turba*) of piebald stone (*ablaq*), with a *nāʿūra* (Persian wheel), over the river. Another house with a subterranean vault and an anteroom (*dihlīz*) above street level led to the Umayyad Mosque from his living quarters. Ibn al-Furfūr was a very rich man. Besides the income from his position of chief

[6] Ibid., 82. According to another version, Selīm gave Ibn al-Furfūr jurisdiction over 'Ṣafad, Gaza, Jerusalem and the entire province'. Ibn Ṭūlūn 1956, 107.

Shāfiʿī qāḍī, he controlled revenue yielding *awqāf* and had several villages as his *iqṭāʿ* from the Mamluk period, which he maintained under the Ottomans as well (ibid., 233–35, 241; Ibn Ṭūlūn 1956, 314; Ibn Ṭūlūn 1964, 2: 93). Ibn Ṭūlūn writes that in 928/1522 Walī al-Dīn b. al-Furfūr traveled to Istanbul to ask the Sultan to appoint him as the chief qāḍī of Egypt or as the *ḳāżīʿasker* of the Arab lands (Ibn Ṭūlūn 2002, 149). It is hard to verify the accuracy of this report, but Ibn al-Furfūr certainly did not lack ambition.

Ibn al-Furfūr also had a cruel side. He ordered the execution of one of his slaves for fornication. A pit was dug and the condemned man was buried up to his neck and then stoned to death. Clearly shaken, Ibn Ṭūlūn writes that this was the only time in his lifetime that such a thing had happened (ibid., 222).

In Shaʿbān 936/April 1530, Ibn al-Furfūr was dismissed. He left Damascus and headed north, no doubt to arrange his affairs in Istanbul. Yet the governor of Damascus, who was hostile to him, had him recalled for an investigation (*taftīsh*) of alleged embezzlement or fraud. Upon their return, Ibn al-Furfūr and his assistants were incarcerated in the Citadel. It was announced that anyone who had claims against him could come forward and demand his rights. The investigation in the presence of the pasha, the qāḍī, the *defterdār* and the Ḥanafī *muftī* extended over fifteen sessions, during which time all his property was sold so that he could pay what he owed. Walī al-Dīn b. Furfūr died in the Citadel on 30 Jumādā I 937/19 January 1531 at the age of 40, possibly by poison.[7]

In a register (*defter*) documenting a survey of *awqāf* and *amlāk* prepared in Damascus about thirty years after the Ottoman conquest, we come across a listing of a family *waqf* made in 909/1503 or 1504. The final beneficiary of the *waqf*'s revenues after following the deaths of all members of that family was a mosque in the Ṣāliḥiyya suburb. Nūḥ Çelebī, the *defterdār*, who soon after the conquest carried out an inspection of all pious endowments and private properties in the province and summarized them in an official register entitled *Defter-i Nūḥ*, had approved the validity of the *waqf*, and issued the owner a certificate (*tedhkere*). It says in the later *defter* that Qāḍī Ibn al-Furfūr seized by force (*jebren*) the owner's documents. Then he

[7] Ibid., 232, 234, 235, 241. The date 1530 that is found in some modern studies as Ibn al-Furfūr's death is erroneous.

blackened a few places in the papers, and registered the property as his own property (*milk*). Hence the investigation (*taftīsh*, almost certainly the events described by Ibn Ṭūlūn), during which the chief qāḍī of Damascus ordered Ibn al-Furfūr in writing to return the property to the trustee. The clerk who wrote the *defter* adds that witnesses testified concerning *waḍʿ al-yad* (*de facto* possession) (*Defter* fol. 60a [my pagination]).

The same *defter* mentions other cases in which members of the al-Furfūr family claimed rights on *waqf* properties where there were strong suspicions of fraud. One concerns a case of a *waqf* whose trustee had lost his rights because he had been in the Ḥijāz (for the *Ḥajj*) during Nūḥ Çelebi's survey. Nūḥ registered several possessions as Ibn al-Furfūr's *milk* and the rest as *timār*.[8] The clerk adds: "Now it is *timār*, but there is no doubt that it is *waqf*. Everybody knows it" (ibid., fol. 78b).

Banū Mufliḥ, a famous family of qāḍīs under the Mamluks and the Ottomans, also appear in this register as trustees of several *awqāf*. Here too the language of the document leaves no doubt that they came to control these assets by illegal means and without possessing the necessary documents, such as a *waqf* deed (*waqfiyya, vakıfname*). Moreover, it was impossible for them to administer the *awqāf* properly, because they had been living in Istanbul for a long time, as is mentioned three times in the *defter*.[9]

The Profile of the Ottoman Qāḍīs of Damascus

In the Ottoman judicial hierarchy, Damascus was in the highest category of provincial judgeships, one of *bilād-i arbaʿa*, the Four Towns, together with Edirne, Bursa and Cairo. Therefore, those who were sent from Istanbul to serve there as chief qāḍī were in most cases chosen from among the elite *ʿulamāʾ* of the center. After the early years of the occupation, all the qāḍīs, with only two exceptions, were Turkish-speaking Ḥanafīs. As we have seen, Ibn al-Furfūr's case was

---

[8] *Timār* is the Ottoman variation of the classical pseudo-feudal military system-the state granted the revenues of government lands to army officers for military services.

[9] *Defter* fols. 113a, 115a, 117a. In Ibn Ṭūlūn's chronicle (2002, 181) there is a reference to Ibn Mufliḥ's being in Istanbul in the year 931.

special, owing to his strong and dynamic personality and experience during the transitional period from Mamluk to Ottoman rule. In 1104/1692 or 1693, Aḥmad Efendi al-Bakrī al-Ṣiddīqī, a member of a prominent *ʿulamāʾ* family, was appointed as the first chief qāḍī since Ibn al-Furfūr (Rafeq 1966, 45). His grandson, Khalīl Efendi b. Asʿad al-Bakrī, was appointed in 1165/1751 as the second Arab chief judge. He was born (in 1098/1687) and educated in Damascus (among his teachers was the great Sufi and scholar ʿAbd al-Ghanī al-Nābulusī), yet he lived most of his years in the Ottoman capital and was thoroughly ottomanized. In Istanbul he was a follower and disciple of *Sheyhülislām* Feyżullāh, and rose eventually to the position of the qāḍī of Istanbul with the title of *ḳāżīʿasker* of Anatolia. Al-Murādī reports that as the qāḍī of Damascus he transferred the court to his house, a common practice in Damascus, 'as his grandfather had done before' (Budayrī 1959, 163–64; Murādī 1966, 2: 83–7). He died in Istanbul in Jumada II 1173/December 1759.

The typical appointee had taught at the most prestigious colleges in the capital; then he would be sent to serve as the chief judge in a major city. Several qāḍīs served first in Aleppo, then in Damascus, Cairo, Medina or another important provincial town. Some of them were promoted after their term as town qāḍī to the position of the *ḳāżīʿasker* of Anatolia, then Rumeli, and a few rose to the top to become the *Muftī* of Istanbul, *Sheyhülislām*. One qāḍī had a Persian background (Būrīnī 1959–63, 2: 161–62). Ḥasan b. ʿAbd al-Muḥsin (appointed in 960/1553) was a former slave (mamluk) of Rüstem Pasha, a Grand Vizier.[10] Aḥmad b. Ḥasan Bey (who arrived in 994) was the son of an army officer (Ibn Ṭūlūn 1956, 335). Al-Sayyid Muḥammad b. Burhān al-Dīn, known as al-Sharīf al-Ḥamīdī (d. *circa* 1040/1630–1), was a *sharīf* who became later the *Naqīb al-Ashrāf* of the Empire (Muḥibbī 1966, 3: 405–8). Several Ottoman qāḍīs impressed the educated elite of Damascus with their perfect knowledge of Arabic (Ghazzī 1981, 1: 102–6, 2: 659–60; Būrīnī 1959–63, 1: 67; Muḥibbī 1966, 3: 405–8). There were qāḍīs who taught in Damascus at one of the *madrasa*s or at home. It appears that their favorite subject was Qurʾānic exegesis, *tafsīr*. Ibn Ṭūlūn tells about a qāḍī who gave public lessons at the Umayyad Mosque (Ibn Ṭūlūn 1956, 118, 334).

---

[10] Ibn Ṭūlūn 1956, 327; Anṣārī 1991, 2: 168. He preferred to sign 'Ibn ʿAbd al-Muḥsin' rather than 'Ibn ʿAbdallāh', like most sons of non-Muslim parents.

Many Ottoman qāḍīs befriended leading *ʿulamāʾ* of Damascus; they attended their lessons and received from them personal diplomas (*ijāzāt*), allowing them to teach what they had learned.

It is noteworthy that quite a few chief qāḍīs in the early Ottoman period were of an advanced age when they arrived in Damascus and they died in office. This is particularly striking, since the terms were usually short, one year or less.[11]

In the eighteenth century, the number of biographies of chief qāḍīs of Damascus is much smaller than in the previous two centuries. If one compares al-Murādī's *Silk al-Durar* to the biographical dictionaries of the authors of the centennial biographical dictionaries that preceded his work, the difference is striking. Al-Murādī was as loyal to the Ottoman state as his predecessors, but he wrote only a few and rather short biographies of Ottoman qāḍīs, although references to them are scattered in the text.[12] It is possible that the involvement of the Ottoman qāḍīs in Damascene society was more limited than in the past. Al-Murādī, who was thoroughly familiar with the Ottoman culture and language, took care to emphasize the differences between the ways of the Ottoman *ʿulamāʾ* and those of the Arab ones. Expressions like 'it is done according to their (the Turks') customs', when he speaks about the Ottoman system of training, patronage and promotion in the capital, abound.

The eighteenth-century chronicle of Aḥmad al-Budayrī al-Ḥallāq gives us a rare perspective of Damascene society, including information about some Ottoman qāḍīs. Budayrī 'the barber', as his surname indicates, was not a scholar. His work offers a few interesting anecdotes about qāḍīs. They show the increased lawlessness in the life of the city and the unruly conduct of various segments of society that could threaten the qāḍī personally.

In Ramaḍān of 1162/1749, the qāḍī was seen drunk in public. He carried a sword and a handgun. He wore a slipper on one foot; the other was bare. It turned out that what brought on such disgraceful

[11] Ibn Ṭūlūn 2002, 308 (Isḥāq Çelebi, d. 944/1537), 303 (Ibn Isrāfīl, d. 943/1536), 315–16 (Abū al-Layth al-Rūmī); Ibn Ṭūlūn 1956, 317 (Shihāb al-Dīn Aḥmad, d. 942/1535), 318 (Isḥāq al-Burṣāwī).

[12] Murādī 1966, 1: 12–13, 32, 42; 2: 6–7; 4: 124. It is worth noting that al-Murādī's chronicle contains many biographies of natives of Damascus who immigrated to Istanbul and pursued careers there as teachers and judges. See, for example, ibid., 2: 107, 183–89; 3: 144, 217; 4: 28.

behavior was his infatuation with a maid. He had divorced his wife for her, on the grounds that she had been nagging and insulting him. He then lost control and threatened his servants with weapons. The divorced wife complained to the Porte and the qāḍī was exiled to Cyprus, while all his property was seized and transferred to her. Al-Budayrī's reaction is the most interesting part of the story. He says that the people felt sorry for the qāḍī, since he was honest and modest. He fed the poor during Ramaḍān and had never taken bribes. His verdicts were always just. So some bad people supported his wife and asked the authorities to dismiss him, it was said (Budayrī 1959, 131–32).

In 1158/1745, there were bread riots. Ruffians were in control, and the population suffered from a scarcity of food and high prices. They complained to the weak Pasha who sent them to the qāḍī. The demonstrators attacked the qāḍī's court with rocks, and the qāḍī's men responded with firearms. One *sharīf* was killed and several demonstrators were wounded. The rabble (*al-ʿāmma*) and some janissaries attacked the court of law and looted it. The qāḍī escaped to the Citadel and swore that he would reside only there. Finally he was compensated by funds obtained from fines on the Janissary regiment and from several rich men.

The qāḍī who was appointed the following year went to the law court surrounded by bodyguards armed with muskets, no doubt owing to the previous events. The chronicler notes that the new qāḍī's appearance was without precedent (ibid., 63–5).

Justice and Injustice in the Public Service

The Ottoman chief qāḍīs were expected to intercede with the authorities to reduce the extraordinary taxes, *avariz* or *nuzul*, payments for the provisions of the army in time of a campaign. If they failed to do so or were unsuccessful, they became the object of the people's wrath, and physical attacks were not unknown.

Muḥammad b. Muḥammad b. Ilyās, known as Çivizāde (d. 995/1587), was considered the best Ottoman judge to come to Damascus. He served there less than one year (from Ṣafar 977/July 1569 to the end of that year) before being transferred to Cairo. He made the full career, from a teacher in the top *madrasa*s of Istanbul to judgeship in Damascus and Cairo, then *ḳāżīʿasker* of Anatolia and Rumeli, and finally *Sheyhülislām*. He was honest and refused to accept any gifts. He reduced the fees for court documents (*ḥujaj*, sing. *ḥujja*) and copies of such papers. He was lenient but strict when it came to combating injustice. He heard complaints against state officials himself. He attended some classes in *tafsīr* and *fiqh* (jurisprudence) of Badr al-Dīn al-Ghazzī, the outstanding Shāfiʿī scholar in Damascus at the time. Najm al-Dīn al-Ghazzī, his son, and the most important historian in the second half of the sixteenth century and the first third of the seventeenth century, tells that Çivizāde was proud that he had obtained an *ijāza* from his father. Upon his return to Istanbul, he arranged for Badr al-Dīn a daily income of 80 akçes, more than any other Arab scholar had received. On the Friday before he left Damascus it was announced in the Umayyad mosque that anyone who had complaints against the qāḍī or his assistants could come forward and claim his rights. All the people in the mosque wept because he was leaving (Ghazzī 1945–59, 3: 27–9).

Küçük Muṣṭafā (d. before 1010/1601–1602) was an example of an honest judge. He was careful to investigate the cases that were brought to him, particularly regarding janissaries who lent money with exorbitant interest. People hurried to him to claim their rights. When he passed through the markets of Damascus, people blessed him, calling him 'the Mahdī, ʿĪsā, son of Maryam' (Ghazzī 1981, 2: 661–62; Muḥibbī 1966, 4: 394).

Ibrāhīm b. ʿAlī al-Iznīkī (d. 1028/1618 or 1619), twice the chief qāḍī of Damascus, was one of the best judges. In 1005/1606, he negotiated with ʿAlī b. Jānbulāṭ, a famous rebel, to prevent him from entering Damascus to settle his accounts with a political rival and the soldiers of the town. The qāḍī gave him money to spare Damascus this incident. He encouraged the soldiers of the Ottoman garrison to guard the gates. The qāḍī also succeeded in reducing the special levies imposed on Damascus by the Grand Vizier who came to fight Jānbulāṭ (ibid., 4: 31–2; Ghazzī 1981, 1: 231–40).

The following are examples of corrupt or oppressive qāḍīs:

Muḥammad al-Ayyāshī (appointed in 1007/1598–1599) was notoriously corrupt. Once demonstrators threw stones at him and soldiers had to defend him. He was attacked in satirical poems (*hijāʾ*) that criticized his oppression. One said: "Under his jurisdiction *waqfs* were sold at auction like cucumbers" (Būrīnī 1959–63, 1: 85–91).

Qāḍī Fayḍallāh (appointed in 999/1591) demanded from the various law courts in Damascus to send him special clothes made by a well-known tailor. He asked for less from courts that were weaker financially (Anṣarī 1991, 208–11).

Kamāl Efendi Ṭāshköprü (appointed as qāḍī of Damascus in 1005/1596) met the *ʿulamāʾ* of Damascus and charmed them with his excellent Arabic and his knowledge. After serving only one month in a satisfactory manner, he asked the *ʿulamāʾ* to write a laudatory report (*maḥḍar*) about him to Istanbul, and they did. Immediately afterwards he revealed his true nature as a greedy grasping man who liked to receive bribes (Ghazzī 1981, 2: 607–10).

The following passage from a chronicle about Aḥmad b. Ḥasan Bey, a judge who arrived in 994, is revealing. The writer praises the qāḍī who appointed him as a deputy qāḍī (*nāʾib*) without taking anything from him, as others were wont to do (Ibn Ṭūlūn 1956, 335).

The fees that the chief qāḍīs charged for their services are called in the Arabic sources *maḥṣūl*, gain. ʿAbd al-Raḥmān, the qāḍī in 1010/1601 or 1602, respected *ʿulamāʾ* and notables and was lenient with them, but charged anyone else excessively. He was the first qāḍī who set his fee according to the financial worth of the case. He was strict and despotic (Ghazzī 1981, 2: 506).

A few Ottoman qāḍīs (and several Damascene deputies as well) had a reputation of being immoral. Two were known to be attracted to *murd* (sing. *amrad*), or beardless youths. Isḥāq al-Burṣāwī was never married. It was rumored in Damascus that he liked to look at handsome young men. But by the time he was 70 years old, he did not go beyond talking with them (Ibn Ṭūlūn 1956, 319).

Muḥammad Akmalzāde (d. 1011/1603), a Ḥanbalī deputy qāḍī, was known for his debauchery. He was involved with a young Egyptian beardless youth (*amrad*) and people composed poems about this relationship. He used an Indian drug made of opium and saffron (*zaʿfrān*), called *barsh*, that is frequently mentioned in the period as being very addictive and used by some *ʿulamāʾ*. He assumed control of *awqāf* properties claiming falsely that the founder of the endowment was one of his ancestors. People mocked him saying: "O, Qāḍī, you have so many ancestors!" Generally, he acted wrongfully towards officeholders in the administration of *awqāf* (Ghazzī 1981, 1: 73–7).

The qāḍī was a central figure in the Ottoman administration. Though not as powerful as the pasha, the governor, there are occasions in which the qāḍī in his decisions demonstrated independence, and even acted in ways that were detrimental to the governor's economic interests. Muḥammad b. Muḥammad b. Maʿlūl (appointed as the qāḍī of Damascus in 975/1567 or 1568) had the reputation of being greedy and difficult. The Ottoman governor built a *khān* and a bathhouse. The qāḍī cancelled the pasha's business transactions concerning these buildings, which had been approved by a previous qāḍī; nor did he allow his deputies to approve them (Ibn Ṭūlūn 1956, 330).

In a rare case in 967/1560, a street fight erupted between the chief qāḍī's retinue and the governor's men. The qāḍī, Muḥammad b. Abūssaʿūd al-ʿImādī, was popular; he was a poet and was kind to the poor. He built a castle in Damascus, planted aromatic plants and arranged an irrigation system for his garden. Aḥmad Pasha was also a builder and developer. While the judge was riding in the street followed by a retinue of notables and many bodyguards, he came across a swing, with a band playing music and drums beating, not paying respect to him. The qāḍī's horse reared and he almost fell off it. The qāḍī ordered his men to tear up the pasha's drum and to remove the swing. The pasha's men cut the mounts' tails. As a result, several deputy qāḍīs fell of their mules. The qāḍī's guards had to protect him. Both the qāḍī and the pasha sent petitions to Istanbul. Both were transferred to other towns (Ibn Ṭūlūn 1956, 328; Būrīnī 1959–63, 1: 73–7; Anṣārī 1991, 2: 170).

The Ottoman chief qāḍīs, more than anyone else, including even the Pasha, determined the location of the law courts in Damascus. The site of the chief qāḍī's court frequently changed.[13]

The qāḍī appointed (sometimes with the pasha) local religious office holders like *muftīs*, *madrasa* teachers and mosque preachers. Often the qāḍī divided one teaching position between two candidates. It also happened that the qāḍī forbade anyone else from writing *fatwās* and attempted to impose censorship on the contents of public lessons (Ghazzī 1981, 1: 14 ff.; Ibn Ṭūlūn 1956, 316–17).

---

[13] For example, Ibn Ṭūlūn 2002, 170; Ibn Ṭūlūn 1956, 312; see also above al-Murādī's report about the two qāḍīs of the al-Bakrī family (p. 94).

The Ottoman Qāḍīs' Personnel and Subordinates

The Chief Qāḍī's principal assistants were deputy qāḍīs (*nā'ib* pl. *nuwwāb*); *mutasallim* (a jurist or official who came to Damascus before a newly-appointed qāḍī to prepare his beginning of his service); *qassām*, 'a divider', who taxed inheritances of members of the military; *qāḍī al-rakb al-Shāmī* (the judge of the annual Syrian pilgrims' caravan going to the *Ḥajj*); *kuttāb*, secretaries of the court; *qāḍī al-kashf*, the magistrate who investigated criminal cases; *kātib al-ʿarḍ*, 'the clerk of the petitions', a Turkish secretary who reported to the sultan on behalf of the qāḍī or the pasha; *qāḍī al-barr*, a judge responsible for the outlying districts of the Province of Damascus; and a judge appointed by the chief qāḍī to be responsible for matters of orphans and missing persons (Ibn Ṭūlūn 1964, 2: 92).

Danishmends, literally learned men, *madrasa* graduates, were, in our context, the clerks whom Ottoman qāḍīs brought with them from Istanbul to assist them in their work. In 999/1591, a new chief qāḍī appointed a *dānishmend* in each court to write in the *sijill* registers and dismissed the *shuhūd* (sing. *shāhid*), the local professional witnesses, or notaries, who had performed this work until then. The *dānishmends* are described sometimes as violent men, occasionally accused of debauchery (Ibn Ṭūlūn 1956, 318, Ibn Ṭūlūn 2002: 321, Būrīnī 1959, 77–84, Anṣarī 1991, 1: 159, 164, 2: 206).

The Arabic sources often refer to the chief Ottoman qāḍī as *al-qāḍī al-kabīr* ('the great qāḍī') or by the old Arabic title *aqḍā al-quḍāt*, the head of the qāḍīs. The only local qāḍī to whom the Damascene chronicles referred as *aqḍā a-quḍāt* was Muḥibb al-Dīn b. Taqī al-Dīn al-Ḥamawī (see below). Those were not official Ottoman titles, however. These refer to the chief judge as simply *qāḍī*, or sometimes *Shehir menlāsı* (the city judge). The Arabic sources call the local deputy judges *nā'ib*, or often *qāḍī*, while the Ottoman sources refer to them merely as *nā'ib*.

The *nuwwāb quḍāt* were subordinate to the Ottoman qāḍī. Yet it is important to remember that they were the real backbone of the judicial and administrative system, and had the continuity and the permanence that the Istanbul-appointed qāḍīs could not obtain in their short terms of office. One Ḥanbalī *nā'ib* served in that post over forty years (Ghazzī 1981, 1: 26–9; Muḥibbī 1966, 4: 143–44; Rafeq 1966, 47).

The Special Case of Muḥibb al-Dīn b. Taqī al-Dīn Abū al-Faḍl al-Ḥamawī (949/1542–1016/1608)[14]

He was an Arab deputy judge who obtained a unique position and prestige in Damascus, more than many Ottoman chief qāḍīs could hope for. Muḥibb al-Dīn al-Ḥamawī was the first one of his family who came from Ḥamāh to Damascus. He was the great-grandfather of the important seventeenth-century historian Muḥammad Amīn al-Muḥibbī (d. 1111/1699). His father was a clerk at a law court in Ḥamāh and was a follower of ʿAlwān b. ʿAṭiyya al-Shādhilī al-Ḥamawī, a famous Sufi Shaykh.

Muḥibb al-Dīn was a great scholar and writer. Among many other works, he authored three travel accounts—on Egypt, Tabriz and Turkey. He studied in Ḥamāh, Aleppo, Damascus, Egypt and the Turkish regions. He changed his *madhhab* from Shāfiʿism to Ḥanafism, citing intellectual preference as the reason. It is more probable that as a Ḥanafī he could rise higher in the Ottoman system. In this period quite a few Shāfiʿīs, and also several Ḥanbalīs, converted to the Ḥanafī *madhhab*; never the other way round. Yet in his personal devotions he mostly followed the Shāfiʿī *madhhab*. Muḥibb al-Dīn mastered Arabic, Turkish and Persian, and maintained close contacts with high Ottoman *ʿulamāʾ*. An especially significant relationship was that with Çivizāde, the future *Sheyhülislām*, whom he accompanied to Damascus, Jerusalem and Egypt. Muḥibb al-Dīn served as qāḍī of Fuwwa near Alexandria, and then in numerous small provincial towns in Syria. Later he was appointed as teacher in several *madrasa*s in Damascus. He married a daughter of Ismāʿīl b. Aḥmad al-Nābulusī, head of a wealthy family of Shāfiʿī *ʿulamāʾ* and qāḍīs. After his wife's death, he married her sister. Muḥibb al-Dīn obtained the right to educate al-Nābulusī's children, and took control of his vast property and his slaves. He became the leading *ʿālim* of Damascus. He was given a stipend from the taxes on the *dhimmī*s, the *jawālī*. He was appointed as teacher in two *madrasa*s that had been designated for Shāfiʿī scholars by the founder of the *waqf*. Yet the Shāfiʿīs forgave him owing to his friendly attitude toward them.

[14] Ṣabbāgh 1986, 48–57; Muḥibbī 1966, 3: 322–31; Ghazzī 1945–59, 3: 206–13.

Later Muḥibb al-Dīn fulfilled several judicial tasks in the Province of Damascus. He was appointed by the Sultan as the Ḥanafī *muftī* of Damascus. He served as the *qāḍī ʿaskar* of the campaign against a rebel in Syria and as the judge of the Syrian *ḥajj* caravan. He was often the interim judge (*qāḍī mā bayn*) until the arrival of a new Ottoman qāḍī. He was given the unique authority to appoint independently all the Ḥanafī deputies, among them several Rūmīs (Turks).

Ethnicity: Awlād ʿArab *and* Arwām

Historians and biographers were sensitive to the relations between the Arabs (*awlād ʿArab*) and Turks (*Rūmīs, Arwām*). They mention only very rare expressions of negative attitudes of Ottoman qāḍīs towards Arabs. There are a few exceptions, however. Aḥmad Efendi b. Muḥammad Sheykhzāde (appointed in 1022/1613) used to call the Arabs "*tat*," a pejorative term used at the time for non-Turks, Arabs in particular. Al-Būrīnī considered him a good qāḍī, but an unpleasant man (Būrīnī 1959, 1: 196–97).

Another Ottoman qāḍī, who served in Damascus toward the end of the sixteenth century, is mentioned by the historian and deputy judge Sharaf al-Dīn Mūsā b. Yūsuf al-Anṣārī as being hostile to his Arab deputies (Anṣarī 1991, 1: 166–67).

Yet the opposite, namely, positive attitudes toward the Arabs are more common. A good example is Muḥammad b. Bustān, who was the qāḍī in Damascus from 981/1573 to 983/1575 or 1576 (d. 1006/1598). Later he was appointed to Cairo then *Ḳāżī ʿasker* in Anatolia and Rumeli, and finally he became *Sheyhülislām*. Najm al-Dīn al-Ghazzī heard him say that while he was serving in Cairo he constantly visited the sepulcher of al-Imām al-Shāfiʿī to ask for his assistance in carrying out his duties, telling him: "Oh, Imām, this is your town. This or that has happened, and I ask for your help." He was a great scholar and his Arabic was excellent. In Damascus he was in contact with Badr al-Dīn al-Ghazzī, the historian's father. He said that the families of Raḍiyy al-Dīn, that is, al-Ghazzīs, the leading *ʿulamāʾ* and Sufis of Damascus, and al-Bakrīs, a famous aristocratic Sufi family in Cairo, would last forever (Ghazzī 1981, 1: 102–6; Muḥibbī 1966, 4: 223–24).

In the eighteenth century, al-Murādī tells in his *Silk al-Durar* about a ranking Ottoman qāḍī and scholar, Isḥāq Efendi Munlajiqzāde

(d. 1195/1781), who studied under the outstanding *ʿulamāʾ* of Damascus, including the historian's grandfather who was the Ḥanafī *muftī* of the town. "He liked the Arabs (*abnāʾ al-ʿArab*) and spoke about their good qualities and spoke in literary Arabic" (Murādī 1966, 1: 221–22).

Al-Būrīnī wrote a highly laudatory biography of Aḥmad Efendi b. Ḥasan Bey who was appointed qāḍī of Damascus in 994 AH. He was an expert on Arabic language and poetry and collected Arabic books. "He liked the Arabs and imitated their clothes, wearing the wide robe (*farjiyya*) with the large and wide sleeves according to the fashion of the Arab judges and jurisprudents (*mawālī*)" (Būrīnī 1959, 1: 66–72).

Religiosity

A distinction must be made between individual qāḍīs' religiosity, as it is described by the local observers, and the policies and attitudes of the Ottoman Empire: generally, it proved as staunchly orthodox as the Mamluk state had been. The individual qāḍīs were judged by public opinion, of which the biographers and chroniclers are reliable exponents, by their personal religiosity and their policies in that all-important sphere. Again, in most cases the impressions of the Damascene were favorable.

In Shaʿbān 940, a new chief qāḍī, Shihāb al-Dīn Aḥmad Karaoğlu, arrived in Damascus. Ibn Ṭūlūn describes him as an old man with Sufi inclinations. He visited all the sacred sites in the town. When he saw people gambling with eggs, he ordered that they be broken, but compensated the owners. In Ramaḍān, he proclaimed that no youthful woman (*imraʾa ṭifla*) should go out in public, on pain of arrest, even if accompanied by her husband or another male relative. The qāḍī also imposed strict rules of modesty in the *ḥammām*—for example that no young beardless youth should enter the Umayyad mosque at night. Ibn Ṭūlūn approved of all these measures and said that they were beneficial.

This qāḍī considered imposing censorship on what the *ʿulamāʾ* of Damascus taught in public. He demanded to see and approve everything that any *ʿālim* would teach. A young scholar showed him his materia, and the qāḍī liked it and allowed everybody to attend. Women were permitted to listen behind a curtain. It is clear that the idea to supervise the texts that were to be taught was the qāḍī's own and not the policy of the central government. This was an isolated case.

The Qāḍī died at the end of 941/1534. During his terminal illness he visited the tombs of the holy men in Damascus and the suburbs. Then forty-one Qur'ān readers, each named Muḥammad, recited from the Qur'ān the chapter of *al-Anʿām* (the Cattle) and prayed for his recovery. He donated meat to the needy and prisoners. He set free prisoners who had light sentences. He manumitted all his slaves, more than thirty in number. He turned his library into *waqf* to be placed at the tomb of his master at the sepulcher of Abū Ayyūb al-Anṣārī in Istanbul. He died reciting his *wird* (Sufi litany). Ibn Ṭūlūn concludes that he was the best of the Turkish qāḍīs (Ibn Ṭulūn 1956: 316–17; Anṣārī 1991, 2: 111 ff.).

On two occasions, in 931/1525 and 939/1532–33, when Damascus was hit by a plague (*ṭāʿūn*), the Ottoman qāḍī sent his family to the villages surrounding the town to protect them. It was of no use—the qāḍī lost his two sons to the plague. The chronicler notes that this behavior (namely, leaving the plague-infested region) was contrary to Islamic law "according to the view of the wise Arab *ʿulamāʾ*" (Ibn Ṭulūn 1956: 311, 315).

Aḥmad b. Sheykhzāde (arrived in Damascus 1022/1613) was a qāḍī who was considered ideal in religious observation and keeping religion in the public space. He was a scholar in the religious sciences and very thorough in his investigations. He attempted to remove anything that was 'objectionable'. For example, he ordered the removal of a certain wooden hut erected by a janissary officer next to the Umayyad mosque, saying that it was forbidden to impose restrictions (on public access to a mosque). He strictly inspected the *awqāf* of the mosques and *madrasa*s in Damascus, criticizing the trustees for excessive expenses. The qāḍī also declared that living in *madrasa*s was wrong. He participated in all pubic payers at the Umayyad mosque. He used to tour the space around the mosque. In his personal ablutions he was strict and renewed the ritual for a white secretion or a tear in his eye (Ghazzī 1981, 1: 296–300; Muḥibbī 1966, 1: 172–73).

Certain variations in the reading of religious texts and performing of rituals, while not theologically controversial in most cases, brought criticism and even ridicule among the Damascene *ʿulamāʾ*. A few examples demonstrate this point: Ibn Ṭūlūn mentions a disagreement between the Shāfiʿīs and the Turks over the details of a prayer (Ibn Ṭūlūn 1964, 2: 380), and another that he had with Qaḍī al-Fenerī at the end of 923/1517 concerning the Ḥanafī system of determining the new month of Dhū'l-Ḥijja (ibid., 75). In 927/1521, the Ottoman governor dismissed Taqī al-Dīn al-Qārī, an important Shāfiʿī scholar, from all his positions and arrested him for saying that it was not permissible to pray behind the Ḥanafīs (meaning the Ottomans) and for calling the Ottomans innovators (*bidaʿiyya*). Someone, an admirer of Muḥyī'l-Dīn b. al-ʿArabī, the famous fourteenth-century Andalusian mystic who is buried in Damascus, interceded for al-Qārī and he was pardoned (Ibn Ṭūlūn 2002, 135).

The admiration of Ibn al-ʿArabī's doctrine was much more widespread among the Turks than among the Arabs, whose Sufism tended to be more orthodox. As soon as Selīm conquered Damascus, he ordered the construction of a mosque on the tomb of Ibn al-ʿArabī. Later, Ibn Zīrik, the *Ḳāżīʿasker* of Anatolia, paid a visit to the site and gave money to its guardians (Ibn Ṭūlūn 1964, 2: 40, 77).

It is reported in the Arabic sources that in 948/1541 Sultan Süleymān *Ḳānūnī* dismissed Çivizāde from his position as *Sheyhülislām* of the Empire, reportedly for opposing the doctrines of Ibn al-ʿArabī "while the majority of the Turks admired them," according to the Arabic sources.[15]

Ibn al-Fenerī, the first Ottoman qāḍī of Damascus, demonstrated his Sunnī zeal when in Muḥarram 924 AH he complied with the demand of the Sufis to disperse the *ʿĀshūrā'* procession of Persian Shīʿīs. He had their flag broken and ordered that they be beaten (Ibn Ṭūlūn 1964, 2: 78–9).

That the well-known Ottoman tolerance of Christians and Jews[16] did not extend to the Shīʿīs was demonstrated in 942/1535 by the public burning to death of two Shīʿīs by the order of ʿOsmān b.

[15] Ibn Ṭūlūn 2002, 341; Ghazzī 1945–59, 1: 116; 2: 28, 49. Evidence about the accuracy of the statement that the Ottomans admired Ibn al-ʿArabī and his ideas—and Sufism generally—abounds. See, for example, ibid., 343 (their veneration of Shaykh al-Ṣamādī). According to Ibn Ṭūlūn (1964, 2: 92), Turkish prominent men visited Ibn al-ʿArabī's tomb before leaving Damascus. Even if the Damascene historian was not well informed about the real reasons behind Çivizāde's dismissal, the fact remains that the impression of educated Arabs was that it would be unsafe to criticize Ibn al-ʿArabī's ideas.

[16] This statement must be somewhat qualified. In 923/1517, in the first year of Ottoman rule, it was proclaimed in Damascus that Jews, Samaritans, local and foreign, and European Christians are not permitted to ride any mounts. See Ibn Ṭūlūn 1964, 2: 66. Of course, this decree was nothing new.

Isrāfīl, another Ottoman qāḍī. When Quṭb al-Dīn b. Sulṭān, the Ḥanafī *muftī* of Damascus was asked about the case, he said that taking such action was not permissible according to Islamic law; the Shīʿīs should have been given the option of repentance (Ibn Ṭūlūn 2002, 299).

A few serious clashes between the Ottoman and the local population are recorded in the early decades of Ottoman rule. For example, in 931/1525, the Ottomans took over the old Ḥanbalī *madrasa* of Shaykh Ibn ʿUmar at al-Ṣāliḥiyya suburb. They destroyed the small rooms of the theology students, threw out the books and had 'the lowliest of the Turks' live there, according to Ibn Ṭūlūn's report (Ibn Ṭūlūn 2002, 175). In 937/1531, ʿOsmān b. Isrāfīl, the Ottoman chief qāḍī, took control of libraries that had been founded by *awqāf* for the benefit of students of religion, and allocated the books for the exclusive use 'of the Turks and those who are under their protection' (Ibn Ṭūlūn 1956, 315).

Ibn Ṭūlūn tells that in 938/1532 he was approached by a bureaucrat in charge of assessing land taxes who tried to get from him a legal ruling that would enable the Ottomans to regard the Province of Damascus as tithe land (*ʿushr*). Ibn Ṭūlūn insisted that it was *kharāj* land (Ibn Ṭūlūn 2002, 246–47).

In 950/1543 or 1544, the Ottoman qāḍī Yūsuf b. Ḥusām al-Dīn b. Ilyās ordered that it be proclaimed to the cafes in Damascus that drinking coffee in a group with singing and the passing around of the cups was forbidden; that those caught doing it would be flogged. When Quṭb al-Dīn Muḥammad b. Sulṭān, the Ḥanafī *muftī*, was asked about this, he said that the chief qāḍī may prohibit drinking the beverage in this manner and selling it, since what may lead to forbidden things (*ḥarām*) is forbidden. The qāḍī thanked the *muftī* for his opinion, and produced a written ruling that drinking coffee is forbidden if it reaches the degree of intoxication, that is, if the user raves, or if one drinks with the purpose of entertainment and rapture. If the purpose of drinking coffee is different, it is still forbidden according to Shāfiʿīs, Mālikīs and the Ḥanbalīs. The Ḥanafīs do not object, if the beverage is consumed privately. Yet if people convene to drink it in the same manner as people drink wine, as is the custom in these places, there is no doubt that it is forbidden, particularly if it is done by passing the cup around, accompanied by singing and the music of the *mizmār* (single-pipe wood-wind instrument). Generally, the harms of coffee outweigh its benefits, and the ruler ought to forbid it, following the principle of caution. So it is right to forbid it in any event. The Ḥanafī *muftī* endorsed that decision. Here we have an interesting case of a qāḍī acting as a *muftī*. This gives an idea of the religious and cultural norms of the Ottoman qāḍīs and the *muftī*s in the sixteenth century. The religious authorities, as seen so often, objected to the people having a good time.[17]

Images of the Ottoman Qāḍīs in Damascus and Cairo: A Comparative Note

There is an abundance of information about the Ottoman, Istanbul-appointed, qāḍīs of Damascus. The principal sources are the excellent biographical dictionaries. Almost all the writers were *ʿulamāʾ*, some of whom or whose family members were deputy qāḍīs (*nuwwāb*), and the world of the *madrasa* and the law courts was the one they knew best. They were interested in the history of the qāḍīs of Damascus from the early days of Islam, particularly since the Ottoman conquest, and they could rely on a long local historiographic tradition on that subject.[18] It is also important to note that almost all of them were natives of Damascus with a strong attachment to their town and country, and to their Arabic culture and Arab identity. At the same time, they can be described as loyal Ottoman subjects, and they expressed their support of the sultans and the Empire on many occasions.

The attitudes of the Damascus historians toward the Ottoman qāḍīs were generally favorable, in contradistinction with the feelings in Egypt. The Ottoman chief qāḍīs of Damascus were judged by the historians on their own merit, and in the majority of cases they were described as pious, knowledgeable and just. They were involved in the religious and scholarly life of Damascus. They had close relations with the leading *ʿulamāʾ* of the town, showing them respect, and they left their impact by their decisions and appointments of local *ʿulamāʾ* to the various teaching, preaching and administrative

[17] Ibid., 355–60. Ibn Ṭūlūn cites similar decisions from the late Mamluk period. He recounts that he himself consumed coffee and did not observe any damage. Professor Amnon Cohen has told me about older texts that are similar or identical to the above-mentioned *fatwā*.

[18] On the historical knowledge about the qāḍīs of Damascus in previous centuries, see Anṣārī 1991, 1: 225 ff.; Güneş 1981, 106, 111.

positions in Damascus. On the other hand, the Ottoman chief qāḍīs of Cairo are barely noticed by the Egyptian chroniclers.[19] The few cases in which they are mentioned only demonstrate their marginality and lack of relevance to the religious, intellectual and social life of Cairo. Moreover, quite a few Ottoman qāḍīs in Damascus are praised by the chroniclers and writers for trying to help the population. I have not come across a single case in which the historians of Cairo regarded the Ottoman qāḍī as being actively on the side of the local population.

The reasons for the marked contrast between the great Arab cities in this respect lies in the special character of each of them. Geography, the proximity of Damascus (and even more so of Aleppo) to Istanbul plays a part. But the special status of Egypt provides the main explanation. Many of the ranking *ʿulamāʾ* of Damascus traveled frequently to Istanbul and learned to speak Turkish: our historians and biographers themselves are outstanding examples. The Egyptians were not given to traveling. Educationally, Cairo was self-sufficient, and al-Azhar attracted students from the Turkish parts of the Empire and from Syria—not the reverse. Bilingualism among the *ʿulamāʾ* was more rare in Cairo than in Damascus.

Another difference between Cairo and Damascus is the huge size of the Egyptian capital. The Turkish presence was considerable in Cairo; many soldiers, administrators, and traders lived there permanently, often in their own enclaves. Evliyā Çelebi, the famous Turkish traveler, who describes Egypt in the second half of the seventeenth century, gives a clear picture of exclusively Turkish congregations in specific mosques (Evliyā Çelebi 1938, 10: 216, 218, 235, 239, 467). In this social and linguistic situation, the Ottoman qāḍīs were quite isolated from the Egyptian *ʿulamāʾ*, despite their high position.

Finally, there was the Ottoman special (and wise) policy towards Egypt. The Ottomans administered it in a manner that would ensure their strategic and economic interests, yet refrained from interfering in Egypt's religious and scholarly life. They respected the unique character of Egypt as the center of Islamic scholarship and culture for centuries. The notable example is the total independence of al-

[19] Ibn Iyās (1961, 5: 467), Ibn Ṭūlūn's Egyptian contemporary, and like him an eyewitness of the Ottoman conquest, describes the Ottoman *Ḳāżīʿasker* as 'more ignorant than a donkey, who does not know anything about *Sharʿī* rules'.

Azhar under Ottoman rule. The office of *Shaykh al-Azhar* was invariably in the hands of either a Shāfiʿī or a Mālikī, never a Ḥanafī, the official Ottoman legal school. Nor did the Ottomans interfere in the inner struggles over that position.

Concluding Remarks

It was necessary to limit the present study to the discussion of those qāḍīs who were sent from the center of the Ottoman Empire to serve in Damascus, as well as other cities. I am preparing a related but separate article about the local Damascene judges who served as *nuwwāb*, or deputy qāḍīs. They were the backbone of the Ottoman judicial and administrative system in the province, often yielding more real influence than the chief qāḍīs who served much shorter periods.

After the first years of Ottoman rule in Damascus, it became clear that the initial suspicions and fears of the Muslim Damascus elite concerning the Ottoman regime's Islamic policies were exaggerated. We have seen that by and large the Ottoman qāḍīs, as the most visible and direct representatives of the Ottoman state in public and religious matters, won the approval and respect of the local public, as expressed by the historians and the biographers of the three first centuries of Ottoman rule in the Province of Damascus.

CHAPTER SIX

PATRONAGE, INTERVENTION AND VIOLENCE IN THE LEGAL PROCESS IN EIGHTEENTH-CENTURY SALONICA AND ITS PROVINCE

Eyal Ginio

Abşir Ağa, the Chief Black Eunuch (*darüssaade ağası*) and administrator of the endowments in favor of the two holy cities of Islam—Mecca and Medina (*harameyn-ı muhtarameyn evkafı*)—petitioned the Imperial Diwan (*divan-ı hümayun*) in November 1752 requesting the release of Nikola, the son of Estamoni, who had claimed (*iddia eden*) to be the *koca başı*, the head of the village of Mukritsa [?]. We further learn from the sultanic decree issued on this matter that Nikola had previously been declared a depraved person who disturbed the public order by performing all kinds of wicked deeds; consequently, he was imprisoned (*kalebend*) in the citadel of Salonica. The relations between the Chief Eunuch, one of the most powerful persons in the Ottoman political hierarchy, and this Christian villager later became apparent: Nikola can be described as a low-ranking semi-official due to his alleged position as a head of a village, one of the few semi-official positions that Christian villagers could hold in the Ottoman state prior to the reforms of the nineteenth century. Nikola's village was part (*mukataa*) of the pious endowments that came under the supervision (*nezaret*) of the Chief Eunuch. This may explain the latter's sudden intervention, claiming that the Christian villager had repented (*islah-ı nefs*) and therefore asking for the Sultan's compassion

* Note of transliteration: In this chapter I opted to use the current Modern Turkish mode of spelling Ottoman terms. The locations mentioned in this chapter are today situated in Greece, Turkey, Bulgaria, Albania and the Former Yugoslav Republic of Macedonia. In the chapter I used the Ottoman names transliterated into Modern Turkish. If different, I also added in parentheses the current name of the location.

* Author's acknowledgments: While preparing this chapter, I benefited, as a Stanley J. Seeger visiting fellow, from the generosity and hospitality of the Program in Hellenic Studies at Princeton University. I would also like to thank Molly Greene for reading my chapter and for her valuable comments.

(*istida-yi merhamet*) and for Nikola's release from prison—on condition that he refrains from interfering in the affairs of his village or of his fellow villagers. Accepting the Chief Eunuch's declaration, the Sultan ordered the inmate freed on the grounds of his repentance (*kendi halinde olup*), thus justifying the release with an explanation that dovetails with the punishment's purpose. The Chief Eunuch affixed his own few lines below the sultanic decree, in which he bid the citadel's commander to abide by the edict, and he added his own signature. The use of the first person in these few lines (*taht-ı nezaretimizde*), a linguistic device normally employed in decrees announcing the Sultan's decisions, emphasizes the Chief Eunuch's interest and involvement in this particular case.[1]

The successful intervention of the Chief Eunuch in favor of his apparent protégé indicates an important feature of the Ottoman legal process, a feature that rarely appears in the written legal manuals: the ability of external elements who did not hold any formal role in one of the official courts and who were not related directly to the case in question, to shape, influence and even alter the legal process found in the various official courts of the Ottoman period. Similarly, this intervention well demonstrates the significance of social networks, sometimes transcending religious boundaries, in Ottoman society in determining one's ability to negotiate his position vis-à-vis the various state agents and to use the legal resources available to him.

This observance is pertinent to the ongoing debate on the efficiency of the Ottoman legal system prior to the westernizing legal reforms of the nineteenth century, and its ability to present an independent, predictable and cohesive judicial process based on a well-known system of rules. The Weberian derisive concept of *kadijustiz*, long prevailing in the study of Islamic law, depicted a Muslim legal system that was devoid of the fundamental elements of Western law: rationality, formality, consistency, predictability and independence from external involvement and extra-legal considerations. Recent studies, however, drawing their conclusions from different Ottoman case studies, refuted such a presentation, at least with regard to the implications of the Ottoman legal system in particular provinces at different times. Haim Gerber's study on seventeenth-century Bursa (Gerber

[1] The Historical Archives of Macedonia, Salonica, *Sicil* vol. 82, p. 35, 3 Muharrem 1166 [10 November 1752].

1994) is a major example of this tendency to reevaluate previous assumptions on the implications of Islamic law in an Ottoman city.[2] This chapter aims to contribute to this discussion by exploring the ability of external factors to intervene in the legal process as registered in the *sicil* of eighteenth-century Salonica, or even to be in a position to compete with official courts and to interfere with issued verdicts. As part of the general discussion on the power relations between the kadi's court and the surrounding society, we can ask to what extent was the kadi directed in his decisions by local interventions, vested interests and even threats or direct violence? What role did the local community play in the legal arena? These questions lie at the center of this chapter.

The Kadi's Court in Ottoman Salonica and Its Place in the Local Legal System

Ronald Jennings' observation about the 'limitation of the judicial powers of the kadi' (Jennings 1979, 151–84), when discussing the function of the kadi's court in seventeenth-century Kayseri, is significant to our discussion. As in Ottoman Kayseri, the kadi's court was not the only forum in which to solve legal problems in eighteenth-century Salonica; nor did the kadi hold a monopoly over the legal process. Salonicans could solve their problems with the help of an assortment of local dignitaries and officials whose names and positions often elude the modern researcher, but their traces are evident in the *sicil*: from local officials, heads of guilds, spiritual leaders of the different religious communities and urban magnates to the governors of Rumeli and to the Sultan himself.

Indeed, at the top of the legal process stood the Sultan, who was obligated to uphold justice in his realm. Suraiya Faroqhi notes that one of the major devices of commoners in the Ottoman lands, to seek redress for their grievances against the state's local agents, including the kadis, was to petition for the Sultan's intervention, through his Imperial Diwan (*divan-ı hümayun*) (Faroqhi 1992, 1–39). Michael Ursinus observes that the Imperial Diwan in Istanbul served in a wider sense as a 'court of appeal' that acted in response to petitions

[2] For a discussion about the current debate, see Kermeli 2002, 129–36; Powers 2002, 23–52.

that came from all corners of the state. In this capacity, it reflected the ruler's obligation to thwart any mistreatment of the subject population by local officials and, thus, ensured a direct link between the ruler and his subjects (Ursinus 2005, 3). Furthermore, while the authority of the Ottoman center clearly diminished in the Balkans during the eighteenth century, the Salonican *sicil* suggests that the image and symbolic perception of the Sultan as the ultimate source of justice remained vigorous and untarnished. People continued during this period to seek justice by addressing the Sultan with petitions and complaints about misdeeds and wrongs that they had endured.

As I showed elsewhere (Ginio 1998, 185–209), the existence of various venues to solve conflicts and to address injustices rendered the kadi's role as a judge only secondary in eighteenth-century Salonica. Therefore, any discussion of the Ottoman legal system in the provinces cannot limit itself to a study of the legal process that took place under the kadi's jurisdiction in his court, the *mahkeme*, and ignore other formal and non-formal institutions of adjudication and conciliation—as most cases registered in the *sicil* were settled through mediation (*sulh*). The kadi's role was limited in such cases to providing the litigants with an official document (*hüccet*) that registered the compromise and thereby empowered it with official recognition. As no other legal archive survived from eighteenth-century Salonica, it seems that such a conclusion can only lead us to an impasse. However, the capacity of the kadi as an administrator casts some light on the legal process that took place in other arenas.

The petition of the Chief Eunuch discussed above is an illustrative example: while we gain access to this particular official's intervention through the kadi's registers, it should be borne in mind that the kadi's role in this case, as in many others, was only marginal from the judicial perspective—he had to ensure the proper execution of the Sultan's will as it appeared in the issued decrees. It was his role as the major administrator in Salonica that required his listing as one of the recipients of the decrees, a step that also ensured the registration of a case in the kadi's records. Put differently, though the *şeriat* played only a secondary role in judging felons in Salonica, the kadi's *mahkeme* was, nevertheless, a central local administrative hub for running the city and its province. Indeed, Leslie Peirce suggests in her discussion on sixteenth-century Aintab that the use of the term 'local court' rather than '*şeriat* court' is much more apt when referring to the kadis' courts in pre-nineteenth-century Ottoman judicial system as the vast responsibilities and multiple roles that were vested in this court implied also administrative, notarial, and legal functions (Peirce 2003, 90–1. See also Ergene 2003, 35–7, 48–55).

These various capacities make the records of the kadi's court a unique source that can shed light on different features of Ottoman urban history. Among other things, the kadi's records provide researchers with insight into individuals whose voices are generally absent from other historical sources (women, slaves, villagers and nomads, just to mention some examples). While similar textual records were compiled by other pre-modern Muslim societies, with some rare exceptions, only the Ottoman records from various places survived the vicissitudes of time.

Therefore, thanks to the survival of the *sicil* in large numbers since the late fifteenth century (in Salonica the earliest surviving volume begins in 1694), the Ottoman period presents a promising case study, already amply used by several scholars, who studied various features of Ottoman urban society as it was portrayed in the *sicil*. Among other merits, these records, compiled by scribes under the supervision of the kadi, provide descriptive documentation that exemplifies the court's judicial practice, as well as indications of the legal activities pertaining to dispute resolution that took place in other formal or non-formal venues in Ottoman Salonica.

Generally speaking, these records are brief summaries, in rigid administrative jargon, that present the spectrum of cases heard in court; their phraseology ostensibly implies seamless order and control. Yet, it should be noted that these records present a very clear discourse that was crafted by the scribes according to a particular set of requirements and representations, and possibly also legal manuals that provided typical formats for different kinds of cases (Peirce 2003, 100–6). The particular unfolding of events over time and the voices of the litigants, the eyewitnesses, the scribes, the kadi and especially those of others who were present in court during the litigation, but did not fill any formal role in court (family members, friends, etc.), virtually disappear in these records; the drama of the judicial process, the emotions involved, are converted into brief, dry reports that follow almost-identical patterns.[3]

[3] On the methodical questions involving the use of the *sicil* as a historical source, see Zeevi 1998, 35–6.

One major exception to this rule is the registration of decrees that arrived from the Imperial Diwan in response to petitions submitted by people from all strata of society. While the wording of these decrees is formal, not to say pompous, it nevertheless gives some indications of the sultan's decisions and the correspondence that led to their issuing. In this manner, we can learn about the strategies of individuals who attempted to manipulate the legal process on their own behalf or in favor of others. Volume 30 of the Salonican *sicil* is a register that overwhelmingly records the responses of the Imperial Diwan to petitions against misdeeds by local officials in the province of Salonica. Many of the cases raised below are found in this volume.

Before proceeding to the discussion on external interference, a brief historical contextualization is required.

The Historical Context: The Rise of Local Powers in the Ottoman Balkans

One of the main arguments of this chapter is that the capacity of local officials and notables (contemporarily known as *âyan*) to successfully intervene in the judicial process was a clear feature of eighteenth-century legal routine in Salonica—a reflection of the deteriorating power of the center to enforce its will in its Balkan provinces. This period saw the rise of local military leaders who seized political power from the center by various means: exploiting the support of certain high officials in the center, forging local networks of patronage with locals, taking possession of economic resources or by sustaining independent armed units. At times during the eighteenth century, some of these local notables actually controlled parts of the Balkans independently of central domination, though they did not challenge the Ottomans' general legitimacy to rule and formally pledged allegiance to the ruling dynasty in Istanbul. This continuing symbolic authority of the Sultan may also explain the endurance of the Sultan's image as the ultimate source of justice, a phenomenon already noted above.

In some cases the central authorities tacitly acknowledged, even if only temporarily, this reality by bestowing official titles and posts upon the upstarts. The competition over power between the representatives of the central authorities in Istanbul and local powerful magnates, mainly military officers and landholders, and the internal clashes among different pretenders to hold provincial power led to a series of mutinies and suppressions that characterized much of the eighteenth century in the Ottoman Balkans.[4]

While the emphasis in historical study is on military and political challenges that the central authorities had to contend with, there were also civilian elements, at least in Salonica, that competed with the authorities by inserting their own agendas. An illustrative example is the rise of the guild that represented Muslim merchants who handled the lucrative commerce with Egypt. Their self-confidence and power were reflected in their ability to construct a Friday mosque, hitherto a privilege enjoyed by the dominant agents of the state (governors, chief administrators, etc.), and to support their mosque with an endowment (Ginio forthcoming).

These influential local people were commonly defined in the *sicil* as *âyan*, 'local notables'. Their potential to meddle in the affairs of local administrators and even to challenge the normative order, as defined by the state, is stated regularly in the records to the extent that warnings against their interference became fixed clauses in many edicts, such as those that dealt with taxes. A telling example is found in the orders that sanctioned the collecting of the Gypsies' poll tax (*kiptîyan cizyesi*). The Gypsies, one of the weakest segments in Ottoman society, served as easy prey for local magnates who could extort taxes from them at the expense of the state—the danger of which the authorities were aware.[5]

During the period under discussion, some *âyan* even challenged the privileged status of those who held positions of *askerî*, who were in the service of the Sultan, and thus were enjoying various privileges, including legal ones. One petition submitted by a group of *askeri* indicates the scale of the problem. This group of privileged men complained that while according to the sultanic law, the *kanun*, they could be summoned to the kadi's court for adjudication only with the consent of their officers, some *âyan* had the audacity to claim against them: 'We [can] apprehend and jail' (*biz ahiz ve hapis ederiz diye*) and to arrest *askeri*s in citadels against the *şerʿi* law and without any formal decree.[6]

---

[4] See, for example, Anastasopulos 2002, 73–88. For a general discussion on this chronic problem, see Brummett 1998, 91–107.

[5] See, for example, the notification of the collectors of the Gypsies' *cizye* against such intrusions by local *âyan: sicil*, vol. 8, pp. 79–80, 2 Rebiüevvel 1113 [5 September 1701].

[6] *Sicil*, vol. 32, p. 71, *evahir-i* Rebiülahir 1132 [2–11 March 1720].

This encroachment on the right to mete out punishment exemplifies the extent of power achieved by local *âyan* at the time. The 'Age of the *Âyan*', as the eighteenth century is sometimes referred to (Sadat 1972, 346–63; McGowan 1994, 2: 658–63), evidently presented more possibilities of local persons, officials and non-officials, to intervene in the legal process. Basing his conclusion on findings from seventeenth-century Bursa, Gerber argues that he was not able to retrieve even one case of officials' interventions in the judicial process. Moreover, he also questions the possibility of finding traces for such interventions in the written records (Gerber 1994, 40). The *sicil* of Salonica does, in fact, unambiguously refer to such interventions. This interference of local magnates—*âyan* or local officials (the distinction between these two groups was not always clear as more and more *âyan* gained official appointments)—could occur at two particular levels of the legal process. The first was found only following the issue of a verdict; in such a case, local magnates attempted to bring about the release of their protégés from their court-ordered punishments. Hints for such interferences generally appear in the framework of a discourse that extolled the Sultan's image as a benign and compassionate leader. Nevertheless, their evident aim was to change the sovereign's decision or, at least, to achieve an early release of the culprit. The second mode of intervention was much more violent and menacing and took place during the judicial process itself, sometimes by overtly defying the legal representatives of the central authorities. Such hindrances of the kadi's, or his local deputy, the *naib*'s, ability to adjudicate felons occurred mainly in small towns in the province of Salonica, but also, more rarely, in Salonica itself.

Negotiating Punishment and Exoneration: Prison and Banishment

Two key terms appear in this part of the chapter: patronage and the reputation of a person in his community. These two terms had an important role in determining one's fate. Leslie Peirce claims that justice in sixteenth-century Aintab varied "according to a person's location in the social landscape—by gender, by class, by place of residence, by religious orientation" (Peirce 2003: 386). A similar approach prevails in the files of the Salonican *sicil*. Indeed, terms that imply some form of patron-client relations appear in the *sicil* as justifications for altering previous verdicts: *istinat* (depending on), *inti-*

sap (affiliation), *hamileri olup* (to be a protector),[7] *sahib çekip* (standing forth as protector).[8] These convey the significance of patronage relations as a key concept in understanding eighteenth-century Ottoman society, including its legal system and practice.[9]

Illustrative examples that testify to the vitality of social connections and to patronage relations in determining one's fate can be found in the sentences of imprisonment and banishment. These were the prevailing modes of punishment in the eighteenth century.[10] Salonica, which served as a seat of a governor and boasted a well-protected citadel (the Kelemeriye *kalesi*; today known as the 'White Tower', and widely known as the symbol of modern Salonica), served as a place of internment for culprits sent from all over the Southern Balkans. It was the Sultan who passed the sentence, and he alone who could order a culprit's release. While this monopoly on punishment can indicate centralization of power, the reality was quite different, as I will demonstrate below. We gain information about these punishments and the entailing legal procedures thanks to the kadi's role as the administrator responsible for the punishment's execution by initiating the procedures of confinement in the citadel or in the place of exile (*meks ve ikamet ettirip*).

The *sicil* records show that exile and incarceration were prone to interference by external pressures as the articulating of these punishments did not refer to the length of the confinement or to its conditions, and these were certainly diversified. Only a general statement about the need of the culprit to repent was pointed out as the prerequisite for his release. For that reason, enough leeway was left for negotiating the length and conditions of the confinement. Sometimes, convicts were able to literally escape from their confinement by receiving some sort of external help. One example, the circumstances of which remain unknown, is the absconding of Kara Kaş ('Black Eye-bow') Musa 'by some means' (*takrib ile*) from his exile in Salonica. He was a Jew who used to torment the local Jewish community of Tekfurdağ by slandering them, giving false testimonies (*şahid-i zûr*) against them and entertaining violent people (*eşed makulesi*)

[7] *Sicil*, vol. 16, p. 153, 7 Şaban 1120 [22 October 1708].

[8] *Sicil*, vol. 31, p. 67, 25 Rebiülevvel 1134 [13 January 1722].

[9] See also the discussion of Cornel Fleischer about the significance of patronage relations for attaining promotion in the Ottoman bureaucracy: Fleischer 1986, 19–20.

[10] On imprisonment and exile as modes of punishments in Ottoman law, see Heyd 1973, 301–3.

in his private home.[11] In another case of escape it was two young Greek women who converted to Islam and later turned into apostates. It was thought (*mazanne*) that they were assisted in their escape by two jailers, both recent converts to Islam. This suspicion led the authorities to sanction that neither converts nor their children would ever serve in prison (*ve sair-i mühtedi ve mühtedi oğulları muhzır başlık vekâletinde ve zindancılıkta istihdam olunmayıp*).[12]

In other cases we find an explicit explanation in the text for the decision to release a culprit. A petition submitted by the inhabitants of Timürhisar (Siderokastron) reveals the extent of banditry in the countryside and the close relations between bandits and high officials that brought about three felons' release on the false assumption of repentance. The petitioners claimed that a certain local *zaim*, named Ömer, and his two brothers, Ebübekir and Osman, were infamous for their malicious deeds; they used to gather rebels together, imbibe wine in public and roam drunk in the city's markets so that ordinary people no longer felt safe to venture out of their homes. They were subsequently apprehended and confined in the citadel of Salonica. However, the petition states, as the brothers were related to the former governor of Rumeli (*mezbur Ömer'in sabıkan rumeli valisi Hasan paşa'ya intisabı olmağıla ba'delyevm kendi hallerinde olmak üzere beyinlari ıslah olunmuşiken*), they were released from the citadel, probably following the issue of a decree on their behalf, on the grounds that they had repented. Upon their release, they gathered around them 30–40 *sekban* (irregular cavalry troops) and rebels and caused even greater havoc than before; the terrorized townsfolk did not leave their homes, even to attend the Friday prayers in the mosques, a recurring formula that indicates the population's extreme sufferings. Consequently, the intimidated inhabitants were not able to pay their taxes either. The Sultan ordered an investigation. Fifteen kadis who had formerly held positions in neighboring towns—Siroz (Serres), Drama, Nevrekop (Goce Delcev), Timürhisar (Sidreokastron), Zihne (Zichna), Petriç (Petric), Menlik (Melnik) and Doyran (Stari Tojran)—together with nineteen impartial (*bi-garaz*) Muslims were summoned to assess the culprits' ignominious character. They all confirmed the evil conduct of Ömer and his two brothers. As a result, the *kazasker* of Rumeli, who had general supervisory authority over all the kadis in the

[11] *Sicil*, vol. 107, p. 51, *evasit-i* Muharrem 1179 [29 June–8 July 1765].

[12] *Sicil*, vol. 41, pp. 28–30, *evahir-i* Cemaziyelevvel 1140 [4–13 January 1728].

Ottoman Balkans, issued a verdict (*ilâm*) according to which the three would be exiled to Salonica. Based on the *kazasker*'s sentence, the Sultan issued a decree affirming the punishment.[13]

We can deduce that this exceptionally long list of religious personnel was necessary in order to confront the significant high status of the culprits' patron—the former governor of Rumeli. Their role in the legal process was to determine the brothers' infamous reputation in the community. Some other conclusions can be drawn from this case: it exemplifies the identity of those who were able to form such patronage relations with high officials—former soldiers who for some reason crossed the line between law enforcers and outlaws—a recurring phenomenon in eighteenth-century Salonica. Another observable fact is the sultanic decision to change the place of adjudication and to substitute the serving judge from the court of a kadi in a small Macedonian town of Avrathisar (Kilkis) to the central court of the *kazasker*—a phenomenon to which I will return below.

But not only people who had some military experience could shape such relations with local magnates. It seems that economic and administrative ties could likewise forge such sought-after relations. One case illustrates the ability of a Jewish convict to gain his instantaneous release from castigation thanks to the intervention of local high dignitaries. In this case, the Sublime Porte notified the kadi of Salonica in July 1722 about the imminent arrival of three Jews from Edirne. Their names were recorded: Haim *veled* Isak, Harun *veled* Haim, and Saçlı Oğlu Isak, all inhabitants of Edirne. They were accused by the 'poor' (a linguistic device often used in the *sicil* to underline the misery of the petitioners) who belonged to the ten Jewish congregations (*cemaat*) of Edirne[14] for interfering in the work of the rabbis and for meddling in others' affairs to the extent that the congregations did not feel secure any more. On the basis of this petition, the Sublime Porte decided to exile the three Jews to the citadel of Salonica until they repented (*ıslah-ı nefs edinceye değin Selânik'e nefiy ve icla*).[15] However, just a few days later, another decree arrived in Salonica from Istanbul. This time, the edict ordered the immediate release of one of the culprits, Harun *veled* Haim. The reason for this sudden reversal of decision becomes clear with the reading of the subsequent lines: the

[13] *Sicil*, vol. 16, p. 81, *evail-i* Zilhicce 1119 [23 February–4 March 1708].
[14] On the Jewish community of Edirne, see Gerber 1985, 35–52.
[15] *Sicil*, vol. 32, p. 68, *evail-i* Şevval 1134 [15–24 July 1722].

comptroller of the customs (*gümrük emini*) of Istanbul submitted a claim to the Sublime Porte stating that the same Harun *veled* Haim was an employee of the administrator (*mutasarrıfı hizmetinde*) of the Edirne customs post that came under the jurisdiction of Istanbul. The comptroller claimed that the said Jew was assiduous and diligent in his work of collecting taxes and showed good conduct (*kendi halinde ve umur-i mîrî'nin tahsilinde mücid ve sai olup*).[16]

This reference to what we might call in modern language a 'personal record' is not rare in eighteenth-century Salonica. The establishing of one's conduct and reputation in his own community prior to the felony upon which he was brought to trial was an accepted mechanism in determining the offender's verdict. However, this scanning of a man's past usually appeared in the Salonican *sicil* only in cases where there was an attempt to present an offender as a habitual criminal who merited capital punishment. Still, in the case of the Jewish culprit, his positive record secured for him a quick release from his enforced exile.

The role of the local 'community' in determining the verdict of a wrongdoer on the basis of his local reputation was an important feature of the legal practice in Ottoman Salonica.[17] Establishing one's personal record could be crucial to the final verdict. This observation is important in understanding the relations between the court and its surrounding society—the 'community' often had a vital role that enabled, and even necessitated, it to be a part of the legal process.

Consider, for example, the following case: a man called ʿAbdi submitted a petition to the Sultan while he was camping near Salonica on his way to the front (*ordu-yi hümayun*). He claimed that he was one of the *âyan* in the *kaza* of Aranaut Beleğradi (Berat) when some people with vested interests (*ashab-ı-ağraz*) tried to have him removed from his position by getting the local subjects (*reaya*) to complain about his conduct to the Sublime Porte. They succeeded, and he was summoned to trial in Istanbul. According to the petitioner, he abided by the decision and came to Istanbul where he was tried in the presence of the kadi. The allegations against him were proven to be groundless (*iddiaları lağv olduğu nümayan olmakla*). Nevertheless,

[16] *Sicil*, vol. 32, p. 69, *evahir-i* Şevval 1134 [4–11 August 1722].

[17] On the significance of this term in understanding the function of urban and rural societies in the Ottoman Balkans, see Gara 1998, 135–62.

he was retried, this time in the presence of the Grand Vizier (*huzur-i asafi'nde dahi murafaa olmak üzere*). The outcome of the second trial was totally different: he was sentenced to exile in Salonica. While he insisted that all the charges against him were sheer lies and fabrication (*kizib-i sarih ve iftira-yi mahz*), he did not ask for his punishment to be revoked on the basis of falsification. Rather, he opted for another strategy: he recruited an impressive group of people from his own province who all confirmed his general good conduct (*hüsn-i hal üzere olduğunu*). Among the petitioners we can find an array of people who could be loosely defined as representatives of the local community: the deputy kadis (*naib*) of neighboring Muzakia, Arnaut Beleğradi (Berat), Timüriçe and Eskerapr (Skrapari). Added to them was a group of people who were generally labeled as the religious personnel of the district, the *âyan* and the poor and the destitute who lived in the province. Basing his request upon this impressive list of people who testified to his good behavior (and not disputing the allegations against him), 'Abdi asked to be allowed to return from exile to his province. The Sultan agreed to release him from his punishment.[18]

In this last case, the declarations made by the representatives of the local community proved to be crucial when weighed against the specific allegations raised against the petitioner. This success proves the importance of a man's reputation in his community in determining a case's outcome. It likewise exemplifies the importance of this vague notion of 'community' in the legal process.

Indeed, the definition of the community varied: it could be the neighborhood or the village, the religious community or a corporate group, like the guild. It could also be merely a random group of people who shared acquaintance with the person who was put to trial and, therefore, consisted of an '*ad-hoc* community' that could testify about the person's character. In one case, for example, a Venetian captain was brought to trial before the kadi in a special court hearing that took place in the Diwan of the governor of Salonica. The captain was accused of the mugging and murder of one of his passengers, a Christian merchant from Tırnov (Tarnovo) who traveled in the Venetian vessel from Salonica to the Aegean island of Sakız (Chios) on his way to Izmir. The Venetian captain

[18] *Sicil*, vol. 43, pp. 54–5, *evail-i* Safer 1143 [16 August 1730].

claimed innocence, arguing that due to a violent storm, the Christian merchant had left the ship already when it docked at the island of İskapolos (Skopelos, one of the Sporadic Islands). To prove that he was not among those 'who venture into similar shameful business' (*ve ben bu misilli emir-i faziha ictira eder makulesinden olmamakla*), he brought to court a group of merchants (*tüccar taifesi*)—six Muslims, two Christians and a Jew—who all testified that the Venetian captain was an honorable and reliable man who never jeopardized his passengers' safety or their belongings.[19] In this particular case, the defending community was composed of merchants who, we can presume, already had commercial relations with the defendant.

The community had another possible role in the legal process: to re-absorb a wrongdoer and sometimes also to serve as guarantor (*kefil*) of his future good conduct. Consider the following case: the kadi of Salonica submitted a petition to the Sublime Porte in which he described the torment of the population that inhabited the village of Katrin (Katerini) at the hands of three men who pretended to be *yeniçeris*. These soldiers triggered constant havoc in the village and succeeded in evading the sultanic order that commanded their imprisonment. However, one of them, Kör Haliloğlu Mustafa, eventually obeyed the order and was imprisoned in the citadel of Kelemeriye in Salonica. While his companions were still evading punishment, a delegation of the district's *âyan* and the keepers (*menzilci*) who worked in the local post stations (*menzilhane*)[20] in Katrin pleaded with the Sultan to bring about the release of the detainee. They claimed that the post station could not function because of his imprisonment (*hapisinden naşi menzil umuru muhtel ve müşeveş olup*). Furthermore, if he remained in jail, they cautioned, the whole system of post stations would be jeopardized. They emphasized the fact that Haliloğlu Mustafa was the only one of the gang who had obeyed the decree and turned himself in. Furthermore, they were ready to guarantee (*kefil*) his good conduct.[21]

As noted by Colin Heywood, the Ottoman post stations were part of a courier network that assured the military and administrative

---

[19] *Sicil*, vol. 69, p. 38, 17 Cemaziyel'ahır 1160 [26 June 1747].

[20] The post station of Katrin (Katerini) stood on the 'left arm', a major route that connected the Capital with the Morea peninsula. On the network of post stations in this area, see Heywood 1980, 179–86; idem 1996, 129–44.

[21] *Sicil*, vol. 30, p. 122, *evail-i* Rebiülahir 1132 [10–19 February 1720].

connections between the Sultan's court in Istanbul and the provinces; its efficient operation was vital for the transmission of goods, administrative correspondence, provision of intelligence about the provinces to the ruler and its entourage, and close inspection of the passage of foreigners and suspicious persons in the Ottoman lands (Heywood 1980, 179–86). In the case above, stressing the importance of these post stations enabled their keepers, overwhelmingly villagers, to pose a hidden threat and to successfully negotiate the release of their co-worker. Furthermore, their readiness to reinstate him and to guarantee his good conduct was pivotal in the decision to release Haliloğlu Mustafa from prison. This last point confirms the importance of the community in shaping the final outcome of the case. The community was perceived by the central authorities as a significant force that should be considered in the legal process.

As demonstrated in this part of the chapter, the intervention of local men of power in favor of their protégés emphasizes their ability in the eighteenth century to grasp some control over the legal process. While it indicates the significance of patronage in negotiating the terms of punishment and its length, such intervention does not necessarily imply an open challenge of authority. On the contrary, the petitioners were asking for the Sultan to use his power in favor of their protégés; their intervention is well established in the confines of a regular process of submitting petitions. The explicit mentioning of the intervention alludes to its normativity. However, other cases, mentioned in the *sicil*, of interference entailed an overt challenge of the kadi's court.

Law Enforcement and the Court's Incompetence

The *naib* of Ağustos (Naoussa) complained about the aggressive conduct of local *sekban* who were harassing the local population and violating the public order in his town. When he had earlier attempted to caution them about their behavior, not only did they refuse to desist, but they overtly challenged his authority by attacking the building of the court under night's cover. The powerless *naib* requested the intervention of the central authorities to bring an end to this mayhem.[22] The physical attack on one of the main symbols of the

[22] *Sicil*, vol. 30, p. 85, *evail-i* Ramazan 1130 [29 July–7 August 1718].

sultanic presence in the region of Salonica clearly demonstrates the potential vulnerability of the kadi's court, at least in the small towns that surrounded Salonica. This incident likewise raises the question of the kadi's ability to enforce the law and to bring justice in the area of his jurisdiction. While we have in the *sicil* indications of the kadi's intervention in the work of rural executive administration—like raising questions about the validity of fines and the use of torture to extract confessions by local officials[23]—we also find references of the kadis' incompetence to execute their own decisions in the face of external interference to the extent that adjudications had to be transferred to better 'secured' courts, a term that I will discuss further below. The formulas, 'The performance of justice was not possible *in situ*' (*mahallinde bir vechile ıcra-yı hak mümkün olmayıp*) or 'The [culprit] did not take notice [of the verdict]' (*müntebih olmayıp*) testify to this shortcoming of the court to execute its own mandate to bring justice.

Consider the following case: Abdüllah, the kadi in Avrathisar (Kilkis), submitted a petition to the Sublime Porte in which he informed the authorities that a delegation of the inhabitants of a neighboring village, named Potaris [?], came to the kadi's court and complained about the misconduct of a certain farm (*çiftlik*) holder, Kavukçu Mehmut. They said that this notorious felon brought two obscene females (*fahişe avrat*) to his farm that was situated in the same village. Together with other men of his company, they 'dissolutely indulged themselves in bodily lust' (*fisk u fücur*); there was no limit to his obscene acts (*fisk ve fahaşet*). The court had given him several warnings, but he refused to desist.[24] The kadi asked for the Sultan's intervention as no solution could be found locally. In this case, we have only the petition without the Sultan's response. However, in other cases the outcome is recorded: cases were sometimes transferred from the local court to a court in a neighboring bigger city, like Salonica, or even to Istanbul.

In one such case a complaint was received about an apparent conspiracy between local *âyan* and the local kadi to assist their four protégés in dodging their debts. Four Jewish moneylenders (*sarraf*)

[23] See, for example, *sicil*, vol. 2, p. 42, 13 Rebiülevvel 1108 [10 October 1696]; vol. 18, p. 40, 20 Cemaziyelevvel 1120 [7 August 1708]; vol. 76, 22 Şaban 1163 [27 July 1750].

[24] *Sicil*, vol. 32, p. 69, 2 Zilkade 1134 [14 August 1722].

benefited from the patronage of the province's *âyan* and the kadi (*âyan-i vilayet ve kadi'ye istinad ile*) in order to evade payment of their debts, estimated at the hefty sum of 3000 *guruş*. We can assume that the patronage relations between these four Jews and the powerful magnates stemmed from past business that they had conducted. However, the result of this complicity was clear: these relations enabled them to carry on with their affairs and ignore the need for accountability. Their debtors remained powerless against the alliance that these moneylenders were able to form. The Sultan's response to their debtors' agonies is illustrative to our discussion: he ordered that the four moneylenders be taken to Istanbul and brought to trial before the sultanic Diwan and the *kazasker*.[25] The solution, therefore, was to move the case hearing from the provincial court to the center, elucidating the inability of the center to enforce justice *in situ*.

A similar justification for transferring the hearing of a claim from a court of a local kadi, this time to another kadi's court occurred in the town of Filorina (Florina). In this case, two brothers and two sisters petitioned the Sublime Porte complaining that the local kadi (*toprak kadısı*) had plotted (*yedgi olup*) with the murderers of their father, Ahmet Ağa. The kadi's conspiracy with the murderers was revealed during his investigation of the victim's corpse to determine the cause of death. The text, however, remains mute about the exact nature of the kadi's intervention. Therefore, the siblings claimed, no justice could be achieved in their home town. The Sublime Porte ordered that the case be transmitted to neighboring Salonica, where justice could be done.[26] It is worth noting that the murdered father was a local military functionary who might had connections with the central authorities, as indicated by his military title, *ağa*, and that when he was attacked he was returning home from a visit to the private residence of the town's *serdar* (chief of police). As for his murderers, there too we find titles, occupations and nicknames that indicate that they were well-known representatives of the local community: craftsmen, local religious personnel (*imam, derviş*) and *yeniçeri*s. This could explain the conspiracy between the assassins and the kadi and their ability to influence his decision. The following entry in the *sicil* indicates that the same kadi of Filorina was ultimately removed from

[25] *Sicil*, vol. 30, p. 121, *evasit-i* Safer 1132 [23 December 1719–1 January 1720].
[26] *Sicil*, vol. 30, p. 90, *evahir-i* Cemaziyel'ahır [1]131 [11–20 May 1719].

office for over-charging the local inhabitants for the local tax levy, contrary to the *kanun*, and extorting from them ungrounded fines.[27]

These last cases, all of them registered in petitions to the Sultan, raise the issue of law enforcement in the Salonica region in the eighteenth century. They provide us with an utterly different picture from the seemingly orderly process that appears in the kadi's records. In these cases the legal process that took place in the kadi's court was vulnerable and exposed to threats, intrusions and even conspiracy between the kadi and local felons. Were these cases representative of the legal process in eighteenth-century Salonica? We can only claim here that the central authorities found them grave enough to order the transfer of their adjudication from the provinces to the center.

Conclusions

This chapter does not claim that the Ottoman legal system was notoriously corrupt; we can assume that other legal systems in other places and times were likewise vulnerable to external pressures and interferences. Neither does it argue that the legal practice observed in Ottoman Salonica represents the legal norm which prevailed in all the Ottoman lands. Rather, its main aim was to discuss the notion of the kadi's judicial monopoly in eighteenth-century Salonica and his power relations with different segments of the surrounding society. The choice of the period should also be emphasized—the registers of eighteenth-century Salonica cast light on the legal process at a time of a severe crisis: the local agents of the central power had to compete with local magnates over authority and the ability to enforce formal decisions. In fact, this chapter provides examples that clearly indicate the external intervention of officials and others in the legal process. The loose definition of the length and conditions of imprisonment and exile provided ample grounds and opportunities for such intervention. What makes the examples that appear in this chapter telling is the explicit mentioning, probably for future reference, of the intervention as crucial to shaping the legal outcome

[27] *Sicil*, vol. 30, pp. 90–1, *evahir-i* Cemaziyel'ahır 1131 [11–20 May 1719].

of the involved parties. Such an explicit reference can indicate the contemporary acceptance of such demarches.

Local men of power—officials and non-officials—occasionally found enough room to negotiate the outcome of the legal process. Local social networks and one's reputation in his community played equally significant roles in the process. Sometimes such intrusions and interventions led to the early release of culprits; at other times it utterly undermined the authority of agents of the law to the extent that adjudications had to be transferred to the center.

Another conclusion of this chapter is that the legal perception of the kadi's judicial monopoly that reigned, for example, in seventeenth-century Bursa (Gerber 1994, 69), is not applicable with regard to eighteenth-century Salonica. While it is true that the *sicil* documents depict a picture of consistent implementation of the *şerʿi* law and also acceptance of the local custom in some particular cases, it should be borne in mind that in many cases the litigation in the kadi's court was only a stage, and not always the final one, in the long process of determining a verdict and its essence. This conclusion had significant ramifications on the kadi's ability to reach a verdict and to enforce it—whether issued by the local kadi or by the central authorities. To begin with, the kadi's court was only one of the possible formal and non-formal venues for sorting out conflicts. But that was not all; the surrounding community also played an important role in the legal process. Such involvement was well established in Ottoman legal practice. Ottoman routine at the time allocated certain power to the local community in determining a culprit's punishment: when needed, local community representatives were summoned to the court to establish a defendant's personal record; their opinion was crucial in deciding the offender's categorization and the subsequent punishment. The local community was sometimes asked to receive the culprit upon his release and to then stand as guarantors for his conduct.

Moreover, the kadi, while habitually sent to Salonica from other provinces, became at times a part of the social and political matrix of the city. As shown here, the boundaries between the agents who represented the central authorities (governors, kadis, etc.) and local *âyan* were sometimes blurred. This involvement in local society also made the kadi vulnerable to external intervention. In some cases we even found signs of a plot that was concocted between a kadi and local magnates to the extent that the kadi assisted his accomplices or their protégés to evade justice. Such cases were reported primarily in the small towns in the area of Salonica, thus indicating the different levels of crisis and the effect of decentralization between Salonica, a major seat of the central power, and the townships around it.

CHAPTER SEVEN

ARCHAIC FORMS OF CONTRACT IN MAX WEBER'S THEORIES AND IN ARAB AND SOMALI CUSTOMARY LAW[1]

Frank H. Stewart

In the nineteenth and early twentieth centuries historians and anthropologists were much interested in archaic forms of contract and advanced a variety of ideas on the subject. Soon after World War I, however, the stream of new theories dried up, and most of the relevant literature dropped below the horizon. The only authorities whose works are still frequently cited are Henry Maine and Max Weber.[2] Maine's famous observation that "the movement of progressive societies has hitherto been a movement from Status to Contract" (Maine 1930, 182 [first published in 1861]) has never been forgotten, but his publications no longer attract much comment.[3] In contrast, books and articles about Weber continue to flow from the press, and his *Sociology of Law*, the work in which he set out his ideas about early contract, remains widely influential.[4] It was written largely in the years 1911–13, and its discussion of early law is based on the conclusions of the leading scholars of the period. The

[1] This paper benefited greatly from comments and references supplied by Michael Cook, Nick Foster, Margaret Gilbert and an anonymous reviewer. To all of them my thanks.

[2] Anthropologists will recall that Marcel Mauss's famous essay on the gift (originally published 1923–24) was seen by him as "part of a series of researches . . . concerning the archaic forms of contract" (Mauss 1990, 5). The phenomena that interested Mauss in this work are not, however, usually discussed nowadays under the heading of contract. Mauss's ideas were taken up with reference to North Africa in an article published in 1927 by René Maunier. A new edition of this work includes a useful introduction by Alain Mahé (Maunier 1998).

[3] For a recent study, see Piccinini 2003. Unfortunately no copy of this work was available to me.

[4] Books devoted exclusively to this part of his work include Romero Pérez 1975; Treves 1981; Kronman 1983; Breuer and Treiber 1984; Rehbinder and Tieck 1987; Lascoumes 1995; and Coutu 1995. All these works include bibliographies, the last two very extensive ones.

writings of those scholars are now rarely cited, even in the German-speaking countries from which most of them came, but through Weber their ideas have been carried into the twenty-first century. In the ninety years that have passed since Weber put pen to paper, no one has come up with any better ideas. In fact, on the particular subject of archaic forms of contract, no one seems to have had any new ideas at all.

In this chapter I shall first try to discover what Weber has to say about the early history of contract—or at least some aspects of it—and will then ask how well what he says fits with what we know about contract in Arab and Somali customary law. For reasons that will immediately become apparent, the first of these tasks is not a simple one.

I

Weber's *Rechtssoziologie* (*Sociology of Law*) is a chapter of his large work, *Wirtschaft und Gesellschaft* (*Economy and Society*), first published in 1921, a year after the author's death. In the early editions of *Wirtschaft und Gesellschaft* the text of the *Rechtssoziologie* was not good, and it was fortunate that in 1957 a typescript with Weber's own corrections and additions was discovered.[5] The eminent Weber scholar Johannes Winckelmann used this typescript to produce a revised German text that was first published separately in 1960 and then incorporated (with some small corrections) in his definitive edition of *Wirtschaft und Gesellschaft* (Weber 1976).

The differences between the 1960 text and earlier ones are substantial. Nonsensical statements are replaced by reasonable ones.[6] For our purposes, the most important change relates to the word *Zwangskontrakt*, a strange term that Weber's translators rendered in English as 'coercing contract'. This term appears several times in the pre-1960 editions, but nowhere at all in the 1960 text. It is everywhere replaced by 'purpose contract' (*Zweckkontrakt*), a term that

[5] For details of this typescript and its discovery, see Weber 1960, 37–49.

[6] It turns out, for instance, that Weber did not refer to "the highly political character of the debt-relationship" in Roman law (Weber 1954, 122, following the pre-1960 German text), but merely to "the strictly personal nature of the debt-relationship" in that law (Weber 1976, 408 = 1978, 682).

refers to a concept that is central to Weber's analysis of the history of contract. This change, however, also illustrates a point that Winckelmann is at pains to emphasize: even the 1960 text cannot pretend to reflect Weber's intentions with certainty. The term *Zwangskontrakt* does actually occur in the typescript, and it is primarily because there is no manuscript authority for it that Winckelmann everywhere replaced it in his 1960 edition with *Zweckkontrakt* (Weber 1960, 48).

An English translation of the *Sociology of Law*, based on the pre-1960 text, was produced by Edward Shils and Max Rheinstein. It appeared, together with their translations of some other materials, in Weber 1954. Max Rheinstein added invaluable notes.[7] This translation was subsequently revised in the light of the 1960 German text, and the revised version was published as part of the English translation of the whole of *Economy and Society* (Weber 1978, originally published 1968). The Shils-Rheinstein translation is a brave effort, and better than many of the other translations that together make up the English version of *Economy and Society*. Nevertheless, even in its revised version, Shils-Rheinstein cannot be used by scholars as a substitute for the original German. For instance, Shils and Rheinstein generally translate *Zweckkontrakt* as 'purposive contract', but at one point, apparently because they misunderstood the context, they render it as 'instrumental contract'.[8]

The best known study in English of Weber's *Sociology of Law* is Kronman's *Max Weber* (1983). Kronman relies exclusively on the Shils-Rheinstein translation. There is no indication that he was aware of the problematic nature either of the original German text or of the English translation; even the fact that the 1968 version of Shils-Rheinstein differs significantly from the 1954 one is not mentioned, though he gives references to both. Differences between Kronman's interpretation of the Weber and mine may in part be the result of our using different texts.

My own interpretation is based on the 1976 German text. The translations from it are by me, though I have consulted the revised

[7] These can be supplemented from the volume of notes (*Erläuterungsband*) that Johannes Winckelmann published together with his 1976 edition of *Wirtschaft und Gesellschaft*. For the *Sociology of Law* the notes are particularly rich, and add substantially to those provided by Rheinstein.

[8] Weber 1978, 673. See further n. 12 below.

Shils-Rheinstein version and give references to it immediately after the references to the original.

To conclude this section, a word of caution: Weber is at the best of times not a very clear or precise writer, and the *Sociology of Law* is notoriously one of his least-polished publications. In all likelihood the work would have undergone further revision had Weber lived. The pages that deal with the early history of contract have often been seen as important and cited with approval, but (as far as my knowledge of the literature goes) the commentators have not dealt in depth with the difficulties that they present. In the next section I shall point out some problems that seem to me to have been neglected (or at least not confronted in the way they should have been), but I do not claim to have offered definitive solutions to them. Given the state of the text, they may in fact not be susceptible to such solutions.

II

1. Weber's most original contribution to the study of early law—and the one that will mainly concern us in this paper—is the distinction he draws between what he calls status contracts and purpose contracts.[9] "These represent two entirely different forms of contractual association, and the passage in which Weber describes their contrasting characteristics is one of the most important in the *Rechtssoziologie* as a whole" (Kronman 1983, 100). Purpose contracts (*Zweckkontrakte*) are the kind of arm's length contracts characteristic of highly developed legal systems (classical Roman, Islamic, modern). Their purpose "is only to bring about some specific, generally economic, performance or result" (Weber 1976, 402 = Weber 1978, 673). Status contracts (*Statuskontrakte*) are those that determine a person's status as child, father, wife, slave, master, clansman, fellow warrior, protector, client, vassal and the like. In archaic society they played a major role in public law, often being used to bring a person into a political or other grouping. Most of them are 'fraternization contracts', meaning that the tie they establish is in some way like that of brother-

[9] Weber 1976, 401–2 = Weber 1978, 672–73. Weber uses the term contract "in the sense of a voluntary agreement as the legal basis for the creation of rights and duties" (Weber 1976, 401 = Weber 1978, 671).

hood. On making such a contract a person's legal status undergoes a radical transformation; the person is viewed (at least in early law) as qualitatively changed, as being entered into by a new soul. Status contracts are always magical in origin—they are formed by procedures like mixing or drinking blood or saliva; and even when they lose this magical character, they long retain traces of it in their symbolism.

Weber's account of the conceptual relationships between the two types of contract is sketchy. He generally writes as if all contracts are either status contracts or purpose contracts, i.e., as if there are no other categories along this dimension, and as if every contract falls clearly into one or the other of these two categories. It is possible, however, given his notion of the ideal type, that he did not mean to exclude the existence of intermediate forms.[10]

The historical relationship between the two types of contract is also somewhat uncertain. Weber is concerned in this context essentially with three types of legal system: primitive ones in which contractual obligation does not exist (Weber 1976, 403 = 1978, 675); those that we may call early or archaic, and that are exemplified by pre-classical Roman law and by early Germanic law; and those that we may call highly-developed or advanced, and that are exemplified by classical Roman law and modern law. Weber believed that status contracts are characteristic of early law and purpose contracts of highly-developed law. This suggests two questions, neither of which finds an explicit answer in Weber's text.

First, do status contracts still exist in highly-developed law? Kronman does not consider the question, but his account of status contracts suggests strongly that he believes that Weber viewed them as absent from advanced legal systems (Kronman 1983, 101–8). Belley, in contrast, says that "Weber did not claim that the status contract had disappeared in modern Western society" (Belley 1995, 230). Belley's view seems to be the right one. Marriage, for example, is evidently a status contract, and obviously Weber knew that it continues to exist in modern society.

Second, do purpose contracts already exist in early law? Neither Belley nor Kronman asks this question, but both seem to believe that the answer is no. Belley implies throughout that Weber viewed

[10] Thus he talks of 'pure purpose contracts' (*blosse Zweckkontrakte*) (Weber 1976, 402 = 1978, 673). This seems to imply that mixed or intermediate forms of contract exist.

purpose contracts as a late development. Thus he writes that "Weber showed how the evolution towards the notion of the purpose contract corresponded also to a major political transformation that was to lead to the pre-eminence of the state as the central political organisation of the society" (Belley 1995, 230). Kronman quotes a passage from the English translation of Weber's work in which the purpose contract is defined as the one that "is peculiar to the exchange or market economy" (Weber 1978, 672, quoted in Kronman 1983, 101). In my view, however, Weber does not mean to say (as the translation might be taken to imply) that the purpose contract is found only in market economies, but rather that the purpose contract is the contract characteristic of commercial relations.[11]

In fact Weber's remarks imply pretty clearly that purpose contracts did exist in early law. He states that exchange is the archetype of all pure purpose contracts,[12] and he realized of course that exchange existed even in archaic societies. He mentions both the exchange of goods and the exchange of women. As so often, the discussion is far from clear, but it suggests that Weber held that the exchange of goods—barter—is in its simplest and earliest forms a transaction that has enough in common with the purpose contract to be called the archetype of the purpose contract, but that still lacks important features of the full-blown purpose contract. The main difference between the two is that the full-blown purpose contract gives rise to a special type of obligation, whereas primitive barter did not. In primitive barter there was merely a simultaneous exchange of goods. To the extent that the transaction was protected by law,

[11] In the original Weber writes, "wollen wir jene urwüchsigen Kontrakttypen als 'Status'-Kontrakte, dagegen die dem Güterverkehr, also der Marktgemeinschaft, spezifischen als 'Zweck'-Kontrakte bezeichnen." Weber 1976, 401.

[12] Weber 1976, 402 = 1978, 673. The English translation of this passage reads, "This type of contract [i.e., the purpose contract], however, does not appear in the most primitive society. In earliest times, *barter*, the archetype of all merely instrumental contracts . . ." This may have misled commentators. The original has, "Urwüchsig ist das nicht. Der Tausch, der Archetypos aller blossen Zweckkontrakte," and between the two sentences is a paragraph break. The first sentence refers not to the purpose contract, but to the use of the oath in the formation of purpose contracts. Weber believed that the earliest form of the oath was magical, and as such suitable only for guaranteeing status contracts. He thought that the oath subsequently changed its nature in that it invoked the gods, and that only in this later form could it be used in purpose contracts. (Perhaps it was the sheer implausibility of these ideas that put Shils and Rheinstein on the wrong track.) The second sentence clearly says (both in the pre-1960 editions and in the subsequent ones) that exchange is the archetype of all pure purpose contracts.

it was protected (according to Weber) not by a law that recognized obligations arising from agreements, but by one that recognized claims against a thief.

Weber also implies that primitive barter lacked a second, less important, feature of the full-blown purpose contract: it did not involve any (legal) formalities. Weber's view seems to be that such formalities (for exchange) only came into being when some kind of currency began to be used, and he goes on to say that the 'money contract' is the "archetype of the purpose contract" (Weber 1976, 403 = 1978, 674).

I will not attempt to disentangle all this, for even if we discount barter, and even if we assume (what I do not believe to be the case) that the introduction of money marks for Weber the boundary between early and advanced legal systems, the logic of Weber's work still demands that we accept the existence of purpose contracts in early law. As we have seen, Weber generally writes as if all contracts are either status contracts or purpose contracts. A class of contract characteristic of early law is the procedural contract. The first type of procedural contract to appear, Weber tells us, is the arbitration contract (*Schiedsvertrag*), that is, the contract that embodies an agreement between sibs to settle a dispute either by arbitration or by ordeal (Weber 1976, 401 = 1978, 678). Since this is clearly not a status contract, it must be a purpose contract; and indeed it fits Weber's definition of purpose contracts, for it is of a kind whose purpose is to bring about a specific performance or result.

This reasoning is, however, not quite consistent with a subsequent remark of Weber's, which seems to say that the arbitration contract is an ancestor of the purpose contract rather than being itself a purpose contract. In the passage that has just concerned us, he states that the arbitration contract developed out of the composition contract (*Sühnevertrag*), that is, the contract that embodies an agreement between two sibs to settle a dispute by some kind of payment rather than by taking revenge. Later he writes that "the composition contract, on which the trial is based, is on the way to being a purpose contract, insofar as it is a contract between enemies and not a fraternization contract, and insofar as it demands a precise formulation of the issue and above all of what it is that is to be proved."[13] It

[13] Weber 1976, 406 = 1978, 678. It is perhaps this passage from Weber's work that led Belley to write that "the composition contract (*contrat de transaction*) by which

looks as if the text needs to be emended here, since Weber seems to be referring to the arbitration contract rather than to the composition contract. In any event, it is not clear why he thinks that the contract in question is merely "on the way to being a purpose contract," rather than actually being a purpose contract. As I have just noted, this type of contract falls within Weber's own definition of the term 'purpose contract'. So once more we have a muddle, and given the nature of the text any attempt to sort it out will be highly speculative. I would simply conclude by saying that the main thrust of Weber's arguments suggests that purpose contracts already existed in early law, though at times he may have tried to hedge his position at the expense of conceptual clarity. One of Weber's weaknesses is that when it becomes clear to him that the concepts he is using do not fit the facts, his reaction, all too often, is not to create new or more refined concepts, but rather to blur the outlines of the ones that he is already using.

2. The distinction between status contracts and purpose contracts obviously owes something to Maine. Weber realized that Maine was wrong if he meant to say that contract is always of little importance in early law, but Weber also realized that the kind of contract characteristic of early law is different, both in form and in subject matter, from the kind characteristic of advanced legal systems. It is this contrast that Weber attempts to capture in the distinction between status contracts and purpose contracts.

Maine describes the evolution of societies from those in which status is the main legal determinant of a person's life to those in which the main legal determinant is contract. Weber no doubt believed that societies whose legal systems characteristically use purpose contracts generally evolved from societies whose legal systems characteristically used status contracts. But he has been read as if he were saying something quite different, as if he were claiming that the status contract evolved into the purpose contract. This is Belley's view,

the parties reach an agreement in order to settle their dispute is [in Weber's view] the conceptual ancestor of the modern purpose-contract" (Belley 1995, 228; no reference is given to a specific statement by Weber). Note the fudging effect of the word 'modern' in this sentence: we are not told whether there is such a thing as a pre-modern purpose contract, and, if so, whether the composition contract is a pre-modern purpose contract.

and he goes so far as to refer to it as "a central thesis in Weber's analysis."[14]

I see no evidence to support such an interpretation. Weber's view is that the ancestor of the modern type of purpose contract (whose exemplar is the commercial contract) is the procedural contract (e.g., the arbitration contract). As we have seen, he is a little vague about whether the procedural contract is actually an early form of purpose contract or merely an ancestor of the purpose contract, that is, a contract that still lacks some (unspecified) characteristic(s) of the true purpose contract. But there is no doubt that in Weber's view the techniques that were used in the procedural contracts for creating legal obligation were subsequently adopted for the creation of contractual obligation in other areas of life.[15] Obviously he did not think that these techniques were used in the formation of status contracts, since status contracts had their own specific techniques. He therefore meant that these techniques were adopted for use in the formation of (non-procedural) purpose contracts.

Among the techniques that Weber mentions are the use of sureties, pledges and hostages (Weber 1976, 406 = 1978, 679). Since these practices appear at quite an early stage outside procedural contexts, the implication of what Weber writes is that even archaic law (preclassical Roman law, Germanic law in the era of the *leges barbarorum*) included some non-procedural purpose contracts.[16]

There is no indication that Weber believed that status contracts evolved into purpose contracts or indeed into any other kind of contract. The implication of what he writes is that status contracts continued to exist into modern times, but that the role they played in law and society became less and less significant as states grew in power and commerce developed. At most one can say that the purpose contract adopted from the status contract one particular technique, the use of the oath (in its later form) (Weber 1976, 402 = 1978, 672–73. Cf. n. 12 above).

---

[14] Belley 1995, 229 (where he writes of "an evolution from status contract to purpose contract," echoing a phrase that appears already on p. 221 of his article).

[15] "Broadly speaking (*in sehr weitgehendem Sinn*), the oldest types of contracts in private law . . . trace their origins to procedural contracts" Weber 1976, 401 = 1978, 671. "The oldest purely contractual obligations were procedural devices that were adopted in non-procedural areas of legal life" Weber 1976, 406 = 1978, 679.

[16] This is also implied by what he says about the *negotia per aes et libram* of preclassical Roman law. Weber 1976, 403 = 1978, 674.

III

1. Those commentators on Weber's *Sociology of Law* whose work I have seen present the distinction between purpose contracts and status contracts in an extraordinarily abstract fashion. Neither Kronman nor Belley, for instance, refers to a single specific example of a status contract. Neither makes the slightest reference to the historical and ethnographic sources that inspired Weber to draw this distinction.[17] Neither makes any attempt to assess its value, and in particular neither tries to discover how far what Weber says corresponds to what is now known about early forms of contract. There is a similar absence of criticism in a recent British collection of cases and materials on contract law that quotes at length the relevant passages from Weber and Kronman. The British authors (like Kronman and Belley) do not so much as hint at the notion that it might be worth comparing Weber's theories with the facts (Wheeler and Shaw 1994, 37–44). This scholastic approach to Weber is totally alien to the spirit of his work, every line of which is written with particular examples in mind. He above all would have demanded that his theories be measured up against the real world, and would have objected to their being treated as a closed system.

I noted at the beginning of this chapter that the flow of ideas about early forms of contract ceased in the early decades of the twentieth century. To a large extent the flow of new data also ceased at that time. Historians no longer paid much attention to the subject, and ethnographers tended to ignore it. The result is that we have relatively little to add to the information that was available to Weber before World War I. But there has been some modest progress, and part of it has occurred because of new information about Arab and Somali customary law.[18]

Even before the World War I, accounts had been published of certain customary law contracts that were current among the Arabs of North Africa, those that the French call the *associations agricoles*

[17] Winckelmann's *Erläuterungsband* (n. 7 above) offers guidance to those sources. Both Kronman and Belley rely exclusively on translations of Weber's work. This suggests that their knowledge of German is limited or even non-existent. If so, then they would in any case be denied direct access to most of Weber's sources.

[18] For a brief general introduction to Arab customary law, see *EI*^{2}, s.v. ʿUrf (F.H. Stewart), and for a fuller account of Bedouin customary law in particular, see Stewart 2006.

(agrarian partnerships).[19] These contracts were of practical importance to the colonists, since they included the various kinds of arrangements by which one man cultivated the land of another or herded animals belonging to another. It is unlikely that Weber knew the relevant literature, but even if he had known it, there is no reason to believe that it would have affected his analysis. These North African contracts are not much different either in form or in content from those recorded from many other times and places, and Weber, who had written extensively on agrarian relations both ancient and modern, was intimately familiar with material of this kind.

Whether in North Africa or elsewhere, agrarian contracts often raise a problem that Weber ignores. If a landowner hires a laborer to help him bring in the harvest, this is clearly a purpose contract; if a free man gives himself into serfdom, this is clearly a status contract; but between the two there are infinite gradations, and Weber offers no hint as to where we might draw a line.

A more particular challenge to Weber's analysis is offered by some of the material on Arab customary law that was not yet available in his day. It comes from two regions of the Arab world. One is Cyrenaica and the Western Desert of Egypt (which I shall refer to together as North-East Africa) and the other is Sinai, the Negev and Transjordan. For the latter region I shall rely on data that I gathered in the field in Sinai; what is true of Sinai is also generally true of adjacent areas to the east. We also have good accounts of the customary law of the Somali of the Horn of Africa,[20] a people whose social structure is similar to that of the Bedouin and whose culture has been profoundly influenced by the Arabs. Until recent times the populations of all these regions consisted largely of nomads, and the

---

[19] Among the best early works on the subject are Salmon and Bruzeaux 1905 and Vaffier-Pollet 1906. For a general treatment, see Milliot 1911, and for the Italian literature on the subject, see the references in Shinar 1983, 415–22. After World War I, the French also investigated customary agricultural contracts in the Levant (see, for instance, Latron 1936 and Maurin 1945). For a well-informed recent discussion of such contracts in pre-colonial Morocco, see Michel 1997, 304–30. Finally, special mention should be made of Marcy 1949. This remarkable study, which is based mainly on material collected in the 1920s, deals with a Moroccan Berber tribe, but much of what it says about contract probably applies equally to the Arabs.

[20] Notably in Cerulli 1957–64 (a collection of papers, several of which deal with the customary law), Colucci 1924 (on which see Cerulli 1957–64, 2:87–94) and Lewis 1961.

traditional political systems were ones in which there was no effective central authority.

2. A fundamental feature of the social structure of the Bedouin (not only those of North-East Africa and the Sinai) and of the Somali is what I shall refer to as the *blood-money group*.[21] Such a group is made up exclusively of adult men.[22] Broadly speaking, if one of their number is obliged to pay blood-money, they will all contribute to the payment, and if one of them receives blood-money, he will share it with the others. If one of them commits a blood-offense, then they are all legitimate objects for revenge; and if one of them is the victim of a blood-offense, then it is the duty of all to help him to get either revenge or compensation. The size of these groups varies greatly: some have only a dozen or so members (as is common in Sinai), while others have hundreds (as is common in North-East Africa)[23] or even thousands (among the Somali).[24] Small groups may be part of larger groups, and there is considerable variation as to the exact nature of the obligations of the members to each other. In general, the smaller the group the broader the obligations of the members to each other. It is essentially on his group that a man depends for the defense of his most important interests, above all his physical safety and that of his womenfolk and children.

---

[21] The existence of such groups among the Bedouin has been known for at least three quarters of a century, and information about them is now available in a number of sources. Among the Somali, in contrast, they were first mentioned in the literature only in 1955 (Lewis 1961, 160 n. 1), and Lewis 1961 remains the only detailed treatment of the subject. Following the practice of the British administration in Somaliland, Lewis uses the term "dia-paying group" to refer to what I call the blood-money group. Somali blood-money groups are very similar to the Bedouin ones, and I have little doubt that the Somali adopted the institution from the Arabs.

[22] Among the Somalis the group "is thought of as having a dominantly male character" (Lewis 1961, 171). This cautious formulation does not reflect a real difference between the Bedouin group and its Somali equivalent, but rather a difference between my analysis and Lewis's. Among the Bedouin women and children are not members of the group, although the group protects them and is liable for any blood-debts that they may incur. Lewis, in his account of the Somali, looks on all those whom the group protects or is liable for as being members of the group. I believe that this view is mistaken, since the parties to the contract that unites the group are, among the Somali precisely as among the Bedouin, men only (Lewis 1961, 176, 197).

[23] See, for instance, Obermeyer 1968, 175; Mohsen 1970, 66; Peters 1990, 60, 87.

[24] The Somali groups vary in size between about 300 and 3,000 men (Lewis 1961, 170).

The members of these groups, or at least of the smaller ones, are often each other's closest agnates. They view themselves, however, as being bound not only (in many cases) by common ancestry, but also by contract. This contract, which I shall refer to as the *blood-money pact*, spells out such matters as what share of any blood-money that a man may receive must be passed on to the other members of the group, and what share of blood-money that he may be obliged to pay will be contributed by the other members. The obligations created by a blood-money pact are of indefinite duration; in the case of the smaller groups, at least, they are not (and perhaps cannot be) sharply defined, for they touch on substantial areas of the members' lives. These pacts are status contracts, in fact precisely the type of status contract that Weber called fraternization contracts.[25]

A boy automatically becomes a member of his father's group upon reaching manhood.[26] This does not, however, make it impossible to view the group as being formed by contract. Though it is most unlikely to occur in practice, a young man may in principle either refuse to join his father's group or, having joined it, leave it. There are also procedures by which individuals or groups can join a group to which they do not belong by birth. These new members may be agnatically remote from the existing ones, or not even agnates at all.

Although the substance of the blood-money pacts is broadly similar in the three regions that concern us, the form in which they are cast is entirely different. In North-East Africa, indeed, it could be said that there is no form. All that is necessary is an agreement between the parties (who are usually not individuals but leaders of smaller agnatic groups). The same appears to be true among the Somali.[27] In North-East Africa the agreement is sometimes drawn

[25] This is not to say that members of a blood-money group look on each other as brothers or even as something like brothers. When Weber wrote of fraternization contracts he merely meant contracts that produced a strong, long-lasting comradely tie between the parties.

[26] Lewis (1961, 170) writes that among the Somali "everyone is born into" a blood-money group. I suspect that this statement is a result of the analytic difference mentioned in n. 22 above.

[27] Lewis 1961, 176. Although Cerulli did not know of the existence of the blood-money group, he was aware of the fact that an individual or a group could be adopted into an alien descent group, and he describes the legal consequences of such adoption at some length. As regards the transaction itself, this is what he writes about one of the Somali groups that he studied. "I did not encounter among the Hawiyya tribe any particular adoption ceremony. Other peoples of East Africa, in

up in writing and signed or sealed by the parties, but this is done in order that there should be a record rather than because it is necessary for the formation of the contract. Similarly, among the Somali the pacts "were apparently only conserved orally and in the memory of those concerned, but they were no less binding." It was only as a result of measures taken by the British administration that blood-money pacts came to be regularly reduced to writing (Lewis 1961, 175–76).

In Sinai, in contrast, the pact (which is rarely reduced to writing) does indeed make use of a particular form, though not one that is special to it. I shall call this form the *three-party contract*, since it normally involves a man who gives an undertaking (the principal), a man who receives the undertaking (the obligee) and a man who guarantees that the principal will perform (the guarantor).[28]

The Bedouin blood-money pact, whether in its North-East African or in its Sinaitic version, does not offer the slightest support for Weber's ideas about status contracts. In both cases, the procedures involved are wholly mundane and carried out by words alone: no blood, no spittle, not the slightest hint of anything magical or religious, not even an oath. It would never occur to a Bedouin that by moving from one blood-money group to another he became a qualitatively different person or acquired a new soul. Joining a new blood-money group is certainly a most important event, but it is viewed in the same sober way as any other legal transaction. As far as I can tell, all this is equally true of the Somali.

3. It is not only in the context of the blood-money pact that the law of the Sinai Bedouin offers an opportunity to test Weber's theories. The Bedouin of this region have a remarkably well-developed set of procedures for settling disputes, and contracts are a central part of those procedures. The law includes both the composition contract and the arbitration contract, each in several varieties, and

contrast, have special rites (they cut their arms and mix drops of blood of the adopter with those of the adoptee; the adoptee pretends to feed from the right breast of the leader of the adopting group; and so on)." Cerulli 1957–64, 3: 68. It appears then that adoption was effected by a mere formless agreement. Just how the transaction that Cerulli calls adoption was related to joining a blood-money group is not clear, but at any rate, what he says shows once more that not all status contracts have a form of the kind that Weber ascribes to them.

[28] For a detailed account of this contract, together with comparative material, see Stewart 2003.

a good many other procedural contracts as well. It will be remembered that in Weber's model the form of these contracts—given that they are either purpose contracts or ancestral to purpose contracts—should be entirely different from the form of the blood-money pact. But among the Sinai Bedouin and their neighbors the opposite is the case: the same three-party form is used for both the blood-money pact and for all the procedural contracts, and indeed for a wide range of other purposes.

In North-East Africa and among the Somali the procedures for settling disputes are much simpler than in Sinai, and it is questionable whether one can talk of the existence of procedural contracts. Instead there are mere formless agreements, which are of no relevance to us here.

4. The distinction between status contracts and purpose contracts is the most original part of what Weber has to say about early forms of contract. Most of the other ideas that he offers do not differ significantly from those that had long been familiar to legal historians (cf. Stewart 2003, 266 n. 373). He accepts, for instance, the idea that contractual obligation arose from personal liability for delict (Weber 1976, 403, 405 = 1978, 675, 677). I have elsewhere tried to show that there is no reason to believe that this is true of Bedouin law in Sinai. Both there and, indeed, throughout the whole huge region (it stretches from northern Syria to southern Yemen) where much the same kind of customary contract is to be found, contractual liability is embedded in a wholly different context, the context of honor (Stewart 2003, 204–12).

5. Weber's suggestion that the techniques that were first used in procedural contracts for creating legal obligation were subsequently adopted for the creation of legal obligation in other areas of life is also one with a long history behind it.[29] This particular idea—I shall call it the *adoption thesis*—is not easy to test among the Bedouin, since we know almost nothing about the history of their customary law. But there are indications that the adoption thesis does indeed describe what happened among them.

We may begin by noting that that our evidence is consistent with a thesis that is not actually advanced by Weber, though it is closely

[29] See, for instance, Heusler 1885–86, 2:237 (on Germanic law).

related to some of those that he does propose. This is the thesis that formal contracts first arise in the context of procedures for dispute settlement.[30] The Bedouin of North-East Africa, like the Somali, do not have the elaborate procedures for the settlement of disputes that are to be found among the Asiatic Bedouin and the sedentary tribes of the Yemen. The Africans get by without the careful definition of the issue, the allocation of the roles of plaintiff and defendant, the public hearing before a judicator, the formal pleadings, the formal judgment, the formal testimony and other similar features of Arab customary law in large areas of the East. Equally, they get by without a formal contract. In other words, the formal contract exists in the customary law of the areas that concern us only where dispute settlement has reached a high degree of procedural elaboration.

If we look now at the way in which the three-party contract is used among those Bedouin who have it, we can find some support for the adoption thesis as well as for the thesis mentioned in the preceding paragraph. In Sinai one of the most common uses of the three-party form is in what Weber calls the arbitration contract, a use to which it is quite well-adapted. We also find it in other more or less procedural transactions, for instance the truce and the quitclaim, for which its structure is no less appropriate. But the three-party form is in addition used for contracts that cannot be called procedural, notably the blood-money pact. It seems likely, however, that the three-party form only came to be used in the blood-money pact after having developed elsewhere. The pact is a multilateral transaction, while the three-party contract is unilateral;[31] some sophisticated legal devices had to be created in order to adapt the three-party contract to this particular use (for details, see Stewart 2003, 256–60), and they are unlikely to have come into being simultaneously with the contract in its basic form. Another non-procedural transaction in which the three-party form is always used is divorce. The transaction is not a consensual one—the Bedouin husband may repudiate his wife at any time—and the contractual form is used

[30] See the passages quoted in n. 15 for Weber's own formulations.

[31] The principal gives an undertaking to the obligee, but the obligee does not (within the framework of a single three-party contract) give an undertaking to the principal. If (as is usually the case) the obligee of this contract wishes also to give an undertaking to the principal of this contract, then that undertaking is embedded in a second three-party contract which will normally have a different guarantor from the first one.

merely in order to give it a particular type of legal enforceability (for details, see Stewart 2003, 188–90). It can be taken as almost certain that the three-party contract existed elsewhere in the law before being adapted to repudiation.

In sum, the Sinai Bedouin data are consistent with the adoption thesis. In fact they are consistent with a strengthened version of that thesis: the notion that formal contracts first arise in the context of procedure, and that the form used for giving legal force to procedural transactions is then adopted elsewhere in the legal system. To say this is not, of course, to claim that the adoption thesis is true; such a claim could only plausibly be made on the basis of a review of the evidence from many different legal systems.

There remain in this context two points on which the Sinai Bedouin evidence does not support Weber. One has already been mentioned: his idea that in early law there are the two kinds of contract, status and purpose, each with its own distinctive form. As has been noted, these Bedouin have both types of contract, but only one form. The evidence suggests that techniques these Bedouin originally used for their purpose contracts (that is, their procedural contracts) were subsequently adapted to one of their status contracts (the blood-money pact) and even to a non-consensual transaction (repudiation).

The second point is that precisely the kind of adoption that most interested Weber—the adoption for commercial transactions of contractual forms originally developed in procedure—does not seem to have occurred among the Bedouin. They do not use the three-party contract for business arrangements, contenting themselves instead with formless agreements (Stewart 2003, 274–76). I have no idea why this is so.

IV

Weber lived in a time when legal history flourished as never before or since. The leading figures in the field—who came mostly from the German-speaking countries—were men of extraordinary learning and acuity. But some of them were also a little too prone to speculation. Elegant legal-historical constructions were erected on inadequate factual foundations. A few hints in the documentation of a later period (and often from another place) were enough to induce scholars to reconstruct with misplaced confidence developments that they believed to have occurred in times from which few or no records survived. And having discovered—as they thought—the way in which Roman and Germanic law developed in their earliest stages, they had little hesitation in concluding that all other legal systems must have gone through essentially the same evolution.

Weber, in his treatment of early law in general, and of the early history of contract in particular, adopted these speculations wholesale. He may be excused: there are respectable historians who cling to them to this day. But these ideas, though still stimulating enough to be worthy of our attention, are often wrong, or at best unprovable. Weber (like his contemporaries) saw clearly that early types of contract are very different from later ones, but his attempt to capture much of this contrast in the single distinction between status contracts and purpose contracts is a failure. The evidence from the Bedouin and the Somali adduced in this paper shows that Weber was wrong in believing that the functional distinction between his two types of contract also always corresponds to a formal difference. More generally, it will be evident that Weber drew the distinction between status and purpose contracts only in a very rough-and-ready fashion. If we want to improve our understanding of early forms of contract, then a different approach will be needed, one that is both more rigorous in its analysis and more closely tied to the facts.

CHAPTER EIGHT

PROVINCIAL JUDGES: THE *SHARĪʿA* JUDICIARY OF MID-TWENTIETH-CENTURY YEMEN

Brinkley Messick

For the highland region known as Lower Yemen, the twentieth century moment of incorporation into the state of the Ḥamīd al-Dīn line of Zaydī Imāms occurred in 1919, following the demise of the Ottoman Empire after World War I. Imām Yaḥyā continued to rule over the unified highlands until his assassination in 1948 at the outset of a brief and unsuccessful coup. After only twenty-four days, his son Imām Aḥmad regained control and then shifted the capital south from Ṣanʿāʾ to the important Lower Yemen city of Taʿizz where he had been serving as the provincial Governor. Imām Aḥmad died in his sleep in 1962, and on September 26 of that year the Revolution began that marked the end of the Imamate and the birth of the Yemen Arab Republic.[1]

At the beginning of this twentieth-century period of independent Imamic rule, the next largest center in Lower Yemen after Taʿizz was Ibb, a small (pop. c. 5,000) but prosperous walled old town which sat to one side of a long and seasonally verdant mountain valley at 6,700 feet above sea level. Initially, as under the Ottomans, Ibb was the seat of an administrative District (*qaḍāʾ*) that was part of the old Taʿizz Province, and the principal local judgeship was that of the District. In the late 1930s, however, when Ibb became the capital of a newly formed Province (*liwāʾ*), a higher level judgeship of Ibb Province was added. With the advent of this Province structure, other local judgeships were instituted, including both a Judge of the Seat (*al-maqām*), who was attached directly to the Governor, and the lower level judge of the Ibb Subdistrict (*nāḥiya*). As Aharon Layish (*EI*[2], s.v., Maḥkama, Viii. Yemen and the People's Republic of Southern Yemen, p. 36) has written, "the powers" of

[1] On this period, see Dresch 2000, chs. 2–3; and on the specifically legal dimensions, Haykel 2003, ch. 7. I also cover this period in Messick 1993.

such pre-revolutionary sharīʿa courts were "very wide," including both "personal status and criminal law."

Focusing upon the phenomenon of the provincial sharīʿa court judge (*ḥākim*), I will introduce four men who served in Ibb. Within the frames of these principal biographies, I also refer to a number of other members of the Imamic-era judiciary, including individuals related to the four main judges by kinship, identity or function. My aim in this biographical approach is to pursue patterns of incumbency in the period judgeship, and to elucidate the intellectual and political culture of the judiciary. The judges in question were the sorts of men charged with the application of the *sharīʿa* at the provincial level. My selection of these four particular individuals has to do with their prominence on the local scene in Ibb and also with the fact that I have analyzed a corpus of their court rulings (e.g., Messick 1995; 1998). I draw here on published and unpublished biographical histories (including separate works by a father and son, Muḥammad and Aḥmad Zabāra,[2] and by the brothers, and sometime Ibb residents, Ismāʿīl (1980, 1995) and Muḥammad (1987) al-Akwaʿ, and also on oral historical materials from my field research in Ibb, which began in 1974 and continued, intermittently, until 1995.[3]

Two further themes in my discussion of these four judges are the relationship between schools of *sharīʿa* interpretation and the relationship of the *sharīʿa* to customary law. A distinctive feature of the legal situation in Ibb (and Lower Yemen generally) was that the Shāfiʿī school of law traditionally predominated there, while the Zaydī school occupied the same position in Upper Yemen, and also was official throughout the Imamic state. Part of the characteristic surround of *sharīʿa* application in the courts was the functioning of out-of-court settlements, and a subset of these were based on custom. The resolution of disputes had been central to the mission of the Zaydī Imamate for a thousand years, from the arrival of the first of these Imāms in the highlands. In the late ninth century, Imām al-Hādī was invited to Yemen to personally settle conflicts among tribes near the northern town of Ṣaʿda. Imāms stood for the regime of the *sharīʿa*, but from the beginning this required entering into dialogue

[2] On the father, see Messick 1993, 123–31; on the son, Haykel 2003, 197–200; Messick 1996.

[3] My research was supported by grants from the Social Science Research Council and from Fulbright.

with the dictates and the representatives of custom. In an Imamic state, with the Imām exercising oversight at the pinnacle, ideally as a *mujtahid*, the essential work of dispute resolution had to be delegated. Central to this delegation was the judicial authority invested in the judges of the sharīʿa court system, which was designed to handle the basic traffic in all types of cases.

As the several careers discussed below illustrate, this system of Imamic state courts involved the posting and transferring of court personnel in all the highland and coastal towns and in many rural districts. This distribution of judgeships effectively demarcated the active sphere of state authority. But Yemenis were, and are, notoriously litigious and the sharīʿa court system could neither handle the great volume of disputes nor satisfy the need for alternative forms and terms of resolution. Within the sharīʿa regime itself, however, in addition to conventional litigation that terminated in judgments based procedurally and substantively on *sharīʿa* principles, there also was an envisioned, and valued, possibility of resolution in the form of a judicial settlement (*ṣulḥ*). Such settlements were to be proposed and facilitated by the court judge.

Beyond the state courts, the *sharīʿa* also was implemented by independent jurists, representatives of the broader interpretive community of trained scholars. In the twentieth century, from the mid-1920s onward, a significant segment of this interpretive community was actively shaped by the instructional institutions of the Imamic state, first by means of Imām Yaḥyā's hybrid school, the Madrasa ʿIlmiyya, founded in the capital Ṣanʿāʾ in 1924, and also in schools modeled on it in other towns, later including, under Imām Aḥmad, a similarly conceived school known as the Aḥmadīya in his capital Taʿizz (see Messick 1993, 99–114; cf. Haykel 2003, 196). Existing pious endowment revenues were reorganized and earmarked to provide for teacher and student stipends in such new schools. However, jurists also continued to be trained beyond state auspices, in mosque lesson circles and in private residential sitting rooms. And beyond these town institutions, as Ismāʿīl al-Akwaʿ (1995) has extensively documented, *sharīʿa* scholars also were trained in numerous small rural centers, known as *hijra*s, which were attached to villages (see also Madelung 1991).

Interventions by independent jurists occurred in two basic ways. The first, which preserved a degree of control by the Imām, involved delegations and transfers from the Imām's *dīwān*, either to members of this circle itself or to outside jurists, to assume jurisdiction in particular cases. The second involved independent jurists being approached directly by the parties to a conflict. Rather than a top-down delegation or transfer of judicial authority from the Imām or his circle, this second sort of conflict resolution was predicated on authority that came from the bottom up, often with a formal legal empowerment (*tafwīḍ*). Authority of this type derived from the parties' 'mutual consent' (*tarāḍī*) to submit their matter to the selected jurist and to be bound by his finding. "We are in your hands" was an opening formula of such an approach. Such out-of-court procedures resulted in a judgment called a *ḥukm tarāḍī*, or in an arbitrated or mediated settlement (*ṣulḥ*). In *sharīʿa* jurisprudence, in the sphere of conflict resolution, as in that of contract analysis, the 'mutual consent' of parties was a source of fundamental legal authority (see Messick 2001).

Beside the identities and reputations of particular presiding judges, what the formal courts offered was the fundamental legitimacy of the sharīʿa regime itself together with whatever coercive power the state had in particular settings to summon and require responses from adversaries, and to restrain or punish. Court rulings also offered the possibility of appeal to a higher court and involved regular oversight by the Imām. What independent jurists offered, by contrast, were their reputations for *sharīʿa* knowledge and their personal skills and records in handling conflicts. Many leading independent jurists were known as private *sharīʿa* practitioners. Thus M. Zabāra (1979, 266) records, in formulaic terms, that prior to his appointment as Presiding Judge of the (Ottoman-era) Appeal Court, Ḥusayn al-ʿAmrī "resolved the conflicts of disputants who resorted to him." A frequently encountered formula is used in reference to both the elder and the junior al-Yamānī family judges (see below): "He resolved many legal matters and divided many estates" (al-Jirāfī 1946, 82; A. Zabāra n.d., 2: 343). According to such formulas, what a presiding or intervening jurist did was to 'resolve' or 'settle' (*faṣl*, lit., 'separate', and thus 'to decide'; or *ḥall*, lit., 'open', 'untie') a dispute (*shijār*), problem (*mushkila*), legal matter (*qaḍīya*), or lawsuit (*khuṣūma*). Estate settlement work, involving the inventorying of properties and the division into shares, was as common among leading *sharīʿa* jurists as it was lucrative, and the reported memorization of inheritance law manuals, by judges such as the junior al-Yamānī, underscores the existence of specific expertise.

Out-of-court dispute resolution also opened into the sphere of custom (*'urf*),[4] and many permutations and combinations were possible. In his social history of villages southeast of Ibb town, Isaac Hollander (2005, 281) presents a document countersigned by then-Ibb District Judge al-Manṣūr (see below), which its local writer describes as involving a "customary judgment with a *sharī'a* orientation" (*ḥukm 'urfī wa wajh shar'ī*). Other such complex articulations of the sharī'a system with tribal custom have been analyzed by Paul Dresch (1989) and Martha Mundy (1995, 268–76) on the basis of settlement documents from rural highland contexts in Upper Yemen. As was true of most such settlements, the governing substantive and procedural rules of tribal customary law also were set down in written texts, so that the relation of *sharī'a* to custom was not simply one of written to oral.[5]

Although in many tribal contexts custom largely held sway without regard to the *sharī'a*, independent jurists resident in some villages also were available to represent its legitimacy. Part of this phenomenon was based on the existence of the numerous and widely dispersed scholarly *hijra*s identified by I. al-Akwa' (1995). Clusters of these village-based *hijra*s dotted great swatches of the central highland map (see al-Akwa' 1995), although there also were spaces, especially to the east and in the far north, nearly devoid of them. Another part of this presence of the *sharī'a* in the domain of tribal custom concerned jurists attached to particular tribal groups. For example, I. al-Akwa' (1995, 126–28) gives biographical entries on jurists who came to be known as the al-Jabrīs, the first of whom, Ṣāliḥ b. Aḥmad (d. 1855), was 'chosen' by the tribesmen of Banī Jabr to handle their legal matters. It is reported of this jurist that "he occasionally ruled, when necessary, with a customary judgment (*ḥukm 'urfī*), so long as it was not in conflict with the *sharī'a*." This man's great grandson is identified by al-Akwa' as "a scholar knowledgeable in the *fiqh* and inheritance." He was 'chosen' by the same tribal group as its 'judge' and it is reported that he, too, issued "customary judgments that were not in opposition to the Islamic *sharī'a*." In addition to such resident exemplars of the *sharī'a*, there was the important institution of 'going out' (*khurūj*) by town-based specialists, on the basis, again, either of an official dispatch or an invitation from the parties.

---

[4] See my discussion in Messick 1993, 182–86.

[5] For general and specific references, see *EI*[2], s.v., Ṭāghūt, 2. As a Legal Term in Yemen; Tha'r; and 'Urf, 2. Arab Customary Law (Frank H. Stewart).

Although large parts of the Upper Yemen countryside were under the demarcated sway of particular tribal rules, custom often interfaced with the *sharīʿa*, and this was true even at the very center of state authority. Rather than consisting of a simple boundary between a state sphere and an entirely separate sphere of custom, *sharīʿa* and custom in Yemen interpenetrated in distinctive ways. A particular strength of the sharīʿa system was in agrarian property relations, so that even in most 'tribal' locales, which were not places of nomadism but of settled cultivation, *sharīʿa* categories of individual ownership (*milk*) and of lease (*ijāra*) quietly predominated. A particular strength of tribal custom was in addressing matters of abused honor, so that even in the towns turbans would be thrown down and bulls sacrificed (in what was known as a *hajr*) as offending parties arrived at the door of an aggrieved family. In many respects *sharīʿa* and tribal custom were complementary, but there also were characteristic points of difference. One of these concerned the individual rights of women, mainly in matters of marriage and inheritance, which the *sharīʿa* generally defended; another was in criminal law, where the *sharīʿa* held for individual responsibility and either a set amount of monetary compensation or the requirement of a 'life for a life', while tribal custom looked beyond individuals to their responsible kinsmen and had highly elaborated penalty structures. In addition to tribal custom, there was the town-based custom of the merchants and also that of the government, and even the custom that pertained to the courts themselves. For all types of prevailing custom the basic *sharīʿa* perspective was that it was accepted provided it did not contravene a *sharīʿa* rule.

Sayyid *Ismāʿīl ʿAbd al-Raḥmān al-Manṣūr (c. 1883–1963)*[6] *Judge of Ibb Province*

Like his colleague Judge al-Iryānī (see below), Judge al-Manṣūr held a number of judicial appointments prior to a final, lengthy posting in Ibb, a position in which he died. He was from Upper Yemen, a Zaydī school jurist posted in a Shāfiʿī district in Lower Yemen. His posting followed a formula dating back several centuries in which

[6] A. Zabāra n.d., 1: 235; I. al-Akwaʿ 1995, 429.

Imāms dispatched northern-born judges (and governors, etc.) to Lower Yemen. In some instances this led to the local rooting of important Ibb town descent groups with scholarly identities, such as the al-Shuwaytir, al-Mujāhid and al-Ānsī families (see Messick 1993, 41, 45, 271).

However, unlike individuals from these families and his three colleagues discussed below—Judges al-Iryānī, al-Haddād and al-Yamānī—all of whom were from what are termed 'qāḍī' families, Judge al-Manṣūr was a *sayyid*, a descendant of the Prophet. In Yemen, the word qāḍī, which ordinarily means 'judge' in Arabic, has an additional broader usage. Thus the title 'al-qāḍī' before an individual's proper name refers to educated individuals who are not of *sayyid* descent. 'Al-qāḍī' indicates either that the individual himself is educated, or that he comes from a family with a reputation for education. Individuals from 'qāḍī' families did serve as judges, but there were many others from such families, also known as 'al-qāḍī So-and-So', who, while adequately educated, never entered the judiciary. Those of *sayyid* descent also had a general reputation for educational achievement, although, as with qāḍī families, there were individuals, branches and whole families that did not pursue instruction. Judge al-Manṣūr was from a *sayyid* line that went back through Imām al-Qāsim (d. 1620). As such, he shared an identity with the ruling family of the Ḥamīd al-Dīn Imāms, including Imām Yaḥyā, his son Imām Aḥmad and also Sayf al-Islām ('Sword of Islam', as the Imām's sons were titled) al-Ḥasan, the younger son of Imām Yaḥyā, who was the Governor of Ibb in the late 1930s and 1940s. Judge al-Manṣūr also shared this identity with the members of many other prominent highland *sayyid* families, such as the al-Wazīrs, and with some local *sayyid* families in Ibb.

Several other Ibb town judges of the period also were *sayyid*s from the northern highlands. One was Sayyid Ḥasan b. ʿAbd al-Wahhāb al-Warīth (al-Jirāfī 1946, 68; al-Ḥaddād n.d., 98), born in Dhamār in 1868, the Judge of the Ibb District prior to Judge al-Manṣūr. Judge al-Warīth also held a series of judicial appointments in the highlands prior to Ibb. In 1926, he was appointed to the Ibb judgeship and he died in this office in 1934. Al-Warīth's legal studies began with his father and other teachers in his natal town of Dhamār, an important center for Zaydī scholarship. Some eighteenth-century Zaydī jurists posted to Ibb used to send their sons to Dhamār for instruction. Talented men such as al-Warīth frequently gravitated to the seat of state power, with its concentration of scholars and possibilities for advanced study, and many were drawn into the employ of the Imām. Al-Warīth's brother became prominent as the co-editor of the literary journal al-Ḥikma and, prior to his final career posting in Ibb, al-Warīth himself served as one of the 'judges of the Imām's administrative circle' (*ḥukkām al-dīwān*).

During his time in Ṣanʿāʾ, al-Warīth pursued advanced studies with the very distinguished Ḥusayn b. ʿAlī al-ʿAmrī (d. 1942), the subject of an extended biographical history by al-Jirāfī (al-Jirāfī 1946; cf. M. Zabāra 1979, 265–66; A. Zabāra n.d.; I. al-Akwaʿ 1995, 1459). Following the Peace Treaty of Daʿʿān between Imām Yaḥyā and the Ottomans in 1911, al-ʿAmrī was appointed by Imām Yaḥyā as the first Yemeni Chief Justice of the Appeal Court in what was still the Ottoman Province of Yemen. Al-Jirāfī refers to al-ʿAmrī as 'Shaykh al-Islām', the highest honorific for a jurist, while al-Akwaʿ calls him 'Shaykh al-Shuyūkh', or 'teacher of teachers' (Cf. Haykel 2003, 200). Al-ʿAmrī's studies continued, M. Zabāra writes, "until he mastered all of the *sharīʿa* sciences." Al-ʿAmrī's formation is detailed in an account he wrote of his teachers and the specific books he studied with each of them (quoted in al-Jirāfī 1946, 13–25; summarized in M. Zabāra 1979, 256–66). This exemplary formation included the study of the authoritative *Commentary on the Flowers* (*sharḥ al-azhār*) with no fewer than six teachers. Notable among the many other works mentioned, in the several disciplines, are the major Sunnī *ḥadīth* works. The complex Zaydī tradition that al-ʿAmrī so fully received and transmitted thus comprised not only the venerable Hādawī mainstream of the school (represented by the *Flowers* literature) but also that of the 'Sunnī' opposition that culminated in al-Shawkānī, the major motif of which was the turn to the utilization of these Sunnī *ḥadīth* sources (Haykel 2003). One of the specific books Judge al-Warīth reportedly studied with al-ʿAmrī was *The Overflowing Sea* (*al-Baḥr al-Zakhkhār*), the cross-school comparative work by Imām al-Murtaḍā, the late fourteenth-century author of the school's authoritative basic text, *The Book of Flowers*. Aḥmad Qāsim al-ʿAnsī, the author of the *Gilded Crown* (*al-Tāj al-Mudhahhab*) the last, twentieth-century commentary on the *Flowers*, also studied with al-ʿAmrī and worked as his secretary. One of the many students to which al-ʿAmrī issued diplomas was the future Imām Aḥmad.

In Ibb, Judge al-Warīth lived in a large, multi-floor old stone house named Dār al-Mulk, which is located just across from the small domed Bayḥānī Mosque on the through-street that passes by two of the town's three large commercial warehouses (*khāns*) on its way from the Great Mosque to the Main Gate. Dār al-Mulk, a name which literally means the 'House of (State) Authority,' was privately owned and had served as a rented government residence since Turkish times. Although there was an official location for his sharīʿa court in the government building (*ḥukūma*), al-Warīth conducted morning court in the partially walled yard (*ḥawsh*) in front of this house. Weather normally permitted the holding of open air morning court year round, since even during the May–August rainy season rain usually fell only in the afternoons. A man I knew remembered that in these sessions Judge al-Warīth would respond properly for disputants who were unable to do so for themselves. The government building of this (pre-provincial) era, which was another unspecialized, multi-storied residential stone house, rose high above a buttressed portion of the town wall near the Main Gate. Its top floor, looking out over the cultivated valley to the northwest, had a room for the District Officer (*ʿāmil*) and another for the District Court; the Treasury (*māliyya*) occupied the floor below; the military administration the next floor down; and the jail (*shabaka*, lit., 'net') the ground floor.

A second judge of *sayyid* ancestry who served in an Ibb judgeship was Sayyid ʿAbd Allāh b. Muḥammad b. Isḥāq (b. 1902),[7] Judge of the Ibb Subdistrict. Of a younger generation than Judge al-Warīth, Judge Isḥāq was trained in the capital at the Madrasa ʿIlmiyya. He, too, had an official location for his Subdistrict Court, which was located together with the office of the Municipality (*baladiyya*) atop one of the bastions of the Main Gate of the town, but it is remembered that Judge Isḥāq received petitioners and litigants elsewhere, including in the street, in the mosque, or at his house, which was in a quarter just north of the Great Mosque.

To return to Judge al-Manṣūr, following his previous appointment in Dhamār, he was posted by the Imām to Ibb in 1934 to follow Judge al-Warīth as the Judge of the District; later, with the administrative change, al-Manṣūr became Judge of the Province. Originally from a village near Shuhāra in the northern mountains, where he began his studies, Judge al-Manṣūr remained in Ibb as the principal

[7] M. Zabāra 1979, 384. I photographed a register from his court, containing case records dated 1954 to 1960, at the Ibb house of Judge Aḥmad Muḥammad al-Ḥaddād.

judge for twenty-eight years. During this time he resided in Dār Daʿfān, an elegant four-storey stone house just west of the Great Mosque, where, across a small cobblestone square, it faces the mosque's porticoed entrance. Although he also had the official court room in the government building, Judge al-Manṣūr worked from Dār Daʿfān, receiving disputants in the morning in front of the house and, after lunch, one flight of stairs up in his afternoon sitting room.

In a theme that is repeated for many prominent jurists, it is reported in his biography that Judge al-Manṣūr continued to teach during his years as a sharīʿa court judge: "He taught whenever he was free and his house was open to all who arrived." Biographer A. Zabāra also mentions a telling detail concerning the social respect given this judge. Recognizing "his worth, due to his knowledge, refinement and integrity," the prominent and powerful Ibb Governor of the 1950s, Aḥmad al-Sayāghī, always stood up when Judge al-Manṣūr entered the room. With the coming of the Revolution of 1962, it is recalled that the eighty-year-old judge was put in jail for two days, and then was released, and that he died a few months later.

Ḥasan b. Aḥmad al-Iryānī (1901–1968)[8]
Judge of the [provincial] Seat

Judge al-Iryāni, who was not arrested at the Revolution, succeeded Judge al-Manṣūr as the Judge of the Province, and he remained in the post until his death six years later. The notion of 'retirement' had yet to be introduced in Yemen and judges commonly died while still occupying their positions. Judges always were supported by their households, and in their later years such jurists usually had the full-time support and assistance of a son, a nephew or a son-in-law. In one case I have read, Judge al-Manṣūr's son plays a subordinate role, and in another case, when his father was sick, he served as the Acting Judge. Nepotism, as we negatively term it, was the norm. Across the old occupations, from jurist and Imām to tailor and cultivator, sons commonly succeeded their fathers and often appren-

[8] M. Zabāra 1979, 205–10; A. Zabāra n.d., 2: 13–17; I. al-Akwaʿ 1995, 79–82; and information from his son Muḥammad b. Ḥasan in Ibb.

ticed with them. Judge al-Iryānī began his career as a personal secretary (*kātib*) to the future Imām Aḥmad, then the Governor of Ḥajja in the northwest. Later, al-Iryānī held a series of five judicial positions, the last three of which were in rural locations in the north of Ibb Province. In the early 1950s, he was appointed in Ibb as the Judge of the [provincial] Seat (*ḥākim al-maqām*), the judgeship of the governorate, and it was in this capacity, in 1961, that he ruled in a murder case I have studied (Messick 1998).

Born in Iryān, the well-known village in the northern part of Ibb Province tied administratively to the District of Yarīm, Judge al-Iryānī studied with two members of his large and influential descent group. The Iryānīs, many of whom held judgeships in locations in the vicinity of their natal village, operated on the frontiers of the Zaydī-Shāfiʿī divide. Their home district was located along one of the boundary zones between Upper and Lower Yemen, and one family member described to me a split in allegiances, explaining that they were Zaydī in jurisprudence but Shāfiʿī in ritual matters.

Judge al-Iryānī's first teacher was Ḥusayn b. ʿAbd Allāh al-Iryānī, in his own judicial career the judge of al-Nādira and later of Khubān, both in northeast Ibb Province. Biographer M. Zabāra writes that the future Ibb judge "acquired knowledge from him" (*iqtabasa min anwārihi*), literally, he 'took from his lights'. The related verbal noun, *iqtibās*, means not only 'learning' but also 'borrowing', and by extension the 'adaptation' of a literary work, and finally, 'quotation'. The transmission of knowledge from teacher to student could be thought of as a kind of quotation. Following this first teacher, the future judge devoted himself as a student to another of the al-Iryānīs, a man who was at the time the principal Judge of Ibb, the very distinguished Yaḥyā b. Muḥammad.

This Yaḥyā b. Muḥammad al-Iryānī (b. 1881 or 1882, d. 1943),[9] a *ḥāfiẓ*, one of the relatively limited number of individuals in his place and time to have memorized the entire Qur'ān, is referred to by biographer al-Akwaʿ in the same exalted terms as Ḥusayn al-ʿAmrī, that is, as a 'shaykh al-shuyūkh', a 'teacher of teachers'. There also was an instructional connection between the two great men: according to biographer al-Jirāfī, al-Iryānī asked for and received a

[9] Al-Jirāfī 1946, 133; M. Zabāra 1979, 635–42; A. Zabāra n.d., 4: 217–26; al-Akwaʿ 1995, 71–7. See also Messick 1993, 192–93, Haykel 2003, 199.

diploma (*ijāza*) from al-ʿAmrī. In 1910, still in the Ottoman period, al-Iryānī received his first appointment, which was to a teaching position in Yarīm. In 1919, the year which marked the end of the empire, the independence of Yemen and the extension of Imām Yaḥyā's control to Lower Yemen, al-Iryānī was appointed as the first Imamic-era District Judge in Ibb. He, too, resided in the large house known as Dār al-Mulk. As al-Akwaʿ states, "his work in the judgeship did not inhibit his teaching those who desired to acquire knowledge." In 1926, however, after a conflict with the District Officer of Ibb, the powerful and wealthy local man, Ismāʿīl Bāsalāma, he retired for a period to his native Iryān to teach and give fatwās.[10] But in 1930, Yaḥyā b. Muḥammad was summoned by Imām Yaḥyā to be a member of the Appeal Court, and soon thereafter, when the court was expanded into two sections, he was made the Presiding Judge of the First Section. While in Ṣanʿāʾ, he continued his instructional work, teaching at the new Madrasa ʿIlmiyya and also at the al-Filayḥī Mosque, where early nationalist discussions were beginning to occur. His important work in the field of *ḥadīth* was published posthumously.[11] Al-Akwaʿ also reports that Yaḥyā b. Muḥammad had a notable personal library (*khizāna*) of manuscripts and printed works he had inherited and acquired, and that he was a prolific poet for whom "not an occasion passed that he did not record in his poetry."

Poetry, oral and written, was, and is, a prime medium of political discourse in the highlands, and one important branch of this prodigious output was produced by jurists.[12] Yaḥyā b. Muḥammad al-Iryānī was one of many in his extended descent group to express himself in verse, and the biographies of these and other jurists are filled with selections from their poems. Yaḥyā Muḥammad's famous son ʿAbd al-Raḥmān al-Iryānī also was a formidable poet. Later the President of the Yemen Arab Republic (1967–74), ʿAbd al-Raḥmān

[10] The two men, al-Iryānī and Bāsalāma, figure together in Muḥammad al-Akwaʿ's two volume biographical history, *ʿĀlim wa Amīr* (1987).

[11] *Hidāyat al-Mustabṣirīn bi-Sharḥ ʿUddat al-Ḥuṣn al-Ḥaṣīn*, based on al-Shawkānī's commentary on a work by al-Jazarī (d. 1429). It was edited by the author' son ʿAbd al-Raḥmān and published in Damascus in 1397/1977. Cf. al-Akwaʿ 1995, 77. Al-ʿAmrī (1985, 176) calls it a "truly remarkable new Hadith work", while also noting that it "depends entirely on Shawkānī".

[12] See recent anthropological studies, including the book by Caton 1990, and dissertations by Lucine Taminian 2001 and W. Flagg Miller 2001.

was an Ibb-based leader of the abortive Coup of 1948 and, prior to that, had held a rural judgeship in Ibb Province. He was jailed for many years after the Coup of 1948 and, several years earlier, in 1944, one of his well-remembered poems also had landed him in jail. This poem, which became an important monument of the 'nationalist' opposition, mounted a sharp attack on the Imamic regime (reproduced in I. al-Akwaʿ 1995, 1748–53, cf. M. Zabāra 1979, 354–55).

In the Imamic period jurists jailed for political reasons often were returned to positions of responsibility. After ʿAbd al-Raḥmān al-Iryānī was released the second time, Imām Aḥmad appointed him to the Sharīʿa Panel (*Hayʾa Sharʿīyya*), the highest judicial review organ.[13] When the early nationalist and historian Muḥammad al-Akwaʿ was released from jail, he assumed a judgeship in Ibb Province (District of Dhī Sufāl). A third example is a man named Aḥmad b. Aḥmad al-Jirāfī (I. al-Akwaʿ 1995, 366) who began his career as a secretary to the Judge of Ṣanʿāʾ in late Ottoman times and who went on to serve as a district officer. In these years he also handled a well-known legal case that involved Imām Yaḥyā as a litigant party. The case concerned the Imām's claim of a right of pre-emption (*shufʿa*) in a house in Ṣanʿāʾ in which al-Jirāfī famously ruled against him. Al-Jirāfī later participated in the nationalist opposition movement of 1948 and was subsequently jailed, but after two months he was released and appointed by Imām Aḥmad to the Appeal Court, and later he served as the Imām's Minister of Justice. The '*sharīʿa* sciences' were the principal focus of advanced academic formation in this period and trained jurists were indispensable members of the highland's limited intelligentsia.

Ultimately, for the Judge of the Seat in Ibb, Ḥasan b. Aḥmad al-Iryānī, it was his non-*sayyid* identity and his broader family credentials of criticism and opposition, and also the specific influence of his relative ʿAbd al-Raḥmān, who would be the first republican Minister of Justice, that kept him out of jail with the coming of the Revolution. M. Zabāra says of Judge al-Iryānī that he, too, was an *adīb*, a literary man, who "worked in literature and the versification of excellent poetry." Excerpts of four of his poems are quoted in his biography. These include verses written to historian Zabāra himself,

[13] The Panel was headed by the later historian and Muftī of the Republic, Sayyid Aḥmad al-Zabāra, at the time related by marriage to the Imām.

then in Ibb, on the occasion of the end of Ramadan that year; a poem written in praise of Imām Yaḥyā, with a response from the Imām; humorous verses sent to Ḥusayn al-ʿAmrī; and a *qaṣīda* of fifty-four verses addressed to Imām Yaḥyā in the venerable 'advice' (*naṣīḥa*) genre. This last concerned the external politics of the day, specifically the treaty the Imām had signed with Italy in 1926. Al-Iryānī pointedly reminded the Imām of what happened to King Husayn, the Sharif of Mecca, after he entered into an alliance with the British against the Ottomans in World War I. Al-Akwaʿ (1995, 80–2), who also excerpts the poem, renders the gist of al-Iryānī's warning to the Imām as follows: "When the English accomplished their aims, they abandoned their ally and took the side of their ally's new enemy, King ʿAbd al-ʿAzīz Al Saʿūd."

A. Zabāra mentions, without elaborating, that early on in his career Judge al-Iryānī was drawn to asceticism and to sufism. Al-Akwaʿ (1995, 82) attributes to him two unpublished historical works: one a biographical history of the scholars of his native Iryān and the other a history of twentieth-century relations between the Ḥāshid and the Zarānīq, the key tribal confederation of the northern highlands and the principal tribe of the Red Sea costal plain. Al-Iryānī knew this particular history personally from his early days in the employ of the future Imām Aḥmad who famously used Ḥāshid forces to subdue the Zarānīq.

Yaḥyā b. ʿAlī al-Ḥaddād, (1890–1955)[14]
First Secretary, Acting Judge

Where the jurists from Iryān situated themselves betwixt and between Zaydī and Shāfiʿī territories and traditions, those of the noted al-Ḥaddād family of Ibb were the quintessential Shāfiʿī jurists of Lower Yemen. In my earlier work (Messick 1993) I focused on the local Shāfiʿī juridical tradition represented by several scholarly descendants of ʿAlī b. Nājī al-Ḥaddād (d. 1893). This man also was the father

[14] A. Zabāra n.d., 4: 166. I. al-Akwaʿ (1995, 1738) does not give a biography but mentions that he wrote a biographical work on Imām Yaḥyā. The biography of his father, ʿAlī Nājī al-Ḥaddād, is in M. Zabāra 1956, 149–57, at the end of which his grandson, my friend Muḥammad b. Yaḥyā b. ʿAlī, is mentioned as "among the secretaries of the Imamic *dīwān* in these days".

of Yaḥyā b. ʿAlī, who was the Acting Judge of a property case from 1931 I have studied.[15]

Two of the Acting Judge's siblings, ʿAbd al-Raḥmān b. ʿAlī (d. 1922) and Abū Bakr b. ʿAlī (d. 1932), were very distinguished men. ʿAbd al-Raḥmān (M. Zabāra 1979, 347–49) was one of the great men of Lower Yemen in the late Ottoman period. He not only attained the highest level of *sharīʿa* scholarship and served in judicial positions, first following his father ʿAlī as *Muftī* in Ibb and then assuming the principal judgeship of Taʿizz Province, but he was also, as the Deputy (*wakīl*) to the Ottoman Governor of Taʿizz Province, a high-ranking Yemeni political leader as well. After Imām Yaḥyā assumed control of Lower Yemen in 1919, he appointed ʿAbd al-Raḥmān al-Ḥaddād as the Presiding Judge of the Taʿizz Appeal Court. For his part, Abū Bakr (M. Zabāra 1979, 39–40) followed his father and brother as the Ibb *Muftī*, and then served in judgeships in Taʿizz and in the Red Sea port town of al-Ḥudayda. Still another brother, Muḥammad, was the father of Aḥmad, who married his uncle ʿAbd al-Raḥmān's daughter and succeeded his uncle Abū Bakr as a third generation *Muftī* of Ibb. In the decade before the Revolution this Aḥmad b. Muḥammad b. ʿAlī al-Ḥaddād was posted as a judge in the western mountains of Ibb Province. Later still, up to his retirement in 1980, I knew him as a town judge in Ibb, who signed himself as 'Judge of Ibb'. When his uncle Yaḥyā b. ʿAlī died in 1955, this future republican-era judge, Aḥmad b. Muḥammad b. ʿAlī, wrote a poem of remembrance.

Although some scholarly families produced noted individuals over many generations and, in some cases, centuries—several *sayyid* lineages and a few 'qāḍī' families, such as the al-Akwaʿs, being examples—there also was a pattern of scholarly credentials being newly achieved by individuals of non-scholarly ancestry. One of the leading scholars of late Imamic and post-Revolutionary Ibb, Muḥammad Nājī al-Wahhābī (d. 1993), a respected teacher and later the town *Muftī*, emerged from an untutored and low-status local background. Talent could be recognized and such boys sometimes found their way beyond Qur'ānic-school to higher instruction, which in Ibb and elsewhere was supported by pious endowment-financed residences and stipends. It may have been the case that the scholarly branch

[15] This case figures in my book in progress on the mid-twentieth century sharīʿa system in the highlands.

of the al-Ḥaddād family actually commenced with their late nineteenth-century scholarly eponym, ʿAlī. During my residence in Ibb, beyond the kinship tree of the scholarly al-Ḥaddāds, there were other, uneducated people in town named al-Ḥaddād (which means 'smith'), including individuals who worked in the grain trade. Also, there is no record of Nājī, ʿAlī's father, being a scholar. The eponym of the scholarly al-Ḥaddāds was not among those described in their biographies as having begun their studies with their fathers. Despite some theories I heard from al-Ḥaddād family members—asserting a connection, for example, to the scholarly al-Ḥaddāds of the Ḥaḍramawt—it appears that ʿAlī b. Nājī was the first of the Ḥaddāds of Ibb to excel in the acquisition of knowledge.

Acting Judge al-Ḥaddād's son Muḥammad b. Yaḥyā b. ʿAlī al-Ḥaddād was my friend in the 1970s. This Muḥammad was one of the secretaries in the *dīwān* of Imām Aḥmad and after the Revolution of 1962 he served as a cabinet minister while pursing his principal career as a historian. I did not become fully aware of the judicial career of his father until years later when I began to study the judgment record of the property case I mentioned. Acting Judge Yaḥyā b. ʿAlī also was less well-known to biographical history. Where there are biographical entries on several of the al-Ḥaddāds, including my friend Muḥammad, the third generation historian (M. Zabāra 1979, 608–9), one did not exist for his father. This omission later was remedied by an entry added in the expanded version of the same historical book by Aḥmad Zabāra (n.d. 4: 166), a work I first saw in 1995. Later still, I obtained a photocopy of the same Yaḥyā b. ʿAlī al-Ḥaddād's still unpublished book, a biography of Imām Yaḥyā.[16]

Like the Zaydī jurists of the north, reared intellectually on the *Book of Flowers* and its commentary literature, the Shāfiʿī jurists of Ibb and elsewhere in Lower Yemen were formed on the concise and authoritative law manuals of their own school. These were the same standard works studied and relied upon by Shāfiʿīs everywhere, including jurists in Egypt, the Levant, Southeast Asia and the nearby Ḥaḍramawt: the *Minhāj al-Ṭālibīn* ('Program for Students') by the Syrian Nawawī (d. 1277), and its large abridgement and commentary literature, including four titles mentioned in the biography of

[16] My thanks for this to John Willis. The original manuscript is in the Western Library, Great Mosque, Ṣanʿāʾ, Tarīkh, 2594.

ʿAbd al-Raḥmān al-Ḥaddād; the *Mukhtaṣar* ('Abbreviation') of Abū Shujaʿ, and its smaller commentary literature, including the late nineteenth-century *Ḥāshiya* by the Egyptian al-Bājurī; and the *Zubad* ('Cream'), a law manual in verse by Ibn Raslān, which was commented on (in prose) by a nineteenth century Ibb jurist named al-Muftī (d. 1866).

Aside from the *madhhab*-specific character of their authoritative *fiqh* texts, there otherwise was a significant overlap in the principal texts studied by Zaydīs and Shāfiʿīs in Yemen, especially in the remaining academic disciplines such as Qur'ānic exegesis (*tafsīr*), *ḥadīth*, and the language sciences (grammar and the rhetorical arts). This may be illustrated by comparing the relatively detailed biographical entries for Ḥusayn al-ʿAmrī, an exemplary Zaydī, and ʿAbd al-Raḥmān al-Ḥaddād, the prominent Shāfiʿī. In Qur'ān exegesis, both studied the *Kashshāf* of Zamakhsharī (d. 1025), while in the field of *ḥadīth*, both studied the *Ṣaḥīḥ* of al-Bukhārī, the *Ṣaḥīḥ* of Muslim and the *Sunan* of Abu Dā'ūd, that is, three of the six standard 'mother texts' of the (Sunnī) discipline. In grammar, Ibn Hishām and the thousand verse (*Alfiyya*) manual by Ibn Mālik were standard in both the Zaydī and the Shāfiʿī traditions as was the *Talkhīs*, by Qazwīnī (d. 1338), in rhetoric.

While they served to mark *madhhab* identities, the different legal texts studied by Zaydīs and Shāfiʿīs should not be seen as an absolute barrier between them. In the first place, Zaydī doctrine was close to that of the Sunnī schools, and points of practical difference between the two schools were both limited in number and relatively well-known among Yemeni jurists. In the second, some scholars received academic certification across these intellectual genealogies. One example is the Acting Judge himself, whose early studies in Ibb began with his father and his older brother ʿAbd al-Raḥmān. According to his own account (al-Ḥaddād n.d., 27), however, he later requested a 'general diploma' (*ijāza ʿāmma*) from Ḥusayn al-ʿAmrī. This al-ʿAmrī issued, but only after al-Ḥaddād also had agreed to give similar licences to al-ʿAmrī's sons. In the next generation, his son Muḥammad b. Yaḥyā al-Ḥaddād, my friend the future historian, studied *fiqh* with the Zaydī *sayyid* and also republican-era historian, Aḥmad Zabāra, who was at the time the Head Judge of the Sharīʿa Panel. For his part, Zabāra had studied the *Commentary on the Flowers* among other works, with both Yaḥyā Muḥammad al-Iryānī (see above) and the distinguished father of Judge al-Yamānī (see below).

Although they had been trained on the texts of a different school of *sharī'a* law and while they also had served in various Ottoman-era appointments, the Ḥaddād siblings, including the future Acting Judge Yaḥyā b. 'Alī, successfully made the transition to function as jurists in the Zaydī state. To this end, they actively adapted themselves to the rule of Imām Yaḥyā and versed themselves in the details of Zaydī legal practice. According to an unpublished biography by his brother Abū Bakr which is mentioned by biographer Zabāra, 'Abd al-Raḥmān al-Ḥaddād's early writings had been on such topics as *jihād* and the old Sunnī issue of the status of miracles attributed to saints. But after the collapse of Ottoman rule he shifted topics, notably to a versification of, and commentary upon Imām Yaḥyā's juridical 'choices' (*ikhtiyārāt*) (See Messick 1993, 48, 211–16; Haykel 2003, 204–5, 213–14). Such 'choices' represented an Imām's personal doctrinal positions on a limited set of troublesome topics and they were meant to guide sharī'a court judges in their rulings in these specific areas of the law. Three decades later, the also Shāfi'ī-trained *Muftī* of Ibb, 'Abd al-Raḥmān's nephew and son-in-law, Aḥmad b. Muḥammad b. 'Alī al-Ḥaddād, wrote a letter of commentary explicating the textual sources of the new set of 'choices' recently issued upon his accession by Imām Aḥmad. For his efforts, Aḥmad b. Muḥammad received a letter of thanks from the Imām and, not long after, an appointment as a rural sharī'a court judge in the western mountains of Ibb Province. In addressing the 'choices' of the ruling Imāms of each of their respective eras these two Ḥaddāds demonstrated both fealty to the ruler and their mastery of the applied doctrine of the official school of *sharī'a* interpretation.

For his part, as noted earlier, the future Acting Judge Yaḥyā b. 'Alī authored a book-length biography (*sīra*) of Imām Yaḥyā. This work contains a life sketch of the 'Imām of our age' and discusses some aspects of his administration before turning to a year-by-year political history from 1904 to 1924. In an early section of his book (pp. 28–33) Yaḥyā b. 'Alī gives a detailed description of Imām Yaḥyā's new school, the Madrasa 'Ilmiyya, which I have described as a 'hybrid' of old and new (Messick 1993, Ch. 5; cf. I. al-Akwa' 1980). One of the innovations of this school was its division into levels and classes. As al-Ḥaddād notes, however, in this new educational regime the *Book of Flowers* remained a set text for the beginning classes, while the study of the *Commentary on the Flowers*, which he mentions six times, recurs in the curriculum of the later years. In addition to its genre identity as a *sīra*, al-Ḥaddād's book is further described as a 'commentary'. The target of the commentary is the author's own verses, amounting to more than a thousand lines and written some years before on the topic of the noble ancestry of the Zaydī Imāms. The book also contains excerpts from some of the poetry written about this earlier work in the testimonial genre (*taqrīḍ*), including some lines from 1922 by Imām Yaḥyā himself (al-Ḥaddād n.d., 27). In his entry on the year 1340 H., Yaḥyā b. ʿAlī covers the death of his well-known brother ʿAbd al-Raḥmān (pp. 199–217). He quotes an obituary that appeared in the Yemeni journal *al-Ḥikma* together with several poems written in remembrance, including poems by their brother Abū Bakr and by the Ibb judge of the time, Yaḥyā b. Muḥammad al-Iryānī. He states that his brother's Ottoman period book on *jihād* was printed in Egypt and he dates ʿAbd al-Raḥmān's treatment of Imām Yaḥyā's 'choices' to 1920. He explains that his brother addressed only those of the Imām's 'choices' he had been aware of, mentioning also that the Imām "required of his judges that their work be in accord with" these doctrinal rules. ʿAbd al-Raḥmān wrote both an initial versification and then a brief prose commentary on the Imām's 'choices'. This commentary both analyzed the textual sources for such rules and also cross-referenced and further supported the Imām's 'choices' with respect to Sunnī jurisprudential thought. He "exposed the clear indications (*adilla*) of these choices and additionally set forth that which strengthened their positions from the views of the jurists of the four [Sunnī] *madhhab*s."

As the example of Yaḥyā b. ʿAlī al-Ḥaddād shows, court secretaries frequently were men of distinction, and as the 1931 property case I have read indicates, they could be delegated authority to decide cases. In his book on Imām Yaḥyā, as he mentions some judicial appointments, including that of the previously mentioned Sayyid Ḥasan al-Warīth in Ibb, Yaḥyā b. ʿAlī states concerning his own career that he refused to accept an appointment that would require him to move away from his native town of Ibb (pp. 97–8). The Imām consequently appointed him as First Secretary to Judge al-Warīth and he remained an Ibb court secretary for many years. Toward the end of his life, however, he relented and was appointed by Imām Aḥmad as Judge of the Subdistrict of Dhī Sufāl, southwest of Ibb, a post in which he died. Another example of such a highly qualified court functionary is Yaḥyā b. ʿAlī al-Iryānī (d. 1939) (M. Zabāra 1979, 625–26; A. Zabāra n.d., 4: 180; al-Akwaʿ 1995,

77), who was a secretary in the court of his cousin, the previous District Judge of Ibb, Yaḥyā b. Muḥammad al-Iryānī, who also was his teacher. In 1932, this al-Iryānī was transferred from his post as an Ibb court secretary directly to a judgeship on the Appeal Court.

ʿAbd Allāh b. ʿAlī al-Yamānī (al-Yadūmī), 1884–1972[17]
Judge of the [Imamic] Seat

A different category of judicial intervention in local sharīʿa proceedings is exemplified by the work of ʿAbd Allāh b. ʿAlī, who signed himself on final judgment rolls as al-Yamānī, but whose correct family name is al-Yadūmī. Originally from Ṣanʿāʾ, Judge of the Seat al-Yamānī remained in Taʿizz for more than twenty years, during which time he built a house and took up residence. Unlike the three preceding judges, Judge al-Yamānī had no regular jurisdiction in Ibb and only took on cases involving important Ibb town families at the behest of the Imām. Unlike independent jurists, men who from time to time received cases transferred from the Imām's circle (*dīwān*) or from one of his governors, or who handled cases after being approached directly by the parties, Judge al-Yamānī had a long-term judicial appointment in Taʿizz as the Judge of the Seat. This was the judgeship attached directly to Aḥmad, initially as the Heir to the Throne and, after 1948, as the Imām. Judge al-Yamānī's rulings in Ibb cases left no record in an Ibb court register and I encountered evidence of his work only through the original judgment rolls held in the private archives of Ibb families. Register copies of such final judgment texts would exist, but these would be found in the capital of the period, Taʿizz.

Like ʿAlī b. ʿAlī al-Yamānī, his esteemed father (and teacher) before him, Judge al-Yamānī represented the highest caliber of Zaydī juridical knowledge. His father was honored by Imām Yaḥyā's father, Imām al-Manṣūr (d. 1904), with the title 'Shaykh al-Islām.' Such distinctions about juristic competence sometimes were connected to the two levels of the legal literature. Represented by standard *fiqh*

[17] As al-Yamānī, al-Jirāfī 1946, 82; M. Zabāra 1979, 378; A. Zabāra n.d., 2: 342–44; as al-Yadūmī, al-Akwaʿ 1995, 806–8. On his father, ʿAlī b. ʿAlī: Jirāfī 1946, 99–101; M. Zabāra 1979, 438; A. Zabāra n.d., 3: 81–5; al-Akwaʿ 1995, 805–6.

texts such as, among the Zaydīs, the *Book of Flowers* and its commentary literature, the 'branches' (*furū'*) of the *fiqh* is the corpus of substantive and procedural law. While the 'branches' of the *fiqh* entailed the positive law designed for application, the separate 'roots' (*uṣūl*) literature of the *fiqh* was concerned with its theoretical and methodological dimensions. This distinction between 'branches' and 'roots' could bear on the qualifications of individual jurists. All jurists, to the extent that they were qualified, had competence at the level of the branches'. Qualified jurists necessarily also had some exposure to and familiarity with the 'roots' of the law, but only a few were considered expert in it. Where Ibb Judge al-Manṣūr (see above) is described by biographer I. al-Akwa' as "verified in the branches" and Judge al-Iryānī (see above) as a "scholar of the *fiqh*," Judge al-Yamānī is differently identified, as "a scholar verified in the branches of the *fiqh* and its roots."

M. Zabāra says that Judge al-Yamānī was "one of the greatest scholars of the era." His profile is comparable to such already mentioned leading twentieth-century Yemeni jurists as Ḥusayn al-'Amrī, Yaḥyā b. Muḥammad al-Iryāni, and, among the Shāfi'īs, 'Abd al-Raḥmān al-Ḥaddād (who, according to his biographer, studied Shāfi'ī *uṣūl* works of jurists such as al-Suyūṭī). Like all of these other leading jurists, al-Yamānī also served for a time as a judge on the Appeal Court, to which he was appointed by the Imām in 1919, under Presiding Judge al-'Amrī. For Judge al-Yamānī, as for both al-'Amrī and al-Ḥaddād, biographical entries give a relatively detailed picture of the specific texts of his formation. Mention of the memorization of basic manuals (*mutūn*, sing. *matn*; or *mukhtaṣarāt*, 'abridged works') at the onset of a scholar's post-Qur'ānic school training is associated only with such major, 'Shaykh al-Islām'-level figures such as al-'Amrī, al-Yamānī's father, 'Alī b. 'Alī, and earlier, Muḥammad 'Alī Shawkānī (in his autobiography). Of al-Yamānī's father, for example, biographer al-Jirāfī (1946, 100–1) says, "many were his memorized works (*maḥfūẓāt*)." In addition to the Qur'ān, of which he was a *ḥāfiẓ*, the senior al-Yamānī "memorized abridged works in his youth and did not omit their study in his adulthood."

Biographer M. Zabāra gives a list of specific texts the father memorized. First on the list is the *Flowers* (*al-Azhār*), followed by *al-Ghāya* [in *uṣūl al-fiqh*, by al-Ḥusayn b. Qāsim], *al-Shāfiya* [in language morphology, by Ibn al-Ḥājib], *al-Talkhīs* [in rhetoric, by al-Qazwīnī], and *al-Kāfiya* [in grammar, by Ibn al-Hājib]. For Judge al-Yamānī the son, minus the text on morphology and adding an unnamed text in inheritance law, the list given of memorized texts is the same. The memorization of such *mutūn* was but the prolegomena to advanced training, which involved the study of commentary literatures that had accumulated around such concise introductory texts together with work in the other major academic fields, notably Qur'ān exegesis and *ḥadīth*.

The connection of the al-Yamānīs, father and son, with the Ḥamīd al-Dīn Imāms, father Yaḥyā and son Aḥmad, was close. In his youth, the future Imām Yaḥyā studied with the senior al-Yamānī and many years later this same teacher also issued a diploma for the future Imām Aḥmad. In addition to these important instructional relationships, the Yamānīs also served the twentieth-century Imāms as troubleshooting emissaries for the handling of important legal matters. Special interventions by the al-Yamānīs on behalf of the Imāms include that of the senior al-Yamānī in the era of Imām Yaḥyā. "In the year 1921," M. Zabāra (1979, 440) reports, "Imām Yaḥyā commissioned him to go to the town of Taʿizz to settle some of its problems, and he resolved lawsuits among its people concerning property and water systems endowed for mosques and schools."[18] Under Aḥmad, as the Heir to the Throne and then as the Imām, the junior al-Yamānī would be dispatched for similar tasks, including, in the late 1940s and in 1958 (at age 74), the sharīʿa resolution of two thorny Ibb town disputes. The expertise of the younger al-Yamānī dated back to the Ottoman era. M. Zabāra (1979, 378) records an instance of unofficial work: "In the year 1911 [at 27], he went to the region of Yarīm [now in Ibb Province] to resolve some disputes."

Conclusion

Provincial judges in the mid-twentieth century Yemeni Imamate were very substantial men, not merely jurists practicing in the local and state-level sharīʿa courts of the period but also, a number of them, major scholars, teachers and literary jurists as well. The accom-

[18] Al-Akwaʿ (1995, 805) is more specific: he was sent to divide the estate of the wealthy shaykh, ʿAlī b. ʿAbd Allāh Pasha. He was unable to resolve the dispute due to the great number of problems associated with endowments for mosques and schools. A critic remarked, "where is the Islām that you are the 'Shaykh' of?"

plishments of such men, from their training in the '*sharīʿa* sciences' to listings of their many students, mentions of their judicial postings and, especially, their incisive poetry, were mainstays of the vibrant Yemeni tradition of biographical historiography. The law itself, their speciality, was the centerpiece of the state system of rule and dominated intellectual life prior to the Revolution of 1962. Nationalists and reformers would come to see this as a fault. One stated, "we define ignorance as a lack of knowledge of Islamic jurisprudence, grammar, morphology . . . [Our] institutions over the past centuries produced hundreds of notable qāḍīs . . . However, it is not possible to find a doctor, . . . there are no experts in agriculture, . . . and no industries" (Aḥmad Nuʿmān, quoted in Dresch 2000, 53–4).

In their careers, sharīʿa court judges exhibited a number of patterns that I have tried to illustrate using the four principal biographies and, within them, the partial biographies of many other individuals who served in appointments in Ibb and elsewhere. Among these patterns are the differences between *sayyid*s and qāḍīs, representing two varieties of educated individuals and descent groups. Instruction and employment relations developed, in part, along genealogical lines. Although the lines of differentiation among the various jurisdictions in Ibb were imprecise, there were formal descending levels of single-judge courts, from the province, down to the district and then the sub-district, together with ascending appellate relations focused ultimately on a multi-judge panel in the capital and the final authority of the ruling Imām. Judges and court secretaries, who were often highly able jurists in their own right, all were appointed directly by the Imām. Ibb was a key province for the Imāms, an important source of agrarian revenue, but also of a large volume of legal matters. Later, under the nation state, Ibb would be known as the 'province of problems.'

Using the details of provincial careers I have also attempted to portray the practical and human side of the venerable dialogue of the Zaydī and Shāfiʿī schools of law in the pre-revolutionary highlands. Finally, I have tried to make a small contribution to the still larger relation of the *sharīʿa* to various systems of custom, a theme that has preoccupied Aharon Layish throughout his distinguished career.

CHAPTER NINE

"ALL OF PALESTINE IS HOLY MUSLIM *WAQF* LAND": A MYTH AND ITS ROOTS

Yitzhak Reiter

In 1988, the fledgling Islamic Resistance Movement in Palestine, Ḥamās, emerged with a new concept, manifested in article 11 of its Charter: ". . . The land of Palestine is an Islamic *waqf* land [endowed] for the benefit of Muslims throughout the generations and until the Day of Resurrection. It is forbidden to abandon it or part of it or to renounce it or part of it . . ." This idea was further elaborated in the following Ḥamās statement: "Palestine in its entirety is *holy* [emphasis added] Muslim *waqf* land."[1] The Ḥamās view of Palestinian land thus incorporates two concepts: one, Palestine is *waqf* land; and two, as such, it is holy land. The popular Islamic concept of the holiness of Palestine was until then based on religious and historical factors, such as being regarded as 'the territory blessed by God (Allāh)'—an interpretation of Qur'ān 17:1, which identified the blessed precincts of al-Aqṣā (*alladhī bāraknā ḥawlahu*) with Palestine (originally with al-Shām) (Jabr 1999, 191; Abū 'Aliya 2000, 41), and as *arḍ al-isrā' wa'l-mi'rāj*—the territory of Muḥammad's nocturnal journey and ascent to heaven (Jabr 1999, 200). With Article 11, Ḥamās added a legal justification to the holiness of Palestine. And once the land was pronounced *waqf*, two additional attributes were added to the public discourse (the religious and nationalist discourse in general, not only that of the Ḥamās activists)—it was now regarded as holy and inalienable.

* Author's note: I am deeply grateful to the Jerusalem Institute for Israel Studies and to the Harry S. Truman Research Institute for the Advancement of Peace at the Hebrew University for their support of my studies since the early 1990s. Thanks as well to Miriam Hoexter and Ron Shaham for commenting on the first drafts of this article and making valuable suggestions regarding its structure. The remaining faults in the article are my sole responsibility.

[1] Quoted from a leaflet Ḥamās disseminated in Gaza on July 22, 2000.

Even though the claim that Palestine is *waqf* land, and as such no part of it could be renounced, was commonly used in the public discourse in the context of the Palestinian-Israeli conflict over the last decade or two, its legal and historical roots have not yet been studied. One expert even wrongly claimed that this new assertion of Ḥamās was not accepted by other Islamic fundamentalist groups, and that "apparently Ḥamās itself was aware of the weaknesses of this claim" (Steinberg 2002, 148–49). As I will show below, the concept that Palestine is holy inalienable *waqf* land is not only a consistent assertion of Ḥamās, but was adopted by the official political and religious actors of the Palestinian Authority (PA) and became common knowledge amongst Palestinians and other Muslim constituencies.

My main argument in this chapter is that the Ḥamās concept is a novel politically-oriented myth, rooted neither in Islamic legal texts nor in historical practice. This myth aims to explain why Palestinians (or Muslims in general) should not cede a single inch of land to Israel or to the Zionist Jews. A myth is generally a political allegory related to events from the past or, alternatively, it is future-oriented. It is normally based on historical reality, but its original factual core is adapted, extended, interpreted and exaggerated. The purpose of a myth is basically twofold: to interpret the reality (mainly to place the present on a historical sequence) and to urge people to behave according to a particular pattern (Sivan 1990, Introduction).

The first section is an attempt to trace the legal grounding of the Ḥamās contention that Palestine is a *waqf* land and to follow the sources and authorities that Ḥamās uses to endorse its new interpretation. I compare the Ḥamās text both with earlier texts, those issued by Ḥājj Amīn al-Ḥusaynī, the Grand *Muftī* and President of the Supreme Muslim Council (SMC) in British Mandate Palestine during the 1930s, and with more recent texts, such as Jordanian and Palestinian *fatwā*s from the 1990s and 2000. In the second section I demonstrate that, contrary to Ḥamās' claims, lands conquered by Islam, including Palestine, were categorized as *fay*ʾ lands rather than as *waqf* lands (I will also explain the differences between these two systems). The third section deals with the practice of land tenure during medieval and Ottoman times. I argue there that *fay*ʾ or *kharāj* lands, known as *mīrī* lands in the Ottoman period, were not considered holy and were transacted freely, including with non-Muslims.

In the fourth section I demonstrate that, even if we accept Ḥamās' erroneous contention that all of Palestine is holy inalienable *waqf* land, both Islamic jurisprudence on the *waqf* institution and historical practice show that *waqf* assets were, in fact, alienable. Palestinian Muslims, including religious authorities during the British mandate period, took part in transactions that altered the original purposes of the *waqf*, changed its charitable character, and even transmitted *waqf* assets to non-Muslim hands. In the conclusion, I explain how the general public, including those considered political rivals of the Islamists, accepts the new radical Islamic religious-based legal innovations.

The Invention of the Myth and Its Political Use

Article 11 of the Ḥamās Charter of 1988 states:

> The Islamic Resistance Movement believes that the land of Palestine is an Islamic *waqf* land [endowed] for the benefit of Muslims throughout the generations and until the Day of Resurrection. It is forbidden to abandon it or part of it or to renounce it or part of it. No Arab State nor the aggregate of all Arab countries, and no Arab King or President nor all of them in the aggregate, have the right to do so; nor does any organization or the aggregate of all organizations, be they Palestinian or Arab, because Palestine is an Islamic *waqf* for the benefit of the Muslim generations to the Day of Resurrection. This is its [Palestine land's] rule in the Islamic *sharīʿa*. This rule applies like any other land conquered forcefully by the Muslims, since the Muslims endowed it at the time of conquest as *waqf* for the benefit of Muslims throughout the generations and until the Day of Resurrection. This [rule also] took place when the commanders of the Muslim armies, upon completing the conquest of al-Shām [Greater Syria] and Iraq, sent [a message] to the Caliph of the Muslims, ʿUmar Ibn al-Khaṭṭāb, consulting him as to what to do with the conquered land, whether it should be partitioned between the troops or left in the possession of its population, or otherwise. Following discussions and consultations between the Caliph of Islam, ʿUmar Ibn al-Khaṭṭāb, and the Companions of the Messenger of Allāh, peace and prayer be upon him, they decided that the land should remain in the hands of its holders to benefit from it and from its wealth; but the abstract ownership (*raqaba*) of the land ought to be endowed as a *waqf* for all generations of Muslims until the Day of Resurrection, while the [original] owners would have usufruct

> rights (*manfaʿa*) only, and this *waqf* will endure as long as heaven and earth last. Any action regarding Palestine [lands] that contradicts this rule of Islamic law is void and those who conducted it will bear the responsibility.[2]

As far as we know, this document—the Ḥamās Charter—was the first to make this legal claim, based on what was believed to be a historical precedent according to which all the Islamic conquered territories (and not only Palestine!) are *waqf*, and therefore should remain under Muslim control. It reveals two features of the outlook of modern Islamist groups. The first is that this outlook draws on a tradition attributed to the second Caliph ʿUmar Ibn al-Khaṭṭāb (r. 634–644), while at the same time ignoring other important Islamic sources and practices. This reflects, as Emmanuel Sivan noted, the Islamist tendency to idealize the age of Muḥammad and the four Righteous Caliphs (r. 622–661), "whereas all laws and injunctions produced after 660 by jurists by means of analogy (*qiyās*) and consensus of experts (*ijmāʿ*) are *ipso facto* suspect, for the jurists were usually more attuned to the needs of the powers that be than to the goals of the Faith" (Sivan 1990, 55, 69–70).

The second feature pertains to the maneuvering between traditional concepts and modern ideology; in our case it is the interplay between ʿUmar's precedent and the modern goal of national (Islamic) territory. The fact that fundamentalist groups tend to sanctify tradition, on the one hand, and to put it in a modern ideological form, on the other, was explored by Eisenstadt. He maintained that in their approach to the old Arab and Islamic literature and holy texts, although the Islamists sanctify tradition, they have altered it from an idealistic, utopian, substantial and totalistic form to a modern ideology (Eisenstadt 2002, 9).

Before I discuss the historical roots of the Ḥamās argument, I would like to shed some light on the questions of who instigated this idea and to what extent it was accepted by the Palestinian public. The circumstances involving the drafting of the Ḥamās Charter are vague. Only a few books have been published on the Ḥamās (Shaked & Shabi 1994; Mishal & Sela 1997; Nüsse 1998; Pavlowsky 2000;

[2] The Arabic text is available at http://www.hashd.org/rr/hamas.htm. My translation deviates from that of Raphael Israeli by using the relevant legal terms (Israeli's translation is available at http://www.palestinecenter.org/cpap/documents/charter.html and taken from: Alexander & Foxman 1990).

Hroub 2000; al-Ḥarūb n.d.; Manṣūr 2003), but none discussed this issue, or even raised the question. Shaykh Aḥmad Yāsīn, the Ḥamās founder and spiritual leader, received no formal education beyond high school in Gaza. There is room to believe that neither Shaykh Yāsīn nor any of his followers drafted the Charter, but rather that Islamic experts from the Jordanian Muslim Brothers organization developed it.[3] An Islamic legal opinion (*fatwā*) published in 1995 indicates that Jordanian Islamists hold similar ideas to Ḥamās. The *fatwā* issued by Jordanian *sharīʿa* experts, signed by seventeen Ph.D. holders (some of them faculty members) and two members of parliament from the Muslim Brotherhood party, refers to the question of selling Jordanian land plots to Jews. The issue was raised in the Jordanian media following reports that Israeli businessmen wished to invest in Jordanian real estate after the two countries achieved a peace treaty, and the *fatwā* was aimed at blocking such transactions. In their legal opinion, published in Ḥamās' international journal, *Filasṭīn al-Muslima* (October 1995, p. 29), the drafters refer to Jordan's land in the same category as the Ḥamās Charter of 1988 refers to Palestine:

> . . . These Jordanian lands and the rest of al-Shām land is *harāj* [sic—should be: *kharāj*] lands whose abstract ownership was endowed to *Allāh* for the public benefit of Muslims. They are not the private property of any leader, regime, party, head of a tribe, or particular person. It is legally (*sharʿan*) prohibited to sell *waqf* lands to the Jews, who are the enemies of *Allāh* and who desire to take it over and to expel the inhabitants of these lands.

In 1994, Zīyad Abū ʿAmr, a Palestinian professor of political science at Bir Zeit University, attributed the perception of Palestine as *waqf* land to Palestinian and other Islamic movements (Abū ʿAmr 1994, 27). When the Oslo peace process deteriorated during the second half of the 1990s, Yasser Arafat also adopted this idea and it was raised frequently in the Palestinian media. For example, in 1998 Fayṣal al-Ḥusaynī, who was a PLO representative to Jerusalem and a PA cabinet member, made the following assertion in a lecture and in an article he published on the peace process:

[3] Roni Shaked, who interviewed Shaykh Yāsīn for his book on Ḥamās, told me this but he did not mention it in his book.

> If you ask a Palestinian, what are the boundaries of Palestine, if he presents his Islamic outlook, then Palestine stretches from the river to the desert, it is an Islamic *waqf* land, not to be sold or traded . . . (Mayor & Hussaini 1998, 10).

During Friday services on December 4, 1998, the preacher (not identified) whose sermon was broadcasted on PA Radio said: "Palestine is an Islamic *waqf* land" (*Ṣawt Filasṭīn*, December 4, 1998). This message was reiterated in another sermon on April 30, 1999, by another *khaṭīb*, Shaykh Yūsuf Abū Sneineh, an official PA preacher (ibid., April 30, 1998); and Yasser Arafat himself repeated these words in December 1999, as reported in the PA's newspaper (*al-Ḥayāt al-Jadīda*, December 12, 1999). The following year, the public message took the form of an official PA *fatwā*. On July 22, 2000, the very day that Arafat declined US President Bill Clinton's proposal for solving the Israeli-Palestinian conflict at the Camp David II summit, Shaykh ʿIkrima Ṣabrī, the Chief *Muftī* of Jerusalem and the Palestinian Territories, issued a *fatwā* ruling that it would be forbidden (*ḥarām*) for Muslims in Palestine to accept compensation or indemnification in return for their land which was seized by the Zionists when the Jewish State was created in Palestine in 1948. The *fatwā*, which was typed on the official stationery of the PA's Chief *Muftī* and signed by Ṣabrī, asserts in its first paragraph:

> Accepting compensation for land in Palestine equals its sale—both are absolutely forbidden by the *sharīʿa*. Whoever accepts compensation for his assets is bound by the *fatwā* issued by the Palestine *ʿulamāʾ* in the 1930s, which totally prohibits [such action], because the Palestine land is not 'goods' to be traded, but rather blessed and holy *waqf* land (*waqfiyya mubāraka muqaddasa*). This *fatwā* was repeatedly supported by *fatwā*s issued by *ʿulamāʾ* of the Muslim nation since it originated and until the present day.

Ṣabrī's *fatwā* went on to state that the Palestinian refugees' [physical] right of return is sacred and eternal and that "the land of Palestine will remain in the hands of those [Palestinians] who are entitled to it and *to all the Muslims until the Day of Resurrection*" [emphasis added].[4] It is unclear from Ṣabrī's wording whether the concept of Palestine as a holy *waqf* is his own ruling or whether he [wrongly,

[4] For an incorrect English translation, see "Muslim Authorities Reiterate Islamic Stance on Palestine, Jerusalem, Refugees", *Palestine Times*, Issue No. 110 (August 2000), at http://www.palestinetimes.net/issue110/index0.htm.

as will be discussed later] attributes it to the 1930s *fatwā*. Undoubtedly, both *fatwās*, though issued sixty-five years apart, are motivated by the same purpose: to prevent the transfer of Arab/Islamic-owned lands to Zionist Jews. Before discussing the political context of Ṣabrī's 2000 *fatwā*, let us draw on the 1930s *fatwā* and compare its legal arguments to those of more recent texts.

Ṣabrī's mention of the 1930s precedent refers particularly to Ḥājj Amīn al-Ḥusaynī, the Grand *Muftī* and President of the SMC in British Mandate Palestine. Al-Ḥusaynī was deeply concerned by the increase of land sales to Jews in Palestine during the 1920s–30s, and he launched a public campaign among the Palestinian Arabs opposing the trend. In this campaign, as well as in issues related to holy places, al-Ḥusaynī was the first Palestinian leader to employ religious arguments in the context of the Arab-Jewish struggle over Palestinian territory.

In his public speeches, al-Ḥusaynī repeatedly stressed that selling land to the Jews was a sin from the Islamic viewpoint and an act of high treason. Addressing a large meeting on 29 December, 1934, al-Ḥusaynī explained, according to a British intelligence report, that since Palestinian land belonged to God it should not be sold to man (Porath 1977, 96). This argument, which was presented in a general form, with no reference to a particular legal or theological text, resembles the position of the Ḥamās Charter. One would expect to find it too in the most important *fatwā* that al-Ḥusaynī issued four weeks after the above-mentioned meeting, but in fact his *fatwā* of January 1935, which was printed at the SMC's Islamic Orphan Press (Dār al-Aytām al-Islāmiyya) and widely disseminated, highlights other arguments for explaining why Palestine land is holy and why Muslims should not sell assets to the Jews:

> . . . These holy lands embody the first *qibla* [direction of prayer—al-Quds/Jerusalem], the third [sacred] Mosque [al-Aqṣā], the destination of the *isrā'* [the nocturnal journey] and *mi'rāj* [ascent to Heaven] of your Prophet Muḥammad, and its soil was molded by the blood of the Muslim righteous warriors, and by [the bodies of] many prophets, saints, martyrs, and pious forefathers, and every inch of it contains their righteous remnants and their eternal glorious deeds which sustained throughout the ages in an Islamic dimension, confirming that 'There is no God but Allāh and that Muḥammad is the Messenger of Allāh'. This holy land which embodies all of what was mentioned is a trusteeship (*amāna*) of Allah, of his Messenger and of the Muslims on their shoulders, and therefore the sale of any inch of this land to

> the Zionists is a betrayal of God and his Messenger and the entire Muslim people (or all Muslims), as well as an extinguishing of the light of Islam from the sacred land and an assistance to remove the Muslims from their territories . . . (al-Ḥusaynī n.d.; see also Zuʿaytar 1984, 374).

The *fatwā* was ratified by 249 *ʿulamāʾ*, *muftī*s, qāḍīs and other officials of the SMC who were subordinated to the Grand *Muftī*. On this occasion they also issued another *fatwā* which specifically attacked the land brokers, who now were threatened with denial of Muslim burial. The latter *fatwā* referred to the entire territory of Palestine as 'the Islamic holy lands' (*al-bilād al-Islāmiyya al-muqaddasa*) without indicating the grounds for why this was so (ibid.).

Thus, although the current Palestinian Chief *Muftī* Shaykh ʿIkrima Ṣabrī mentioned in his July 2000 legal opinion the 1930s *fatwā* to support his argument regarding the holiness of Palestine, al-Ḥusaynī's *fatwā* provided different justifications for this; nor did al-Ḥusaynī argue, as does Ṣabrī, that Palestine is a *waqf* land and that those who possess it are entitled only to enjoy the right to use it.

The attributes for Palestine's holiness enumerated by al-Ḥusaynī, who himself had no education in Islamic law (Porath 1974, 191), were taken from the literature extolling Jerusalem (*faḍāʾil bayt al-maqdis/al-quds*).[5] Unlike Ṣabrī (and the Ḥamās Charter), al-Ḥusaynī grounded the holiness of all of Palestine in Islamic history and heritage. The battles occurred on Palestinian soil and the Islamic prominent figures, be it those who sacrificed their lives for its conquest or those who operated, lived or were buried there, all turned it into a sanctified patrimony. Al-Ḥusaynī claimed that the Islamic conquest of the land and its history under Islam turned it into a trusteeship that Allāh, his Messenger and the successive Muslim generations obligated present-day Muslims to uphold, and this entailed a ban on transferring any of the land to non-Muslims. However, al-Ḥusaynī did not use legal claims, as Ḥamas and the PA's *Muftī* do today, that the land of Palestine is *waqf* and inalienable. Moreover, in the mid-1930s, al-Ḥusaynī himself appealed to the local Palestinian Arabs to endow their private lands as *waqf* in order to prevent their sale to the Jews. His appeal was backed by another special *fatwā* that he issued for this purpose (*al-Jāmiʿa al-ʿArabiyya*, January 24, 1935). Since the SMC controlled the sharīʿa courts, which were entitled by law

[5] For the literature lauding Jerusalem, see Livne-Kafri 1985 and 2000; al-Wāsiṭī 1979.

to approve every transaction of *waqf* properties, the Grand *Muftī* hoped that granting the lands *waqf* status would give his SMC the legal power to control land sales. This very fact proves that in his mind Palestine was not *waqf* territory, as Islamists today claim; rather, he recognized private ownership of lands but he wished to change its legal status to *waqf*. However, Palestinian Arabs did not respond positively to his appeal.

Let us return now to the PA *Muftī*'s legal opinion of July 2000. The political context of Ṣabrī's *fatwā* was to protect his Chairman—Arafat—from allegations of relinquishing the Palestinian refugees' right of return. It was urgently issued a few hours after a similar manifesto signed by senior Islamist and Ḥamās figures was circulated in the Gaza Strip. The Ḥamās leaflet stated that:

> Palestine in its entirety is holy Muslim *waqf* land and no person, group, organization or State is authorized to concede any part of its soil to the enemy (ibid.).

The rivalry between the two Palestinian political factions—Fateh headed by Arafat and Ḥamās headed by Yāsīn—led the PA to adopt the concept that 'Palestine land is a holy *waqf*,' which was a Ḥamās innovation.

Though a relatively new argument, this notion was soon inculcated into segments of the Islamic public in Palestine and across the Muslim world. For example, Dr. Muṣṭafā Rushwān, a faculty member in one of al-Azhar's affiliated colleges, refers to Palestine as *waqf* land and cites the same argument as the Ḥamās Charter (Rushwān 2001, 46–53). Another example is a *fatwā* issued by Shaykh Yūsuf al-Qaraḍāwī, one of the most popular contemporary *muftīs*, based in Qatar, who referred to all of Palestine as *waqf* land.[6]

Between Waqf *and* Fay'

The Islamist drafters, as we have seen, base their claim regarding the *waqf* status of the forcefully conquered Palestine and al-Shām (Greater Syria) lands on an early tradition (*ḥadīth*) which refers to these lands as '*kharāj* lands.' The tradition is taken from the early Arab literature regarding conquered lands (*futūḥ al-buldān*) (al-Ḥarūb

[6] "*al-Aqṣā wa-khaṭar al-tahwīd*" dated July 24, 2001, at www.qaradawi.net.

n.d., 77) which the *Imām* transferred for the public good as *fay*ʾ. The system of *fay*ʾ totally differs from the institution of *waqf*.

It is worth outlining the differences between the two institutions, *fay*ʾ and *waqf*, in order to understand the method that today's Islamists employ in adopting new interpretations and uses to early traditions. *Waqf* is a privately-initiated endowment of a completely privately-owned (*mulk*) property, based on the Islamic pious concept of charity. The endower is an individual who wishes to turn a property he owns into an eternal endowment for charitable purposes. Charitable action in Islam is based on eternal remuneration of the endower in the afterworld (Anderson 1951, 292; *EI*[2], s.v. *Ṣadaḳa*, 709), and therefore the founder of a *waqf* is entitled to such reward while the endowment could exist in this world forever. Hence, the ban on the sale, long-term rental or mortgage of *waqf* assets (Qadrī Pasha 1902, 3). The verb *waqafa* means 'to stop', 'to block' or 'to suspend,' implying one of the basic rules of the *waqf*: once endowed, the donated property loses its abstract ownership (*raqaba*) which, according to the Ḥanafī school of law (official school of the Ottoman state), goes to Allāh, as a metaphor for its eternal status, and the beneficiaries are entitled to usufruct (*manfaʿa*) only; that is, no one has ownership rights of the endowed property. The founder of the endowment can stipulate the charitable purposes of the *waqf*, the beneficiaries and their entitlement at the time of the donation, and the rules of devolution for generations to come. He can also nominate the administrator of the endowment, as well as stipulate the conditions for future nominations and the rules of the endowment's administration.

*Fay*ʾ, on the other hand, is the name given to land which was conquered by the Muslims but remained in the hands of the original owners to benefit from, provided that they pay a special tax signifying that the abstract ownership belongs to the State Treasury for the benefit of the Muslim community. In order to understand how the Ḥamās Charter drafters arrived at the conclusion that *fay*ʾ lands (all forcefully conquered lands) have the status of *waqf*, it is necessary to outline the historical development of these two institutions.

In pre-Islamic tribal society *fay*ʾ applied to immoveable items taken as booty (*EI*[2], s.v. Ghanīma, 1005–6), to be divided between victors, either in fifths or fourths, the leader being entitled to one of the parts. This custom was upheld by the Prophet Muḥammad after the battle of Badr (624), and Qur'ān 8: 42 mentions five uses for the prophet's one fifth. The Prophet actually designated his fifth for public use. The other four fifths were divided among the conquering troops (*EI*[2], s.v. Fay', 869; Berchem 1886: 47–8). The Prophet's practice was part of the custom of *ghanīma* since the Qur'ānic text says: *fa'in ghanimtum* (if you take booty), and not *fay'*. The subsequent battles which ended with the surrender of Banū al-Naḍīr, and the Jews of Khaybar and Fadak led to a new precedent which involved the institution of *fay'*, as distinct from *ghanīma*. The Banū al-Naḍīr surrendered after a siege in 625, and Qur'ān 59: 7–10 states that since the victory resulted from God's interposition in favor of his Apostle, it [the entire land and not only one fifth] was *fay'* for him exclusively, to the ultimate benefit of the Muslim society (*EI*[2], ibid.). In this case, the Qur'ān uses the verb *afa'a*, namely to bring back (and not the verb *ghanīma* as in the case of Badr), which indicates that the new custom marks the principle of *fay'*. Khaybar estates were left in the hands of their Jewish inhabitants who, after their surrender in 628, had to pay half of their date crops as tax to the Muslim conquerors.

The conquest of Khaybar, a Jewish-inhabited oasis, was more complicated—a matter that entailed many interpretations regarding the legal precedent in terms of land tenure, booty and taxes. It was first conquered by force (*'anwatan*) and then the Prophet reached an agreement with the local Jewish inhabitants according to which they would surrender and remain on their lands, but in the future would have to hand over half of their date and grain crops as tax to the Muslim conquerors. From a legal point of view, the pact was defective, since it did not say whether they were to remain the owners of the soil which they were to cultivate. Traditions tell that the Prophet divided the lands into plots and gave every Muslim beneficiary from among the warriors the right to collect from a particular Jewish cultivator half of the yield of his specific plot (*EI*[2], s.v. Khaybar, 1137–43).

In the Banū al-Naḍīr and Khaybar precedents the foundations of the future State Treasury (*bayt al-māl*) were established. The principle was that in territories surrendered without a battle (*ṣulḥan*) the lands (completely) belong to the entire Muslim community, which may benefit from its taxes. However, when land was conquered by force (*'anwatan*), it was divided between the warriors and only one fifth went to the Prophet (or his successors as leaders of the Muslim army and community), who could donate it for the benefit of the Muslim community (*EI*², s.v. Bayt al-Māl, 1143–44).[7]

What joined the concept of *fay*ʾ and *waqf* and the fate of estates acquired *ṣulḥan* and *ʿanwatan* was apparently the reform initiated by the Caliph ʿUmar b. al-Khaṭṭāb. The urge for the reform grew as the Islamic conquests increased, and it became economically damaging to divide conquered lands between the Muslim troops. The following *ḥadīth* cited in Abū Yūsuf's *Kitāb al-Kharāj* marks the change of policy by ʿUmar:

> Bilāl and his companions asked ʿUmar b. al-Khaṭṭāb to distribute the booty acquired in Iraq and Syria: "Divide the lands among those who conquered them," they said, "just as the spoils of the army are divided." But ʿUmar refused their request . . . saying: "Allāh has given a share in these lands to those who shall come after you" (ibid., 1141).

The tradition indicates the essence of ʿUmar's new policy according to which the conquered lands (*ʿanwatan*),[8] and not only the lands captured after a peaceful surrender (*ṣulḥan*), belong to the Muslim community, and should not be allocated to the warriors for private ownership.

Another tradition narrating this reform tells that after al-Shām (Greater Syria) was conquered, the leaders of the Islamic camp:

> . . . wrote to the Caliph ʿUmar b. al-Khaṭṭāb: This *fay*ʾ of which we allotted you one fifth, the rest belongs to us and nobody has any share in it, following the Prophet's example . . . in [the case of the conquest of] Khaybar [referring to a different version of the above-mentioned tradition, according to which the Prophet distributed shares of Khaybar to the warriors].[9] ʿUmar replied: I am not bound by what you said, rather, I shall endow it (*aqifuhu*).[10]

---

[7] In early Islam the difference between *ghanīma* and *fay*ʾ was also not clear. See, for example, Sarāj and Muḥammad 2001, 168. On *fay*ʾ, see *EI*², s.v. Fayʾ, 869.

[8] Lokkegaard (1978, 76) holds that in Greater Syria the towns were taken *ṣulḥan*, while the land was taken *ʿanwatan*.

[9] al-Khaṣṣāf (1904, 3–5) cites *ḥadīth*s maintaining that both the Prophet and ʿUmar b. al-Khaṭṭāb dedicated their personal booty from Khaybar to charitable purposes.

[10] Ibn ʿAsākir 1995, 2: 196–97. The Arabic text is: *Aṣāba al-nās fatḥ bil-Shām . . . fa-katabū ilā ʿUmar b. al-Khaṭṭāb inna hādhā al-fay*ʾ *alladhī aṣabnā laka khumsuhu, wa-lanā mā baqiya laysa li-aḥad minhu shay*ʾ *kamā ṣanaʿa al-Nabī ṣallā Allāhu ʿalayhi wa-sallama bi-Khaybar, fa-kataba ʿUmar: laysa ʿalayya mā qultum wa-lākinnī aqifuhu . . .*; I am grateful to Professor Amikam Elad for this reference and for his assistance.

In a second version of this tradition the last word *aqifuhu*, namely 'I shall endow it', is replaced with the words *aḥbisuhu fay'an*, meaning: 'I shall endow it as *fay'*' (*ḥabasa* is a synonym for *waqafa*, used commonly in the Maghrib). This particular version of the *ḥadīth* reflects the combination between *waqf*, or *ḥabs*, and *fay'*. The second version actually shows that the verb root h.b.s.—endow—by itself is not enough, or too general, and needs specification—endow as what? The second version of the *ḥadīth* cited above specifies 'endow it as *fay'*'.

There is also another interpretation of the verb *waqafa* in this context as meaning 'withheld' and 'refrained from dividing the conquered lands' (Ben Shemesh 1967, 24 n. 9; 112 n. 9). This is based on a literal understanding of the verb w.q.f. before the term *waqf* was used to express an endowment. Those who accept this interpretation would rule out the Ḥamās contention.

A third approach was provided by W. Heffening, who (wrongly, in my opinion) maintains that *waqf* has two meanings: one is pious endowment and the other is the fiscal system explained above as the *fay'* system (*Shorter EI*, s.v. Waḳf). In other words, one legal term—*waqf*—signifies two different institutions.

'Umar's reform created a confusing mixture, which affected the meaning of the terms. The public could no longer use the term *ghanīma* (booty) for the lands conquered *'anwatan* because they were also re-allocated for public purposes. Thus, the verb w.q.f. or ḥ.b.s. was used in this connection, because it had the connotation of an act of withdrawing the abstract ownership from a specific person and designating lands for public use. The principle of *fay'* lands was that the newly captured territories were left in the hands of the indigenous inhabitants who were entitled only to usufruct rights without the abstract ownership (*raqaba*), which was retained by the treasury. The indigenous owners were liable to pay the *kharāj* land tax (and in the case of non-Muslims also *jizya*), as a sort of tenure to the state, which was legally transferred to the State Treasury (*bayt al-māl*) (*EI*[2], s.v. Fay', 869). *Fay'* lands were not actually state lands. The separation between the abstract ownership and the usufruct was only a theoretical legal device that enabled the imposition of taxes.

The inter-relationship between *fay'* and *waqf* can be explained thus: in the formative period of Islamic statehood, before the jurists attached specific meanings and rules to the various terms, denoting different institutions, the Muslims made use of different terms to express a particular practice or, alternatively, the same term was used for different practices. The main reason for this complexity was that since the institutions followed earlier systems, they varied from one region to another and were controversial even before Islam.[11] Claude Cahen points to a very fluid use of terminology in the early generations of Islam. The example he gives is that of *kharāj* and *jizya*, which were used interchangeably and finally were determined as poll tax on non-Muslims for *jizya* and land tax for *kharāj* (*EI*[2], s.v. Kharādj, 1030; ibid., s.v. Djizya, 559; ibid., s.v. Bayt al-Māl, 1143–44; Cf. ibid., s.v. Waḳf, 58). The jurists defined them and specified only at a later stage that the one meant land tax and the other poll tax. In the same manner, all kinds of pious donations were made by the first generations of Islam. They could all be included in the very general term of charity (*ṣadaqa*). Only later, with the elaboration of Islamic law, did jurists differentiate between the various kinds of donations, attaching a specified meaning, a precise definition and rules, as well as a different term to each of the charitable acts. The various kinds of charities made by the first generations of Islam were not all considered *waqf* by later jurists. Some of the early donations fell within this definition, while others were classified as gifts or ordinary charity (Cahen 1961, 45). Moreover, the first generations of Islam used derivatives of the verb w.q.f. in a fluid or loose way. Only later did the jurists attach to the noun *waqf* (and its synonym *ḥabs*) and its derivatives a specific meaning; it became a technical term implying exclusively the institution of Islamic endowment. Only those early charities, which fulfilled the rules pertaining to this specific institution, were then considered as *waqf*.

The Ḥamās and current Islamists disregard the *fay*ʾ system and refer to ʿUmar's action as *waqf* in the new form, that is, as it was shaped by jurists from the second/eighth century onwards (perhaps by making use of the first above-mentioned *ḥadīth* version, which uses the verb w.q.f., 'to endow,' without specifying 'as what' and neglecting the second version which specifies the *fay*ʾ). The Ḥamās interpretation of that *ḥadīth* says:

> . . . The land should remain in the hands of its holders to benefit from it and from its wealth; but the abstract ownership of the land ought

[11] On the changes of tax institutions over time, see Simpson 1988, 149–50. On the differences according to regions, see Dennett 1950.

> to be endowed as *waqf* for all generations of Muslims until the Day of Resurrection, while the [original] owners will have usufruct rights only (see n. 1).

It is true that the *fay'* shared one legal characteristic with what later became the Islamic endowment institution of *waqf*—the separation of ownership and usufruct. This is, however, the only characteristic shared by the two institutions. The *fay'* came into being as a result of conquest, and taxes imposed on *fay'* lands were, in fact, the major source of revenue for the Muslim State Treasury. The *waqf*, on the other hand, was never owned by the state and never formed part of its fiscal revenues; it was employed in strict conformity with the private founder's stipulations. These particularities of the two different institutions were formulated during the first two centuries of Islam.

In sum, the basic element of the new concept is based on attributing the early Islamic *fay'* system to the *waqf*. According to the present-day interpretation, land is transferable between Muslims, who have only usufruct rights. The Islamists use the ambiguity and the multi-faceted meaning and practice of the term and institution of *waqf* in the formative period of Islam and manipulate it for their political purposes in the context of the Israeli-Palestinian conflict over territory.

State Land in Medieval and Ottoman Practice

The next question to be addressed is whether under Islamic rule *fay'* land could not be sold by its actual holders, and whether non-Muslims were excluded from acquiring rights on *fay'* or other sorts of state lands. The emphasis in this section will be on the practice in Palestine.

Cahen wrote that during the Medieval Period, *fay'* lands were viewed as quasi-*waqf*, [only] in the sense that they were devoted to the benefit of the Muslim generations to come. In other words, by using the term *waqf* in the context of land tenure, the early Muslims meant to distinguish the *fay'*, i.e., lands in which a share (from the tax revenues) was given to the public benefit, from other privately-owned lands (upon which lower taxes were imposed). Cahen, however, emphasizes that the landholders, whether Muslims or not, were entitled to absolute ownership on *fay'* lands and they could exploit them in that capacity [and conduct transactions] (Cahen 1970, 108).

Put another way, state control of these lands was limited to one major public interest: safeguarding the state's income from the *kharāj* taxes. The Muslim state of medieval times did not interfere in matters such as who the actual owner of the land was (or its beneficiary), or his religious denomination, as long as he paid the required taxes.

Granovski wrote that during the Mamluk and Ottoman periods a new kind of state-owned lands was granted to military commanders by a kind of feudal tenure (*iqṭāʿāt*). The landlord and the state received revenues from the tenant farmers. Under the Ottomans, *kharāj* lands—formerly *fayʾ* lands—were regarded as privately-owned, whereas only the relatively new feudal estates were considered state-owned (Granovski 1949, 322 n. 20). The new non-possessed lands conquered by the Ottomans were transferred to the State Treasury and re-allocated to cultivators in return for a payment (*ṭāpū*), according to the principle of *fayʾ* (abstract ownership of the State, and usufruct to the cultivator), but they were now called *arāʾḍī amīriyya* or, in short, *mīrī* (ibid., 16). In introducing the new *mīrī* system the state aimed to ensure the productive nature of the land (Stein 1984, 11).

All non-private and non-cultivated lands, and more importantly all sown lands, but not fruit trees and the like, were categorized as *mīrī* and were regarded as state lands. The peasants could not sell, grant or endow these lands. However, *mīrī* land was not state land in the modern sense of public land not to be sold to private individuals. It could be acquired by possession and actual working of the land for a ten-year period. In the later years of the Ottoman state, ways were found to circumvent these restrictions by the establishment of *waqf ghayr ṣaḥīḥ*, that is, an endowment of estates of the *mīrī* kind established with the special approval of the state in which the endower donated only those rights he was entitled to—usufruct rights—i.e., the revenues from the land (*EI*², s.v. Mīrī, 125).

Gabriel Baer states that privately-owned land (*mulk*) not only existed during the successive Muslim periods in Palestine and other Muslim-controlled territories, but that the lands were liable to change owners and non-Muslims were also able to purchase them (Baer 1962, 51). Ottoman non-Muslim subjects (*dhimmī*s) could legally purchase lands, and Palestine, or Greater Syria, was not an exception. Indeed, the Ottoman Sharīʿa Court records of Jerusalem from the sixteenth century testify that Jews purchased lands and houses from Muslim buyers (Cohen & Simon-Picali 1993, 304–21; Cohen 2003, 238–396).

Foreign non-Muslims who resided in the Ottoman territory (*musta'mins*) could only purchase land following the reforms of 1856 (Baer 1962, 51), and consequently a *musta'min* became a *dhimmī* and had to pay the *kharāj* and/or *jizya*.

The 1858 Ottoman Land Law determined five categories of land, among them completely privately-owned land (*mulk*), *waqf*, and *mīrī*. *Mīrī* land could be transacted under certain restrictions, but the buyer of such land was entitled to usufruct rights only. The consent of the Sultan was required to turn *mīrī* land into *mulk* in a procedure known as *tamlīk* (Granovski 1949, 84). The purpose of this system was to ensure that the land would be cultivated, and if neglected, the state could reclaim it. It is believed that many feudal landlords succeeded in turning their *mīrī* lands into private (*mulk*) land (Heyd 1973b, 81). Thus, the land tenure reality in Palestine was that most of the *mulk* land was confined to urban sites, mostly buildings and gardens; most of the agricultural land was of the *mīrī* category (Stein 1984, 11).

During the last third of the nineteenth century the Ottoman government sold large-scale worthless lands in the plains of Palestine to entrepreneurs—among them non-Muslims—who undertook to cultivate them. For example, the lands of the Sarona colony in northern Palestine were sold to the German Templers and tracts in Umm Labs were sold to Jews who established the colony of Petaḥ Tikva (today a city). On the eve of World War I, 172 large landholders in Palestine possessed, as private owners, over five million dunams (4.425 dunams = 1 acre). One Arab family from Beirut, the Sursoqs, alone owned 230,000 dunams, incorporating a few Arab villages on the Esdraelon Plain, which they sold to the Zionist movement in the 1920s (Granovski 1949, 75). Unlike the plain areas, in the mountainous sections of Palestine private owners held only small plots, and they registered their ownership already in the second half of the nineteenth century (Gerber 1987, 80). Between 1878 and 1914 some 245,000 dunams in Palestine were purchased by individual Jews and by Jewish agencies (Porath 1977, 109).

The very fact that thousands of private Muslims—and non-Muslims—endowed their real estate in Palestine as *waqf* for the benefit of the public as well as their family members is further proof that the ownership of lands in Palestine during centuries of Islamic rule was also private. The practice of *waqf* endowment in Palestine (and elsewhere in the Ottoman state) followed the legal theory according to which the land or urban property could be donated as *waqf* by individuals only, not by an organization or by the state apparatus as such. Even large *waqf*s for public purposes endowed by governors and other statesmen were registered as private endowments. If the land was state-owned, the official who endowed it had to receive a special decree from the Sultan (*tamlīknāme*), turning the land over for his private disposal and, in so doing, making it possible for him to legally endow it. Only the Sultan or his deputies had the right to endow *mīrī* land as *waqf*, and even if *mīrī* land was endowed for public purposes, the land itself was not the endowed property since the abstract ownership could not be transferred; only the income tax from these lands was diverted from the State Treasury to other public purposes. Consequently, no private person could endow land, unless he received a *tamlīk* (Ben Shemesh 1953, 32).

Thus, the actual situation regarding land tenure in Palestine during the Ottoman period refutes the Ḥamās claim that the land of Palestine was all state-owned or that its sale to non-Muslims was forbidden. The Ḥamās contention disregards the Islamic medieval and Ottoman practices according to which *fay'* lands could change hands and non-Muslims were not excluded from buying such lands. Even the Ottoman newly-created state land—*mīrī* land—could become privately-owned and, again, non-Muslims were not excluded. From the last third of the nineteenth century, *mīrī* lands in Palestine (and elsewhere) were sold to entrepreneurs, including Jews.

The "Holy" Inalienable Nature of Waqf—*Twentieth-century Practice in Palestine*

Even if we accept the Islamists' contention that lands in Palestine are *waqf* lands from the Islamic legal perspective, which we do not, the question arises as to whether they are holy by nature, and whether, according to both Islamic jurisprudence and practice, they are, indeed, inalienable.

The political use of the alleged *waqf* nature of all Palestine draws on two attributes of this system. The first is the claim that *waqf* land, due to the pious nature of the institution of *waqf* and of the principle of respecting the endower's stipulations as if they were the Legislator's [God's] text (*sharṭ al-wāqif ka-naṣṣ al-shāriʿ*), is holy and intact. This assertion draws on the *waqf*'s pious character as a charitable endowment usually associated with religious institutions and holy places, since in the eyes of Muslims *waqf* is instinctively associated with basic Muslim tenets, with piety in general, and especially with the holy nature attributed to places of worship and burial.[12] True, *waqf* as an act of charity is a desired deed in Islam. However, the endowed properties *per se* have no holy nature. In a previous study I showed that what was of a pious ('holy' in the eyes of many Palestinians and Islamists) nature and should be eternal is the charitable purpose of the *waqf* and not the endowed lands or other properties (Reiter 1997a, 82).

The second principle that the Palestinian and Islamist advocators draw on is the inalienable nature of *waqf* property. Basically, *waqf* properties were regarded as inalienable. Their eternal nature stems from the principle of *waqf* as a charitable act for which the endower should be eternally remunerated in the afterworld. Indeed, in most endowment deeds (*waqfiyyāt*) known to us, the founders stressed their opposition to a property change (Anderson 1951).[13]

In spite of this principle, Islamic jurists ruled that a *qāḍī* is empowered to overrule the founder's stipulation if the property in question becomes valueless and unproductive. Their opinions developed not as an abstract theory, but as a response to actual challenges. Their rulings, thus, reflect practical problems regarding the administration of *waqf* properties and solutions that they grounded in the principles

---

12 The *Waqf* al-Ḥaramayn is an example. See Hoexter 1998, 7–11.

13 As an example, the following is a stipulation laid down in 1856/57 by the founder of a *waqf* for the benefit of a Sufi lodge in the village of Tarshīḥa in northern Palestine: "Eternal and enduring charity, whose [properties] or any part of it should not be sold, granted, mortgaged, acquired, appropriated, wasted, exchanged, transferred, abandoned, violated, ruined in any way, or transferred to private ownership of any Muslim or creature. As time passes, the more it would be assured, and as more periods elapse, the stronger it becomes, and it is protected by the prohibitions of Allāh and is defended by the might of Allāh. [The founder] seeks Allāh's gratitude, and fears Allāh's wrath. Anyone who believes in Allāh and doomsday and knows that he will go to his Lord in the afterworld should not defect this *waqf* and not change, replace or exchange it. Whoever damages this *waqf* or ruins or changes any part of it will be subjected to the curses of Allāh, of his angels and of all humankind, and he will be defeated by the mighty Qur'ān and be judged by the almighty God and his chosen messenger in the day in which no property or offspring would help, but only the one who comes to Allāh guiltless [will be saved]. Allāh, the most reliable speaker said: 'If anyone changes the bequest after hearing it, the guilt shall be on those who make the change, for Allāh hears and knows." The last phrase, citing Qur'ān 2: 181, aimed at sanctifying the *waqf* founder's stipulations and putting them on the same level as the divine revelation regarding the change of heirs and shares of a will. For the unpublished *waqfiyya* photocopy, see Reiter 1986, 152.

of Islamic law (Reiter 1996, 171; idem 1997a, 65). The two major justifications to legitimize transactions of *waqf* assets were *maṣlaḥa* or *manfaʿa*—benefit for the endowment—on the one hand, and *ḍarūra*—duress regarding the physical or economic condition of the estates, on the other (Qadrī Pasha 1902, art. 133; Abū Zahra 1971, 6).

Two major methods of alienating *waqf* assets were legitimized by the jurists under these circumstances. The first was leasing *waqf* properties for long periods in a variety of forms (Hoexter 1984 and 1997).[14] The second method abandoned the interpretation of viewing the asset as an absolute perpetual element and allowed, under certain conditions, the exchange or even sale of properties as a means of ensuring the charitable purpose of the *waqf*. Thus, the *waqf*'s income could fund the charity and perpetuate the charitable nature of the endowment and satisfy its eternal nature (as opposed to the eternal nature of the properties originally endowed). The method was *istibdāl*, the exchange of a *waqf* property for a substitute property that would become *waqf*. This method was developed as an exchange for money—*istibdāl bi'l-darāhim*—which should be invested in the purchase of a substitute property for the *waqf*.

The very existence of the *istibdāl* system in the *sharīʿa* and in judicial practice refutes the contention of Islamists that *waqf* land is holy. The endowed land could be exchanged or sold to purchase another property. Moreover, as I will show in the following paragraphs, long-term lease, exchange and even the sale of *waqf* real estate were common practices in Palestine and were authorized by Muslim religious authorities even when the buyers were Jews or other non-Muslims.

The following examples, showing that *waqf* land was in fact sold with the approval of established religious figures, are taken from British Mandate Palestine and from the records of the sharīʿa courts in Israel. Under British rule, between 1917–48, thirty-two out of fifty-six real-estate transactions in Jerusalem involved *waqf* properties that changed hands through *istibdāl bi'l-darāhim* (Reiter 1996, 177). In most cases, the *waqf* sold unused urban land and invested the proceeds in the construction of new buildings for the *waqf* on other vacant plots in its possession, or in purchasing houses or warehouses.[15]

[14] On long-term transactions such as *ḥikr, ijāratayn, muqāṭaʿa*, and *khulū* in the Ottoman period, see Gerber 1988; Baer 1979; Clavel 1895; Mercier 1899; Abribat 1901 and Hoexter 1984 and 1997.

[15] For examples, see Jerusalem Sharīʿa Court records [henceforth: Jerusalem *sijill*]

One of these transactions was a sale by the family *waqf* of ʿAlī Karīm al-Dīn al-Nammarī of a twenty-dunam stretch in Jerusalem to the English Sports Association for use as an athletic field. The qāḍī who permitted the transaction was employed by the SMC, which also approved the sale. Given the political sensitivity of selling such a large *waqf* plot in Jerusalem, it is implausible that the qāḍī, who was subordinate to Ḥājj Amīn al-Ḥusaynī, did not receive the latter's consent prior to giving his approval. Hence, al-Ḥusaynī, who ruled that lands in Palestine are a holy asset that should not be transferred to non-Muslims, did not prevent the sale of a twenty-dunam plot of *waqf* land in Jerusalem to a British foundation.

Al-Ḥusaynī, as president of the SMC, was also involved in selling *waqf* properties administered by the council[16] by the legal device of *istibdāl bi'l-darāhim*, without investing the money received to purchase a substitute property. Among these transactions was the sale of a twelve-dunam plot belonging to the al-Bira mosque *waqf*.[17] True, the land was sold to Muslims, but it lost its *waqf* status and became privately owned.

During the British Mandate period, *istibdāl bi'l-darāhim* was also used by Muslim authorities as a legal means for approving government expropriation of *waqf* land to be used for the benefit of the public (Arabs and Jews alike), for a substantial amount of money as reparation (ibid., 180). The SMC also leased to private Arab investors uncultivated agricultural *waqf* lands for long periods, on the basis of special civil contracts issued according to civil Mandatory (and not *sharīʿa*) law. The *waqf* inspector of the SMC criticized these transactions as contrary to *waqf* interests and leading to the loss of its land, but despite this criticism, the transactions took place (ibid., 187).

After 1948, Israeli qāḍīs found a technical method of using *istibdāl* to approve the selling of *waqf* assets, some of them to non-Muslims—Jews or Bahais (Layish 1966, 41–76; Reiter 1989, 21–45).

455/147/150 [vol. 455, p. 147, no. 150], 453/64/315; 453/89/210; 461/11/17; 453/87/209.

[16] In some cases, the SMC also administered family *waqf*s which the sharīʿa court had rendered to its administration due to mal-administration of their *mutawallī*s. See Reiter 1996, 140.

[17] Jerusalem *sijill*, 500/101/114. There is evidence (Israel State Archives, SMC files, P/989, file 84) that SMC officers were looking for an estate to sell in order to raise money for renovating and developing other *waqf* assets, and that the al-Bira plot was chosen for this purpose.

For example, two large urban plots belonging to the ʿAlī Pāshā *waqf* in Acre were sold to the Bahais, one in 1962 (6.5 dunams in a village east of Acre) and the other in 1974 (6 dunams in Acre's al-Majādala neighborhood).[18] In another case, the qāḍī approved the sale of a *waqf* house in Haifa without asking the price or the name of the buyer, who was a Jew. In his records, he wrote that he relied on the judgment of the *waqf* administrator's (civil) attorney, who also happened to be a Jew, and that the sale would benefit the *waqf*.[19] The attorney was interested in selling this house without committing himself to a specific purchase and the qāḍī separated between the two parts of the *istibdāl*, selling and buying, by granting the *waqf* administrator general permission to sell and specific permission to buy, and vice versa. In an interview I conducted with the qāḍī who authorized these transactions, he expressed his motivation as 'satisfying present-day economic requirements,' that is, maximizing the endowment's profits.[20] In so doing, the qāḍīs eased the restrictions on selling *waqf* assets according to market needs, even when the buyers of the *waqf* estates were non-Muslims, namely, Jews and Bahais.

In sum, the debate regarding the eternal nature of *waqf*, that is, whether the charitable purpose of the *waqf* or the original endowed properties should be preserved, was determined by medieval Islamic jurists in favor of the former one. The legal devices which authorized transactions of *waqf* estates were adapted by the qāḍīs in a flexible manner. *Istibdāl*, the exchange of *waqf* properties, was used in the last century by Muslim official authorities to legalize state expropriation of *waqf* land, as well as in exceptional cases to sell *waqf* estates even to non-Muslims. Even Ḥājj Amīn al-Ḥusaynī, who attempted to use the *waqf* system in order to prevent Palestinian Muslims from selling lands to Jews, approved both the sale and long-term lease of *waqf* lands. Perhaps the present-day Islamists and Arab nationalists who proudly base their opinion on his *fatwā*s are unaware of his contribution to the loss of the status of *waqf* of large plots of land in Palestine during the Mandatory period.

[18] Acre *sijill*, *Qarārāt*, 11/83/74.

[19] Acre *sijill*, *Qarārāt*, 5/22/68.

[20] Interview with Shaykh Muḥammad Ḥubayshī, conducted on February 27, 1986.

Conclusion

The current Islamic argument that Palestine in its entirety is *waqf* land is a political myth, based on a *ḥadīth* interpretation. The new concept is threefold: first, it claims that all seventh-century conquered lands enjoy the status of *waqf*; second, as such, these lands are a holy Islamic patrimony; and, third, these lands are inalienable in the sense that they could not be sold or transferred to non-Muslims, and particularly not to Jewish Zionists. The invention of this concept by the Ḥamās during the first *intifāḍa* was driven by modern political goals: to prevent Arab moderate leaders from ceding any land to Israel and to stop Muslims from selling Arab-owned estates to Jews. When the Oslo process crumbled in the second half of the 1990s, the concept was rapidly inculcated into many Palestinians and other Muslim communities outside Palestine, and it was adopted by Yasser Arafat and the PA *Muftī*.

The new myth is based on a *ḥadīth* referring to the seventh-century Islamic fiscal reform, putting it into a present political concept involving control of land and territory and giving it a new, anachronistic interpretation. The huge body of Arab and Islamic literature contains millions of traditions that Islamists could use as 'artifacts,' to borrow Benedict Anderson's term (Anderson 1991), in the process of constructing a new myth.

Our case study sheds some light on the process of constructing a religious-based political myth by Islamist groups. It reveals the sources—*ḥadīth* literature as historical precedents, reflecting the ideal period of the prophet and the first Righteous Caliphs, and the method that they used in endorsing a new legal interpretation. This method demonstrates selectivity in choosing the traditions, according to a literal criterion, without any research into the original meanings of the early terms and institutions as long as the literal text serves their political end. The Islamists' method in this case is also based on ignoring a significant proportion of other authentic literature that reveals alternative approaches. Furthermore, it is based on an absolute disregard of the accumulative practice of fourteen hundred centuries of Muslim rule.

The Ḥamās concept regarding land tenure in Palestine reflects the Salafī orientation of authenticity, which implies slavish imitation of the past, or a contemporary reading of the past. As Sivan noted, Islamists tend to idealize the age of Muḥammad and the four Righteous

Caliphs. As this study shows, through a legal contention, the new concept of Ḥamās is narrated by present-day Islamists without indicating a particular reference to the literature. By so doing, the Islamists present their concept as an axiomatic precedent and they avoid being challenged by non-radical *ʿulamāʾ*.

This case study explores how Islamists maneuver between two worlds, as Eisenstadt argued, between the worlds of tradition and modernism. The Ḥamās Charter presents the organization's modern ideology and political ends in the context of the current Middle East conflict. However, their modern outlook is based on tradition. Early Arab and Islamic literature (and history) is being sanctified and anachronistically re-interpreted to cope with modern challenges.

Another interesting phenomenon related to the modern myth invented by fundamentalists is the rapid process of dissemination of such a myth until it becomes accepted wisdom. In the case of Palestine, the claim that it is a holy *waqf* in its entirety was adopted by PA officials and by many Palestinian and even some Muslim religious figures, as well as the general public outside Palestine. Why was the new myth so easily and rapidly accepted and how did it become common knowledge? Moreover, how is it that an ideologically-based religious-legal myth which was constructed by the Ḥamās Islamist movement to distinguish its political goals from those of its nationalist opponent—the non-religious Fateh—has been welcomed and used in the political discourse by Fateh itself and other political rivals? Here, the actual context of the PA's *Muftī* ʿIkrima Ṣabrī's *fatwā* is important: Yasser Arafat's participation in the peace summit talks of July 2000 at Camp David was presented by Ḥamās as a surrender and a compromise on the issue of the Palestinian claim of return. As such, Arafat's political rivals charged that he was planning to cede sacred territory. Once it became clear that the peace talks collapsed (on July 22, 2000)—the PA's apparatus made use of the Ḥamās myth as a means of overall Palestinian and Islamic consolidation. The broader Islamic World now became a strategic hinterland for the Palestinians. In order to achieve political unity and to face the new challenge, the PA recruited a religiously-based myth. However, Ṣabri's *fatwā* differs from the Ḥamās text by grounding the legal opinion on a different historical precedent. Whereas Ḥamās idealizes the first century of Islam (seventh century), the PA refers to the 1930s Palestinian nationalist hero—Ḥājj Amīn al-Ḥusaynī. The rapid and wide acceptance of the new myth can also be explained by a number of additional reasons: first, the need for Palestinian unity opposing Israeli policy since 1997, with the demise of the Oslo process; second, the fact that Palestinian society is mostly religious; and, finally, the lack of high-level Islamic scholarship, that is, the fact that Palestinian laypeople are not acquainted with the religious and historical knowledge which could refute such newly-invented myths. This particular point was even raised by senior Islamist scholars, such as the Syrian Saʿīd Ḥawwā, who referred to the ignorance in religious matters of the masses who in his eyes are being misled by official *ʿulamāʾ*. Ḥawwā wrote that "things have come to such a point that somebody can say to the Muslims: 'This is Islam' or: 'This does not contradict Islam,' and they would always believe that" (Sivan 1990, 54). Our case study shows that what Ḥawwā attributes to the official *ʿulamāʾ* applies to the Islamists themselves. Thus, "What is Islam?" in any particular case undergoes a process of interpretation, and the methods of interpretation vary according to the political ends of those who are engaged in this process.

CHAPTER TEN

LEGAL REFORM, INTERPRETIVE COMMUNITIES AND THE QUEST FOR LEGITIMACY: A CONTEXTUAL ANALYSIS OF A LEGAL CIRCULAR[1]

Ido Shahar

The purpose of this article is to take up Brinkley Messick's (1995) suggestion and produce a 'textual ethnography', in which a particular 'local document will serve as point of departure for an interrelated contextual, doctrinal, and discursive analysis' (ibid. 157). The document to be analyzed and contextualized here is a legal circular (*marsūm qaḍā'ī*) issued in 1995 by the president of the Israeli Sharīʿa Court of Appeal. Under the title, "The Role of Informants in Cases of Maintenance" (*waẓīfat al-mukhbirīn fī qaḍāyā al-nafaqa*), this circular—one of three issued between 1994–96[2]—deals with the matter of determining the size of maintenance awards allotted to women in cases of family dispute. The circular directs that instead of relying on information supplied by informants for the purpose of evaluating the financial ability of husbands, qāḍīs presiding in Israeli sharīʿa courts should rely primarily on official documents (e.g., paychecks and income tax forms).

The circular therefore heralded a reform that entailed a shift from a reliance on the oral testimony of witnesses, who must be present

---

[1] An early version of this article was presented at the conference, "Law in Islamic Societies: Historical Issues and Current Directions", held at the Institute of Asian and African Studies, the Hebrew University of Jerusalem on June 10, 2002. I would like to thank the participants in this conference for their valuable comments, and especially Qāḍī Aḥmad Nāṭūr, who chaired the session in which the paper was presented. I would also like to express my gratitude to Aharon Layish, Ron Shaham, Moussa Abou Ramadan, Dror Zeevi, Nimrod Hurvitz, Sam Kaplan and David Powers, who read earlier versions of this paper and helped me to sharpen my arguments. Needles to say, any remaining faults are my own.

[2] The first circular (promulgated in 1994) deals with the prohibition to sell all *waqf* properties to non-Muslims; the second is the one at issue here; and the third and last circular (1996) deals with 'obligatory bequest' in favor of the orphaned grandchild. All three circulars appeared in a collection of judgments issued by the Sharīʿa Court of Appeal that was published in *al-Kashshāf* 1999, vol. 3.

in court, to a reliance on written, official documents. The reform also brought about a certain shift in the power distribution in Israeli sharīʿa courts: the status of the qāḍīs was strengthened at the expense of informants—that is, at the expense of non-professional elements involved in the judicial process. In this sense, the reform promoted processes of professionalization, rationalization and bureaucratization in the Israeli sharīʿa court system.[3] Moreover, although the reform was procedural in nature, its impact has been far-reaching: since 1995, a significant increase has been noted in the sums of maintenance payments that Israeli sharīʿa courts apportion to women.

One peculiar feature of this reform had to do with the mechanism that the President of the Sharīʿa Court of Appeal chose in order to realize it—namely, the legal circular. This is a highly unusual legal instrument, both within the framework of the Israeli legal system and in the context of Islamic law. Aharon Layish, in a lecture delivered at the Van Leer Jerusalem Institute on May 14, 1997, described the circumstances under which the idea of issuing a legal circular was conceived. Layish recounted that Qāḍī Aḥmad Nāṭūr—President of the Sharīʿa Court of Appeal and a former graduate student of his—had been searching for a mechanism that would allow the introduction of a legal reform without resorting to statutory legislation by the Israeli parliament (the Knesset).[4] Having studied legal documents from the period of the Sudanese Mahdī (Layish 1996; 1997), Layish suggested the mechanism of the 'legal circular' (*manshūr qaḍāʾī*), which the British applied in the Sudan after the Mahdī's defeat. Shaykh Nāṭūr embraced the idea, and the Israeli legal circulars (*marsūmāt qaḍāʾiyya*, as they were called locally) came into being.

Nevertheless, whereas the Sudanese circulars were legally ratified by the British colonial administration, those issued by the President of the Israeli Sharīʿa Court of Appeal have no legal standing whatsoever.[5] From the viewpoint of the Israeli legal establishment, the

---

[3] See Messick 1993 for an illuminating discussion of such processes in Islamic law over the last 150 years.

[4] From the point of view of the qāḍīs presiding in Israeli sharīʿa courts, any interference by the Knesset in procedural and material laws applied in the sharīʿa courts is highly problematic, for it might undermine the Islamic legitimacy of these courts. See below for further discussion of the legitimacy problems encountered by Israeli sharīʿa courts.

[5] Indeed, Abou Ramadan (2003, 287, n. 153) claims that the *marsūm*, as an act of legislation, violates the principle of separation of powers. Prof. Layish also wondered in his lecture at the Van Leer Institute what would happen "if someone

qāḍīs' choice of initiating a procedural reform by way of promulgating a legal circular is unconventional, to say the least. Qāḍīs, like civil judges, may instigate legal reforms either by handing down a precedent verdict[6] or by promoting legislation in the Knesset, but not in any other way. It may be argued, therefore, that the qāḍīs exceeded their authority, and that the reform introduced by the circular is not binding.

The attempt of self-appointed reformers—qāḍīs presiding in Israeli sharīʿa courts—to instigate a reform in *sharʿī* procedures is also dubious in the context of Islamic law. In this context, the prerogative of performing *ijtihād* and of suggesting new, innovative interpretations of the *sharīʿa* is usually limited to *muftīs*—jurisconsults, who are considered well-versed in Islamic law and related sciences. Qāḍīs, by contrast, are appointed by the government, and rarely earn the status of moral authorities and the required proficiency in the classical sources. All the more so when the appointing government is non-Muslim and when the appointed qāḍīs have no *sharʿī* education, as is the case in Israel (Reiter 1997b; Shahar 2000; Abou Ramadan 2005).

Two intriguing questions therefore arise concerning this legal circular: first, why did the qāḍīs initiate this particular reform at this particular time; and second, why was it that an unconventional and problematic mechanism—the legal circular—was chosen for that purpose? This chapter seeks to provide some answers to these questions. I argue that the nature of the reform, as well as the legal instrument that was chosen to accomplish it, were partly determined by a unique political constellation that prevailed around 1990. Specifically, concurrent with the promulgation of the circular (January 1995), a struggle had been taking place over the jurisdiction of Israeli sharīʿa courts. A proposal to reduce their broad jurisdiction was initially raised within Palestinian feminist circles. Beginning in the early 1990s,

would appeal to the High Court of Justice against a judgment based on these circulars". Yet he also quoted Qāḍī Nāṭūr, who had claimed that the *marsūmāt* may be defended in the High Court of Justice on the grounds that they fall within the interpretive authority of the qāḍī (Layish, lecture at the Van Leer Jerusalem Institute, May 14, 1997, and personal communication. See also Layish, forthcoming).

[6] Of course, only precedent judgments issued by the High Court of Justice are binding and, likewise, only precedent judgments issued by the Sharīʿa Court of Appeal are binding for the other sharīʿa courts. As a matter of fact, treating judgments of the Sharīʿa Court of Appeal as binding is an innovation introduced by Qāḍī Nāṭūr. See Abou Ramadan 2003; Layish, forthcoming.

Palestinian feminist activists began to voice loud criticisms of the 'conservative' and patriarchal sharīʿa courts, which, in their view, persistently and systematically discriminate against women. In particular, the feminists protested against the meager maintenance payments that sharīʿa courts regularly awarded to women.

In the mid-1990s, several women's organizations waged a campaign for conferring jurisdiction on civil family courts in matters pertaining to the personal status of Muslims. Such a move would have naturally meant a decrease in the power of sharīʿa courts, which previously enjoyed exclusive jurisdiction in these matters (excluding succession), and the qāḍīs were therefore eager to prevent it. The qāḍīs' initiative to reform the procedure by which maintenance payments are determined should therefore be viewed in the context of this political struggle: the procedural reform was intended to endow qāḍīs with greater control over the process of determining maintenance payments, so that they could increase the sums allotted to women. In this manner, they strove to placate the feminist criticisms that were directed at them and to thwart the initiative to reduce sharīʿa courts' jurisdiction.[7]

But why, then, was the legal circular chosen as a means for realizing the reform? I suggest that this choice was also driven primarily by political considerations: the reform needed not only to be executed, but also to be seen; it had to be made public so that the sharīʿa court system would gain legitimacy among its various constituencies in the Muslim-Palestinian community in Israel. A less visible reform, by way of legal precedents established by ordinary judgments of the sharīʿa court of appeal, would not have achieved the desired publicity. Moreover, by initiating and implementing an internal reform—without resorting to Knesset legislation—the president of the sharīʿa court of appeal conveyed a clear message of autonomy and independence from state patronage. At the same time,

[7] It is noteworthy, however, that Qāḍī Nāṭūr's own account of the motivations leading to the reform is different from my own. When this paper was presented to Qāḍī Nāṭūr during the above-mentioned conference (see n. 1), he rejected my interpretation and explained that the only motivation behind the reform was his desire to rectify a mistaken legal interpretation which had harmed a large number of women. Indeed, as noted by Barthes (1977, 142–48), the author of a text cannot be held responsible for the multiple meanings that readers may discover in it. The same goes for Nāṭūr and the legal circular under consideration.

he reinforced his personal authority vis-à-vis the other presiding qāḍīs.[8]

An attempt to portray the political framework within which Israeli sharīʿa courts operate yields, therefore, a complex picture. In order to properly function, sharīʿa courts in contemporary Israel have to maintain 'good working relations' with various communities and interest groups. First, sharīʿa courts are part of the Israeli legal system and are accountable to it. Second, since sharīʿa courts exercise significant authority in the realm of Muslim personal status, they are engaged in an intense dialogue with feminist circles in Palestinian society, as well as with other civil society organizations. And third, sharīʿa courts also seek the recognition and approval of the Islamic movement in Israel, which is a major religious and political force in the Palestinian community. Sharīʿa courts and the qāḍīs officiating in them cannot afford to lose legitimacy among any of these groups.

The qāḍīs are therefore obliged to maneuver between the opposing demands of various audiences. The textual fabric of the circular reflects this need very well. The circular implicitly addresses all of these diverse—even antagonistic—interpretive communities, and attempts to anticipate their responses to the reform and thwart their criticisms. Accordingly, it relies on diverse sources, discourses and styles, each of which is valued by a different community. It is therefore a heterogeneous text, which easily lends itself to an intertextual analysis (Bakhtin 1981, 1986; Kristeva 1986) that traces the various references, quotations and allusions that constitute it.[9] Moreover, since the 'legal circular' is an unconventional genre, with almost no precedents, its intertextuality is even more salient. It is in fact a bricolage of different genres—a *fatwā*, a modern, Western-style legal

[8] For an analysis of the centralization process in the Israeli sharīʿa courts system over the last decade, see Abou Ramadan 2003. According to the latter, the President of the Sharīʿa Court of Appeal, Qāḍī Aḥmad Nāṭūr, has managed during this period to fortify the status of the Court of Appeal vis-à-vis the regional sharīʿa courts, as well as his own authority vis-à-vis the other qāḍīs.

[9] The term 'intertextuality' was coined by Julia Kristeva in her influential accounts for Western audiences of the work of Mikhail Bakhtin (see Bakhtin 1981, 1986; Kristeva 1986). In a nutshell, 'intertextuality' refers to the fact that texts are not isolated, self-contained entities, but rather include numerous allusions, quotations and references to other texts. Snatches of other texts may be explicitly demarcated or implicitly merged in the text, and the text may assimilate them, contradict them, remark on them ironically and so forth. On intertextuality, see also Still & Worton 1990; Fairclough 1992; Allen 2000.

tract and an administrative circular at one and the same time—which are woven together to produce a new textual form.

The objective of this chapter is therefore to read the context of the legal circular into its text, and to read the text within its context. I argue that this legal text, and the reform that it promotes, should be understood in the context of political pressures that were exerted on Israeli sharīʿa courts by external constituencies. The text itself engages in cross-cutting dialogues with various interpretive communities, and seeks to gain legitimacy among all of them. A close reading of this complex, multifaceted document may reveal the implicit messages that it conveys to each group of readers, and the intricate strategies that it employs in order to establish the legitimacy of the reform, as well as of the Israeli sharīʿa court system as a whole.

In the next section, I briefly describe the legal-political context in which the circular was produced. I then move on, in the third section, to a close textual analysis, which traces the various voices and influences that may be detected in the text. The final section offers an integrative discussion of text and context, as well as some general conclusions.

The Legal-Political Context

The origins of the sharīʿa court system in contemporary Israel are to be found in the legal systems of the late-Ottoman and Mandatory periods.[10] Perhaps the most significant vestige of the Ottoman legal legacy has been the preservation of a *millet*-like legal system under both Mandatory and Israeli rule (Friedmann 1975, 206). The millet system of the Ottoman Empire was a 'personal status regime',[11] under which some non-Muslim religious minorities (Jews and several Christian denominations) were granted extensive religious and cultural autonomy. These religious communities were allowed to

[10] Sharīʿa courts within Israel serve primarily the Muslim-Palestinian minority residing within the 1948 borders. The Muslim population of the occupied territories has its own system of sharīʿa courts, administered currently by the Palestinian Authority. For detailed discussions of Israeli sharīʿa courts—their history, status and jurisdiction—see Eisenman 1978; Layish 1965, 1971, 1975, forthcoming; Peled 2001; Shahar 2006.

[11] A personal status regime, according to Galanter and Krishnan (2001, 271), is a system of 'legal arrangements for the application within a single polity of several bodies of law to different persons according to their religious or ethnic identity.'

establish their own autonomous courts, which employed religious law, and which had jurisdiction in matters of personal status relating to their respective community members (*EI*[2], s.v. Millet (M. Ursinus)). The *millet* system thus produced a state of 'weak legal pluralism' (Griffiths 1986), in which different groups in the population were allocated to different tribunals.[12]

Under Mandatory and Israeli regimes sharīʿa courts lost their residual jurisdiction over matters pertaining to the personal status of non-Muslims. However, until November 2001[13] they maintained greater jurisdiction than any other religious court in Israel. They maintained a virtual judicial-religious monopoly over the definition of the personal status of Israeli Muslim citizens—e.g., their identity as Muslims, bachelors, married, divorcees and parents of children. Notably, the jurisdiction of the sharīʿa courts has been broad not only as compared to that of Christian and Druze courts, but also as compared to that of the rabbinical courts (Yifraḥ 1955–56; Layish 1965).[14]

Why is it, then, that the Israeli legislator has refrained from changing this legacy of the Ottoman legal system? It seems that the 'conservative' policy adopted by Israeli policymakers with regard to issues of personal status was driven primarily by internal tensions within Jewish society in Israel. Specifically, the preservation of the *millet* system enabled Israeli policymakers to avoid the imminent clash between those sectors of the Israeli public that view Israel as a Jewish (religious) state, and those that view it as a democratic (secular) state. The tensions between these two opposing sectors have been inherent to the Israeli polity ever since the state was established. Because

[12] On weak vs. strong legal pluralism, see chapter 2 in Shahar 2006.

[13] On November 5, 2001, the Knesset passed Amendment No. 5 of the Family Courts Law, 5755–1995, which gave jurisdiction to the civil family courts in all matters of personal status affecting Muslims, except for marriage and divorce. By this act, the Israeli legislator made the jurisdiction of sharīʿa courts equal to that of the other religious courts in Israel. See further below.

[14] The reason for this situation was twofold: first, the definition of 'personal status matters' diverged between Muslim courts and all other communal courts. Whereas in the case of all the other courts, such matters were defined by Article 51 of the Palestine Order in Council, for Muslim courts they were defined more inclusively by Article 52, with reference to Article 7 of the Ottoman Code of Procedure for Sharīʿa Courts, 1917; second, Muslim courts were accorded exclusive jurisdiction in *all* matters of personal status (Article 52), while the other courts were accorded exclusive jurisdiction in *some* matters, and concurrent jurisdiction in others (Articles 53, 54 of the Palestine Order in Council, 1922–1947). See Bentwich 1926, 1, 14.

Israeli policymakers lacked the will and/or the political power to resolve this conflict positively, they chose to leave the situation as is. In other words, they chose to preserve the status quo in matters of religion and state relations (Friedman 1995). As a result, the religious courts—including the sharīʿa courts—have maintained their autonomy and their broad jurisdiction.

The preservation of the status quo was not limited to the courts' jurisdiction—it was also applied to the religious laws practiced in Israel. Ostensibly, the Knesset refrained from interfering with the religious laws: the Jewish *halakha*, the canonical codes, and the Islamic (codified) *sharīʿa*. Thus, the Ottoman Family Rights Law of 1917 and the Ottoman Law of Procedure for Sharīʿa Courts have remained intact and unchanged in Israel, and are still employed in the sharīʿa courts until this very day.[15] Indeed, some civil and criminal Knesset legislation has had considerable impact on the functioning of these courts (Layish, forthcoming), but in the absence of effective state supervision, the interpretation and implementation of Knesset legislation in sharīʿa courts is left to the qāḍīs' discretion. The qāḍīs have therefore acquired considerable powers and authority: they not only hold office in an important legal institution, embracing a broad jurisdiction, but also function in a sort of 'legal void', which leaves them significant degrees of freedom and agency.[16]

Thus, in recent decades the sharīʿa courts in Israel have become an almost-autonomous kingdom. The absence of effective state control, combined with far-reaching jurisdiction, broad judicial agency and insufficient procedural and material codes (the Ottoman codes are almost ninety years old), have transformed Israeli sharīʿa courts into an important arena for the practice of autonomous action, not

[15] This is true only to the extent that the Ottoman Family Law does not contradict Israeli statutes pertaining to family law that have been explicitly directed at religious courts.

[16] The only effective limitation on the judicial agency of qāḍīs is posed by the Israeli High Court of Justice, which is required by petitioners, from time to time, to probe the lawfulness of sharīʿa court decisions. In recent years the High Court of Justice has overturned some controversial judgments issued by sharīʿa courts, in general, and by the Sharīʿa Court of Appeal, in particular. See, e.g., HCJ judgment 8906/04, http://elyon1.court.gov.il/files/04/060/089/n07/04089060.n07.HTM; HCJ judgment 6452/96, http://elyon1.court.gov.il/files/96/520/064/n07/96064520.n07.HTM.

only for the qāḍīs, but also for Muslim-Palestinians in general (Shahar 2001). And yet, these characteristics have also transformed sharīʿa courts into a site of social and ideological struggle between opposing groups within Palestinian society. Particularly active in the struggle to reform matrimonial issues are various Palestinian women's rights organizations. These organizations work in close cooperation with both Jewish-Israeli women's organizations and Palestinian women's organizations in the West Bank. In recent years, feminist activists have promoted several initiatives related to sharīʿa courts, ranging from submitting a scheme for a comprehensive reform in sharīʿa law to establishing a professional course that qualifies women as *sharʿī* attorneys (Sulitzeanu 1999).

Criticizing the qāḍīs presiding in sharīʿa courts for being 'conservative', and viewing the procedural and material laws applied by sharīʿa courts as inherently discriminating against women (Bishara & Toma-Suliman 1997), these feminist activists have begun to demand that Muslim and Christian women—like Jewish and Druze women—be able to choose whether to resort to religious courts or to civil courts (rather than being obliged to resort to religious courts). Several women's groups and civil rights organizations have joined hands in this struggle and, by 1995, a "Working Group for Equality in Personal Status Matters" (WGEPS) was established.[17] The proclaimed goal of this group was to "combat discrimination against Arab women in the area of personal status, and change social norms by promoting significant changes in attitudes and behavior toward Arab women and their personal status issues."[18]

The WGEPS has waged a public campaign to make the legal status of Muslim and Christian women equal to that of Jewish and

[17] The following organizations participated in the working group: Women against Violence; The Association for Human Rights in Israel; The Arab Association for Human Rights; al-Ṭufūla: Pedagogical and Multipurpose Women's Center; Israel Women's Network; Shatīl: Equal Access Project; al-Siwār: Arab Feminist Movement in Support of Victims of Sexual Violence; Haifa Women's Shelter; The Association for Nurturing Family Relations; The Social Workers Association.

[18] Most of the information that I have gathered on the activities of the Working Group for Equality in Personal Status Matters is drawn from other civil society organizations that cooperate with it. See, for example, the websites of the Association for Human Rights in Israel (http://www.acri.org.il/hebrew-acri/engine/story.asp?id=496) and the New Israel Fund (http://www.nif.org/content.cfm?id=1370&currbody=1).

Druze women. In 1995, shortly after the Knesset passed the Family Courts Law,[19] the group initiated a bill to amend this law.[20] The main objective of the proposed amendment was to give Muslim and Christian women the option of recourse—in all matters of personal status except marriage and divorce—to the civil family courts. In an annexed clarification to the legislative bill, the drafters presented statistical data compiled by the National Insurance Institute which indicate that the sums of wife- and child-maintenance payments awarded by sharīʿa courts are significantly lower than those awarded by family courts. They concluded that in order to improve the status of Muslim and Christian women, it is mandatory to accord these women greater access to the civil family courts. The underlying assumption was that substantial and complete legal equality between men and women can be achieved only in the civil courts, and not in the patriarchal sharīʿa courts.[21]

The relatively meager maintenance payments that sharīʿa courts accorded to Muslim women therefore not only attracted criticism, but also motivated women's organizations to demand a restriction of these courts' jurisdiction. As expected, this initiative was met by fierce opposition from the courts' presiding qāḍīs. Realizing the danger for sharīʿa rule, and seeking to prevent any reduction of their status and authority, the qāḍīs—led by the charismatic, recently-nominated President of the Sharīʿa Court of Appeal, Aḥmad Nāṭūr—initiated a legal reform of their own.

Striving to take the sting out of the initiative, Qāḍī Nāṭūr sought a method that would yield a systematic increase in the sums of maintenance payments adjudicated in sharīʿa courts. The solution he found was—as explained above—to initiate a reform that transfers the authority to determine maintenance levels from appointed informants (*mukhbirūn*) to the qāḍīs themselves. Instead of relying on informants to gather information concerning a husband's financial status,

---

[19] The Family Courts Law, 5755–1995, was enacted in the Knesset on July 31, 1995. The main purpose of the Family Courts Law was to concentrate all the judicial jurisdictions of the various civil courts dealing with family disputes under the auspices of one civil tribunal—the family court. Furthermore, the law concentrates all legal litigations relating to a single family dispute in the hands of a single judge, presiding in the civil family court (Arbel and Geifman 1997; Shava 1998, 49).

[20] See report on the website of the Association for Human Rights in Israel (http://www.acri.org.il/hebrew-acri/engine/story.asp?id=496).

[21] A draft bill prepared by the Working Group for Equality in Personal Status Matters; no individual author or date is mentioned.

Nāṭūr suggested that the qāḍīs themselves would determine the amount of maintenance payments, relying, for that purpose, on official state documents, such as income tax and national insurance forms.

As noted, the mechanism chosen to bring about the desired reform was the unconventional 'legal circular'. According to my interpretation, the benefits of this method resulted primarily from its public and relatively dramatic and ceremonial nature. The qāḍīs needed to convey the message that they are taking measures to improve the treatment of women, and they needed to convince both the Knesset legislators and liberal and feminist circles in the Palestinian community. Alternative mechanisms—such as issuing precedent judgments by the Sharīʿa Court of Appeal—would have attracted much less attention in the public sphere. Moreover, the promulgation of legal circulars is an autonomous act of the qāḍīs, performed outside the auspices of the state and its legal system. In light of the tense relations between the Israeli state and its Muslim-Palestinian minority, such an autonomous act probably would improve the courts' reputation in this community.

All the qāḍīs holding office in Israeli sharīʿa courts signed the circular, thereby committing themselves to apply the procedural reform.[22] It seems, however, that the qāḍīs committed themselves not only to the procedural reform, but also to allotting more generous maintenance awards. The fact is that in the months following the promulgation of the circular, maintenance awards in the Sharīʿa Court of West Jerusalem have increased by 50 percent.[23]

Nevertheless, despite the public pressure and the substantial increase in maintenance awards adjudicated by sharīʿa courts, the initiative to confer jurisdiction on the family courts refused to die. The following years saw a heated debate within the Palestinian community in Israel between feminist and liberal circles which called for conferring jurisdiction on the civil family courts and Islamist circles (allied

[22] The qāḍīs gathered for a three-day seminar, at which they discussed the implications of this reform (personal communication from Qāḍī Ziyād ʿAsaliyya, former qāḍī in Jerusalem and Haifa).

[23] My data are based on a sample of maintenance files that were adjudicated in the Sharīʿa Court of West Jerusalem between 1994–98. I have no systematic estimates of maintenance awards in other sharīʿa courts in Israel, but I was told (proudly) by Qāḍī Nāṭūr, the author of the legal circular, that the maintenance awards have increased significantly following the issuance of the circular (interview with Qāḍī Nāṭūr, January 1998). It is therefore reasonable to assume that the same rise in maintenance awards also occurred in other courts (see also Reiter 1997b, 226).

with the qāḍīs), which insisted that sharīʿa courts must retain exclusive jurisdiction. On May 2, 1997, for example, the official journal of the Islamic movement, *Ṣawt al-Ḥaqq waʾl-Ḥurriyya,* published a *fatwā* signed by two qāḍīs presiding in the Sharīʿa Court of Appeals and by three prominent leaders of the Islamic movement.[24] The *fatwā* declared that the legislation bill is a harmful, erroneous endeavor; that it causes damage to Islam in Israel; and that it contradicts the holy Qurʾān and the benevolent *sharīʿa,* by facilitating the application of non-*sharʿī* rules to matters of the personal status of Muslims (*Ṣawt al-Ḥaqq waʾl-Ḥurriyya,* May 2, 1997, p. 8).

Despite this 'heavy artillery' and all the qāḍīs' efforts,[25] the legislation bill was presented to the Knesset in July 1997[26] by Nawwāf Maṣāliḥa, a Muslim member of the Knesset representing the Zionist labor party. Fifty-three members of the Knesset (including four Muslims and all the female members of the Knesset) added their signatures to it. At this phase, the confrontation between the opposing parties shifted primarily to the parliamentary arena, where members of the Knesset affiliated with the Islamic movement did their best to forestall and thwart the legislative process. Consequently, this process lasted more than four years, generating impassioned and heated debates whenever the bill was discussed—both in the Constitution, Justice and Law Committee and in the Knesset plenum.[27]

During these four years of bitter struggle the bill draft has been modified, but the main suggestion raised by it—that family courts

---

[24] The *fatwā* was signed by Qāḍī Nāṭūr and Qāḍī Dāʾud Zīnnī, and by Shaykh Rāʾid Ṣalāḥ, Shaykh Kāmil Riyān, and Tawfīq Khaṭīb of the Islamic Movement. As noted by Abou Ramadan (2005), although this document is entitled 'a *fatwā*', it cannot be viewed as a proper *fatwā*, for it was not issued in response to a petition or a query.

[25] Qāḍī Aḥmad Nāṭūr was particularly active in this struggle. Not only has he personally participated in meetings of Knesset committees that dealt with this bill, he also wrote and spoke against this legislation reform on various occasions. See, for example, Nāṭūr 1998.

[26] Legislation Bill No. p/1421, presented on July 16, 1997. See *Official Acta,* Legislation Bills, 2749, p. 570.

[27] See, for example: Legislation Bill The Family Courts (Amendment—Equalization of Jurisdiction), 1997, Knesset Minutes, July 16, 1997 (http://www.knesset.gov.il/Tql//mark01/h0001253.html#TQL); Legislation Bill The Family Courts (Amendment No. 5), 2001, Knesset Plenum Minutes, October 23, 2001 (http://www.knesset.gov.il/Tql//mark01/h0001245.html#TQL); See also Minute No. 208, The Constitution, Justice and Law Committee, June 28, 1998; Minute No. 91, The Constitution, Justice and Law Committee, February 22, 2000 (http://www.knesset.gov.il/protocols/data/html/huka/2000-02-22.html).

should be granted jurisdiction in matters pertaining to the personal status of Muslims and Christians—remained as it was. The bill finally passed into law on November 5, 2001, bringing the confrontation to an end. The implications of this law are yet to be assessed, but one thing is clear: the internal reform initiated by the qāḍīs as part of their struggle to thwart the bill had dramatic consequences in terms of the maintenance awards adjudicated in sharīʿa courts. Let us now turn to a closer reading of the text that brought about this reform.

The Document

The first thing that comes to mind as one reads this document is its plain, informal language: it contains eighteen folios, printed in Arabic in multiple fonts—undoubtedly with the aid of a word processor—numbered at the bottom and pinned together at the upper-right-hand corner.[28] At the top of page 1 (see Figure 1), under the *basmala*, appears the logo of the High Sharīʿa Court of Appeal, in 'noble' Jerusalem (*Maḥkamat al-Istiʾnāf al-Sharʿiyya al-ʿUlyā, al-Quds al-Sharīf*); below comes a title, 'Legal Circular Number 2' (*Marsūm Quḍāʾī Raqm 2*), and on the left side, 'The President's Office'. The subject of the document is then announced: 'The Role of Informants in Maintenance Cases' (*Waẓīfat al-Mukhbirīn fī Qaḍāyā al-Nafaqa*), followed by an introductory paragraph:[29]

> The use of informants by the sharīʿa courts in Palestine for the evaluation of maintenance payments is so deeply rooted that they [the informants], rather than the qāḍīs, have become the ones who determine [the level of] the maintenance granted. This procedure created [change of font in original] an unbearable situation, in which the adjudication is both wrong and unjust. We have decided, therefore, according to truth and justice, to restore [the correct] order. Since governance according to the *sharīʿa* (*siyāsa sharʿiyya*) was meant to open the gate of *sharʿī* mercy before the people, and—by returning to the source of the law—to implement the most lenient opinion in a matter that may bring either general well-being (*maṣlaḥa ʿāmma*) or general injury, we hereby approach your honors as follows [. . .]

[28] As noted above (see n. 2), this circular, as well as the two others that were issued, were later published in a collection of judgments issued by the Sharīʿa Court of Appeal (*al-Kashshāf* 1999).

[29] All excerpts from the text are my translations.

بسم الله الرحمن الرحيم
محكمة الإستئناف الشرعية العليا
القدس الشريف

مرسوم قضائي رقم (٢)

ديوان الرئيس

الى أصحاب الفضيلة قضاة الشرع الشريف

السلام عليكم ورحمة الله ،

الموضوع : وظيفة المخبرين في قضايا النفقة .

لقد تجذّر إستخدام المخبرين في عملية تقدير النفقات لدى المحاكم الشرعية في فلسطين منذ زمان بعيد ، حتى أصبحوا هم الذين يقدرون النفقة المفروضة دون القاضي ، *الأمر الذي أدى* الى حال لا يمكن المقام معه من سوء الأحكام وبُعدها عن العدل فارتأينا انه لا بدّ من إعادة الأمور الى نصابها إحقاقاً للحق وإقامة للعدل . ولما كان من السياسة الشرعية أن يُفتح للناس باب الرحمة من الشريعة ذاتها وأن يُرجعَ الى أصل الحكم ويُؤخذ بالرأي الذي هو بالناس أرفق ولهم أوفق ، الأمر الذي من شأنه جلب مصلحة عامة أو دفع ضرر عام ، فإننا نتوجه الى فضيلتكم بما يلي :-

Figure 1: Front page of Legal Circular No. 2, 'The Role of Informants in Maintenance Cases'

A few words of interpretation must be added to this opening paragraph, which lays the ground for the subsequent legal discussion. First, some ambiguity arises as to how binding the reform is for the qāḍīs presiding in Israeli sharīʿa courts in Israel. On the one hand, the circular is formulated as a straightforward directive, issued by the President of the Sharīʿa Court of Appeal, and addressed to the qāḍīs subordinate to him. On the other hand, it appears that the qāḍīs' consent to enact the reform was needed, for their signatures at the bottom of the document appear under the words: "I agree and commit myself" (*uwāfiq wa-altazim*). The same ambiguity arises on the recently-established website of the sharīʿa courts' administration. A Hebrew paragraph, posted on the web page currently hosting the three legal circulars, states:

> The legal circulars are issued by the President of the Sharīʿa Court of Appeal, *in agreement with his fellow qāḍīs*, as a means of designing *sharʿī* judicial policy in material and procedural issues, and they are binding for all sharīʿa courts in the country [emphasis added].[30]

Thus, it appears that Qāḍī Nāṭūr, the author of this text, was well aware of its problematic legal status and therefore sought to attain the cooperation of his fellow qāḍīs in promulgating the circular and in implementing the reform suggested by it. Bearing in mind Qāḍī Nāṭūr's strength and centrality in the sharīʿa court system in the last decade (see Abou Ramadan 2003), it is reasonable to assume that the other qāḍīs—especially junior ones—did not have much choice in this matter.

Second, another salient characteristic of the document stands out clearly in the logo, titles and opening words: there is no reference to the state of Israel or to any of its governmental institutions. We have seen that the text refers to a judicial problem in the sharīʿa courts of Palestine, not Israel; moreover, unlike the standard pages used for every sharīʿa court judgment in Israel, the logo of the Ministry of Religious Affairs,[31] as well as the official logo of the state of Israel, cannot be found on this document. The only logo, appearing at the top of page 1, is that of the High Sharīʿa Court of Appeal in 'noble' Jerusalem, as if this court functions in a legal-political void.

This impression of acting/writing in a political void is reinforced by the author's usage of the term 'governance according to the *sharīʿa*' (*siyāsa sharʿiyya*). In classical Islam, the term *siyāsa sharʿiyya* referred to the ability of a Muslim ruler to enact ordinances and to employ other practices of governance in order to serve the public well-being (*maṣlaḥa ʿāmma*), as long as direct *sharīʿa* rules are not violated (see Anderson 1976, 12; Schacht 1964, 54; al-ʿAṭaune 2001). Yet, in this text, the author himself uses the term *siyāsa sharʿiyya*—and this is indeed a pretentious act (see also Abou Ramadan 2003, 286).

The lack of reference to the state of Israel is apparent throughout the whole text: in fact, the word 'Israel' does not appear anywhere in the text. The author, it seems, invested great effort to

---

[30] See: http://www.justice.gov.il/MOJHeb/BatiDinHashreim/MaagreiMeida/Minsharim/.

[31] During the years 1948–2001, the sharīʿa courts in Israel functioned under the administration of the Ministry of Religious Affairs. In 2001, the administration of the sharīʿa courts was transferred to the Ministry of Justice.

distance it from any official Israeli authority. The unofficial, plain nature of the document, and the lack of Israeli attributes in it, are directly related—I contend—to the intricate dialogues conducted by the text with its various audiences. Specifically, these characteristics are related to the twofold appeal to both the Israeli legal establishment and the Palestinian-Muslim community. As noted above, bureaucratically and legally speaking, the qāḍīs may have exceeded their authority by reforming the law without resorting to Knesset legislation. Apparently, by eliminating any vestige of official Israeli authority, they were trying to diminish the irregularity of the document, lending it the appearance of an internal circular of negligible importance. At the same time, by distancing themselves from the Israeli authorities they also were trying to persuade the Muslim-Palestinian public that the legal circular is not a product of Israeli interests, produced by Israeli-appointed qāḍīs, but a respected moral-legal opinion (that is, a *fatwā*), which should be valued accordingly. As we can see, the text's rhetoric and its form of presentation are employed to disguise problems of authority, as well as to build authority, towards all targeted audiences.

The introductory paragraph is followed by the first section of the document. Under the title 'Legal Background', the author presents the procedural precept which stands at the base of the problem:

> In their use of the informants 'regime' (*niẓām al-ikhbār*), the sharīʿa courts have been relying on Clause 31 of the [Ottoman] Sharīʿa Courts' Law of Procedure from year 1333 (fiscal year)—1917 (A.H.), which reads as follows: "If the parties disagree on matters such as the evaluation of the sum of maintenance and the appropriate rental [cost] (*ajr al-mithl*)[32]—matters in which gathering of information from people of knowledge is needed (*al-khuṣūṣāt al-muḥtāja ilā ikhbār ahl al-khibra*)—or if the defendant is absent, people of knowledge will immediately be appointed on behalf of the court".

The text then analyzes Clause 31:

> [We] need to notice that the text of the above-mentioned Clause 31 poses several substantive questions, which should be studied carefully! What is the meaning of 'to inform' (*ikhbār*) and what is its legal sta-

---

[32] The *sharʿī* concept of *mithl*, usually rendered as 'appropriate', refers to financial matters such as dower or rental costs. The appropriate sums of dower or rent are determined according to local accepted conventions (*al-maʿrūf*) and local custom (*al-ʿāda*). See Meron 2001, 207.

> tus? Is it a part of the plaintiff's evidence, or is it perhaps impartial information delivered to the qāḍī concerning the [financial] state of the defendant? Then, to whom does the title 'people of knowledge' refer and what are their qualifications and attributes? Does the term 'is needed' in the text denote an obligation to appoint informants in every case of 'evaluation of the sum of maintenance', or does it denote 'a need', which is open to the qāḍī's deliberation? [. . .] For if it is 'obligatory' for the qāḍī to rely on informants, does eschewing from appointing them impair his verdict? In order to answer these questions, one needs to scrutinize the text and to interpret the intents of the legislator concerning the need for informants.

As we can see, the above paragraph is formulated as an analytical legal discussion. Clause 31 of the Ottoman Law of Procedure is skillfully deconstructed by a series of Socratic questions, which bring to light its vagueness. Not only is it not clear in which cases informants are needed, and who may be considered a qualified informant, it also is unclear how the qāḍī should employ the information supplied by the informants.

This kind of legal analysis is obviously addressed to readers who are professional jurists, rather than to the general public. Indeed, whereas the author tries to avoid any reference to Israeli authority, this paragraph seems to incorporate the language of the Israeli legal establishment. Paradoxically, the author endeavors to conceal the document from the institutional eye, but goes out of his way to express his fluency in the legal discourse characteristic of this very same institution. In other words, although the text does not refer directly to Israeli legal sources, it does resort at times to a formalistic mode of argumentation that is often to be found in Israeli legal discourse. This internal tension makes one wonder if the document's author is not waiting for someone to appeal against the proposed reform, so that it can be tested in the High Court of Justice.

Thus, the formalistic mode of argumentation found in the above excerpt stands in contrast with other, informal elements in the text. The text employs various rhetorical devices that are formalistic and 'modern'[33] in nature: it is analytically well-structured, both in content and in form, moving skillfully from presenting the problem to analyzing its causes in malpractice and in misinterpretation, continuing

[33] As argued by Weber (1978) and by many other commentators who followed in his footsteps, the most salient characteristic of modern law is its aspiration to rationality, certainty and orderliness.

with the presentation of legal references that substantiate an alternative interpretation, and concluding with the suggestion of a corrective reform. The analytical and formalistic nature of the text is clearly demonstrated in the next section of the document, which is entitled, 'The Implementation [of Clause 31] and Actual Reality' (*al-Taṭbīq wa'l-Wāqiʿ al-ʿAmalī*). This section is subdivided into four clauses, presenting the numerous causes that unwittingly produced the overuse of informants in maintenance cases.

Clause (a) of this section opens with a discussion of the typical maintenance claim, which usually does not include information concerning the financial status of the defendant. Even in cases in which wives claim that their husbands are well-to-do and therefore demand substantial sums of maintenance, they usually fail to support their claims with sufficient *sharʿī* evidence. As a result,

> [. . . after the qāḍī has established the wife's entitlement to maintenance, he] moves on to nominate 'informants' in order to evaluate the sum of maintenance that should be granted [to the wife]. Now, we have to remember that those [informants] are usually not recruited from among the litigants (*mutaqāḍiyyīn*), [but from among people] who are brought especially for the purpose of evaluation [of the size of the maintenance award]. Bearing in mind that this task [viz., the evaluation] constitutes the most important phase in the process of resolving the legal case—they [viz., the informants] are the ones who bring the case to an end, by determining a sum. Since they may be sinful and ignorant people (*al-fāsiqīn al-jahla*), it is inevitable to question their integrity, and their favoritism—as a way of nature—towards the beneficiary party. [. . .] The result of this procedure is nothing but a falsification of justice and truth, due to the handing over of the scales of justice to [persons] other than the qāḍī, and to favoritism rather than to objectivity and justice.

Clause (b) deals with the equivocality of the term 'people of knowledge' (*ahl al-khibra*). Drawn from the root kh.b.r., this term may be understood as referring either to experts (*khubarā'*) in a specific field, or to informants (*mukhbirūn*). The clause concludes that in the present context, the latter meaning is the correct one, since the qāḍī, rather than the informants, should be regarded as an expert in the field of maintenance. Clause (c) deals with the prevalent use of informants in maintenance cases:

> The sharīʿa courts do not distinguish between cases in which adjudication may be reached without resorting to informants and cases in which the qāḍī must be aided by informants in order to adjudicate.

> Instead [of distinguishing between such cases] the courts always resort [to informants], whether a case is one of basic maintenance (*nafaqat kifāya*) or of wealth maintenance (*nafaqat yasār*).[34] The Sharīʿa Court of Appeal has nevertheless taken this issue to the extreme, by nullifying any judgment issued by the first instance courts that was not based on information [supplied by informants]. Thus, [the Sharīʿa Court of Appeal] regards [the failure to use informants] as a substantive flaw [in the trial procedure], obligating the nullification of the judgment.

Finally, clause (d) concludes this section by describing the unfortunate results of the procedure of information gathering by nominated informants:

> As one might expect, the result of this procedure is by and large a predisposition towards the party that is closer to the informants. [. . .] Bearing in mind that the woman is usually the injured party, because of her being less competent [than the man] in regard to the preparation and the management of the legal claim, there is no wonder that certain—justifiable—voices have been heard, calling for a rectification of the harm which is being inflicted on Muslim women. Nonetheless, these voices are still vague, unable to offer a remedy, [because they tend to] generalize rather than scrutinize [the problem] in detail. A few [of these voices] even go so far as to accuse the sharīʿa courts and the *sharīʿa* itself of iniquity, proposing therefore to transfer the jurisdiction over [Muslims'] maintenance cases from the sharīʿa courts to the regional [civil] courts. Surely, from the start we have understood that such calls emanate from a grave misapprehension and from incredible shallowness and myopia. Instead of calling for the destruction of the sharīʿa courts, and for shoving Muslims' affairs into the grip of worldly laws, it was proper to call—and, moreover, to struggle—for a reform in the sharīʿa courts, which are the most just and most truthful among all [courts]. We firmly believe that the sharīʿa court is the only official Muslim institution left for the Muslims in this country, [and therefore it is] our duty to strengthen it, in order to apply the *sharīʿa* and to further establish adherence to the principles of faith in God's land. The preservation of sharīʿa courts is, therefore, a basic Islamic demand, provided that they implement justice and equity.
>
> [A space of four blank lines in original]
>
> Since [women] constitute half of society and the origins of life, Islam has granted special rights of equality and honor to them, and dedicated to them a wide array of its rules. [Islam] also measures in the

[34] The distinction between 'basic' or 'sufficient' maintenance (*nafaqat kifāya*), 'hardship' maintenance (*nafaqat iʿsār*) and 'wealth' maintenance (*nafaqat yasār*) is further developed in section 3 of the document.

> scales of justice the correct balance between the duties of the individual toward [other] individuals and toward society, so that a just equality will prevail among family members in a balanced manner [. . .]. To quote a maxim, if injustice is caused to a human being following the implementation of a *sharīʿa* judgment, the fault must be found in erroneous implementation, not in the law itself.

These four clauses demonstrate the twofold dialogue implicit in the text with the feminist movement on the one hand and with the Islamic movement on the other. As one might expect, the author speaks harshly to those 'voices' that call for a restriction of the sharīʿa courts' jurisdiction, accusing them of shortsightedness, shallowness, and the like. Nevertheless, the text is manifestly sympathetic towards women and the improvement of their status. Not only does it justify the voices calling for a correction of the injustice inflicted on women by the use of informants, it also devotes a full paragraph to praising the just and equitable manner in which women are treated in Islam. These grandiloquent phrases are meant to express the qāḍīs' familiarity with the discourse on women's rights. Instead of confronting feminist ideology, the qāḍīs prefer to embrace elements of the women's rights discourse and to incorporate them into Islamic discourse.

Incorporating new ideologies and discourses—usually of Western origin—into Islamic discourse has characterized the frame of mind of 'Modernist Islamists' since the second half of the nineteenth century (see Anderson 1971, 1976; Layish 1978; Ramadan 1998). However, this tactic has met with opposition—from the nineteenth century to this very day—from 'fundamentalist' circles, which view the efforts of Modernists to adapt Islam to these ideologies as a manifestation of submission to Western values. Indeed, this kind of confrontation between 'modernist reformists' and 'fundamentalists' is implicit in the document under focus. Surprisingly, from the point of view of Israeli qāḍīs, the Islamist circles may constitute a relatively hostile audience, no less, and perhaps even more, than the feminist circles. Nominated by a non-Muslim state and a non-Muslim appointing committee, and lacking official Islamic education,[35] Israeli qāḍīs are usually treated

[35] Although five of the nine members of the qāḍīs' appointing committee are Muslims, this committee by no means can be regarded as Islamic (see Abou Ramadan 2005). None of the qāḍīs holding office nowadays has a proper *sharʿī* education. See Reiter 1997b.

by Islamists with suspicion, and sometimes even disparagement.[36] In such an atmosphere of distrust, it is especially difficult for the qāḍīs to persuade their Islamic audience that the noble *sharīʿa* really is being implemented in their courts. Likewise, it is difficult for them to persuade their Islamic audience that their proposed reforms are not inspired by secular ideologies and do not serve state interests. It is possible, therefore, that the description of sharīʿa courts as the last resort of official Islam in this country is addressed to Islamists and feminists alike. Both groups threaten (each for its own reasons) to restrict the sharīʿa courts' jurisdiction and authority.

As the head of 'the last resort of official Islam in this country', the President of the Sharīʿa Court of Appeal has to establish his proficiency in classical Islamic sources, as well as in interpreting these sources. The next section of the document (section 3)—entitled, 'The Method of Evaluating [the Sum] of Maintenance' (*Kayfiyyat Taqdīr al-Nafaqa*)—attempts to achieve precisely this goal. Here the author develops a meticulous discussion of the different kinds of maintenance (wealth maintenance; sufficient maintenance; distress maintenance) to which a wife may be entitled in various circumstances (pp. 5–9). Drawing in an eclectic fashion (*takhayyur*) on diverse sources, the text quotes Ḥanafī scholars such as al-Khaṣṣāf (d. 261/874), al-Sarakhsī (d. 483/1090), al-Kāsānī (d. 587/1191), the author of *al-Hidāya* (al-Maghrīnānī, d. 593/1196), al-Zaylaʿī (d. 743/1342), and Ibn ʿĀbidīn (d. 1252/1836), as well as scholars from other schools of law (*madhāhib*), such as the author of *al-Mudawwana al-Kubrā* (Mālik Ibn Anas, d. 179/795), al-Shāfiʿī (d. 204/820), al-Karkhī (d. 340/941) and the Ḥanbalī author of *al-Mughnī* (Ibn Qudāma, d. 620/1223).[37] The discussion concludes with the assertion that although there is no general agreement among these scholars, it is clear that the husband's financial status should be considered in the evaluation of the maintenance award. As a rule of thumb, the wife should be entitled to 'sufficient' maintenance, according to local conventions (*kifāya bi'l-maʿrūf*), and in the unusual cases of well-to-do couples, the sum will be determined according to the evidence.

---

[36] See, for example, the harsh criticism that was pronounced by Shaykh Hāshim ʿAbd al-Raḥmān, speaker of the Islamic movements, with regard to the lack of Islamic education of presiding qāḍīs in Israeli sharīʿa courts (*Ṣawt al-Ḥaqq wa'l-Ḥurriyya*, July 1, 1994, p. 28). See also Landau 1969, 10; Dumper 1994; Peled 2001, 121; Abou Ramadan 2005.

[37] On the extensive usage of *takhayyur* by Qāḍī Naṭūr, see Layish, forthcoming.

Section 4 of the document, 'Who Will Evaluate the Maintenance [award]' (*Man Yuqaddir al-Nafaqa*), is subdivided into two subsections. The first part (pp. 9–11), which deals with the issue of the actual evaluation of maintenance awards, concludes:

> [. . .] Since the qāḍī is the one who is solely in charge of the evaluation, without the participation of anyone else, the discussion of the role of informants should be regarded as belonging not to the section of 'who will evaluate the maintenance award,' but to the section on 'the method of evaluating the maintenance award'. Their [viz., the informants'] role is thus to assist [the qāḍī] in cases of wealth maintenance (*nafaqat al-yasār*) in the process of clarifying the evidence regarding the husband's financial status [. . .] (p. 10).

The argument laid down thus far is twofold: first, the qāḍī, and not the informants, has the authority to determine the maintenance award; and second, the procedure of information-gathering by informants is reserved for special cases—those of wealth maintenance (*nafaqat al-yasār*). This conclusion is further developed in the second part of section 4. Under the subtitle, 'The Source for Provision of Information' (*Maṣdar al-Ikhbār*), the opinions of several scholars are reviewed. In addition to classical Islamic authorities, such as al-Kāsānī, al-Zaylaʿī and al-Sarakhsī, the text also refers to statutory legislation in neighboring Arab states such as Iraq, Syria and Egypt. The picture that emerges from this review is of a general consensus among these sources, according to which in cases of wealth maintenance (that is, cases in which the wife claims that the husband is well-to-do), the qāḍī may resort—if he wishes—to the procedure of appointing informants. The purpose of such a course of action is to gather information regarding the husband's financial status. The testimony of the informants may be regarded, therefore, as

> 'informative evidence' (*shahādat istikshāf*)—a term denoting, in Ḥanafī jurisprudence, evidence gathered by the qāḍī in the course of studying a particular issue (*maʿrifat amr min al-umūr*). This is most evident in the Egyptian statute (number 78, year 1931), where it is clearly stated that testimonies regarding maintenance are treated as informative evidence, and therefore they are not given under oath. [. . .] Clause 174 of the Egyptian statute states that 'it is not necessary to adjure [a witness] supplying informative evidence. Rather *it is sufficient merely to hear* [emphasis in original] from someone who is trustworthy.' Al-ʿAmrūsī (*al-Marjaʿ al-Wāfī fī Qaḍāʾ al-Aḥwāl al-Shakhṣiyya lil-Muslimīn*, Cairo, 1963) adds that informative evidence is one of three possible procedures to be implemented in order to prove claims regarding the husband's

affluence: 'There are three ways to prove the husband's [financial] status:

1. The husband's acknowledgement and his agreement with the wife's claims.
2. The court clerks' search [for evidence] using administrative procedures.
3. Informative evidence (*shahādat istikshāf*).'

The meaning of 'search for evidence using administrative procedures' (*al-taḥarrī bi'l-ṭarīq al-idārī*) is that [the qāḍī] may rely on diverse state agencies, such as the police, or even the secret police, or any other official institution, in order to inquire into the husband's [financial] status [. . .].

The lengthy quotes from the Egyptian statute and from a modern commentator (al-ʿAmrūsī) are clear-cut: the procedure of providing information (*ikhbār*) is treated as a mechanism for gathering informative evidence. It is one of three methods of information gathering that may serve the qāḍī—but that by no means obligate him. The most interesting element in the above quote is, of course, the qāḍī's prerogative to employ different state agencies (including the secret police!) to gather information regarding a husband's financial status. The text expands upon this option in the subsequent summation. But before we move on to the summation, it is worth noting another salient feature of the above section: that is, the extensive use of references—in the form of direct and indirect quotes—to modern statutes.

These references, I contend, constitute another component of the dialogues that the text conducts with the Israeli legal establishment and with the Palestinian-Muslim community. Of course, reference to the legal situation prevailing in neighboring Arab-Muslim countries may serve as a source of legitimacy in the simple sense of "If they do it, why can't we?" However, it goes further than this. First, the reference to statutory legislation in neighboring countries is meant to appease the Israeli legal establishment because, on several occasions, Israeli civil courts have themselves resorted to such sources. In several cases in which matters pertaining to sharīʿa courts have been brought before regional civil courts or the High Court of Justice, the prime references in the judgments issued by these institutions were modern statutes of neighboring Arab-Muslim countries. Thus, for example, the High Court of Justice ruled, in a famous verdict, that "a modern state such as Israel cannot allow polygynous marriage", and urged the qāḍīs of the sharīʿa courts to follow the example of neighboring countries which have nullified this custom altogether, or at least restricted it (HCJ 49/54, P"D 16, 70–75). In a similar vein, the Regional Court of Tel Aviv expressed its hope that "[t]he qāḍīs in Israel will follow the lead of religious reformers in the Muslim world, in order to adapt religion to the needs of the modern world" (Tel Aviv R.C. verdict, 376/59, quoted in Layish 1963, 32).

These words of reproach, directed at the Israeli qāḍīs, ignore the fact that in Israel, unlike in neighboring countries, the legislator refrains from directly interfering with religious laws. As a result, the ancient (in legal terms) Ottoman Family Rights Law of 1917 is still intact, and the qāḍīs are obliged to rule according to its precepts.[38] Nevertheless, it seems that the qāḍīs have finally taken the advice of their colleagues from the Israeli civil courts, for they have resolved to reform the law. In doing so, they were careful to legitimize their proposed reform by providing ample references to statutes of neighboring countries. Here again, the efforts of the author to create a text compatible with the expectations of the Israeli legal establishment makes one wonder whether it was not his intent from the start to produce a document that would withstand scrutiny from the High Court of Justice.

As for the Muslim-Palestinian community, the references to the statutes of neighboring countries convey a clear message of resemblance between the situation here—that is, in Palestine/Israel—and the situation beyond the border, in Muslim sovereign states. Like their counterparts in those countries, Israeli qāḍīs apparently are able to implement *siyāsa sharʿiyya*—governance according to the *sharīʿa*—and to initiate reforms for the general public's benefit (*maṣlaḥa ʿāmma*). Thus, by referring to statutory legislation in neighboring countries, the author of the text clearly aims to accentuate the qāḍīs' agency, their independent position vis-à-vis non-Muslim state authorities, and their ability to 'modernize' their courts in accordance with the *sharīʿa*.

The document ends with a summation (*khulāṣa*) (pp. 15–17) that brings together the principal arguments made in the text: the role of informants is not to determine the size of the maintenance award,

[38] Again, this is true only to the extent that the Ottoman Family Law does not contradict Israeli statutes pertaining to family law that have been explicitly directed at religious courts.

but to provide the qāḍī with information regarding the husband's financial status; the qāḍī alone is charged with determining the size of the maintenance award. In addition, it is noted that if the Egyptian statute allows [the qāḍī to] resort to various state agencies in order to gather information, then

> [. . .] Bearing in mind that the *sharīʿa* regarded official evidence as a special kind of hearsay (*al-shahāda al-samāʿiyya*), and therefore permitted its use as lawful evidence, why should the sharīʿa courts of our times not be able to rely on written evidence, produced by formal institutions, in order to verify the husband's financial status? After all, whether the husband is a salaried employee, self-employed, unemployed, a pensioner or a temporary worker, there is always an official agency which is capable of supplying information—in written and officially signed documents—concerning his financial circumstances. [Documents such as] paychecks, income tax forms, national insurance papers, ministry of welfare certificates, and so on may serve this purpose.
>
> There is no doubt that these [documents] are closer to the truth and to justice [than information supplied by informants], for they are considered as merely informative. Therefore, by relying on them, justice will both be done and be seen.

The text continues, repeating the principles mentioned above and then sketching the advisable procedure of adjudication in maintenance cases:

> First, [the qāḍī] has to establish the entitlement of the plaintiff to maintenance, and thereupon, to demand that the plaintiff specify her needs in her suit, so that the defendant and the court will have a clear notion of how she determined the sum [that she asked for], and that [the defendant] will be able to defend himself. If she asks for sufficient maintenance (*nafaqat al-kifāya*), and her entitlement to it has been legally established, the qāḍī will grant her a sum as he sees fit. However, if she asks for wealth maintenance (*nafaqat al-yasār*), and her entitlement to maintenance has been established, but the defendant denies that he is well-to-do, then the qāḍī will ask her [to prove her claim] by supplying lawful *sharʿī* evidence. [These evidences] should be considered immune to the two faults: fabrication and reproduction (*taṣnīʿ*); what we have in mind here are official documents such as paychecks, tax forms and so on. We say so, because in those cases in which [the defendant] denies [the plaintiff's claims], it is impossible to adjudicate without resorting to evidence or to oath [. . .]. Moreover, it is forbidden [for the qāḍī], in any case, to share the evaluation of the sum of maintenance with anyone else, for as we have seen, there is neither basis nor sense for that procedure. Thus, we hereby remove a grave detriment from the Islamic community (*al-umma*), and we get closer—in the implementation of God's law—to His intent and His will.

This conclusion is followed by the qāḍīs' signatures: first that of Qāḍī Nāṭūr, the author of the text and the President of the Sharīʿa Court of Appeal; then the signatures of his two permanent colleagues on this court, and then those of the rest of the qāḍīs. Each of them, except for Qāḍī Nāṭūr, signs his name—as noted above—under the words "I agree and commit myself" (*uwāfik wa-altazim*).

Conclusion

Technically speaking, the document analyzed here deals with the seemingly straightforward issue of a procedural reform in maintenance lawsuits. The text argues that the 'informants' regime' that has been applied in Israeli sharīʿa courts in such lawsuits emanated from a misguided interpretation of the Ottoman ordinance. It proposes, accordingly, to change this regime by transferring the authority to evaluate the size of maintenance awards to the qāḍīs themselves. Furthermore, instead of relying on informants for the purpose of gathering information on the defendant's financial status, the qāḍīs are encouraged (that is, only if they wish) to rely on official state documents.

This document therefore fosters a transition in Israeli sharīʿa courts (in maintenance suits) from reliance on oral testimony to reliance on written texts—from logocentrism (Derrida 1974) to a regime that accords a central role to written documents. While it might appear that such a transition is a 'natural' result of modernization—part of a linear, deterministic process of the gradual elimination of 'oral residues' (Ong 1965) from contemporary sharīʿa courts—the present case suggests otherwise. As I tried to show, the reform was motivated to a large extent by local political considerations and constraints, and not by a 'modernization impulse'. Such local constellations may sometimes foster a movement away from a culture of orality, but at other times they may foster a movement in the reverse direction—that is, towards according more authority to oral testimonies.[39]

[39] Such processes occur in Israeli sharīʿa courts as well. For example, until recently, couples who wanted to ratify foreign marriage contracts (usually Jordanian or Palestinian contracts) were not required to attend the court in person. Instead, they could file a petition for the ratification of their marriage, and add to their petition an original copy of their marriage certificate and a signed declaration, stating that their marriage is valid and still intact. The former presiding qāḍī of the Sharīʿa

The primary motivation for the reform, as argued here, was to thwart the initiative to reduce the jurisdiction of Israeli sharīʿa courts. This initiative, raised by feminist and liberal circles in the Muslim-Palestinian community in Israel, threatened to undermine the status and authority of sharīʿa courts and of the qāḍīs presiding in them. The reform was meant, therefore, to bring about a significant rise in maintenance awards to women in sharīʿa courts, and hence to appease the voices criticizing these courts. Another consequence of the reform, which perhaps was welcomed by the qāḍīs, was to strengthen their authority vis-à-vis non-professional individuals involved in the judicial process (i.e., the informants).

The need to placate feminist and liberal groups in the Palestinian society, as well as Knesset legislators, can be detected in a close reading of the circular. The text alludes to Israeli legal discourse, and incorporates elements of feminist discourse. However, I argued that the text engages in dialogue not only with the Israeli legal establishment and with feminist and liberal groups, but also with groups affiliated with the Islamic movement in Israel. It exhibits considerable proficiency in *sharʿī* sources, and seeks to establish its own legitimacy as an authoritative *sharʿī* text as well as the status of Israeli sharīʿa courts as respectable Islamic institutions. In a way, the document's 'triple-voiced' appeal (Bakhtin 1981, 344)[40] to three distinct audiences promotes the establishment of a common denominator of 'Islamic modernism', which has the potential of being accepted by all three interpretive communities.[41] It may therefore be argued that the document constitutes a dialogic text not only in the Bakhtinian sense of a bricolage of discourses, references and influences, but also in the sense of creating and facilitating a dialogue between its various interlocutors.

But what about the legal mechanism that was chosen to bring about the reform—the unconventional mechanism of the 'legal circular'? I argued that this mechanism was preferred primarily due to

---

Court of West Jerusalem settled for this evidence. However, the current presiding qāḍī annulled this practice, and he now requires that the happy couple attend the court and testify to the validity of their marriage. For more details on this issue, see Shahar 2006, ch. 4.

[40] Bakhtin (1981, 344) refers to a double-voiced discourse; 'triple-voiced' is therefore my paraphrase of his words.

[41] As described by Peletz (2002), a similar function is performed by the sharīʿa courts in contemporary Malaysia. See especially chapter 4 of his book.

its public, ceremonial nature, which helped to convey the message that serious measures are being taken to improve women's status in sharīʿa courts. Moreover, this mechanism also served to convey a message of autonomy: the promulgation of a 'legal circular' enabled the qāḍīs to ceremonially declare their independence of state patronage. Unlike their critics (i.e., women's organizations), they do not need the Knesset in order to introduce a legal reform. They are autonomous, proud Muslims (and Palestinians), safeguarding—even at the price of exceeding their authority—the last resort of Muslim institutions in the country (that is, in Palestine).

Thus, it is no surprise that any explicit reference to the state of Israel and its governmental apparatus is meticulously avoided in the document, and that the author of the text carefully refrains not only from referring to Israeli sources of legitimacy, but also from using the word 'Israel'. Nevertheless, as argued above, this *prima facie* avoidance of anything Israeli is misleading. A close reading of the text reveals a deep engagement in a complex dialogue with the Israeli legal establishment. Moreover, we should bear in mind that the bottom line of the reform was to promote the utilization of official documents issued by the state of Israel (instead of testimonies of righteous Muslims) as legitimate evidence in sharīʿa courts. We may therefore conclude that the circular actually promotes the inclusion of the Palestinian-Muslim community within the Israeli polity, and not its exclusion from it.

In other words, while the *form* of this document conveys a message of autonomy and independence, its *content*—though concealed behind nationalist and Islamist rhetorics—conveys a message of integration and incorporation into the state. It may be argued, therefore, that the qāḍīs do not employ their powerful position and their agency in order to further alienate the Palestinian-Muslim public from the state, but to achieve the opposite: to turn the state (through its official documents) into a tangible—perhaps, even positive—part of the community's life. Thus, in spite of its dubious lawfulness, it would be erroneous to view this document as a subversive text, which challenges the legitimacy of Israeli law. The opposite view is more to the point.

The intricate, concealed message conveyed between the lines of the legal circular is a complex and dialectic one. It argues, on the one hand, for the Palestinian community's independence from state patronage and for the establishment of Islamic solidarity and, on the other hand, for the co-optation of the Palestinian community within the framework of the Jewish state. The text conveys, therefore, a powerful message of Muslim religio-cultural autonomy *within* the political structure of the Jewish state. In other words, in the spirit of the Ottoman *millet* system, the subtext of the document is that so long as the state of Israel endows the Palestinian-Muslim citizens with communal autonomy, those citizens, for their part, will be willing to accept the legitimacy of the state.

The importance of this legal text appears, then, to be political no less than legal. Following Clifford Geertz (1973), we may conclude that this document constitutes a cultural artifact that is, at one and the same time, a *model of* and a *model for* social relations. To be more precise, it is a model *for* and *of* a specific kind of political arrangement between the state of Israel and its Muslim-Palestinian citizens. Compared to other models for (and of) these relationships, which abound nowadays, this one is perhaps the more optimistic.

LIST OF CONTRIBUTORS

Eyal Ginio is Lecturer at the Department of Islamic and Middle Eastern Studies at the Hebrew University of Jerusalem. His research and publications have focused on social history of the Ottoman Empire with a particular emphasis on 18th-century Salonica.

Miriam Hoexter, Associate Professor of Islamic and Middle Eastern Studies, the Hebrew University of Jerusalem. Her publications include: *Endowments, Rulers and Community: Waqf al-Haramayn in Ottoman Algiers*; editor with Shmuel N. Eisenstadt and Nehemia Levtzion, *The Public Sphere in Muslim Societies* and articles on the social and legal history of North Africa and the Middle East.

Nimrod Hurvitz teaches at Ben Gurion University in the Department of Middle Eastern Studies. He has published several articles on Ahmad Ibn Hanbal and Hanbalism and is the author of the book *The Formation of Hanbalism: Piety into Power*.

Brinkley Messick is Professor and Chairman of the Department of Anthropology at Columbia University. He is the author of *The Calligraphic State* (California, 1993) and a co-editor of *Islamic Legal Interpretation* (Harvard, 1996).

David S. Powers (Ph.D., Princeton University, 1979) is Professor of Arabic and Islamic Studies at Cornell University. He is the author of *Studies in Qur'an and Hadith: The Formation of the Islamic Law of Inheritance* (California, 1986); and *Law, Society, and Culture in the Maghrib, 1300–1500* (Cambridge, 2002); and Editor of the journal *Islamic Law and Society*.

Yitzhak Reiter teaches modern history of Islam and the Middle East at Ashkelon Academic College and is adjunct lecturer at the Hebrew University of Jerusalem, the MA program in conflict studies. Dr. Reiter is also a fellow of both the Harry S. Truman Research Institute for the Advancement of Peace and the Jerusalem Institute for Israel Studies.

Ron Shaham, Ph.D. (1992) in Islamic Studies, Hebrew University of Jerusalem, is a senior lecturer at the Hebrew University. Author of *Family and the Courts in Modern Egypt* (Brill, 1997), he has published extensively on Egyptian modern family law reform, and on the legal status of non-Muslims.

Ido Shahar is Yonathan Shapiro post-doctoral fellow at the Department of Sociology and Anthropology, Tel Aviv University. He is a legal anthropologist, specializing in the study of sharīʿa courts. His research interests include the study of Islamic law, legal pluralism, and the Palestinian population in Israel.

Frank H. Stewart is an anthropologist who teaches in the Department of Islamic and Middle Eastern Studies, Hebrew University of Jerusalem. His publications include *Fundamentals of Age-Group Systems* (1977), *Texts in Sinai Bedouin Law* (1988–90), and *Honor* (1994).

Michael Winter is Professor Emeritus of Middle Eastern history at Tel Aviv University. He has published extensively on the history of the Arab lands under the Mamluks and the Ottomans, including *Egyptian Society under Ottoman Rule, 1517–1798* (Routledge, 1992) and *The Mamluks in Egyptian and Syrian Politics and Society*, co-edited with Amalia Levanoni (Brill, 2004).

BIBLIOGRAPHY

Archives

Defter. Muallim Cevdet O.83:936. Atatürk Kitaplığı, Istanbul.

Ḥaddād, Yaḥyā b. ʿAlī b. Nājī. N.d. *Kitāb ʿUmdat al-Qāriʾ fī Sīrat Imām Zamāninā Sayf al-Bāriʾ*. Ms. Western Library, Great Mosque, Ṣanʿāʾ, Tarīkh, 2594.

The Historical Archives of Macedonia, Salonica; Archives of the *Şeriat* Court, *Sicil* vols. 1–111 (1694–1768).

Zabāra, Aḥmad. N.d. *Nuzhat al-Naẓar* (expanded version, handwritten), 4 vols. Ms. Private archive of Brinkley Messick.

Published Works

ʿAbd al-Jabbār, Abū al-Ḥasan. ca. 1965. *al-Mughnī fī Abwāb al-Tawḥīd waʾl-ʿAdl*. Ed. Muṣṭafā al-Saqqā. 20 vols. Cairo: al-Dār al-Miṣriyya lil-Taʾlīf waʾl-Tarjama.

ʿAbdarī, Ibn al-Ḥājj al-. N.d. *al-Madkhal*. 4 vols. Cairo: Idārat al-Azhar.

Abou Ramadan, Moussa. 2003. "Judicial Activism of the Sharīʿa Appeal Court in Israel 1994–2001: Rise and Crisis." *Fordham International Law Journal*, 27: 254–303.

——. 2005. "The Religious Discourse of the Decisions of the Sharīʿa Appallete Court in Israel (1992–2001): A Critique." A paper presented at the workshop: *Courts of Law and Legal Cultures in Past and Present Muslim Societies: A Socio-Legal Perspective*. Ben-Gurion University of the Negev, Beersheba, April 12, 2005.

Abribat J. 1901. "Essai sur le contrats de quasi-aliénation et de location perpétuelle auxquels l'institution du hobous a donné naissance." *Revue Algérienne et Tunisienne de Législation et de Jurisprudence*, 17: 121–51.

Abū ʿAliya, ʿAbd al-Fattāḥ Ḥasan. 2000. *al-Quds, Dirāsa Taʾrīkhiyya ḥawl al-Masjid al-Aqṣā waʾl-Quds al-Sharīf*. Riyāḍ: Dār al-Mirrīkh lil-Nashr.

Abū ʿAmr, Ziyād. 1994. *Islamic Fundamentalism in the West Bank and Gaza: Muslim Brotherhood and Islamic Jihad*. Bloomington : Indiana University Press.

Abū Salīm, ʿĪsā Sulaymān. 2000. *al-Aṣnāf waʾl-Ṭawāʾif al-Ḥirafiyya fī Madīnat Dimashq khilāl al-Nisf al-Awwal min al-qarn al-Thāmin ʿAshar*. Amman: Dār al-Fikr lil-Ṭibāʿa waʾl-Nashr waʾl-Tawzīʿ.

Abū Yūsuf. 1969. *Kitāb al-Kharāj*. Trans. A. Ben Shemesh as *Taxation in Islam*. Leiden: Brill.

Abū Zahra, Muḥammad. 1949. *Ibn Ḥanbal*. Cairo: Dār al-Fikr al-ʿArabī.

——. 1957. *al-Aḥwāl al-Shakhṣiyya*. 3rd ed. Cairo: Dār al-Fikr al-ʿArabī.

——. 1971. *Muḥaḍarāt fīʾl-Waqf*. 2nd ed. Cairo: Dār al-Fikr al-ʿArabī.

Ahmed, Leila. 1992. *Women and Gender in Islam: Historical Roots of a Modern Debate*. New Haven & London: Yale University Press.

Aït-Zaï, Nadia. 1995. "Le Droit musulman et les coutumes kabyles." *Revue algérienne des sciences juridiques, économiques, et politiques*, 32: 305–12.

Akwaʿ, Ismāʿīl al-. 1980. *al-Madāris al-Islāmiyya fī al-Yaman*. Damascus: Dār al-Fikr.

——. 1995. *Hijar al-ʿIlm wa-Maʿāqiluhu fī al-Yaman*. 5 vols. Beirut: Dār al-Fikr al-Muʿāṣir.

Akwaʿ, Muḥammad al-. 1987. *Ḥayāt ʿĀlim wa-Amīr*. 2 vols. Ṣanʿāʾ: Maktabat al-Jīl al-Jadīd.

Alexander, Yonah & Abraham H. Foxman (eds.). 1990. *The 1988–1989 Annual on Terrorism*. Dordrecht & Boston: Martinus Nijhoff.

Ali, Ahmed. 1993. *al-Qur'ān: A Contemporary Translation*. Princeton: Princeton University Press.

Allen, Graham. 2000. *Intertextuality*. London and New York: Routledge.

ʿAlwānī, Ṭāhā J. al-. 1996. "The Testimony of Women in Islamic Law." *The American Journal of Islamic Social Sciences*, 13: 173–96.

ʿAmrī, Ḥusayn al-. 1985. *The Yemen in the 18th and 19th Centuries*. London: Ithaca Press.

Anastasopulos, Antonis. 2002. "Lighting the Flame of Disorder: *Ayan* Infighting and State Intervention in Ottoman Karaferye, 1758–59." *International Journal of Turkish Studies*, 8 (1–2): 73–88.

Anderson, J. N. D. 1951. "The Religious Element in *Waqf* Endowments." *Journal of the Royal Central Asian Society*, 38: 292–99.

——. 1971. "Modern Trends in Islam: Legal Reform and Modernization in the Middle East." *International and Comparative Law Quarterly*, 20: 1–21.

——. 1976. *Law Reform in the Muslim World*. London: Routledge.

Anderson, Benedict R. 1991. *Imagined Communities: Reflections on the Origin and Spread of Nationalism*. London: Verso.

Anṣārī, Sharaf al-Dīn Mūsā b. Yūsuf al-. 1991. *Nuzhat al-Khāṭir wa-Bahjat al-Nāẓir*. Ed. ʿAdnān Muḥammad Ibrāhīm. Damascus: Wizārat al-Thaqāfa. Iḥyāʾ al-Turāth al-ʿArabī.

Arbel, Dan & Yehoshuʿa Geifman. 1997. "Family Court Law, 1995—Critical Analysis." *Hapraklit*, 43.3: 431–52 (in Hebrew).

Asyūṭī, Shams al-Dīn Muḥammad al-. N.d. *Jawāhir al-ʿUqūd wa-Muʿīn al-Quḍāt wa'l-Muwaqqiʿīn wa'l-Shuhūd*. 2 vols. 2nd ed. [Cairo]: N.p.

ʿAṭaune, Muḥammad al-. 2001. "Sharīʿa and Politics in Saudi-Arabia: al-Siyāsa al-Sharʿiyya as a Mechanism for Stabilization of the Government and the Society." *Jamaʿa*, 8: 54–83 (in Hebrew).

Bābartī, Muḥammad b. Maḥmūd al-. 1316/1898–99. *Sharḥ al-ʿInāya ʿalā al-Hidāya*. Printed in the margins of Ibn al-Humām, Kamāl al-Dīn. 1316/1898–99. *Sharḥ Fatḥ al-Qadīr*. 8 vols. Būlāq: al-Maṭbaʿa al-Kubrā al-Amīriyya.

Baer, Gabriel. 1962. *A History of Landownership in Modern Egypt, 1800–1950*. London: Oxford University Press.

——. 1964. *Egyptian Guilds in Modern Times*. Jerusalem: the Israel Oriental Society.

——. 1979. "The Dismemberment of *Awqāf* in Early 19th Century Jerusalem." *Asian and African Studies*, 13: 220–41.

Baghdādī, Aḥmad Muḥammad al-. 1998. *al-Ta'rīkh al-Ijtimāʿī lil-Tajrīm wa'l-ʿIqāb fī Miṣr fī al-ʿAṣr al-ʿUthmānī*. Cairo: Dār al-Nahḍa al-ʿArabiyya.

Bakhtin, Mikhail M. 1981. *The Dialogical Imagination*. Austin: University of Texas Press.

——. 1986. *Speech, Genre and Other Late Essays*. Eds. C. Emerson and M. Holquist. Trans. V. W. Mcgee. Austin: University of Texas Press.

Bargaoui, Sami. 1998. "Sainteté, savoir et autorité en Kabylie au XVIIIe siècle: La de Warthīlānī," in *L'autorité des saints: perspectives historiques et socio-anthropologiques en Méditerranée occidentale*. Ed. Mohammed Kerrou. Paris: Institut de Recherche sur le Maghreb Contemporain- Editions Recherche sur les Civilizations, 249–76.

Barkan, Ö. L. and E. H. Ayverdi. 1970. *Istanbul Vakıfları Tahrîr Defteri: 953 (1546) Târîhli*. Istanbul: Baha Matbaasi.

Bar-On, Yaʿarah. 2000. *The Crowded Delivery Room: Gender and Public Opinion in Early Modern Gynecology*. Haifa: University of Haifa & Zmora-Bitan (in Hebrew).

Barthes, Roland. 1977. "The Death of the Author," in *Image—Music—Text*. Ed. Roland Barthes. Trans. Stephen Heath. London: Fontana, 142–48.

Baumgarten, Elisheva. 2000. "Thus Sayeth the Wise Midwives: Midwives and Midwifery in Thirteenth-Century Ashkenaz." *Zion*, 65: 45–74 (in Hebrew).

Belley, Jean-Guy. 1995. "Max Weber et la théorie du droit des contrats," in *Actualité de Max Weber pour la sociologie du droit*. Ed. Pierre Lascoumes. Paris: Librairie Générale de Droit et de Jurisprudence, 221–241, 272.

Ben Shemesh, Aharon. 1953. *Land Law in the State of Israel*. Tel Aviv: Massada (in Hebrew).

——. (Ed. and trans.). 1967. *Taxation in Islam*. Vol. 1: Yaḥyā b. Ādam's *Kitāb al-Kharāj*. 2nd ed. Leiden: Brill.

Bentwich, Norman. 1926. *Legislation of Palestine, 1918–1925*. 2 vols. Alexandria: Whitehead Morris.

Berchem, Max Van. 1886. *La propriété territoriale et l'impôt foncier sous les premiers califes; etude sur l'impôt du kharāg*. Genève: Imprimerie C. Schuchardt.

Berkey, Jonathan. 1992. *The Transmission of Knowledge in Medieval Cairo: A Social History of Islamic Education*. Princeton: Princeton University Press.

Bishara, Suhad, & Toma-Suliman, Aida. 1997. "Personal Status and Family Laws." in *NGO Report: The Status of Palestinian Women Citizens of Israel*. The Working Group on the Status of Palestinian Women in Israel, 66–73. http://www.arabhra.org/publications/reports/PDF/cedaw.pdf.

Bos, Gerrit. 1993. "Ibn al-Jazzār on Women's Diseases and Their Treatment." *Medical History*, 37: 296–312.

Boulifa, S. 1925. *Le Djurjura à travers l'histoire (depuis l'Antiquité jusqu'à 1830): Organisation et indépendence des Zouaoua (Grande Kabylie)*. Alger: Bringau.

Breuer, Stefan and Hubert Treiber (eds.). 1984. *Zur Rechtssoziologie Max Webers*. Opladen: Westdeutscher Verlag.

Brockopp, Johnathan. 2002. "Competing Theories of Authority in Early Maliki Texts," in *Studies in Islamic Legal Theory*. Ed. Bernard G. Weiss. Leiden: Brill, 3–22.

Brummett, Palmira. 1998. "Classifying Ottoman Mutiny: The Act and Vision of Rebellion." *The Turkish Studies Association Bulletin*, 22.1: 91–107.

Brunschvig, Robert. 1965. "Justice religieuse et justice laïque dans la Tunisie des Deys et des Beys jusqu'au milieu du XIXe siècle." *Studia Islamica*, 23: 27–70.

Budayrī, Aḥmad al-Ḥallāq al-. 1959. *Ḥawādith Dimashq al-Yawmiyya, 1154–1175/1741–1762*. Ed. Aḥmad ʿIzzat ʿAbd al-Karīm. Damascus: Maṭbūʿāt Lajnat al-Bayān al-ʿArabī.

Bukhārī, Muḥammad b. Ismāʿīl. 1862–98. *Ṣaḥīḥ*. Edited M. Ludolf Krehl and Th. W. Juynboll. 4 vols. Leiden: Brill.

Būrīnī, al-Ḥasan b. Muḥammad al-. 1959–63. *Tarājim al-Aʿyān min Abnāʾ al-Zamān*. Ed. Ṣalāḥ al-Dīn al-Munajjid. 2 vols. Damascus: al-Majmaʿ al-ʿIlmī al-ʿArabī bi-Dimashq.

Cahen, Claude. 1961. "Réflexions sur le *waqf* ancien." *Studia Islamica*, 14: 37–56.

——. 1970. *L'Islam: dès origines au début de l'Empire Ottoman*. Paris: Bordas.

Calder, Norman. 1993. *Studies in Early Muslim Jurisprudence*. Oxford: Clarendon Press.

——. 1996. "al-Nawawī's Typology of *Muftis* and Its Significance for a General Theory of Islamic Law." *Islamic Law and Society*, 3: 137–64.

Caton, Steven. 1990. *Peaks of Yemen I Summon*. Berkeley: University of California Press.

Cerulli, Enrico. 1957–64. *Somalia*. 3 vols. Rome: Amministrazione Fiduciaria Italiana della Somalia (vols. 1–2); Ministero degli Affari Esteri (vol. 3).

Çizakça, Murat. 1995. "Cash *Waqfs* of Bursa, 1555–1823." *Journal of the Economic and Social History of the Orient*, 38: 313–54.

Clavel, Eugene. 1895. *Droit musulman, le waqf ou habous*. Paris: Larose.

Cohen, Amnon. 2001. *The Guilds of Ottoman Jerusalem*. Boston: Brill.

——. In collaboration with Elisheva Simon-Picali and Eyal Ginio. 2003. *Jews in the Muslim Religious Court: Society, Economy and Communal Organization in the XIXth Century. Documents from Ottoman Jerusalem*. Jerusalem: Yad Izhak Ben-Zvi (in Hebrew).

—— & Elisheva Simon-Picali. 1993. *Jews in the Muslim Religious Court: Society, Economy and Communal Organization in the XVIth Century. Documents from Ottoman Jerusalem.* Jerusalem: Yad Izhak Ben-Zvi (in Hebrew).

Colucci, Massimo. 1924. *Principi di diritto consuetudinario della Somalia italiana meridionale.* Florence: La Voce.

Conermann, Stephan. 2004. "Ibn Ṭūlūn (d. 955/1548): Life and Works." *Mamluk Studies Review*, 8.1: 115–39.

Cook, Michael. 2000. *Commanding Right and Forbidding Wrong in Islamic Thought.* Cambridge: Cambridge University Press.

Coulson, Noel James. 1957. "The State and the Individual in Islamic Law." *The International and Comparative Law Quarterly*, 6.1: 49–60.

——. 1964. *A History of Islamic Law.* Edinburgh: Edinburgh University Press.

——. 1996. "Muslim Custom and Case-Law," in *Islamic Law and Legal Theory*. Ed. Ian Edge. Aldershot, England: Dartmouth Publishing Company, 259–70. Appeared also in *Die Welt des Islams*, 6 (1959): 13–24.

Coutu, Michel. 1995. *Max Weber et les rationalités du droit.* Paris: Librarie Générale de Droit et de Jurisprudence.

Crone, Patricia. 1987. *Roman, Provincial and Islamic Law: the Origins of the Islamic Patronate.* Cambridge: Cambridge University Press.

——. 2000, March 31. "Human reasoning sacred text?" *Times Literary Supplement.*

—— & Martin Hinds. 1986. *God's Caliph.* Cambridge: Cambridge University Press.

Dennett, Daniel C. 1950. *Conversion and Poll Tax in Early Islam.* Cambridge Mass.: Harvard University Press.

Derrida, Jacques. 1974. *Of Grammatology.* Trans. Gayatry Chakaraverty Spivak. Baltimore: John Hopkins University Press.

Dresch, Paul. 1989. *Tribes, Government and History in Yemen.* Oxford: Clarendon Press.

——. 2000. *A History of Modern Yemen.* Cambridge: Cambridge University Press.

Dumper, Michael. 1994. *Islam and Israel: Muslim Religious Endowments and the Jewish State.* Washington, D.C.: Institute for Palestine Studies.

EI² = *Encyclopaedia of Islam*, 2nd ed. 1954–2004, Leiden: Brill.

Eickelman, Dale F. 1981. *The Middle East: An Anthropological Approach.* Englewood Cliffs: Prentice-Hall.

Eisenman, Robert. 1978. *Islamic Law in Palestine and Israel: A History of the Survival of Tanẓīmāt and Sharīʿa in the British Mandate and the Jewish State.* Leiden: Brill.

Eisenstadt, Shmuel Noah. 2002. *Fundamentalism and Modernity.* Tel Aviv: Ministry of Defense Publishers (in Hebrew).

El-Rouayheb, Khaled. 2004. "Sunni Muslim Scholars on the Status of Logic, 1500–1800." *Islamic Law and Society*, 11: 213–32.

EQ = *Encyclopedia of the Qurʾān. 2001–.* Leiden: Brill.

Ergene, Boğaç E. 2003. *Local Court, Provincial Society and Justice in the Ottoman Empire: Legal Practice and Dispute Resolution in Çankırı and Kastamonu (1652–1744).* Leiden: Brill.

Evliyā Çelebi. 1938. *Seyahatname.* 10 vols. Istanbul: Devlet Basīmevi.

Fadel, Mohammad. 1996. "The Social Logic of *Taqlīd* and the Rise of the *Mukhtaṣar.*" *Islamic Law and Society*, 3: 193–233.

——. 1997. "Two Women, One Man: Knowledge, Power, and Gender in Medieval Sunnī Legal Thought." *International Journal of Middle East Studies*, 29: 185–204.

Fahmy, Khaled. 1998a. "Law, Medicine and Society in Nineteenth-Century Egypt." *Egypte Monde Arabe*, 34: 17–51.

——. 1998b. "Women, Medicine and Power in Nineteenth-Century Egypt," in *Remaking Women: Feminism and Modernity in the Middle East.* Ed. Lila Abu-Lughod. Princeton: Princeton University Press, 35–72.

Fairclough, Norman, 1992. *Discourse and Social Change*. Cambridge and Oxford: Polity Press.
Farḥāt, Muḥammad Nūr. 1988. *al-Qaḍā' al-Shar'ī fī Miṣr fī al-'Aṣr al-'Uthmānī*. Cairo: Al-Hay'a al-Miṣriyya al-'Āmma lil-Kitāb.
Faroqhi, Suraiya. 1992. "Political Activity among Ottoman Taxpayers and the Problem of Sultanic Legitimation (1570–1650)." *Journal of the Economic and Social History of the Orient*, 34: 1–39.
Fleischer, Cornell. 1986. *Bureaucrat and Intellectual in the Ottoman Empire: The Historian Mustafa Âli (1541–1600)*. Princeton: Princeton University Press.
Friedman, Menachem. 1995. "The Structural Foundation of Religio-Political Accommodation in Israel: Fallacy and Reality," in *Israel: The First Decade of Independence*. Eds. Ilan S. Troen and Noah Lucas. New York: State University of New York Press, 51–82.
Friedmann, Daniel. 1975. "The Effect of Foreign Law on the Law of Israel: Remnants of the Ottoman Period." *Israel Law Review*, 10: 192–206.
Galanter, M. & J. Krishnan. 2001. "Personal Law Systems and Religious Conflicts: A Comparison of India and Israel," in *Religion and Personal Law in Secular India: A Call to Judgment*. Ed. G. J. Larson. Bloomington: Indiana University Press, 270–300.
Gara, Eleni. 1998. "In Search of Communities in Seventeenth Century Ottoman Sources: The Case of the Kara Ferye District." *Turcica*, 30: 135–62.
Geertz, Cliford. 1973. *The Interpretation of Cultures*. New York: Basic Books.
Gerber, Haim. 1985. "The Jews of Edirne (Adrianople) in the 16th and 17th Centuries." *Sefunot*, New Series 3 (18): 35–52 (in Hebrew).
——. 1987. *The Social Origins of the Modern Middle East*. Boulder: Lynne Rienner Publishers.
——. 1988. *Economy and Society in an Ottoman City: Bursa 1600–1700*. Jerusalem: The Hebrew University of Jerusalem.
——. 1994. *State, Society, and Law in Islam: Ottoman Law in Comparative Perspective*. Albany: State University of New York Press.
——. 1999. *Islamic Law and Culture 1600–1840*. Leiden: Brill.
Ghazzī, Muḥammad Najm al-Dīn al-. 1945 59. *al Kawākib al-Sā'ira fī A'yān al-Mi'a al-'Āshira*. Ed. Jibrā'īl Sulaymān Jabbūr. Beirut, Jonnieh and Harissa: al-Maṭba'a al-Amīrikāniyya.
——. 1981. *Luṭf al-Samar wa-Qaṭf al-Thamar min Tarājim A'yān al-Ṭabaqa al-'ūlā min al-Qarn al-Ḥādī 'Ashar*. Ed. Muḥammad al-Shaykh. Damascus: Wizārat al-Thaqāfa wa'l-Irshād al-Qawmī.
Giladi, Avner. 1992. *Children of Islam: Concepts of Childhood in Medieval Muslim Society*. New York: St. Martin's Press.
——. 1999. *Infants, Parents and Wet Nurses: Medieval Islamic Views on Breastfeeding and Their Social Implications*. Leiden: Brill.
Ginio, Eyal. 1998. "The Administration of Criminal Justice in Ottoman Selânik (Salonica) during the Eighteenth Century." *Turcica*, 30: 185–209.
——. Forthcoming. "When Coffee Brought about Wealth and Prestige: The Impact of Egyptian Trade on Salonica." *Oriente Moderno*.
Granovski (Granot), Avraham. 1949. *The Land System in Palestine*. Tel Aviv: Dvir (in Hebrew).
Griffiths, John. 1986. "What Is Legal Pluralism?" *Journal of Legal Pluralism*, 24: 1–55.
Güneş, Aḥmad Halil. 1981. *Das K. Ar-Rauḍ al-'āṭir des Ibn aiyūb*. Berlin: Klaus Schwarz Verlag.
Hacoun-Campredon, Pierre. 1921. *Etude sur l'évolution des coutumes kabyles spécialement en ce qui concerne l'exhérédation des femmes et la pratique du habous*. Alger: Carbonel.
Hallaq, Wael B. 1984. "Was the Gates of *Ijtihād* Closed?" *International Journal of Middle East Studies*, 16: 3–41.

——. 1994. "From *Fatwās* to *Furūʿ*: Growth and Change in Islamic Substantive Law." *Islamic Law and Society*, 1: 29–65.

——. 1996. "Introduction: Issues and Problems." *Islamic Law and Society*, 3: 127–36.

——. 1997. *A History of Islamic Legal Theories*. Cambridge: Cambridge University Press.

——. 1998. "The *Qāḍī*'s *Dīwān* (*sijill*) before the Ottomans." *Bulletin of the School of Oriental and African Studies*, 61: 415–36.

——. 2001. *Authority, Continuity and Change in Islamic Law*. Cambridge: Cambridge University Press.

——. 2002. "A Prelude to Ottoman Reform: Ibn ʿĀbidīn on Custom and Legal Change," in *Histories of the Modern Middle East: New Directions*. Ed. Israel Gershoni, Hakam Erdem & Ursula Woköck. Boulder: Lynne Rienner Publishers, 37–61.

——. 2004. "Can the sharīʿa be restored?" in *Islamic Law and the Challenge of Modernity*. Eds. Yvonne Y. Haddad & Barbara F. Stowasser. Walnut Creek Ca.: Altamira Press, 21–53.

Hannemann, Tilman. 2002. "Recht und Religion in der Großen Kabylei (18./19. Jahrhundert): Zu rechtskulturellen Wandlungsprozessen im tribalen Gewohnheitsrecht." Ph.D. Thesis, Universität Bremen.

Haram, Nissreen. 1996. "Use and Abuse of the Law: A Mufti's Response," in *Islamic Legal Interpretation: Muftis and Their Fatwas*. Ed. Muhammad Kh. Masud, Brinkley Messick & David S. Powers. Cambridge, Mass.: Harvard University Press, 72–86.

Ḥarūb, Khālid al-. N.d. *Ḥamās, al-Fikr waʾl-Mumārasa al-Siyāsiyya*. Beirut: Muʾassasat al-Dirāsāt al-Filasṭinīyya.

Ḥaṣkafī, ʿAlāʾ al-Dīn Muḥammad ʿAlī al-. 1386/1966. *al-Durr al-Mukhtār*. Printed with Ibn ʿĀbidīn. 1386/1966. *Ḥāshiyat Radd al-Muḥtār ʿalā al-Durr al-Mukhtār*. 8 vols. 2nd edition. Cairo: Maṭbaʿat Muṣṭafā al-Bābī al-Ḥalabī.

Haykel, Bernard. 2003. *Revival and Reform in Islam: the legacy of Muhammad al-Shawkani*. Cambridge: Cambridge University Press.

Heusler, Andreas. 1885–86. *Institutionen des deutschen Privatrechts*. 2 vols. Leipzig: Duncker & Humblot.

Heyd, Uriel. 1969. "Some Aspects of the Ottoman *Fetvā*." *Bulletin of the School of Oriental and African Studies*, 32: 35–56.

——. 1973a. *Studies in Old Ottoman Criminal Law*. Oxford: The Clarendon Press.

——. 1973b. *The Ottoman Institutions* (lectures edited by Rachel Simon and Yehoshua Porath). Jerusalem: the Hebrew University of Jerusalem (in Hebrew).

Heywood, Colin. 1980. "The Ottoman *Menzilhane* and *Ulak* System in Rumeli in the Eighteenth Century," in *Türkiye'nin Sosyal ve Ekonomik Tarihi (1071–1920)*. Eds. Osman Okyar and Halil İnalcık. Ankara: Meteksan Şirketi.

——. 1996. "The Via Egnatia in the Ottoman Period: The *Menzilhānes* of the *Sol Kol* in the Late 17th/Early 18th Century," in *The Via Egnatia under Ottoman Rule (1380–1699)*. Ed. Elizabeth Zachariadou. Rethymnon: University of Crete Press, 129–44.

Hilmi, Ömer. 1922. *A Gift to Posterity on the Laws of Evqaf*. Trans. C. R. Tyser & D. G. Demetriades. 2nd edition. Nicosia: Government Printing Office.

Ḥimyarī, Muḥammad b. ʿAbd al-Munʿim al-. 1984. *al-Rawḍ al-Miʿṭār fī Khabar al-Aqṭār: Muʿjam Jighrāfī*. 2nd edition. Beirut: Maktabat Lubnān.

Hoebink, Michel. 1994. "Two Halves of the Same Truth: Schacht, Hallaq, and the Gate of Ijtihād: An Inquiry into Definitions." *Middle East Research Associates (MERA) Occasional Papers*, 24: 1–19.

Hoexter, Miriam. 1982. "La *shurṭa* ou la répression des crimes à Alger à l'époque turque." *Studia Islamica*, 56: 117–46.

——. 1984. "Le contrat de quasi-aliénation des *awqāf* à Alger à la fin de la domination turque: étude de deux documents d'ʿanāʾ." *Bulletin of the School of Oriental and African Studies*, 47.2: 243–59.

———. 1995. "*Ḥuqūq Allāh* and *Ḥuqūq al-ʿIbād* as Reflected in the *Waqf* Institution." *Jerusalem Studies in Arabic and Islam*, 19: 133–56.

———. 1997. "Adaptation to Changing Circumstances: Perpetual Leases and Exchange Transactions in *Waqf* Property in Ottoman Algiers." *Islamic Law and Society*, 4: 319–33.

———. 1998. *Endowments, Rulers, and Community: Waqf al-Haramayn in Ottoman Algiers*. Leiden: Brill.

———. 2002. "The *Waqf* and the Public Sphere," in *The Public Sphere in Muslim Societies*. Eds. Miriam Hoexter, Shmuel N. Eisenstadt & Nehemia Levtzion. Albany: State University of New York Press, 119–38.

Hollander, Isaac. 2005. *Jews and Muslims in Lower Yemen: A Study in Protection and Restraint, 1918–1949*. Leiden: Brill.

Horster, Paul. 1935. *Zur Anwendung des Islamischen Rechts im 16. Jahrhundert*. Stuttgart: Verlag W. Kohlhammer.

Hroub, Khaled. 2000. *Hamas: Political Thought and Practice*. Washington DC.: Institute for Palestine Studies.

Hurvitz, Nimrod. 2002. "The *Miḥna* (Inquisition) and the Public Sphere," in *The Public Sphere in Muslim Societies*. Eds. Miriam Hoexter, Shmuel N. Eisenstadt & Nehemia Levtzion. Albany: State University of New York Press, 17–29.

Ḥusaynī, Ḥājj Amīn al-. N.d. *Fatwā Samāḥat al-Muftī al-Akbar al-Sayyid Amīn al-Ḥusaynī bi-Shaʾn Bayʿ al-Arāḍī bi-Filasṭīn lil-Ṣahyūniyyīn*. Jerusalem: Maṭbaʿat Dār al-Aytām al-Islāmiyya.

Ibn Abī al-Dām, Ibrāhīm b. ʿAbd Allāh. 1987. *Kitāb Adab al-Qaḍāʾ aw al-Durar al-Manẓūmāt fī al-Aqḍiya waʾl-Ḥukūmāt*. Brirut: Dār al-Kutub al-ʿIlmiyya.

Ibn Abī Yaʿlā, Muḥammad b. Muḥammad. 1952. *Ṭabaqāt al-Ḥanābila*. Ed. Muḥammad Ḥāmid al-Fiqqī. 2 vols. Cairo: Maṭbaʿat al-Sunna al-Muḥammadiyya.

Ibn ʿĀbidīn, Muḥammad Amīn b. ʿUmar. 1301/1884. *Nashr al-ʿUrf fī Bināʾ Baʿḍ al-Aḥkām ʿalā al-ʿUrf*. Damascus: Maṭbaʿat Maʿārif Sūriyya al-Jalīla.

———. 1311/1893–94. *Minḥat al-Khāliq ʿalā al-Baḥr al-Rāʾiq*. Printed on the margins of Ibn Nujaym, Zayn al-ʿĀbidīn. 1311/1893–94. *al-Baḥr al-Rāʾiq Sharḥ Kanz al-Daqāʾiq*. 8 vols. N. p.: al-Maṭbaʿa al-ʿIlmiyya.

———. 1966. *Ḥāshiyat Radd al-Muḥtār ʿalā al-Durr al-Mukhtār Sharḥ Tanwīr al-Abṣār fī Fiqh Madhhab Abī Ḥanīfa al-Nuʿmān*. 8 vols. 2nd ed. Cairo: Maṭbaʿat Muṣṭafā al-Bābī al-Ḥalabī.

Ibn ʿAsākir, ʿAlī b. al-Ḥasan. 1995–2001. *Taʾrīkh Madīnat Dimashq*. Ed. ʿUmar b. Gharāma al-ʿAmrawī. 80 vols. Beirut: Dār al-Fikr.

Ibn Farḥūn, Burhān al-Dīn Ibrāhīm. 1986. *Tabṣirat al-Ḥukkām fī Uṣūl al-Aqḍiya wa-Manāhij al-Aḥkām*. 2 vols. Cairo: Maktabat al-Kulliyyāt al-Azhariyya.

Ibn Ḥanbal, ʿAbdallāh b. Aḥmad. 1981. *Masāʾil al-Imām Aḥmad b. Ḥanbal*. Ed. Muḥammad Zuhayr al-Shāwish. Beirut: al-Maktab al-Islāmī.

Ibn Ḥanbal, Ṣāliḥ b. Aḥmad. 1999. *Riwāyat Abū al-Faḍl Ṣāliḥ*. Riyad: Dār al-Waṭan lil-Nashr.

Ibn Ḥazm, ʿAlī b. Aḥmad. 1984. *al-Muḥallā biʾl-Athār*. Ed. ʿAbd al-Ghaffār Sulaymān al-Bandārī. 12 vols. Beirut: Dār al-Fikr.

Ibn al-Humām, Kamāl al-Dīn. 1316/1898–99. *Sharḥ Fatḥ al-Qadīr*. 8 vols. Būlāq: al-Maṭbaʿa al-Kubrā al-Amīriyya.

Ibn Iyās, Muḥammad b. Aḥmad. 1961. *Badāʾiʿ al-Zuhūr fī Waqāʾiʿ al-Duhūr*. Ed. Muḥammad Muṣṭafā. 5 vols. 2nd ed. Cairo and Wiesbaaden: Franz Steiner.

Ibn Khaldūn. 1958. *The Muqaddimah: An Introduction to History*. Trans. Franz Rosenthal. 3 vols. New York: Pantheon Books.

———. 1967. *Taʾrīkh*. 7 vols. Beirut: Dār al-Kitāb al-Lubnānī.

Ibn Nujaym, Zayn al-ʿĀbidīn b. Ibrāhīm. 1311/1893–94. *al-Baḥr al-Rāʾiq Sharḥ Kanz al-Daqāʾiq*. 8 vols. N. p.: al-Maṭbaʿa al-ʿIlmiyya.

Ibn Nujaym, Zayn al-Dīn b. Ibrāhīm. N.d. *al-Baḥr al-Rā'iq Sharḥ Kanz* al-Daqā'iq. 8 vols. N.p: Dār al-Kitāb al-Islāmī.

Ibn Nujaym, Zayn al-ʿĀbidīn b. Ibrāhīm. 1322/1904–05. *al-Ashbāh wa'l-Naẓā'ir.* Cairo: al-Maṭbaʿa al-Ḥusayniyya al-Miṣriyya.

Ibn al-Qayyim al-Jawziyya, Muḥammad b. Abī Bakr. 1969. *Iʿlām al-Muwaqqiʿīn ʿan Rabb al-ʿĀlamīn.* Ed. ʿAbd al-Raḥmān al-Wakīl. 4 vols. Cairo: Dār al-Kutub al-Ḥadītha.

——. N.d. *Al-Ṭuruq al-Ḥukmiyya fi'l-Siyāsa al-Sharʿiyya.* Beirut: Dār Iḥyā' al-ʿUlūm.

Ibn Qudāma, ʿAbd Allāh b. Aḥmad Muwaffaq al-Dīn. 1970. *al-Mughnī.* 12 vols. al-Madīna: al-Maktaba al-Salafiyya.

——. 1990. *al-Mughnī.* 15 vols. Cairo: Hajr.

Ibn Rushd, Muḥammad b. Aḥmad. 1415/1995. *Bidāyat al-Mujtahid.* Ed. Muḥammad Ṣubḥī Ḥasan Ḥallāq. 4 vols. Cairo: Maktabat Ibn Taymiyya.

——. 1996. *Bidāyat al-mujtahid wa Nihāyat al-Muqtaṣid.* Trans. Imran Ahsan Khan Nyazee. 2 vols. Reading UK: Garnet.

Ibn Taghrībirdī, Yūsuf. 1963. *al-Nujūm al-Ẓāhira fī Mulūk Miṣr wa'l-Qāhira.* 16 vols. in 9. Cairo: Wizārat al-Thaqāfa wa'l-Irshād al-Qawmī.

Ibn Ṭūlūn, Shams al-Dīn Muḥammad. 1956. *Quḍāt Dimashq: al-Thaghr al-Bassām fī Dhikr Man Wulliya Qaḍā' al-Shām.* Ed. Ṣalāḥ al-Dīn al-Munajjid. Damascus: Al-Majmaʿ al-ʿIlmī al-ʿArabī bi-Dimashq.

——. 1384/1964. *Mufākahat al-Khillān fī Ḥawādith al-Zamān.* Ed. Muḥammad Muṣṭāfa. 2 vols. Cairo: al-Mu'assasa al-Miṣriyya al-ʿĀmma li'l-Ta'līf wa'l-Tarjama wa'l-Ṭibāʿa wa'l-Nashr.

——. 2002. *Ḥawādith Dimashq al-Yawmiyya Ghadāt al-Ghazw al-ʿUthmānī li'l-Shām 926–951 A.H. Ṣafaḥāt Mafqūda Tunsharu li'l-Marra al-'ūlā min Kitāb Mufākahat al-Khillān fī Ḥawādith al-Zamān li-Ibn Ṭūlūn al-Ṣaliḥī al-Dimashqī.* Ed. Aḥmad Ībish. Damascus: Dār al-Awā'il.

Ibrāhīm, Aḥmad. 1985. *Ṭuruq al-Ithbāt al-Sharʿiyya, maʿa Bayyān Ikhtilāf al-Madhāhib al-Fiqhiyya wa-Sawq al-Adilla wa'l-Muwāzana baynahā thumma Muqārana bi'l-Qānūn wa-Muʿallaq ʿalayhi bi-Aḥkām al-Naqḍ.* 3rd ed. Cairo: Maṭbaʿat al-Qāhira al-Hadītha lil-Ṭibāʿa.

Imber, Colin. 1996. "Eleven Fetvas of the Ottoman Sheikh ul-Islam ʿAbdurrahim," in *Islamic Legal Interpretation: Muftis and Their Fatwas.* Eds. Muhammad Kh. Masud, Brinkley Messick & David S. Powers. Cambridge, Mass.: Harvard University Press, 141–49.

——. 1997. *Ebu's-suʿud: The Islamic Legal Tradition.* Stanford: Stanford University Press.

ʿĪsā, ʿAbd al-Rāziq Ibrāhīm. 1998. *Ta'rīkh al-Qaḍā' fī Miṣr al-ʿUthmāniyya (1517–1798).* Cairo: al-Hay'a al-Miṣriyya al-ʿĀmma lil-Kitāb.

Jabr, Aḥmad Fahīm. 1999. *Wujūdunā al-Ḥaḍarī fī Bayt al-Maqdis.* Jerusalem: Markaz al-Quds lil-Abḥāth wa'l-Tawthīq.

Jackson, Sherman A. 1992. "al-Qarāfī's Tips to the Jurisconsult." *Muslim World,* 82: 201–17.

——. 1996. *Islamic Law and the State: The Constitutional Jurisprudence of Shihāb al-Dīn al-Qarāfī.* Leiden: Brill.

Jazīrī, ʿAbd al-Raḥmān al-. 1980. *Kitāb al-Fiqh ʿalā al-Madhāhib al-Arbaʿa.* 4 vols. Cairo: Dār al-Irshād lil-Ṭibāʿa wa'l-Nashr.

Jennings, Ronald. 1979. "Limitations of the Judicial Powers of the Kadi in Seventeenth Century Ottoman Kayseri." *Studia Islamica,* 50: 151–84.

Jirāfī, ʿAbd Allāh b. ʿAbd al-Karīm al-. 1946. *Tuḥfat al-Ikhwān.* Cairo: Maṭbaʿat al-Salafiyya.

Johansen, Baber. 1979. "Eigentum, Familie und Obrigkeit im hanafitischen Strafrecht." *Die Welt des Islams,* 19: 1–71.

——. 1981. "Sacred and Religious Element in Hanafite Law—Function and Limits of the Absolute Character of Government Authority," in *Islam et Politique au Maghreb*. Eds. J. C. Vatin and E. Gellner. Paris: Éditions du CNRS, 281–302.

——. 1993. "Coutumes locales et coutumes universelles: aux sources des règles juridiques en droit musulman hanéfite." *Annales Islamologiques*, 27: 29–35.

——. 2002. "Signs as Evidence: The Doctrine of Ibn Taymiyya (1263–1328) and Ibn Qayyim al-Jawziyya (d. 1351) on Proof." *Islamic Law and Society*, 9: 168–93.

Juynboll, G. H. A. 1983. *Muslim Tradition: Studies in Chronology, Provenance and Authorship of Early Ḥadīth*. Cambridge: Cambridge University Press.

Kāsānī, ʿAlāʾ al-Dīn Abū Bakr b. Masʿūd al-. 1328/1910. *Kitāb Badāʾiʿ al-Ṣanāʾiʿ fī Tartīb al-Sharāʾiʿ*. Cairo: Maṭbaʿat al-Jamāliyya.

Kashshāf 1999. *al-Kashshāf ʿan Qarārāt al-Istiʾnāf al-Ṣādira ʿan Maḥkamat al-Istiʾnāf al-Sharʿiyya al-ʿUlyā fī al-Quds al-Sharīf*. 6 vols. Herzeliyya: The Interdisciplinary Center.

Kermeli, Eugenia. 2002. "Review Article." *Eurasian Studies*, 1: 129–36.

Khaṣṣāf, Abū Bakr Aḥmad b. ʿAmr al-Shaybānī al-. 1322/1904. *Kitāb Aḥkām al-Awqāf*. Cairo: Maṭbaʿat Dīwān ʿUmūm al-Awqāf al-Miṣriyya.

Khiraqī, Abū al-Qasim al-. 1964. *Mukhtaṣar*. Ed. Muḥammad Zuhayr al-Shāwish. Damascus: al-Maktab al-Islāmī.

Kristeva, Julia. 1986 [1967]. "Word, Dialogue and Novel," in *The Kristeva Reader*. Trans. A. Jardine, T. Gora & L. S. Roudiez. Ed. T. Moi. Oxford: Oxford University Press, 34–61.

Kronman, Anthony T. 1983. *Max Weber*. Stanford: Stanford University Press.

Kuhnke, LaVerne. 1990. *Lives at Risk: Public Health in Nineteenth-Century Egypt*. Cairo: The American University in Cairo Press.

Landau, Jacob M. 1969. *The Arabs in Israel*. Oxford: Oxford University Press.

Lane, Edward William. 1954. *Manners and Customs of the Modern Egyptians*. London: J. M. Dent.

Laoust, Henri. 1959. "Le hanbalisme sous le califat de Baghdad (241/855–656/1258)." *Revue Des Etudes Islamiques*, 27: 67–128.

Lascoumes, Pierre (ed.). 1995. *Actualité de Max Weber pour la sociologie du droit*. Paris: Librarie Générale de Droit et de Jurisprudence.

Latron, André. 1936. *La vie rurale en Syrie et au Liban*. Beirut: Institut Français de Damas.

Layish, Aharon. 1963. "Muslim Religious Law in Israel." *The New East*, 13: 19–39 [in Hebrew].

——. 1965. "Muslim Religious Jurisdiction in Israel." *Asian and African Studies*, 1: 49–79.

——. 1966. "The Muslim *Waqf* in Israel." *Asian and African Studies*, 2: 41–76.

——. 1971. "*Qāḍīs* and *Sharīʿa* in Israel." *Asian and African Studies*, 7: 237–72.

——. 1974. "Sharīʿa u-Minhag ba-Mishpaha ha-Muslemit be-Yisraʾel." *Hamizrah Hehadash*, 23: 377–409 (in Hebrew).

——. 1975. *Women and Islamic Law in a Non-Muslim State: A Study Based on Decisions of the Sharīʿa Courts in Israel*. New York, Toronto & Jerusalem: John Wiley & Israel University Press.

——. 1978. "The Contribution of the Modernists to the Secularization of Islamic Law." *Middle Eastern Studies*, 14: 257–77.

——. 1982. *Marriage, Divorce and Succession in the Druze Family. A Study Based on Decisions of Druze Arbitrators and Religious Courts in Israel and the Golan Heights*. Leiden: Brill.

——. 1987. "Saudi Arabian Legal Reform as a Mechanism to Moderate Wahhābī Doctrine." *Journal of the American Oriental Society* 107.2: 279–92.

——. 1991. *Divorce in the Libyan Family. A Study Based on the* Sijill *of the* Sharīʿa *Courts of Ajdābiya and Kufra*. Jerusalem: The Magnes Press & New York: New York University Press.

——. 1993. "The Status of the *Sharīʿa* in a Non-Muslim State: The Case of Israel." *Asian and African Studies*, 27: 171–87.

——. 1996. *The Mahdi's Legal Methodology and its Application in the Sudan: A Selection from the Mahdi's Documents (1881–1885)*. Jerusalem: Akademon (in Hebrew).

——. 1997. "The Legal Methodology of the Mahdi in the Sudan, 1881–1885: Issues of Marriage and Divorce." *Sudanic Africa*, 8: 37–66.

——. 2004. "The Transformation of the *Sharīʿa* from Jurists' Law to Statutory Law in the Contemporary Muslim World." *Die Welt des Islams*, 44.1: 85–113.

——. Forthcoming. "Adaptation of a Jurists' Law to Modern Times in an Alien Environment: The Case of the Sharīʿa in Israel." *Die Welt des Islams*.

—— & Gabriel R. Warburg. 2002. *The Reinstatement of Islamic Law in Sudan under Numayrī: An Evaluation of a Legal Experiment in the Light of Its Historical Context, Methodology, and Repercussions*. Leiden: Brill.

Lev, Yaacov. 1987. "The Fāṭimid Princess Sitt al-Mulk." *Journal of Semitic Studies*, 32: 319–28.

Lewis, I. M. 1961. *A Pastoral Democracy: a Study of Pastoralism and Politics among the Northern Somali of the Horn of Africa*. London: Oxford University Press.

Libson, Gideon. 1997. "On the Development of Custom as a Source of Law in Islamic Law." *Islamic Law and Society*, 4: 131–55.

Livne-Kafri, Ofer. 1985. "The Sanctity of Jerusalem in Islam According to the *Faḍāʾil al-Quds* Literature: Including a Critical Edition of the Manuscript of *Kitāb Faḍāʾil al-Quds waʾl-Khalīl wa-Faḍāʾil al-Shām* of al-Musharraf b. al-Murajjā Abū al-Maʿālī al-Maqdisī." Ph.D. Thesis, the Hebrew University of Jerusalem (in Hebrew).

——. 2000. *Studies in the Status of Jerusalem in Early Islam*. Jerusalem: Yad Izhak Ben-Zvi (in Hebrew).

Lokkegaard, Frede. 1978. *Islamic Taxation in the Classic Period, with a Special Reference to Circumstances in Iraq*. Philadelphia: Porcupine Press.

Longinotto, Kim & Claire Hunt (with Safaa Fathay). 1990. *The Hidden Face*. A documentary film on Nawwāl al-Saʿdāwī produced by 20th Century Vixen for British Channel Four.

Madelung, Wilferd. 1991. "The Origins of the Yemeni Hijra," in *Arabicus Felix*. Ed. Alan Jones. Reading: Ithaca Press, 25–44.

Maher, Vanessa. 1974. *Women and Property in Morocco: Their Changing Relation to the Process of Social Stratification in the Middle Atlas*. Cambridge: Cambridge University Press.

Maine, Henry Sumner. 1930. *Ancient Law*. Introduction and notes by Frederick Pollock. London: John Murray.

Makdisi, John. 1996. "Legal Logic and Equity in Islamic Law," in *Islamic Law and Legal Theory*. Ed. Ian Edge. Aldershot: Dartmouth Publishing Company, 229–58. Appeared also in *The American Journal of Comparative Law*, 33 (1985): 63–92.

Makhlūf, Muḥammad b. Muḥammad. 1975. *Shajarat al-Nūr al-Zakiyya fī Ṭabaqāt al-Mālikiyya*. 2 vols. in 1. 2nd ed. Beirut: Dār al-Kitāb al-ʿArabī.

Mandaville, Jon E. 1979. "Usurious Piety: The Cash Waqf Controversy in the Ottoman Empire." *International Journal of Middle East Studies*, 10: 289–308.

Manṣūr, Aḥmad. 2003. *al-Shaykh Aḥmad Yāsīn Shāhid ʿalā ʿAṣr al-Intifāḍa*. Beirut: Dār Ibn Ḥazm.

Maqrīzī, Taqī al-Dīn Abū al-ʿAbbās Aḥmad al-. 1270/1853–54. *al-Mawāʿiẓ waʾl-Iʿtibār fī Dhikr al-Khiṭaṭ waʾl-Āthār*. 2 Vols. [Cairo]: Būlāq.

Marcus, Abraham. 1989. *The Middle East on the Eve of Modernity: Aleppo in the Eighteenth Century*. New York: Columbia University Press.

Marcy, Georges. 1949. *Le droit coutumier Zemmoûr*. Paris: Larose.

Marghīnānī, Burhān al-Dīn al-. 1316/1898–99. *al-Hidāya Sharḥ Bidāyat al-Mubtadā*. Printed in the margins of Ibn al-Humām, Kamāl al-Dīn. 1316/1898–99. *Sharḥ Fatḥ al-Qadīr*. 8 vols. Būlāq: al-Maṭbaʿa al-Kubrā al-Amīriyya.

Marin, Manuela. 1985. "*Şūrà* et al-*Şūrà* dans al-Andalus." *Studia Islamica*, 62: 25–51.
Marland, Hilary. 1993. "Introduction," in *The Art of Midwifery: Early Modern Midwives in Europe*. Ed. Hilary Marland. London & New York: Routledge, 1–8.
Masters, Bruce. 1988. *The Origins of Western Economic Dominance in the Middle East: Mercantalism and the Islamic Economy in Aleppo, 1600–1750*. New York: New York University Press.
Masud, Muhammad Khalid, Brinkely Messick & David S. Powers. 1996. "Muftis, Fatwas, and Legal Interpretation," in *Islamic Legal Interpretation: Muftis and Their Fatwas*. Eds. idem. Cambridge, Mass.: Harvard University Press, 3–32.
Maunier, René. 1998. *Recherches sur les échanges rituels en Afrique du Nord*. Ed. Alain Mahé. Paris: Bouchène.
Maurin, C. 1945. "Quelques Contrats de Métayage en Afrique du Nord et Syrie." *Institut des Belles Lettres Arabes*, 8: 158–88.
Mauss, Marcel. 1990. *The Gift*. New York: W. W. Norton.
Mayor, Frederic & Faysal al-Hussaini. 1998. *Jerusalem et la Culture de la Paix*. Beirouth: CEEA.
McGowan, Bruce. "The Age of the Ayan, 1699–1812," in *An Economic and Social History of the Ottoman State, 1300–1914*. Eds. Halil İnalcik and Donald Quataert. Cambridge: Cambridge University Press, 637–758.
Melchert, Christopher. 1997. *The formation of the Sunni schools of law, 9th–10th centuries C.E.* Leiden: Brill.
Mercier, Ernest. 1899. *Le code du hobous, ou Ouakf, selon la législation musulmanne*. Constantine: Impr. D. Braham.
Meriwether, Margaret L. 1999. *The Kin Who Count: Family and Society in Ottoman Aleppo, 1770–1840*. Austin Tex.: University of Texas Press.
Meron, Ya'akov. 2001. *Muslim Law in Comparative Perspective*. Jerusalem: The Magness Press (in Hebrew).
Messick, Brinkley. 1993. *The Calligraphic State: Textual Domination and History in a Muslim Society*. Berkeley, Los Angeles & Oxford: University of California Press.
——. 1995. "Textual Properties: Writing and Wealth in a Sharī'a Case." *Anthropology Quarterly*, 68.3: 157–70.
——. 1996. "Media Muftis: Radio Fatwas in Yemen," in *Islamic Legal Interpretation: Muftis and Their Fatwas*. Eds. Muhammad Kh. Masud, Brinkley Messick & David S. Powers. Cambridge Mass.: Harvard University Press, 310–20.
——. 1998. "L'écriture en procès: les récits d'un meutre devant un tribunal shar'i." *Droit et Société*, 39: 237–56.
——. 2001. "Indexing the Self: Intent and Expression in Islamic Legal Acts." *Islamic Law and Society*, 8.2: 151–78.
Michel, Nicolas. 1997. *Une économie de subsistances: le Maroc précolonial*. Cairo: Institut Français d'Archéologie Orientale.
Miller, W. Flagg. 2001. "Inscribing the Muse." Ph.D. Thesis, University of Michigan.
Milliot, Louis. 1911. *L'association agricole chez les musulmans du Maghreb (Maroc, Algérie, Tunisie)*. Paris: Arthur Rousseau.
——. 1918. *Démembrements du Habous*. Paris: Éditions Ernest Leroux.
——. 1953. *Introduction à l'étude du droit musulman*. Paris: Recueil Sirey.
Mishal, Shaul & Avraham Sela. 1997. *Hamas: A Behavioral Profile*. Tel Aviv: Tel Aviv University, the Tami Steinmetz Center for Peace Research (in Hebrew).
Mohsen, Safia. 1970. "The Quest for Order among Awlad Ali of the Western Desert of Egypt." Ph.D. Thesis, Michigan State University. University Microfilms No. 71–31, 266.
Moors, Annelies. 1995. *Women, Property, and Islam: Palestinian Experience, 1920–1990*. Cambridge: Cambridge University Press.
——. 2004. "Women, Gender and Inheritance: Arab States," in *Encyclopaedia of Women in Islamic Countries*. Leiden: Brill, 2: 299–302.

Motzki, Herald. 2002. *The Origins of Islamic Jurisprudence: Meccan Fiqh before the Classical Schools*. Leiden: Brill.

Muḥibbī, Muḥammad Amīn al-. 1966. *Khulāṣat al-Athar fī Aʿyān al-Qarn al-Ḥādī ʿAshar*. Reprinted from the Cairo 1868 ed. 4 parts in 2 vols. Beirut: Maṭbaʿat al-Khayyāt.

Mundy, Martha. 1995. *Domestic Government: Kinship, Community and Polity in North Yemen*. London: I. B. Tauris.

Murādī, Muḥammad Khalīl al-. 1966. *Silk al-Durar fī Aʿyān al-Qarn al-Thānī ʿAshar*. 4 parts in 2 vols. Baghdad: Maṭbūʿāt al-Muthannā.

Musallam, B. F. 1983. *Sex and Society in Islam: Birth Control before the Nineteenth Century*. Cambridge: Cambridge University Press.

Muslim b. Ḥajjāj. 1930. *Ṣaḥīḥ*. 6 vols. Cairo: al-Maṭbaʿa al-Miṣriyya.

Nāṭūr, Aḥmad. 1994. *Marsūm Qaḍā'ī Raqam 1: Tathbīt Qudusiyyat al-Muqaddasāt al-Islāmiyya wa-Manʿ Iṣdār Fatāwā bi-Khilāf Dhālik*. Jerusalem: The Sharīʿa Court of Appeal.

——. 1995. *Marsūm Qaḍā'ī Raqam 2: Waẓīfat al-Mukhbirīn fī Qaḍāyā al-Nafaqa*. Jerusalem: The Sharīʿa Court of Appeal.

——. 1996. *Marsūm Qaḍā'ī Raqam 3: al-Waṣiyya al-Wājiba*. Jerusalem: The Sharīʿa Court of Appeal.

——. 1998. "Moslem Shari'a Court Should Be Left to Its Own Creative Devices. Conversation with Qāḍī Ahmad H. Natur." *Justice*, 17: 16–22.

Nawawī, Yaḥyā b. Sharaf al-. 1992. *Rawḍat al-Ṭālibīn*. 8 vols. Beirut: Dār al-Kutub al-ʿIlmiyya.

Nüsse, Andrea. 1998. *Muslim Palestine: the Ideology of Ḥamās*. Amsterdam: Harwood Academic Publishers.

Obermeyer, Gerald J. 1968. "Structure and Authority in a Bedouin tribe: The 'Aishaibat of the Western Desert of Egypt." Ph.D. Thesis, Indiana University. University Microfilms No. 69–10572.

Ong, Walter, J. 1965. "Oral Residue in Tudor Prose Style." *Publications of the Modern Language Association of America*, 80.3: 145–54.

Osswald, Rainer. 1993. *Schichtengesellschaft und islamisches Recht: Die Zawāyā und Krieger der Westsahara im Spiegel von Rechtsgutachten des 16–19 Jahrhunderts*. Wiesbaden: Harrassowitz.

Patorni, F. 1895. "Déliberation de l'année 1749 dans la Grande Kabylie." *Revue africaine*, 39: 315–20.

Pavlowsky, Agnès. 2000. *Hamas, ou, Le miroir des frustrations palestiniennes*. Paris: L'Harmattan.

Peirce, Leslie. 2003. *Morality Tales: Law and Gender in the Ottoman Court of Aintab*. Berkeley: University of California Press.

Peled, Alisa R. 2001. *Debating Islam in the Jewish State: The Development of Policy toward Islamic Institutions in Israel*. New York: State University of New York Press.

Peletz, Michael. 2002. *Islamic Modern: Religious Courts and Cultural Politics in Malaysia*. Princeton NJ.: Princeton University Press.

Peters, Emrys L. 1990. *The Bedouin of Cyrenaica*. Cambridge: Cambridge University Press.

Piccinini, Mario. 2003. *Tra legge e contratto: una lettura di Ancient law di Henry S. Maine*. Milan: Giuffrè.

Porath, Yehoshuʿa. 1974. *The Emergence of the Palestinian-Arab National Movement: 1918–1929*. London: Frank Cass.

——. 1977. *The Palestinian-Arab National Movement 1929–1939: From Riots to Rebellion*. London: Frank Cass.

Powers, David S. 1986. *Studies in Qur'ān and Ḥadīth: The Formation of the Islamic Law of Inheritance*. Berkeley: University of California Press.

——. 1993. "Legal Consultation (*Futyā*) in Medieval Spain and North Africa," in *Islam and Public Law*. Ed. Chibli Mallat. London: Graham and Trotman, 85–106.

——. 1994. "*Kadijustiz* or *Qāḍī*-Justice? A Paternity Dispute from Fourteenth-Century Morocco." *Islamic Law and Society*, 1: 332–66.
——. 2001. "Parents and their Minor Children: Familial Politics in the Middle Maghrib in the Eighth/Fourteenth Century." *Continuity and Change*, 16: 177–200.
——. 2002. *Law, Society, and Culture in the Maghrib, 1300–1500*. Cambridge: Cambridge University Press.
Qadrī Pasha, Muḥammad. 1902. *Kitāb Qānūn al-ʿAdl waʾl-Inṣaf liʾl-Qaḍāʾ ʿalā Mushkilāt al-Awqāf*. 3rd edition. Būlāq: al-Maṭbaʿa al-Kubrā al-Amīriyya.
——. 1928/29. *Kitāb al-Aḥkām al-Sharʿiyya fiʾl-Aḥwāl al-Shakhṣiyya ʿalā Madhhab al-Imām Abī Ḥanīfa al-Nuʿmān*. Cairo: Al-Maṭbaʿa al-ʿUthmāniyya al-Miṣriyya.
Qarāfī, Aḥmad b. Idrīs al-. 1967. *al-Iḥkām fī Tamyīz al-Fatāwā ʿan al-Aḥkām wa-Taṣarrufāt al-Qāḍī waʾl-Imām*. Aleppo: Maktab al-Maṭbūʿāt al-Islāmiyya.
Qutb, Sayyid. 1999. *In the Shade of the Quran (Fī Ẓilāl al-Qurʾān)*. Trans. and eds. M. A. Salahi & A. A. Shamis. 5 vols. Leicester UK: the Islamic Foundation.
Rafeq, Abdul-Karim. 1966. *The Province of Damascus, 1723–1783*. Beirut: Khayats.
——. 1994. "The Syrian *ʿUlamā*ʾ, Ottoman Law and Islamic *Sharīʿa*." *Turcica*, 26: 9–29.
Ramadan, Tareq. 1998. *Aux sources du renouveau musulman: d'al-Afghānī à Ḥassan Al-Bannā un siècle de réformisme islamique*. Paris: Bayard Editions/Centurion.
Ramlī, Khayr al-Dīn al-. 1893/94. *Kitāb al-Fatāwī al-Khayriyya li-Nafʿ al-Bariyya ʿalā Madhhab al-Imām al-Aʿẓam Abī Ḥanīfa al-Nuʿmān*. 2 vols. N.p: al-Maṭbaʿa al-ʿUthmāniyya.
Rapoport, Yossef. 2003. "Legal Diversity in the Age of *Taqlīd*: The Four Chief *Qāḍīs* under the Mamluks." *Islamic Law and Society*, 10: 210–28.
Rehbinder, Manfred and Klaus-Peter Tieck (eds.). 1987. *Max Weber als Rechtssoziologe*. Berlin: Duncker und Humblot.
Reiter, Yitzhak. 1986. "The Islamic Endowment Institution in Acre." M.A. Thesis, the Hebrew University of Jerusalem (in Hebrew).
——. 1989. "An assessment of the Reform in the Islamic *Waqf* Institution in Israel: Acre as a Case Study." *Hamizraḥ Heḥadash*, 32: 21–45 (in Hebrew).
——. 1996. *Islamic Endowments in Jerusalem under British Mandate*. London and Portland OR.: Frank Cass.
——. 1997a. *Islamic Institutions in Jerusalem: Palestinian Muslim Administration under Jordanian and Israeli Rule*. The Hague, London & Boston: Kluwer Law International.
——. 1997b. "Qāḍīs and the Implementation of Islamic Law in Present Day Israel," in *Islamic Law—Theory and Practice*. Eds. Robert Gleave & Eugenia Kermeli. London: Routledge, 205–31.
Repp, Richard C. 1986. *The Müfti of Istanbul*. London: Ithaca Press.
Riḍā, Rashīd. 1999. *Tafsīr al-Qurʾān al-Ḥakīm [Tafsīr al-Manār]*. 4 vols. Beirut: Dār al-Kutub al-ʿIlmiyya.
Roded, Ruth. 1979. "The *Waqf* in Ottoman Aleppo: A Quantitative Analysis." Paper presented to the International Seminar on Social and Economic Aspects of the Muslim Waqf, Jerusalem, 24th to 28th June, 1979.
Romero Pérez, Jorge Enrique. 1975. *La sociologia del derecho en Max Weber*. N.p.: N.p.
Ruedy, John. 1992. *Modern Algeria: The Origins and Development of a Nation*. Bloomington In.: Indiana University Press.
Rushwān, Muṣṭafā ʿAbd al-Jawwād Aḥmad. 2001. *al-Masjid al-Aqṣā, ʾūlā al-Qiblatayn wa-Thālith al-Ḥaramayn*. Cairo: al-Wahba.
Ṣabbāgh, Laylā al-. 1406/1986. *Min Aʿlām al-Fikr al-ʿArabī fī al-ʿAṣr al-ʿUthmānī al-Awwal: Muḥammad Amīn al-Muḥibbī al-Muʾarrikh wa-Kitābuhu Khulāṣat al-ʿAṣr fī Aʿyān al-Qarn al-Ḥādī ʿAshar, 1061–1111/1651–1699*. Damascus: Al-Sharika al-Muttaḥida liʾl-Tawzīʿ.
Sadat, D.R. 1972. "Rumeli Ayanlari: the Eighteenth Century." *The Journal of Modern History*, 44.3: 346–63.

Salmon, G. and L. Bruzeaux. 1905. "Contribution à l'étude du droit coutumier du Nord-Marocain: De l'association agricole et de ses différentes formes." *Archives Marocaines*, 3: 331–412.

Sarāj, Maḥmūd Aḥmad & ʿAlī Jamāʿa Muḥammad (eds.). 2001. *Al-Amwāl* of Abū Jaʿfar al-Dāʾudī. Cairo: Dār al-Salām.

Sarakhsī, Shams al-Dīn al-. N.d. *Kitāb al-Mabsūṭ*. 2nd edition. Beirut: Dār al-Maʿrifa liʾl-Ṭibāʿa waʾl-Nashr.

——. [1324]-1331/ [1906–1907]-1912–1913. *Kitāb al-Mabsūṭ*. 15 vols. Cairo: Maṭbaʿat al-Saʿāda.

——. 1993. *Kitāb al-Mabsūṭ*. 30 vols. Beirut: Dār al-Kutub al-ʿIlmiyya.

Schacht, Joseph. 1955a. "The Schools of Law and Later Development of Jurisprudence," in *Law in the Middle East*. Eds. Majid Khadduri & Herbert J. Liebesny. 2 vols. Washington D.C.: The Middle East Institute, 1: 57–84.

——. 1955b. "Pre-Islamic Background and Early Development of Jurisprudence," in *op. cit.*, 1: 28–56.

——. 1964. *An Introduction to Islamic Law*. Oxford: Clarendon Press.

Shāfiʿī, Muḥammad b. Idrīs al-. 1903. *Kitāb al-Umm*. 7 vols. Cairo: Al-Maṭbaʿa al-Kubrā al-Amīriyya.

Shaham, Ron. 2003. "Revealing the Secrets of the Body: Medical Tests as Legal Evidence in Personal Status Disputes in Modern Egypt." *Medicine and Law*, 22: 131–54.

Shahar, Ido. 2000. "Palestinians in an Israeli Court: Culture, Control, and Resistance in the Sharīʿa Court of Western Jerusalem." M.A. Thesis, the Hebrew University of Jerusalem (in Hebrew).

——. 2001. "Constructing Identity and Building Relationships: Israeli Palestinians in Israeli Islamic Courts." Paper presented at *the Israeli Oriental Society Annual Conference*. Interdisciplinary Center, Herzliya, May 29, 2001.

——. 2006. "Practicing Islamic Law in a Legal Pluralistic Environment: The Changing Face of a Muslim Court in Present Day Jerusalem." Ph.D. Thesis, Ben-Gurion University of the Negev, Beersheva.

Shaked, Roni & Aviva Shabi. 1994. *Ḥamās, from Belief in Allāh to the Road of Terror*. Jerusalem: Keter (in Hebrew).

Shatzmiller, Maya. 1994. *Labour in the Medieval Islamic World*. Leiden: Brill.

Shava, Menashe. 1998. "The Relationship between Jurisdiction of Family Court and Rabbinical Court." *Hapraklit*, 44.1: 44–71 (in Hebrew).

Shinar, Pessah. 1983. *Essai de bibliographie sélective et annotée sur l'Islam maghrébin contemporain: Maroc, Algérie, Tunisie, Libye (1830–1978)*. Paris: Éditions du Centre National de la Recherche Scientifique.

Shuval, Tal. 1996. "La pratique de la *muʿāwaḍa* (échange de biens *ḥabūs* contre propriété privée) à Alger au XVIIIe siècle." *Revue du Monde Musulman et de la Mediterranée*, 79–80: 55–72.

Sijistānī, Sulaymān b. al-Ashʿath Abū Dāwūd al-. 1353/1934. *Kiṭab Masāʾil al-Imām Aḥmad*. Ed. Muḥammad Rashīd Riḍā. Beirut: Muḥammad Amīn Damj.

Simpson, Jorgen B. 1988. *Studies in the Genesis and Early Development of the Caliphal Taxation System*. Copenhagen: Akademisk Forlag.

Sivan, Emmanuel. 1990. *Radical Islam, Medieval Theology and Modern Politics*. New Haven and London: Yale University Press.

Sonbol, Amira El-Azhary. 1991. *The Creation of a Medical Profession in Egypt 1800–1922*. Syracuse: Syracuse University Press.

——. 2003. *Women of Jordan: Islam, Labor, and the Law*. Syracuse: Syracuse University Press.

Spectrosky, Susan. 1993. *Chapters on Marriage and Divorce, Responses of Ibn Ḥanbal and Ibn Rāhwayh*. Austin: Texas University Press.

Stein, Kenneth W. 1984. *The Land Question in Palestine, 1917–1939*. Chapel Hill and London: the University of North Carolina Press.

Steinberg, Matti. 2002. "Religion and Nationalism in the Ḥamās Doctrine," in *Religion and Nationalism in Israel and the Middle East*. Ed. Nerri Horowitz. Tel Aviv: Am Oved and the Yitzhak Rabin Center for Israel Studies, 126–78 (in Hebrew).

Stewart, Frank H. 2003. "The Contract with Surety in Bedouin Customary Law." *UCLA Journal of Islamic and Near Eastern Law*, 2: 163–280.

——. 2006. "Customary Law among the Bedouin of the Middle East and North Africa," in *Nomadic Societies in the Middle East and North Africa*. Ed. Dawn Chatty. Leiden: Brill, 239–79.

Still, Judith and Michael Worton. 1990. "Introduction," in *Intertextuality: Theories and Practices*. Eds. J. Still & M. Worton. Manchester and New York: Manchester University Press, 1–44.

Sulitzeanu, Orit. 1999. "Qualifying Women as Sharʿī Attorneys." *The Women's voice* [Kol Hanashim], 3: 3–5 (in Hebrew).

Talmon-Heller, Daniella. 2002. "Religion in the Public Sphere: Rulers, Scholars, and Commoners in Syria under Zangid and Ayyubid Rule (1150–1260)," in *The Public Sphere in Muslim Societies*. Eds. Miriam Hoexter, Shmuel N. Eisenstadt & Nehemia Levtzion. Albany: State University of New York Press, 49–63.

Taminian, Lucine. 2001. "Playing with Words." Ph.D. Thesis, University of Michigan.

Ṭarsūsī, Najm al-Dīn al-. 1344/1926. *al-Fatāwā al-Ṭarsūsīyya aw Anfaʿ al-Wasāʾil ilā Taḥrīr al-Masāʾil*. Cairo: Maṭbaʿat al-Sharq.

Toledano, Ehud R. 1998. *Slavery and Abolition in the Ottoman Middle East*. Seattle & London: University of Washington Press.

Treves, Renato (ed.). 1981. *Max Weber e il diritto*. Milan: Franco Angeli.

Ṭulayṭulī, Aḥmad b. Murīth al-. 1994. *al-Muqniʿ fī ʿIlm al-Shurūṭ*. Introduction and critical edition by Francisco Javier Aguirre Sadaba. Madrid: C.S.I.C.

Tyan, Emile. 1945. *Le notariat et le régime de la preuve par écrit dans la pratique du droit musulman*. Harissa, Lebanon: Imp. St. Paul.

——. 1960. *Histoire de l'organisation judiciaire en pays d'Islam*. Leiden: Brill.

Ursinus, Michael. 2005. *Grievance Administration (Şikayet) in an Ottoman Province: The Kaymakam of Rumelia's 'Record Book of Complaints' of 1781–1783*. London and New York: Routledge Curzon.

Vaffier-Pollet, E. 1906. "Les associations agricoles au Maroc," *Renseignements Coloniaux, Supplément au Bulletin du Comité de l'Afrique Française*, 234–39, 263–65.

Wansharīsī, Aḥmad al-. 1401–03/1981–83. *al-Miʿyār al-Muʿrib wa'l-Jāmiʿ al-Mughrib ʿan Fatāwī ʿUlamāʾ Ifrīqiyā wa'l-Andalus wa'l-Maghrib*. 13 vols. Rabat: Ministry of Culture and Religious Affairs.

Wāsiṭī, Muḥammad b. Aḥmad al-. 1979. *Faḍāʾil al-Bayt al-Muqaddas d'Abū Bakr Muḥammad b. Aḥmad al-Wāsiṭī*. Edité et annoté par Isaac Hasson. Jerusalem: Magnes Press.

Weber, Max. 1954. *Max Weber on Law in Economy and Society*. Ed. Max Rheinstein, trans. Max Rheinstein and Edward Shils. Cambridge, Mass.: Harvard University Press.

——. 1960. *Rechtssoziologie*. Ed. Johannes Winckelmann. Neuwied: Hermann Luchterhand.

——. 1976. *Wirtschaft und Gesellschaft*. Ed. Johannes Winckelmann. Tübingen: J. C. B. Mohr.

——. 1978. *Economy and Society*. 2 Vols. Eds. G. Roth and C. Wittich. Berkley: University of California Press.

Wheeler, Sally and Jo Shaw. 1994. *Contract Law*. Oxford: Clarendon Press.

Winter, Michael. 2004 (February). "The Civil Bureaucracy of Damascus in the Late Mamluk Period." *Vostok: Asian and African Studies in Saint Petersburg* [vol. no. not indicated], 47–66.

Yanagihashi, Hiroyuki. 1996. "The Judicial Function of the *Sulṭān* in Civil Cases According to the Mālikīs up to the Sixth/Twelfth Century." *Islamic Law and Society*, 3: 41–74.

Yāqūt, Shihāb al-Dīn b. ʿAbd Allāh al-Ḥamāwī. 1866. *Kitāb Muʿjam al-Buldān*. 5 vols. Leipzig: F. A. Brockhaus.

Yifraḥ, Shlomo. 1955–56. "The Sharīʿa Courts Compared with the Other Religious Courts in Israel." *Mishpat ve-Kalkala*, i–ii: 151–58 (in Hebrew).

Zabāra, Muḥammad. 1956. *A'immat al-Yaman*. Cairo: Maṭbaʿat al-Salafiyya.

——. 1979. *Nuzhat al-Naẓar*. Sanʿā': Markaz al-Dirāsāt.

Zaman, Muḥammad Qāsim. 1997. "The Caliphs, the *ʿUlamā'*, and the Law: Defining the Role and Function of the Caliph in the Early ʿAbbāsid Period." *Islamic Law and Society*, 4: 1–36.

Zaydān, ʿAbd al-Karīm. 1994. *Al-Mufaṣṣal fī Aḥkām al-Mar'a wa'l-Bayt al-Muslim fi'l-Sharīʿa al-Islāmiyya*. 11 vols. Beirut: Mu'assasat al-Risāla.

Zeevi, Dror. 1998. "The Use of Sharīʿa Court Records as a Source for Middle Eastern Social History: A Reappraisal." *Islamic Law and Society*, 5: 35–56.

Zuʿaytar, Akram. 1984. *Wathā'iq al-Ḥaraka al-Waṭaniyya al-Filasṭīniyya (1919–1939) min Awrāq Akram Zuʿaytar*. Beirut: Mu'asasat al-Dirāsāt al-Filasṭīniyya.

INDEX